"Africa can still be mined for stories, and *A Monkey's Wedding* is gold. It is the grit and serendipity, the bravery and the unexpected, that gives depth and fascination to Lloyd's multi-generational tale. Compelling!" Rick Antonson, author of *To Timbuktu for a Haircut: A Journey Through West Africa.*

"A fascinating, sweeping tale of one extended family's roots and lives in wild places and tumultuous times." Tony Park, best-selling author of *Far Horizon.*

"A rollicking adventure, written with wit and grace, about a remarkable family that spanned an empire and helped forge a continent. I loved it." Douglas Rogers, author of *The Last Resort* and *Two Weeks in November.*

A MONKEY'S WEDDING

A Pioneering Family's
Seven-generation Saga
in Southern Africa

STUART LLOYD

CatMatDog Publishers, Australia.
ABN: 85312594003

stuartlloyd.net
Contact the author: stulloyd.worldsmith@gmail.com

Cover design and photo pages: Stuart Lloyd.

Interior typesetting: Shahid Aziz.

A catalogue record for this book is available from the National Library of Australia

Paperback ISBN: 978-0-6453280-6-6
eBook ISBN: 978-0-6453280-7-3
Also available in audiobook through most major platforms.

And they say it is danger to cross the street,
yet one must needs cross it.

Alan Paton, *Cry the Beloved Country*

To Jennifer and George (Mum and Dad)
who brought together two amazing family trees.
Sine qua non.

A Note on the Title

The title draws on a well-known colonial Southern African idiom. In Zulu and Xhosa the expression *inkawu iyashada* literally means 'the monkey is getting married' to describe the curious phenomenon of bright sunshine streaming through steady rain. It is a sight that occurs frequently across Southern Africa.

Somewhere along the line, settlers adapted this to 'a monkey's wedding'.

Creedence Clearwater Revival, one of my favourite bands, captured a similar image in *Have You Ever Seen the Rain*? I remember that song blasting from the radio one afternoon in the early 1970s just as a monkey's wedding caught us playing in a friend's backyard near Umdloti, Natal. A memorable moment of synchronicity.

The phrase serves here as a metaphor. Much of the family story that follows unfolds under clear, hopeful skies, yet it is repeatedly shadowed by gathering storms, both personal and national, over two turbulent centuries. The title reflects those shifting fortunes across seven generations.

CONTENTS

Spotify playlist:

A lot of music features in this journey, especially African and international hits from the 60s, 70s, 80s that illustrate the stories and themes of the book.
Search *'A Monkey's Wedding -- A Southern African Saga'* by Stuart Lloyd.
Or try this link: http://bit.ly/4rCN9Ew

FOREWORD

This is not the book I set out to write. The intended story cast me fair and square as the hero, full of fond reminiscences of how a near-idyllic childhood in southern Africa was lived … and then lost.

I imagined there might be a few paragraphs about my forebears on both sides of the family — maybe extending to a chapter — to give some historical context to the whole shebang.

As it turned out, once I'd researched my family's history in Africa, there was no shortage of actual real heroes in the mix. Pioneers of not just one but two countries, adventurers, prospectors, and decorated (and undecorated) war heroes. Turns out I am not even the hero in my own life story!

In the process I discovered that my family's connections to the mighty continent went back two generations further than had ever been discussed around the dinner table. It turns out I am sixth-generation Southern African.

Where my memory faltered or conflicted (increasingly more common these days), I deferred to brothers and relatives, family documents and correspondence, military records, land deeds, and contemporary accounts. Where the archive was silent, I have tried to say so.

Regardless, I was relegated to playing a minor part in my own movie. And happily so. Because this voyage of discovery has proved to be the most fascinating journey I've ever been on — and one I didn't even have to buy a ticket, nor suffer seasickness nor malaria, for.

I've had to confine the scope to forebears in my family tree who directly contributed DNA to me, and contemporary immediate cousins, otherwise this would be an endlessly sprawling undertaking.

It took the passing of my mum for me to write this book. It sat as a work-in-progress folder in my laptop for years, and I periodically jotted notes into the dump file. But with clearing out Mum's stuff, came photographs, letters, documents, a trove of nostalgia and memorabilia. And questions. Like, *Gee, why didn't I ever ask Mum about that time? Who are those kids in that photo?* But mostly I ended up with, *Who the hell am I?* (Yes, I've arrived in my 60s with an existential crisis of the type that cannot be solved with buying another motorbike or another guitar!)

Another impetus was Christmas 2023, when my son Justin gave me a MyHeritage.com DNA kit. The narrative round the dinner table with a name like Llewellyn Lloyd was always that we were Welsh on Dad's side, Irish on Mum's side. The results were fascinating: English 33.6%, Scottish and Welsh 28.6, Irish 15.5, Dutch 5.8, Germanic 5.8, Danish 4.4, French 3.3, Breton 3.0.

Interestingly the greatest number of DNA matches I have on that site are from Germany, followed by New Zealand and Canada, Netherlands and Sweden, with South Africa a few places behind.

Furthermore, my identity has been clouded by my peripatetic life. Yes, I spent 15 very formative years in Africa. I've also spent 22 years (over three separate chunks of time) in Australia. But I've spent 24 years living across Asia, with two Eurasian children (and two Eurasian grandchildren), a Thai wife, and Thailand has the dubious distinction of being the country I've lived in the longest continually — 11 years. I also spent a decade in Singapore, where I relished its colonial history and the flavour that imbued to it.

Let's talk about the giant African elephant in the room. As I write this, the very mention of the term 'colonialism' stirs strong reactions, much like the smell of a *galjoen* fish left too long in the African sun. The word alone evokes a past many would rather consign to the depths, alongside the statues of figures like Cecil Rhodes. I understand the discomfort — it's a sensitive subject, and rightly so.

Colonial history is always a difficult thing to face for many Europeans. There have been moments when I've had to confront the reality of how colonialism unfolded: claims laid on land that belonged to others, often accompanied by violence and dispossession. This wasn't, and isn't, easy to reconcile. This journey has forced me to examine uncomfortable truths about the roles my ancestors played. It's been an eye-opening and deeply transformative process.

These events took place over a period spanning the last two centuries, a time when actions and beliefs now deemed inappropriate were often considered normal. That doesn't excuse them, particularly the brutalities that occurred. Yet history is what it is. We cannot reshape the past to fit our modern moral framework. This book does not seek to exonerate or prosecute the past — it seeks to describe it honestly. The best that we can do is acknowledge the facts and learn from them, recognising that the lenses through which we view the past are inevitably shaped by the present.

As Dr Shashi Tharoor, former UN delegate, once said: 'You can't put right what has happened in the past. But at least acknowledge it was wrong, for the future generations to understand that.' Let's go with that.

Another useful mindset to adopt in all of this is that history belongs to the past, but understanding it is our duty in the present.

Many events depicted here, and the protagonists including myself, were people and products of their time. It doesn't exonerate them or us, but it gives a context for behaviour.

It can be likened to surgeons of old. The supposed remedy for a headache was to drill a hole in the patient's head, and drain out the blood, a process called trepanation. We can't judge doctors for doing that because that was the common wisdom and accepted practice of the day and only phased out as recently as the 1800s. Happily we've learned and grown since then. And now have more enlightened approaches.

Suffice to say, no offence is intended in general with this book, but I make no apologies to those with a thin skin.

To me the lamest woke expression is 'I don't see colour.' Well, that is to miss the point entirely. I see colour everywhere, not the least in my own beautiful wife, children, and grandchildren. But everywhere else too. In fact, I actively seek colour, because it often leads to fascinating discussions about heritage, music, food, and culture. And frankly more soulful exchanges.

The use of racial terminology is again always loaded: potentially controversial and potentially offensive. This is particularly the case in the South African context in which, unfortunately, its extensive presence in historical commentaries and records makes it impossible to avoid. For the sake of consistency, in this book those references that imply a place or country of origin are given in upper case (for example African, Afrikaner, European, and Indian). References that denote classification by skin colour are given in lower case (for example, black, coloured, and white).

Growing up, I just knew or understood that we were of British stock, living in the English-speaking province of Natal. I had no idea of Natal's turbulent history regarding the Voortrekkers and Afrikaners. And I also had no idea we had several Afrikaners in our bloodline too. For in my memory, we were far more 'racist' against them — our fellow whites — than we were to any other groups: for example, our 'Polish joke' equivalent always involved the hapless Van Der Merwe as the acme of stupidity. And of course, they lived in the distant lands of Transvaal and Vrystaat (Orange Free State) safely on the other side of the border. The reality of course was much more dynamic and fluid, as I've come to understand.

This is not intended as a memoir of lost innocence, nor a nostalgic elegy for a vanished Rhodesia or colonial South Africa. Instead, childhood memories appear here as first-person fragments of lived experience that should be weighed against records, archives, and the longer sweep of history. This book is an examination of how ordinary families like ours became entangled in extraordinary historical forces, and how those forces shaped lives, identities, and moral choices across generations. And continue to do so, with some of our immediate family still living in South Africa, and other relatives having moved back to Zimbabwe more recently.

At heart, this is a book about how history moves through families, and what remains when empires recede.

I've thoroughly enjoyed this voyage of discovery and truly hope you do too.

Hamba kahle (go well).

Stuart Lloyd
NSW, Australia
April 2026.

THE CAST

(The main family characters featured in this seven-generation saga, listed earliest to latest, with their relationship to the author.)

Henry Llewellyn Lloyd (1784-1844) and **Alicia Mary (nee Whittle) (1789- 1848).** My paternal great-great-great grandparents.
George Seymour (1812-1900) and **Mary Ann (nee Walls)(1816-1899).** Maternal great-great-great-grandparents.
Ephraim Frederick Rathbone (1812-1882) and **Anne (nee Williamson) (1818-1910).** My maternal great-great-great grandparents.
John Seymour (1846-1915) and **Annie Alice Chieftain (nee Rathbone) (1848-1910).** Maternal great-great grandparents.
Henry Llewellyn Lloyd (1856-1931) and **Marie Louisa (nee Meyer) (1874-1945).** My paternal great-great grandparents.
George Frederick Seymour (1872-1950) and **Wilhelmina 'Minnie' Frederica (nee Diffenthal) (1879-1964).** My maternal great-grandparents.
Michael McGee (1859-1940) and **Bridget (nee Sarsfield) (1860-1958).** My maternal great-great grandparents.
Henry 'Dick' Llewellyn Lloyd (1901-1966) and **Eileen Patricia (nee Macfarlane) (1907-1989).** Paternal grandparents.
George Edgar Seymour (1903-1971) and **Alys Eileen (nee Tait)(1907-1981).** Maternal grandparents.
George 'Buster' Llewellyn Lloyd (1929-1995) and **Jennifer Ann (nee Seymour) (1936-2024).** My parents.
Michael 'Mick' John Flint (1934-2024) and **Kathleen 'Kay' Maud (nee Lloyd) (1935-).** Kay is a paternal aunt.
David George Seymour (1931-2026) and **Jill Mary (nee Scott)(1940-).** David is an uncle on the maternal side.
Dorothy 'Dot' Nita Daniel (nee Lloyd) (1932-). Paternal aunt.
Henry 'Mick 'Llewellyn Lloyd (1938-2006) and **Patricia 'Paddy' Mabel (nee Williams)(1940-).** Mick is a paternal uncle.
Roger Michael Seymour (1944-) and **Renee (nee Rossler) (1945-).** Roger is an uncle on maternal side.

Tim Kelley Henwood (1951-) and **Wendy Patricia (nee Avery) (1953-).** Wendy is a first cousin on Dad's side.

Ian Charles Daniel (1954-). First cousin on Dad's side.

Geoffrey Richard Flint (1959-) and **Bridgette (nee Morrison) (1958-).** Geoff is a first cousin on Dad's side.

Lloyd Alan Flint (1960-) and **Carol Denise (nee Little) (1959-).** Lloyd is a first cousin on Dad's side.

Glendon Llewellyn Lloyd (1961-). Brother.

Roger Llewellyn Lloyd (1966-). Brother.

Michael David Seymour (1967-). First cousin on Mum's side.

John Roger Seymour (1974-) and **Nicola 'Nicci' (nee Bruyns) (1976-)**. John is first cousin on Mum's side.

Arthur 'Arch' Meader Harley (1983-) and **Sandy Jane (nee Henwood) (1980-).** Sandy is a second cousin on Dad's side.

SOUTH AFRICA : A CHECKERED HISTORY

1652: Jan van Riebeeck, an official of the Dutch East India Company (VOC), established a refreshment station at Table Bay (Cape of Good Hope), the site of present-day Cape Town.

1799–1802: The Khoi-San people initiate the Third War of Dispossession, a prolonged but ultimately unsuccessful rebellion against colonial authorities in the Eastern Cape.

1806: British forces occupy the Cape Colony for the second time after defeating the Dutch at the Battle of Blaauwberg, marking the beginning of permanent British control.

1807: The British Parliament passes the Abolition of the Slave Trade Act, ending the importation of slaves into the Cape Colony, though slavery itself remains legal.

1816: Shaka Zulu rises to power, unifying various clans into the formidable Zulu Kingdom, significantly altering the region's political landscape.

1819: Xhosa prophet Nxele leads an attack on Grahamstown during the Fifth Frontier War; the assault fails, and Nxele is captured and later dies in custody.

1820: Approximately 4000 British settlers arrive in the Eastern Cape, establishing new settlements and intensifying conflicts over land with indigenous populations.

1834: Slavery is officially abolished in the Cape Colony, leading to significant social and economic shifts within colonial society.

1835–1840: The Great Trek sees thousands of Boers (Voortrekkers) migrate inland to escape British rule, resulting in the establishment of independent Boer republics.

1838: Voortrekkers, under Andries Pretorius, defeat the Zulu army at the Battle of Blood River, a pivotal moment in Boer-Zulu relations.

1843: The British annex the short-lived Natalia Republic, incorporating it into the Colony of Natal, further expanding British influence.

1852: The Sand River Convention grants the South African Republic (Transvaal) independence from British control, recognising Boer self-governance. That created the South African Republic (ZAR) as a self-governing Boer state.

1854: The Orange Free State gains independence through the Bloemfontein Convention, establishing another Boer republic.

1879: The Anglo-Zulu War culminates in the British defeat of the Zulu Kingdom, leading to its eventual annexation.

1880–81: The First Anglo-Boer War ends with the Boer victory at the Battle of Majuba Hill, resulting in the restoration of Transvaal's independence.

1886: Discovery of gold on the Witwatersrand leads to a gold rush, rapid urbanisation, and the founding of Johannesburg, transforming South Africa's economy.

1906: Chief Bambatha kaMancinza leads a Zulu uprising against British colonial rule and taxation in Natal; the rebellion is suppressed with significant Zulu casualties.

1910: Formation of the Union of South Africa: Following their defeat in the Second Anglo-Boer War, the former Boer republics of the South African Republic (Transvaal) and the Orange Free State — now British colonies — joined the Cape Colony and Natal Colony to form the Union of South Africa, consolidating white minority rule and marginalising indigenous political structures, including the Zulu monarchy.

1913: Natives Land Act: Legislation restricts Black South Africans from owning land outside designated areas, exacerbating land dispossession, including in Zululand.

1920s–1930s: Expansion of sugar industry. The sugar cane industry flourishes in Natal, with areas like Sezela and Pongola becoming key production centres, relying heavily on African and Indian labour.

1948: Apartheid policy implemented: The National Party institutionalises racial segregation, affecting all aspects of life, including land ownership and labour in regions like Zululand.

1959: Promotion of Bantu Self-Government Act. The apartheid government establishes homelands, including KwaZulu, aiming to segregate Black South Africans into separate territories.

1960: Sharpeville Massacre. Police kill 69 protesters opposing pass laws, leading to increased resistance against apartheid and the banning of liberation movements.

1970: KwaZulu Homeland established: KwaZulu is officially designated as a homeland for the Zulu people, with limited self-governance under apartheid policies.

1975: Formation of Inkatha Freedom Party. Prince Mangosuthu Buthelezi establishes the IFP, promoting Zulu nationalism and playing a complex role in South African politics.

1976: Soweto Uprising: Mass protests erupt against the enforcement of Afrikaans in schools; the government's violent response galvanises international opposition to apartheid.

1980: Intensification of anti-apartheid struggles: Resistance movements gain momentum, with increased internal unrest and international sanctions pressuring the apartheid regime.

1989: FW de Klerk was the last head of state from the era of white-minority rule. His Nationalist government dismantled the apartheid apparatus, introducing universal suffrage.

1994: First democratic elections. South Africa holds its first fully inclusive national elections, ending apartheid rule and ushering in a new democratic era under Nelson Mandela. FW de Klerk serves as joint deputy president.

Present day: South Africa remains a constitutional democracy, with regular elections and peaceful transfers of power since 1994. Under the long-dominant African National Congress — most recently led by Cyril Ramaphosa — the country has made strides in political freedom and institutional stability, but continues to face deep challenges including inequality, unemployment, crime, and energy insecurity, alongside growing political competition and public frustration with governance.

Map of SOUTH AFRICA

Highlighting main areas of family activity

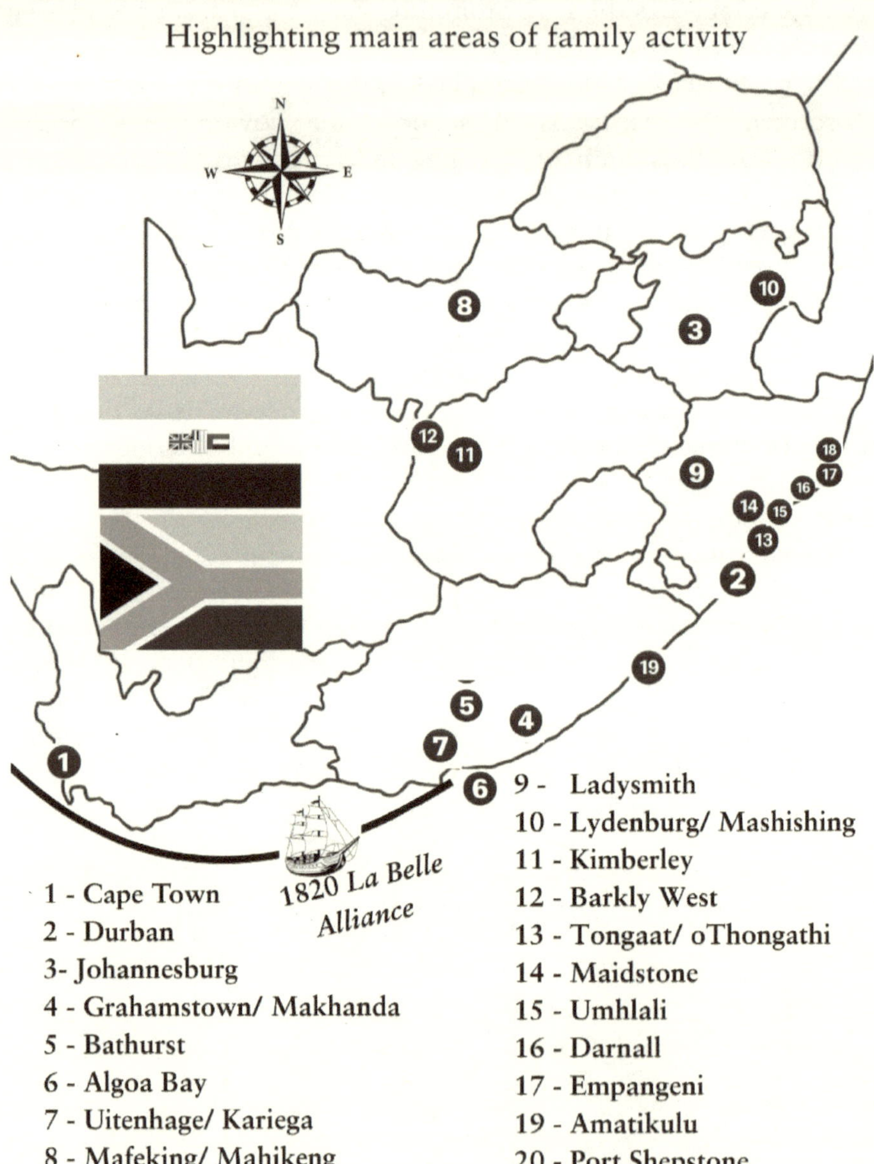

RHODESIA/ZIMBABWE: A POTHOLED HISTORY

1830s: Ndebele migration. The Ndebele people, led by King Mzilikazi, migrate northward from present-day South Africa, establishing the Matabele Kingdom in southwestern Zimbabwe.

1859: Inyati Mission established. Robert Moffat and the London Missionary Society set up the first permanent white settlement in Zimbabwe at Inyati.

1888: Rudd Concession: King Lobengula grants Cecil Rhodes' British South Africa Company (BSAC) mining rights, leading to increased British influence.

1889: BSAC Charter. Queen Victoria issues a royal charter to the BSAC, granting it authority to administer and develop territories in southern Africa.

1890: Pioneer Column. BSAC's Pioneer Column raises the Union Jack in Salisbury (now Harare), marking the beginning of colonial settlement.

1893: First Matabele War: Conflict erupts between the Ndebele and BSAC forces, resulting in the occupation of Bulawayo by the British.

1896–97: First *Chimurenga*: A major uprising by the Ndebele and Shona peoples against BSAC rule; leaders like Nehanda and Kaguvi become national symbols.

1898: Execution of spiritual leaders Nehanda and Kaguvi by colonial authorities, further fuelling resistance narratives. The region south of the Zambezi River is officially named Southern Rhodesia.

1899: Legislative Council established. A part-elected Legislative Council is formed in Southern Rhodesia, marking the beginning of settler self-governance.

1902: Pass Laws introduced: The colonial government mandates that all natives over the age of 14 carry registration passes (situpas).

1923: Responsible government: Southern Rhodesia becomes a self-governing British colony, moving away from BSAC administration.

1930: Land Apportionment Act: Legislation segregates land ownership, allocating the majority of fertile land to white settlers.

1953: Federation formed: Southern Rhodesia joins Northern Rhodesia and Nyasaland to form the Federation of Rhodesia and Nyasaland.

1963: The Federation is dissolved, leading to increased nationalist movements in Southern Rhodesia.

1965: Unilateral Declaration of Independence (UDI): Prime Minister Ian Smith declares independence from Britain, leading to international sanctions.

1970: Republic declared: Rhodesia declares itself a republic, further entrenching white minority rule.

1972: Guerrilla war intensifies: The Rhodesian 'Bush War' escalates as nationalist forces increase attacks against the government.

1976: Mozambique closes border: Mozambique shuts its border with Rhodesia, impacting trade and military logistics.

1978: Internal settlement: An agreement is reached to establish a transitional government, leading to the creation of Zimbabwe Rhodesia.

1979: Lancaster House Agreement. Negotiations in London result in an agreement to end the 'Bush War' and transition to majority rule.

1980: Independence achieved: Zimbabwe gains independence on April 18, with Robert Mugabe becoming the first Prime Minister. Land Reform initiated: The new government begins efforts to redistribute land from white farmers to black Zimbabweans. Zimbabwe is admitted to the United Nations and the Commonwealth, gaining international recognition.

1982–87: *Gukurahundi*: Government security forces conduct a counter-insurgency campaign in Matabeleland against perceived dissidents, resulting in widespread civilian deaths and long-term political and ethnic trauma.

1997: War Veterans payments: Un-budgeted payouts to liberation war veterans trigger currency instability, signalling mounting fiscal pressures and weakening investor confidence.

2000: Fast-Track Land Reform: Large-scale, often chaotic land seizures redistribute white-owned commercial farms, profoundly reshaping agriculture while accelerating economic decline and international isolation.

2015: Currency demonetisation: The Zimbabwe dollar is officially scrapped after years of non-use, cementing the shift to foreign currencies.

Present day: Zimbabwe remains under the long-ruling ZANU-PF, now led by Emmerson Mnangagwa following the ousting of Robert

Mugabe in 2017. While political continuity has been maintained, the country continues to grapple with economic instability, currency volatility, and governance challenges, alongside periodic efforts at reform and re-engagement with the international community.

Map of RHODESIA/ ZIMBABWE

Highlighting main areas of family activity

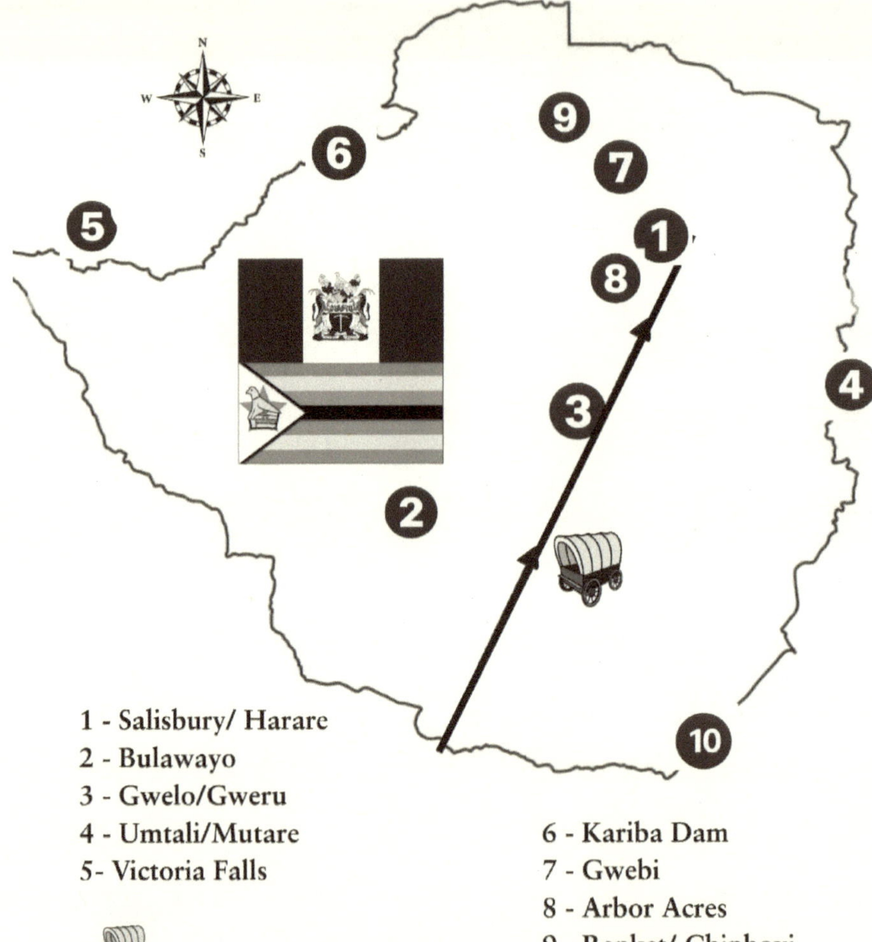

1 - Salisbury/ Harare
2 - Bulawayo
3 - Gwelo/Gweru
4 - Umtali/Mutare
5- Victoria Falls
6 - Kariba Dam
7 - Gwebi
8 - Arbor Acres
9 - Banket/ Chinhoyi
10- Vila Salazar

1890 Pioneer Column route

PROLOGUE 2008

I'd never left a $12 million tip before, but I must admit it was a pretty damn good curry lunch!

However, it wasn't the curry that was making me sweat as I tossed and turned in the heat of the Zambian January night. Although my bed at The Royal Livingstone hotel was wonderfully comfortable, and the air-conditioning took care of the humidity, sleep proved elusive.

Because I was wrestling with a big decision: to return to Zimbabwe — the country of my birth — for the first time in 40 years … or not.

In recent years, I had witnessed the nose-diving of the country from one which was the 'breadbasket' of Africa to one which became the 'basket case' economy poster child of Africa.

Zimbabwe under Robert Mugabe had become one of the world's greatest failed states. A country without food, petrol, money, and one of the highest rates of AIDS infection in the world. Hardly the stuff of travel dreams.

None of that tallied with my memories of a beautiful, peaceful, and fertile land, rich with wildlife, teeming with adventure and possibility, and cherished family memories of farmhouses, tennis parties, and exotic holidays.

Our family left Rhodesia when my father was head-hunted (this being Africa, not literally, thankfully!) for a plum job in South Africa in 1968. The exchange rate then was R$1 = US$1.20. Yes, the Rhodesian dollar was stronger than the US dollar.

With such vivid memories of this country, I did not want to tarnish them by revisiting Zimbabwe when I took my own young family on a five-country visit to southern Africa. My children — from my 20-year marriage to Michelle, a Filipina — were Eurasians, Justin born in Singapore, Jasmine born in Australia, the latter where we resided and had citizenship.

So, our itinerary for their first African adventure included South Africa, Lesotho, Botswana, Zambia and … possibly, *just possibly* … Zimbabwe.

Which is why I lay there sweating on the choice. I had decided not to go to Harare or further into Zimbabwe. But was still deliberating on whether to cross the dramatic bridge which linked Zambia to Zimbabwe. This way, we could experience Zimbabwe without going near any areas where I had pristine memories. Although I still had nagging security concerns for my children then aged 17 and eight stepping into this desperate country. After all, many families we knew had been chased off their farms at gunpoint and dispossessed in recent years.

I had tipped off my uncle Mick and aunt Kay, our only remaining immediate family in the country then, that I might be visiting and it would be great if we could possibly rendezvous. They replied saying meeting at Victoria Falls would be impossible because they had no petrol, so could we possibly make our way to the capital instead?

Hmmm, that's exactly what I didn't want to do.

As the first glimmer of daylight crept its way around the curtains of the lodge, I made the decision: "OK, let's go across to Zimbabwe, guys."

I would return to Zimbabwe, the country of my birth, for the first time in exactly 40 years since I had left it.

After a hearty country-style breakfast, we packed our daypacks and headed to the southern exit of the resort. To where the constant roar of Victoria Falls thunders and the Zambezi River marks the border between the two countries.

Mosi-oa-Tunya is the local name for the falls. 'The Smoke that Thunders'. Indeed, the falls can be heard for kilometres around, long before you see it. Fine misty spray rises from the plunging waters, projecting rainbows into the sky around the area on the clearest of blue, blue days.

Victoria Falls is the largest 'curtain' waterfall in the world, one of the famed Seven Natural Wonders of the World. It's twice the size of Niagara Falls. But no descriptions can possibly do it justice. The sound is incessantly deafening as one thousand tonnes of water per second — 500 million litres of water every minute! — plunge 100 metres on to jagged rocks below, across a front of nearly two kilometres.

We were offered plastic spray jackets to take and use along the pathways traversing the face of the falls. These proved useless. We were absolutely soaked within minutes. Already wet, I decided to take another path leading to a small metal bridge, directly in the spray line of the churning main falls.

I stood under this, feeling completely powerless and insignificant in the natural order of things. Nature is so massive in its awe and power. At that point I felt if the earth just opened up and swallowed me whole, I would not care. I relished that feeling for a few minutes (and indeed revisited the same spot the next day to relive that rush).

But we still had a way to trudge to reach the border. Zambian passport formalities were completed at the northern end of the steel-arched Victoria Falls Bridge.

The 200m bridge itself was built in Britain and shipped out in pieces and later assembled in place over the Second Gorge. It was the brainchild of Cecil Rhodes — a central figure in my family's African adventures, as you'll see — who had instructed engineers to ensure that it should be close enough to the falls that spray from the falls could drench any trains passing over it. All part of his visionary plans for the seamless Cape-to-Cairo rail route.

The bridge was closed during the so-called 'Bush War' that enveloped this region from 1964-79, to limit guerrilla squad infiltrations. However, opposing units often took pot shots at each other across the river from here.

I feel the violent sunshine of Zambia on my back. It's already 31 degrees, with a cloying blanket of humidity wrapped around my body.

I'm absolutely no good with heights, and the 128-metre drop down to the rocky gorges below had me hugging the inner lane of the walkway. Others were clearly not afraid — there's a bungee jump set up along the bridge. You have got to be kidding me! Who in their right mind … ?

Soon we were accosted by a charming entrepreneurial young black fellow, William, who declares himself 'The King of ZimZam.' It's the one metre of no man's land right in the centre of the bridge. 'ZimZam is not Zimbabwe or Zambia … it is my country right in between the two.' He lives on donations, literally royalties, from people passing through his little patch marked on the bridge.

As we reached the Zimbabwe side of the bridge, I felt suddenly apprehensive. The first thing I saw was a camouflaged bunker but could not see who was watching us from within its gloomy interior. We handed over our passports and got stamped into Zimbabwe.

I made it. We're here.

In that designated tourist area, it was easy enough to find a Sprite and some chips. Hard to believe that just a few kilometres away, the local population was struggling to find the basic everyday necessities and foodstuffs to survive.

We then explored the Zimbabwean side of the falls, with stunning views back across to the main falls. A statue of David Livingstone towered over us — the Scottish missionary, explorer and scientist, who became synonymous with Africa and the expression, 'Dr Livingstone I presume' when met by Henry Stanley after years adrift in the wilderness. He stands outsized, in legionnaire-style cap gazing out across the falls and was purportedly the first white person to ever view them, back in 1855. I am surprised that his likeness still stands after all the post-colonial purging of many other colonial-related relics.

Another thing on my 'to do' list was lunch at the Victoria Falls Hotel, standing nearby in splendid contrast to its rather drab urban surrounds. Imagine the Raffles Hotel in Singapore transplanted to the savannah of Africa. Its Edwardian structure is magnificently poised with deliberate grandstand views of the falls, strategically positioned as though by ancient engineers aligning, say, the pyramids or Machu Pichu or Stonehenge with the planets. Its buffalo grass lawns are perfectly manicured, and waiters in crisp white hark back to the height of the colonial Raj. I was at once 'home' again. I love all that mien — be it in Africa, South East Asia, or India.

We chose a table on Stanley's Terrace outside, with views across the sweeping lawns, framed by centuries-old sprawling shade trees.

The hot day demanded thirsts be slaked with lime and sodas all round. We ordered mains — I plumped for the chicken curry. The service was a little tardy but the meal was fine. I looked at my children in the country of my birth. Slightly surreal. Shared some anecdotes of their father as a cheeky youngster having the time of his life in a country and time that I couldn't possibly know wouldn't last forever.

Life on a tobacco farm. Surrounded by beautiful African bush. Rivers. Monkeys. Pet dogs Zeta, Peter, and Zimba. Even a pet pig! Our playground was as far as the eye could see. That was the life I knew here.

Lunch finished, I asked for the bill. There were signs posted on the wall saying that Zimbabweans must pay only in Zimbabwean Dollars. The bill arrived and I gasped: lunch for four people was costing me 128 million Zimbabwe dollars! (In real terms that was then around USD$100 or so). I decided to tip a further 12 million dollars. Grand total 140 million.

I handed over my visa card, and we laughed about the 'astronomical' bill. But our laughter was short lived:

'Sorry, sah, your card is declined,' said the waitress.

'Er, declined? It can't be declined.'

'Yes, sah, declined.'

I fidgeted in my seat. I was sure there was enough money in it for it to be operational. Now I was double guessing myself.

'Can I speak with the manager or something?'

She ushered me to the cashier's area. I detected sweat on my palms which was not all due to the humidity of the day.

'I believe there is a problem with my card?' I said.

'Yes, sah, our connection is down.'

Phew! Well, that's a different story. Zimbabwe's connectivity was abysmal at best, and power outages were more prevalent than power supply.

So now I had a different problem — I needed to pay the bill in cash. I fumbled though my wallet, knowing I'd not really brought a lot of cash because of my security concerns. I started with Zimbabwe dollars and counted those out. Not enough. Sweating. Then some USD. Not enough. Sweating more. I have some Zambian Kwacha. Count those out. And finally, even some Botswanan Pula. We got over the line!

Relieved smiles all round.

Outside the hotel we got into a taxi, a smallish white car, and James — a lovely local with the broadest grin you've ever encountered in your life, something like Isaac from *The Love Boat* — was our driver.

'We'd like to go back to the border, but first two things … I want to buy some Zimbabwean music CDs, and I want to go to the post office please.'

James was amiable and positive. His daughter was living in the US and he wore an 'I Heart New York' T-shirt. We chatted about African music — one of my deep passions in life — especially Southern African music. I am an out-and-out African music junkie. All styles. It speaks to me from deep within, whether I understand the lyrics or not.

But I was ironically not really familiar with many Zimbabwean artists.

'Thomas Mapfumo,' he says. 'He is the best.' Thomas Mapfumo cemented his place in folklore as 'the Lion of Zimbabwe' by developing the Chimurenga style, (meaning 'struggle' in his Shona language). His lyrics were heavily political, urging the black people to rise against the white minority government. Eventually, he was seen as an activist and thrown into jail — without charges — in 1979.

Once Mugabe came to power, he was released. Mapfumo was initially supportive of Mugabe. But then his viewpoint began to change and he started writing protest songs against the new government. His 1989 album title was none too subtle: *Corruption.* The government set about framing him and he was eventually forced to seek exile in the USA, where he continues to live.

Not surprisingly, the music shop where James dropped me had quite a few Thomas Mapfumo CDs.

'Which one do you recommend?' I asked the owner.

'It doesn't matter, it is all good,' he responded.

So I took the lot. About five in all. As I paid with my card, I saw another cover on the 'best seller' shelf: *The Greatest Speeches of Robert Mugabe.* But

I passed on it, and regret that now. Just as a souvenir of the man who was clearly a great orator and started off in the right direction but seemed to have taken a decidedly wrong turn somewhere. But it seems that US governments wouldn't intervene in toppling this manic and genocidal despotic dictator — as they've done with Saddam Hussein, Anwar Ghaddafi, Ayatollah Ali Khamenei, and others — because Zimbabwe had run out of mineral wealth and had no economic benefit to offer America.

Mapfumo has a decidedly low-key singing style. Elegiac in many ways. But distinctive, along with his thumb-piano plucking away in the background.

African music touches me in a very primal way. It was the soundtrack of my youth. And perhaps sub-consciously I tried to recapture that by having my iTunes collection rounded out by 61 albums of African music from all over (West African and swinging African jazz being my preferred genres alongside Southern African *maskandi* and *mbaqanga* styles), and a Spotify playlist ('Afrika!') of 1088 of my favourite songs which runs to nearly 80 hours of music.

Next stop for us was the post office. I wanted to send a couple of postcards with Zimbabwean stamps to friends. I went in with my last remaining USD$2.

The cashier announced that two postcards and two stamps was 450,000 dollars!

'Yes, but you accept US Dollars right?'

'No, Zimbabwean Dollars only.'

That made no sense. You'd think the country would be screaming out for hard foreign currency at desperate times like those. I handed back the postcards and slunk disconsolately out to the carpark.

'Never mind, James, they won't accept my US dollars, so let's just go back to the border now.'

'Well, how much do they want?'

'Four hundred and fifty thousand dollars!' I said.

He sort of grinned, opened his ashtray, pulled out a thick wad of notes, and peeled one single 500,000 dollar note off the top. 'There you go.'

So back I went into the post office and paid for my postcards and stamps. And waited. But the teller started serving the next person. After a while she looked up quizzically. 'Yes?'

'I'm waiting for my change please.'

She harrumphed. And whispered something out of the side of her mouth. The next teller giggled. And said something. The whisper/giggle soon travelled the rounds of the busy post office: Everyone looking at the funny white man asking for his 50,000 dollars change.

I didn't quite get it.

Eventually, an older local with salt-and-pepper coloured curly hair said, 'You want your change? Here …' He rifled through his wallet before pulling out a crumpled bill and passing it to me.

'Um, thanks,' I said, pleased if a little perplexed.

Later I related this story to a friend who asked how much that change was. No idea — I reached for my calculator. 'Oh, shit, no wonder they were laughing at me … it's 0.09 of one US cent. Oops!'

And so it was back to James' taxi, and back to the border.

We got stamped out and walked back to our hotel on the Zambian side, sharing more friendly greetings again with the King of ZimZam en route.

It had been a very emotional day for me, with the sun setting spectacularly over the Zambesi River, and me reflecting with a chilled Mosi beer on the experience of returning to Zimbabwe.

Overall, I'm glad we went. To enjoy the views. Have a fine meal. Tap into some new music, which I'm listening to as I write this (and which you'll find on this book's companion Spotify playlist). To step foot on that soil again and reconnect with my African roots. We had selectively seen only the best of what Zimbabwe then had to offer, which made me feel for the plight of the rest of the country and its citizens.

But mainly, I had kept my wonderful childhood memories intact and untarnished. They still live brightly in my memory. And I now have a thumb piano and multi-coloured Zimbabwean flag in my living room at home.

For years I'd tell people that I was from Rhodesia, and they'd correct me: 'Oh that's politically incorrect; don't you mean Zimbabwe?'

'No, I was born and lived in a place called Rhodesia. I never lived in Zimbabwe.'

Then gradually over the years I started saying I was from Zimbabwe and people would say, 'Don't you mean Rhodesia?'

Either way, I feel now I have a notional 'home', even though that home doesn't exist as I knew it anymore. I've comfortably integrated my African heritage into my being, having turned my back on it as a teenager trying to integrate into Australia.

Happily for Zimbabwe, the country now has petrol and food again. And today you can even pay for goods and services in the country using Chinese RMB. From tentative, opportunistic engagement around the Global Financial Crisis, China's footprint in southern Africa has expanded into a defining presence — through infrastructure finance, mining investment, and trade — positioning China as a central economic 'partner' across the region today.

The economic influences and geopolitical chess games that caused my family's forebears to be in Africa in the first place continue apace as empires rise and fall, countries morph, and people do their best to seek greener pastures and fairer trade winds wherever they can.

And it is their amazing stories that are the beating heart of A Monkey's Wedding.

Part 1

VIOLENT SUNSHINE

1

SOLD DOWN THE RIVER

ENGLAND EARLY 1800s. The Bridge Foot, Bermondsey, was an assault on the senses. The air around that southern end of London Bridge was thick with coal smoke, and through that, cut the bittersweet odour of rotting fruit from the Borough Market stands, the sweat and clang of coopers banging wine barrels into shape, the salty tang of crusted sea spray from wooden vessels docked on the Thames, the acrid smell of leather tanneries, the bells of St Saviours and St George's competing to mark time, the clippety-clop of horse hooves along narrow granite-surfaced roads. Plus overwhelming top-notes of horse shit.

London was mired in megatons of manure, thanks to the tens of thousands of horses harnessed into transportation in the city. But the main problem was another kind of loo: Britain had finally won the Napoleonic Wars at the decisive Battle of Waterloo in 1815.

Britannia ruled the waves, but 140,000 unemployed and often drunken sailors had now returned to Britain, loitering in search of What's Next? Worse still, Britain had spent around £1,650,000,000 in securing the victory, Europe's crops had failed catastrophically a couple of years earlier, and Britain had just announced the re-introduction of the gold standard, upon which deflation set in. The haves and the have-nots increasingly sniped at each other, and the stratification of English class became even more nuanced and pronounced. Financially and socially things were sour as a lime from a market barrow.

So, not ideal for Henry Llewellyn Lloyd, an orange merchant at Bridge Foot.

In the 1800s, citrus fruits were a luxury, much prized by Londoners. If you had a bowl of oranges on the table at Christmas dinner, you were someone.

Oranges were grown aplenty across the waters in Spain and Portugal, especially in the Azores islands belonging to the latter. Many estates had lookout towers erected so they could spot the British merchant ships approaching and start picking the fruit so it would be super-fresh for its journey back to Blighty. Many of the bigger British merchants set themselves up on Sao Miguel (St Michael), a Portuguese-held volcanic island about 1500km west of that country, in the middle of the North Atlantic Ocean. Elaborate mansions known as *solars* sprang up around the capital Ponta Delgada on the back of tens of millions of oranges and limes being exported to the UK.

Henry's father, er, Henry, was one such merchant, with Henry junior and his siblings born on Sao Miguel in the Azores. By the way, get used to the name Henry Lloyd … just about every second person in this story (apart from the ladies) is a Henry Llewellyn Lloyd!

Charles Lloyd, Henry's grandfather, was reportedly the private secretary to Lord Mansfield, a judge who set the legal course for the abolishment of slavery in the British empire, sent 102 people to the gallows, and had 448 others transported. When an angry mob known as the Gordon Rioters decided they'd had enough of rich folks in 1780, hundreds marched on Mansfield's mansion with flames held aloft and set about torching it. Quick-thinking Charles managed to save some valuable documents, for which — in gratitude — Mansfield paid him a £500 pension for life. Charles seems to have been quite an eccentric chap, apparently eschewing great-coats in all weather, and favouring the more youthful dressing style of knee-breeches, silk stockings, and silver buckles. And powdered wigs. One can't help picturing a Gilbert and Sullivan musical extravaganza — *HMS Pinafore* perhaps — with all its brass-buttoned buffoonery.

Back at Bridge Foot, Henry had been a middleman importing the luxury fruit from the Azores, Portugal, and Spain. This entailed financing and consigning, and paying customs duties to the Port of London. The Mediterranean trading boats would offload their golden cargo at Southwark, adjacent Bridge Foot. He'd also traipse through the narrow gas-lit lanes of four-storey houses, across the bridge to Lloyd's Coffee House at Lombard Street. Founded by Edward Lloyd in 1688, this shop was a convivial place for merchants like Henry and captains to meet, swap news, and begin informally sharing marine risks. The cafe smelt equally of coffee and salt, and maritime news and opportunities were posted on the notice board, becoming the go-to list of everything that was worth knowing about the maritime trade ... a trusted information network, a marketplace of individual underwriters, with animated betting on storms and survival rates of crew and cargo. In 1811 it became a corporate body but would not become 'Lloyd's of London, the insurance market' until an act of parliament enshrined it 60 years later.

There are rumoured connections of Henry's family being connected to that line of the Lloyd's, yet no ready evidence I could find.

But this whole lucrative barrow was tipped over when France demanded the Portuguese and Spanish stop trading with Britain, and the Peninsular War broke out on the Iberian Peninsula with the home teams of Portugal and Spain joining the UK to take on the French. Bloody noses ensued, and Napoleon deposed the Spanish House of Bourbon, installing his brother Joseph Bonaparte as king. The Lloyd family lost a part of its fortune in this downturn.

In 1811 Henry made his own overture to Alicia Whittle, who was the daughter of Col Samuel Whittle (later killed in battle) and Catherine de Visme. She too had been born on Sao Miguel. Their wedding was a rather grand affair in London's St James Cathedral, where a long line of Lloyds had been baptised and married, but there would have been some raised eyebrows in polite circles: Alicia was the ex-wife of Count Gerrard de Visme, another Portuguese-based English merchant, who was the benefactor of the British Hospital in Lisbon, and collector of antiquities, who lived in baronial splendour.

Henry and Alicia had two children while living for two or three years in Portugal; Catherine and Francisca. At Francisca's baptism in the Roman Catholic church, Sao Miguel, Lord Mansfield and his wife Emily de Visme (yes, it all sounds very nepotistic), stood as sponsors, along with Lord Packenham.

Perhaps having two young daughters amid all this Napoleonic drama was the catalyst for returning to Britain. Soon, sons Henry and Samuel were born.

And so, they had swapped the pleasant Mediterranean mildness of the Azores for the coldness of Britain. But the winter of 1819-20 was the coldest anyone could remember. Arctic winds kept the mercury pinned below zero. No wonder so many wanted to get the hell out!

With so many disaffected by economic downturn and unemployment, the brains trust at Whitehall decided to export their restless population problem and put a budget of £50,000 against it. The plan was to send settlers out to one of their newly captured territories, the Cape of Good Hope. *Bottom of Africa, old chap. A much better life, you know.*

The average Brit, if they had any preconceptions of Africa, would've thought of it as nothing more than a place of violent sunshine, waterless wilds, death-winds from the deserts, and perhaps certain death from its malicious wildlife.

Tenders were invited for team leaders to put together groups of 10 or more men (and their families) of various trades and skills, and all families were offered free passage to the Cape, free food on board, plus 100 acres of land when they got there. Sounds like a good deal. Many thought so, and signed up when they heard of it, usually through networks of friends and colleagues.

One such aspiring team leader was Thomas Willson, a rather ambitious architect, also now facing difficult times with the shrinking economy. He soon had 307 men, women, and children signed up to his team. Including one Henry Lloyd, who registered himself as a humble harness maker. A trade they'd need in the territory, surely. (It is not clear whether his orange merchant business had soured completely to the point he had to take up that trade to survive.)

Now 35, Henry and Alicia had four children under the age of eight. And he also signed up his sister-in-law Mary, a spinster in her mid-30s, to be their 'servant' possibly to boost her chances of selection on the adventure.

Tender applications poured in and were vetted. Finally, approvals were granted. In all there would be 3487 settlers, divided across a fleet of 14 vessels to sail from London to Port Algoa in the Cape Colony, in December 1819.

Willson collected £5 'deposits' from all families — before his party was officially confirmed — against which later supplies and materials could be drawn.

Most parties were assigned to one vessel, although some larger parties were split across multiple vessels. Party 1, the Bailie Party, was allocated to sail on the *Chapman*. In this group were Henry's cousin Henry James Lloyd (a worsted twister aka wool yarn maker), his wife Rebecca, and four children. The *Chapman* had just returned from delivering a load of convicts to Sydney, Australia, and would later make further convict transport trips to Hobart and Sydney.

The Willson Party (Party 17) was assigned to the three-masted barque *La Belle Alliance*: 38 metres in length, just over 10 metres across, and launched just a couple of years earlier. Scheduled date of departure: 23 December 1819. Embarkation point: Deptford on the River Thames.

Deptford carried the weight of British maritime history on its shoulders, being the jumping-off point for notables such as Sir Francis Drake and Captain James Cook. But this day was not very promising: for there lay eight three-masters completely iced-in along the dock.

Luckily the *Chapman* had loaded earlier in December, sailing to the Downs anchorage at Gravesend. Here the tidal flow and salt water kept the channel more open. They would be the first to sail.

England was at the tail-end of a mini–Ice Age, and the gales on the Thames were said to be the severest in forty years. So maybe death-winds from the desert were relatively attractive.

But still the largely artisanal Willson Party of assorted farmers, cabinetmakers, butchers, carpenters, tailors, glaziers, shoemakers, bakers, architects, weavers, labourers and locksmiths (and a harness maker) went about checking in to the *La Belle Alliance* (or the 'Bell of Lions' as some wag nicknamed it). The idea was to have self-contained settler parties. There were a few odd inclusions in the party: a lawyer, a piano tuner, and a taxidermist.

But, taxidermist or not, *everybody* was stuffed, with no chance of the vessel departing anytime soon. Passengers were able to walk across the frozen Thames to the other vessels, even to shore without a boat or gangplank. The kids took to playing games on the ice. Dances were also held on the ice, as a fiddler played his heart out, and refreshments stalls soon mushroomed. New Years Eve came with rousing renditions of *Auld Lang Syne* that resonated poignantly. The Cape of Good Hope awaited them. But as we know, hope is not a strategy. Others gave up, riddled with gnawing doubts about this new better life in the colonies, and went home. *Cape of Good Riddance*!

Perhaps it was the extra £10 Willson requested from each settler, indicating it could be offset against materials and supplies on the voyage and at their destination, that tipped the balance for some. He also stated that a 5 per cent service fee on all amounts was payable to him for his troubles.

It was early afternoon on 19 January that *La Belle Alliance* could shake itself free of the ice enough to set sail. It made it as far as Blackwall, not five kilometres distant, before once again the weather imprisoned them, like a novelty ice block. Five kilometres an hour is a frustratingly slow speed … five kilometres a *month* brought out the worst in the impatient passengers, tempers often boiling over on the crowded vessel with its cramped conditions.

Valentine's Day finally saw them make it to the open sea.

They left behind a Britain teetering on the edge of the rather repressive Victorian era, and all the hardships depicted by Dickens. Better out than in.

The food was passable but plentiful. Biscuits and beef, pork and mustard. Tea, cocoa, sugar. A ration of rum was also dispensed. But it paid to be sick: apart from other preserved meats, those in poor health were given wine to buck them up!

The ship's crew had a doctor, but there were also two surgeons on the passenger manifest, Drs Cock and Pawle. Regular airing and fumigation took place to control the rats and and cockroaches, but illnesses such as whooping cough, measles, and smallpox relished the crowded conditions to run rampant. Sadly, Cock's wife and three of his five children succumbed to smallpox and were buried at sea (read: tipped overboard).

Some took to shark fishing. The heat and monotony got to others. Other times the high seas would force a battening of the hatches, with passengers confined below decks. Four guns were fired to mark their passing over the equator, initiation including walking the plank over a tub of water on deck.

It was now that Willson put his cards on the table, calling for a meeting with the heads of families, and making a claim to be considered and treated as 'Lord of the Manor'. Furthermore, he claimed exclusive rights to hunt, fish, and cut timber on any settler's land. And he could call on them to work for his benefit without fair compensation for at least the first two years. Deep resentment bubbled.

Especially when later conversations went along the lines of settlers who paid a specified sum into his personal 'Fund of Indemnity' would sway his allocation of certain prized land to settlers. He was monetising access to land: free land, as decreed by the government.

Not a moment too soon, on 1 May 1820, Table Mountain was sighted. Excited cries of 'Land!' went up. Cape Town, settled by the Dutch since Jan van Riebeeck claimed the Cape for the Dutch East India Company (VOC) as a strategic revictualling point on the southern tip of the continent. But after anchor was weighed, they were told that, due to the smallpox on board, only party leaders could disembark. They were to proceed directly to their final destination: Algoa Bay.

They skirted the fertile coast, admiring the bluish mountains as they headed eastward along Africa's southernmost coast. But this gave way around Cape Recife to more desolate sand hills and rocky outcrops, and they dropped anchor further north-east in Algoa Bay, noting its barren, dreary, windswept appearance.

This is the promised land? All they could see were a few houses and many, many, many tents. With the jovial-looking Sir Rufane Donkin, acting governor of the colony, there to welcome them.

But not just yet.

The *Chapman* (with Henry's cousin Henry onboard) was the first settler boat to land in Algoa Bay, followed by six other vessels. The tents of 'Settlers Town' were bursting with earlier arrivals — would they mind waiting on board for, oh, another a week or two? Finally, after around 160 days at sea, they were loaded into lighter barges (like whaling boats) for a rather lively ride into shore: after all just nearby is what would one day become known as the famous Jeffries Bay surf break. At the beach, Scottish soldiers of the 72nd Regiment — stationed there in the Fort Frederick blockhouse, tents, and pavilions — helped carry the women and children ashore. The men waded in best as they could or hitched a ride on the back of a native porter.

So this was Africa.

They spent the first month living in the tented settler town, awaiting transport to their designated area, Zuurfeld, roughly halfway between the present townships of Grahamstown and Bathurst. Willson tried again to gain recognition as Lord of the Manor, now upping the ante that he should get 1000 acres, not 100 like the ordinary settlers. One disgruntled settler threatened to put a gun to his greedy head unless he backed down.

Finally, their ride arrived, and jaws dropped at the sight of 60 Dutch-owned ox wagons, pulled by long-horned cows.

'Tall Dutch-African Boers, with broad brimmed white hats, and huge tobacco pipes in their mouths, were shouting in Colonial-Dutch,' noted Thomas Pringle of the Scottish Party. 'Whips were smacking, bullocks bellowing, wagons creaking; and the half-naked Hottentots, who led the long teams of draught oxen, were running and hallooing, and waving their long lank swarthy arms in front of their horned followers, like so many mad dervishes.'

Their gear was loaded onto the wagons, and they trundled over to the government stores to avail themselves of axes, hammers, picks, spades, and saws, covered by their initial deposits. Then off into the desolate bushland. Many rivers were forded. They struggled up Addo Hill, gobsmacked by the sighting of wild elephants in their hundreds. Springboks bounded and wild flowers abounded. Delightful distractions.

Then the long column diverged, each party heading in different directions. Willson's party trundled towards the plains between Waayplaats and Kowie, rich in elephants, which some immediately tried to down with fowling-pieces, long-barreled muzzle-loaders, more suited to guinea fowl and ducks.

After nearly two weeks of bouncing around in the back of the ox carts via Lombard's Post, they finally arrived at an area on the Bush River, a right-bank tributary of the Torrens River, their party's allocated area in the Albany District (despite Willson's wishes to call it Angloville). Tents were pitched, and all their trunks, boxes, and baggage were offloaded. Then the Boers rode off, back towards the coast. Leaving the Lloyds sitting alone on their suitcases on their patch of land. That was it. No instructions, no directions, no anything. This was their new life.

'Our roughly-kind carriers seemed, as they wished us good-bye, to wonder what would become of us,' wrote Rev Henry Hare 'HH' Dugmore, who'd arrived as a 10-year-old with his family on the *Sir George Osborn* with Gardner's party. 'There we were in the wilderness, and when they were gone, we had no means of following, had we wished to do so. We must take root and grow or die where we stand.'

Willson, having dispatched his party to their destination, stayed the night, did an about-turn and returned to Algoa Bay, and thence to England, in an act that proved his self-serving intentions. Twenty-five of his party sued him for return of around £300 they believe he still owed them, once all his fancy accounting deductions and claw-backs had been deciphered.

At which point, a major deceit surfaced. The British had a garrison at Grahamstown, but what they really needed was a buffer between the natives and the Boers to fill the vacuum. A few thousand exported English settlers would prove a win-win. The ultimate club sandwich.

The main reason the settlers were here was as human shields. Nowhere had the government mentioned that the KhoiKhoi (aka Hottentots, the pastoral branch of the Khoi-San people) and 20,000 Xhosa people who traditionally owned this land had been displaced in a series of concerted battles just eight years earlier. The Xhosa are generally considered more democratic and consensual than, say, the Zulus, but make no mistake they are tough buggers — as young men they are circumcised with assegais!

The Kap River area was the frontline, and Scott's Party and the Irish Party dangerously occupied Kaffir's Drift. Bailie's Party was a human buffer in the tense border area of the Great Fish River, near Bathurst. But it was Mahoney's party at an area called the Clay Pits who first bore the brunt of every native plundering raid.

They had all been sold down the river.

2

WELCOME TO AFRICA

ALBANY, 1820. The first order of business was securing water (easy: rivers and tributaries nearby) and making fires each night to keep the animals at bay (hyenas could be heard cackling and cajoling each night).

Over the next few weeks, there was much jockeying for the land grants. About 40 of the families had direct experience in agriculture, so knew better what they were looking at. Some prioritised water access, the sentimental sought out scenic views. Some wanted flat lands, some wanted higher blocks to protect against floods and natives. The nervous chose defensible positions. Some got what they wanted, others took what they got. But everyone was now the proud owner of 100 acres of African bushland, never mind that there was no title to go with it because, well, the land wasn't actually the British government's to give away in the first place.

But they felt they were finally standing on their own ground, the first time for many. No records remain as to where exactly Henry chose to set up his family.

In the absence of Willson, the Rev William Boardman was appointed the party's new leader, and he proved popular. After all there was a lot to pray for here. (He himself was praying that the government would pay his stipend as minister to the party: it would take nearly two years to agree an amount let alone get any cash.)

Basic sleds and wagons were hewn from hard yellowwood trees. Carrots were planted. Corn. Wheat. All would take time to mature. Some never did, because it turns out that when carrots are planted two-feet under, and onions are planted roots-upward, or maize is planted still on the cob, they don't actually grow. Who knew? But some soon had peas, beans, and potatoes to add to their pots. Along with antelope, wild pigs, guinea fowls, and ducks.

They thrilled in spotting leopard, zebras, monkeys and baboons in the exotic landscape. Less delighted at seeing scorpions and snakes. A story got around that at least one child had been bitten by a *pofadder* (puff adder), one of the most dangerous snakes on the continent.

Government-provided rations covered this period while they were becoming established. Provided at cost, they were drawn down against the group's deposit and they had to collect these themselves. Not so easy when the collection points were Cape Town, Grahamstown, and Bathurst, and there were no roads, you had no horses yet anyway — so much for Henry's harness making skills — and there were no ox-carts available. Each time, the ten live sheep had to be herded along on foot, and 200 lbs of maize meal lugged by hand.

One time a pack of hunting dogs took after the sheep, scattering them in every direction. The aghast settlers dropped their maize bundles and tried to regather their sheep. But darkness closed in, they got lost, their sheep were lost, and finally they couldn't even find where they'd left their maize!

A few days later another party returning from Bathurst with sheep realised they'd forgotten something in the town. They asked a little boy to stay behind and mind the sheep while they double-backed. To ensure the sheep didn't scarper, they bound the sheep's legs together. The boy could only look on in mixed wonder and horror as a pack of vultures swiftly descended on the immobilised sheep!

Housing was a priority, as protection against typical days of 30-35 degrees (more during heatwaves), while winter offered up only 5-10 degree days, with freezing point reached on colder nights. Sheepskin became popular for garments, often trimmed with jackal fur by the more fashionable. Local *veldskoen* shoes took the place of traditional English Wellington boots.

As per the plan for self-sufficient communities, there were a few carpenters and labourers in the party. 'Wattle and daub' designs were the quick and easy solution, with materials freely available nearby. Father-and-son teams roamed the hills, axes across shoulders, looking for solid rafters and door posts. Roofs were thatched.

Clay was plentiful in the escarpment and proved an effective plaster. The local Khoikhoi people had been using it for centuries, and friction arose when 600 KhoiKhoi turned up, but it was deemed they should now pay to collect it from the Clay Pits. Three settlers were killed at the area quickly nicknamed 'The Forlorn Hope'.

Trade was soon flourishing between the English and the Dutch, who happily accepted china and silverware in exchange for their cows and milk. Later the Dutch would realise it was a sellers' market and raised prices of their goods to intolerable levels (and palmed off the scrawniest of their herds on to the ignorant Brits).

The government imposed strict controls, settlers requiring a pass to be procured to go from the settlements to Grahamstown, at the risk of spending a night in the *tronk* (prison). This rubbed many up the wrong way, as they thought they'd left behind in England such behavioural strictures. It was almost like they were under house arrest here. In desperation, some sold their government-issued stores such as blankets.

As horses were progressively introduced and procured, Henry's prospects were good because halters and harnesses were much in demand, but he was presumably too busy with trying to get his crops going to pay much heed to his former trade.

When not herding cattle, the children attended classes run by Rev Boardman: initially outdoors, then later as things got more fancy, in a marquee tent. He also started Sunday services from the get-go.

Overall, the Albany valley seemed pleasant and fertile, and everyone knuckled down to make a go of it. It was a one-way ticket after all.

But then the harsh realities of farming in Southern Africa knocked on their front door. First it was red rust, causing the wheat crops to wither and die. At least one farmer, John Jarman, decided there was an easier way to make a living than farming. He built The Bathurst Arms Inn and discovered a more lucrative life. Africa can be thirsty work.

The following year, crops were decimated again. And again the following year.

By 1823 rust was no longer a problem, because there was a severe drought. Followed by incessant rains which not only violated their crops, but also their homes, washing some of the lower-lying structures away downstream in the ensuing squalls (despite having been warned of this risk beforehand by Lt Robert Hart). The Fish River rose by 30 feet in a single day, another 10 feet the next. Then came the locusts. Truly biblical!

But Albany proved suitable for cattle, and maize — which they called mealies — and floury Clumber potatoes. A Mrs James, probably the wife of Thomas James of Bathurst/ Lower Albany, gained fame in the district for her Green Fountain cheese, named for their farm. Dairying and cheese-making were household-level survival crafts, typically done by women, turning perishable milk into something more durable and tradable.

Cattle rustling by the KhoiKhoi was at an all-time high, with thousands of cattle being stolen or slaughtered each year, plus there was harassment by the same tribes.

To bolster protection, a proclamation was made by Lord Somerset, governor of the Cape Colony, requiring all males between 16 and 60 years old to be called out to serve on a commando force, The Albany Levy, and they all had to undergo training and swear allegiance to King George IV, which didn't sit well with many. It proved ineffectual and was later scrapped.

Two settler children — aged just 8 and 11, and playmates of Rev Boardman's kids — were murdered while herding cattle by marauding natives. This was too much for the Reverend to bear. On top of this, his stipend as minister was still in arrears. To overcome his woes he moved to nearby Bathurst, and opened a grammar school.

Henry Lloyd was similarly disaffected. I wonder if he learned a certain word from the Dutch Boers: *gatvol.* It means entirely fed up with something. He gave up his 100 acres and moved his family to Grahamstown, where he became a schoolmaster. Grahamstown would eventually become an important education centre, with famous schools like St Andrew's and Kingswood soon established, and flourishing till now. Settlers' children educated here became governors, legislators, and generals across the colony over time.

Henry was imbued with an entrepreneurial spirit. Many of the tradesmen and artisans of Albany did the same, forfeiting their grants and moving to urban centres to ply their trade and earn a Pound.

Those who exited early might've fared best, because for the next three years, failure was the main harvest. Bricklayers and carpenters and shoemakers found better livings in Grahamstown.

■ □ ■

Grahamstown had been established around 10 years earlier as a frontier garrison post by Col John Graham. It was in Xhosa territory, and the Cape Frontier Wars between Cape colonists and the indigenous pastoralists had flared on and off since 1779.

Henry and Alicia obviously felt more comfortable in their new inland locale and produced eight more children — one per annum from 1825 (some barely nine months apart!) — for a total of 12 (the last one Margaret given the middle name Boardman in honour of the good reverend). One would become a chemist, another a blacksmith, and son James would later become a carpenter/joiner. One son would die aged 4, another daughter died aged 12.

Grahamstown boomed around them with the influx of settlers and traders, going from hundreds to thousands; houses in High Street and New Street crowding the military buildings, barracks, and hospital that previously dominated the town's centre. A new courthouse and jail were constructed, and housing sprawled beyond Hill and Bathurst Streets, and up the hillside beyond the market, an area for the less prosperous dubbed 'Settlers' Hill'.

Not all Brits prospered here: some were impoverished coming off their failed farms, and others failed in their trades (£6 a month was the going rate for many craftsmen). But mechanics generally fared well fixing pumps, ploughs, and milling gear. Meanwhile Africans moved into the town sensing opportunity with the settler population, creating their own space in and around the town, a complex melting pot which would develop across the country in years to come: Cosmopolitan. Chaotic.

Many tried to make a city and lifestyle in the image of England, but this was not entirely possible because of the blended interactions between the British, KhoiKhoi, and other Africans, typical of a frontier trading town. The latter wanted to live in their own traditional style. Land was ultimately set aside as a dedicated KhoiKhoi 'location' near the cemetery, which became something of a ghetto of straw hovels.

The Brits meanwhile went about wearing English clothing (black neckerchiefs, velveteen, and patent leather anyone?), reading English books and magazines, consuming English goods, and eating English staples. Many sat in the grounds of the churches and reminisced wistfully about the 'dear old land' which most would never again visit. They celebrated their Sovereign and royal occasions. As the *Grahamstown Journal* expressed it: 'In devoted attachment to the land of their forefathers, we hesitate not to say there are no people on earth who surpass the British settlers of Albany.' Ironic, given they'd paid to escape it.

Construction of that most English of things — a spired church — kicked off in 1824, with St George's Church still dominating the city's skyline to this day.

But they developed a distinct 'settler identity' forged in the hot fires of their dependence on African communities they not-so-secretly feared, and the insecurity that bred. Unique local customs developed, such as the 'African welcome' for dignitaries, which involved a signaller firing a shot in the air, at which anyone in the town who owned a gun would fire a shot or volley of shots, the echoes ringing around the hills.

Just like London, Grahamstown stunk of horse manure, and added to that was the putrid stench from the abattoir. Stray dogs were everywhere, dangerous and dirty. The solution: let prisoners out in teams, with sticks, to club them to death in front of outraged shoppers.

While the settlers hoped that British working-class labourers would be available to assist them, that immigration policy never materialised, so the default became the hiring of local Africans at cheaper rates.

A lively public market fair at Fort Willshire on the Keiskamma River, a good few hours' ride, was the epicentre of symbiosis. 'A place of some animation, and that of a strange and wild character,' observed HH Dugmore. 'The motley throng of black and white and brown, varied by the red, green, and blue uniforms of Line, Rifles, and Artillery.' Interpreters named their price, amid the general mangling of several languages. Wagons laden with ivory, native weapons and fabrics, ostrich feathers, hides, horns, even live wild animals attracted curious crowds. Butter, tallow, and salted meat were always best-sellers.

One product caught on immediately: *biltong*. It was a practical way to preserve game and beef in the harsh climate, propagated in the 17th century among Dutch settlers, probably borrowing the idea from the Khoi-San and Portuguese, who both had meat-curing traditions. (Domestic fridges only became popular 130 years later.) You can imagine the moment they were introduced to *biltong* — a heavenly chorus of 'Hallelujah! 'as their tastebuds danced a merry jig to that salty sensation.

One side effect of all this protein: the Settlers soon noticed the next generation — of even some of the shortest fathers — had no trouble reaching six feet in height.

Later, wool from merino sheep would become a major export from this area, once the farmers had worked out what the land was actually good for. Good news if you were a worsted twister.

But luckily Henry, Alicia, and family were off the land now. In 1829, the Kaffir Wars exploded across the frontier territory — some believe stoked by smugglers of guns and gunpowder — with houses set on fire, settlers murdered, and cattle driven off.

'Kaffir' comes from the Arabic Arabic word *kāfir*, meaning non-believer or infidel. Through Indian Ocean trade routes, the term drifted down the East African coast and was picked up by Europeans. By the time of the Cape frontier in the early 1800s, British settlers were using *'Kaffir'* to refer broadly to Xhosa-speaking peoples, especially those east of the frontier. It was a general ethnic label, rather than the slur it would become much later.

The Xhosa territories beyond colonial control were generally referred to as Kaffirland or Kaffraria.

The Afrikaner Voortrekkers, unhappy with their lot under stifling British rule, headed off from the Eastern Cape on the Great Trek in 1834 to take parts of Natal to claim as their own Boer republic, with Pietermaritzburg as its capital. Simple folks — all they really wanted was to be left alone, and all they needed were a Bible and a blunderbuss — it was to become a big part of the future psyche of this land.

The Brits dug in even further. 'Every storm has left the English oak that has been transplanted to this Southern clime more deeply rooted,' reflected Rev Dugmore.

More troops were sent, Grahamstown expanded even further. Major Selwyn built himself an ostentatious castellated villa named 'Selwyn Castle'. Time was counted off the cannon shot from Fort Selwyn, and red-coated troops frequently marched through the streets in a show of force. Army bands provided entertainment. But arguably the best entertainment came from Khoikhoi — perhaps a few beers deep — falling in behind the red coats, playfully dancing and mimicking them often with rude gestures thrown in for good measure. Such was life's rich tapestry in the Cape frontiers.

But relations with the KhoiKhoi neighbours were always at a flashpoint, the natives proving themselves to be brutal warriors. They torched and razed many of the dwellings at Lower Albany — the area where wool man Henry Thomas Lloyd's family were — forcing many to leave their settled farms, and flee to the safety of Grahamstown, women and children seeking refuge inside the church. 'The burning homesteads of Lower Albany lighted up the horizon night after night, and imagination was left to paint its most fearful pictures,' recalled Rev Dugmore.

Then the unimaginable: the British garrison abandoned Fort Willshire in 1836, which fell into the hands of local chiefs, Tyali and Maqoma. The displaced settlers could only watch horrified and helpless as the KhoiKhoi carted away all the spoils of war.

Amid this unrest, Henry and Alicia moved further inland — as did a few of their now-grown children — to Uitenhage which was transforming from a Cape Dutch town into a beautiful English-style town with wide tree-lined streets, and gaining prominence, as the eastern coastline still suffered from the Frontier Wars and general unrest.

Historians estimate 10 to 15 per cent of the original settlers eventually went back to Britain, at least temporarily. Settler Henry and Alicia were among those returning for a trip to London, most likely to visit family and see the old country.

On return, Henry would die in Uitenhage, aged just 60. Possibly spooked by the renewed frontier conflicts of 1846/47 in Eastern Cape, Alicia headed back to England where she passed away in 1848.

By 1852 most of the land from the Cape up to the Limpopo River was invaded, annexed, and under 'white' — either Dutch or British — control.

Intrepid settler Henry and Alicia had planted the seeds of a family tree in Africa — which would thrive far better than their farming attempts — and last at least the next two hundred years.

3

GREEN GOLD

MAURITIUS 1830s. If you trace a line with your finger east from the coast of Southern Africa you'll come across the tiny island of Mauritius. It is isolated now: back in the early 19th century, doubly so. It had morphed from a French colony 'Isle de France' to being under British rule after Napoleon's thrashing but still retained a very French air in its way of life, even its legal system.

There, lived an interesting character named Ephraim Rathbone. English by birth — from Tiverton, Devon — he'd been a sugar planter in the colony for 16 years. Ephraim had married a French-Mauritian woman, Josephine Modet, and — contrary to the famous expression 'Not tonight, Josephine' — she'd borne two sons to him, eccentrically giving them middle names after famous British war ships: Thomas Britannia and Frederic Dart. But she sadly died (diseases like malaria, cholera, typhoid, and TB were endemic). He remarried, this time to an English lass called Anne Williamson.

In 1842 Ephraim was on a study tour to the embattled region known as the Republic of Natalia (now KwaZulu-Natal). The Boers had recently prevailed over King Dingane's Zulus, and the Brits were keen to restamp their authority in the region and regain control of it.

There they inspected the Natal Cotton Company's fields on the Umdloti River. Ephraim was unimpressed by the potential of the crop, given how thirsty it was for irrigation, and suggested to its manager — Edmund Morewood, an Englishman — that maybe sugar cane was a better prospect.

The gents formed a mutual admiration society. Rathbone convinced him to experiment with five acres initially and found some cane growing on a farm at Umgeni, which he purchased for Morewood. (A local variant *imphe* was also growing but deemed to be too low in sugar content to be viable.) He also imported four "Mauritian coolies" to work the farm, because they had the know-how.

Immediately successful, two things happened: Morewood resigned his cotton job to focus on his own sugar cane enterprise, and Rathbone moved his young family to Natal to become manager of Morewood's new 40-acre farm at Compensation (around 50km north of Durban, now eThekwini).

Late in 1850, Morewood set up South Africa's first simple sugar mill, and the first local product was available. Natal had found what would become its most viable staple crop, sugar cane, which became dubbed 'green gold'. Land prices shot up from one shilling per acre to ten, as farmers switched over from cotton, wheat, beans, potatoes and coffee, to cash in.

Soon Morewood would have 100 acres under cultivation, but he soon ran into financial troubles and headed off to Brazil. Rathbone then got enterprising.

He moved up north in 1852, following the main wagon road and finding suitable land "10 miles beyond the Tugela" (*thukela*, meaning 'something that startles' in Zulu). This is where Zinkwazi is today. His occupation was listed at this time as a "Zulu trader". Read into that what you will, but the general understanding is he ran a trading store. He concerned himself with trading exotic fabrics and rugs, but also military outfits.

Morewood had been on good terms with the new Zulu king Mpande — half-brother of the great Shaka and Dingane — after he'd been involved in a peace treaty following the earlier Voortrekker frictions. He'd introduced Rathbone to him, and Mpande granted him use of some land, which Rathbone called Mauritius Farm. He set about establishing his own cane farm, where he and Annie also proceeded to have more children, continuing the British naval middle-name theme: John Mexican, Annie Chieftain, Alfred Legionier, Flora Blade, Harriet Ponguin, Caractacus Reliance, Boedicia Industria, Alfred Leyricer, Constance Rosemont, and finally — running out of inspiration or steam or nautical names — their last daughter was simply Elizabeth Edith (possibly the only one not bullied about their name at school). While Ephraim was my great-great-great grandfather, Annie Chieftain and Caractacus Reliance would later play a key part in our family's story.

But all was not peaceful around them. Mpande's sons — half-brothers Cetshwayo and Mbuyazi — got embroiled in a sibling shouting match which got a little out of hand. You see, Mpande favoured the younger son Mbuyazi to succeed him, but Cetshwayo, the rightful heir by age, sought to secure his own claim to the throne. It escalated with various factions supporting each brother until the whole Zulu nation was involved, and it boiled over near the Tugela River in 1856. Known as the Battle of Ndondakusuka, the brutal battle resulted in the deaths of thousands of Mbuyazi's supporters.

Poor old Rathbone's family was caught up in the middle of this, their house and farm severely trashed, and 80 oxen rustled.

The aftermath is that Cetshwayo won the battle, although his father remained king for many years after. But it cemented a model of centralised military power within the tribe that would shape the Zulu nation and foment future battles for its sovereignty.

Rathbone claimed damages from Mpande in 1859, set out in a two-page letter of legal pomposity or pompous legality — lots of 'heretofores ' and 'notwithstandings' — to the tune of £1876 (worth around £50,000 today). A cheeky 12 per cent interest rate had been applied and backdated. Plus, while we're on the front foot, how about we extend the boundaries of the farm to go all the way from "bounded on the north by the Amataculu, on the south by the Tugela, on the east by the main waggon road, and on the west by the river Umguinue." That's roughly from KwaDukuza (Stanger) to eThekwini (Durban), extending inland towards the Umgeni River near Pietermaritzburg. Over 3000 square kilometres; nearly half of all Zululand!

A chastened Mpande agreed to this, though he never signed the contract, and it created rather bad blood between him and Rathbone. There were whispers and reports and finger-pointing from the Zulu quarter. Cetshwayo took matters into his own hands in 1862: he acknowledged Rathbone's right to live there but ordered him to leave anyway. English law is one thing but a Zulu assegai to the ribs is another. Rathbone did the smart thing and left.

It was some consolation when a couple of years later Cetshwayo admitted any accusations against Rathbone were falsehoods and invited him to return and resume the friendship with the Zulu royal family. Thanks, but no thanks.

Ephraim moved to Utrecht near the Swaziland border, perhaps still fearful of the Zulus. Here he ran the farm Tiverton (named after his Devon birthplace). Ever the entrepreneur, Ephraim was later petitioning to run a passenger cart service in that town.

Ephraim Rathbone's promotion of the sugar industry, and indentation of imported labourers, would change the face of Natal forever. Over 150,000 Indians, mainly Tamils, were indentured from 1860 over the next few decades to meet demand for labourers, growing into a diaspora of 1.5 million Indians today. eThekwini is believed to be home to the largest Indian population outside of India, and often called 'Little India'.

His second son Frederick settled in the Tongaat area, where he was a farmer and shopkeeper, amassing farms and land that would be worth well over a million US dollars today.

These days there are over half a million acres of sugar cane under cultivation in KwaZulu-Natal, generating nearly $1 billion for the South African economy.

4

THE DESERT DUNES OF DURBAN

ENGLAND, 1861. Yorkshireman George Seymour, junior, was toiling away in the vast grounds of the Redbourne Estate in Lincolnshire, where he'd worked for 23 years. As head gardener it was his job to keep the 150 acres of landscaping around Redbourne Hall looking splendid for his employer — take a deep breath first — William Amelius Aubrey de Vere Beauclerk, the 10th Duke of St Albans. George's 15-year-old son John would also help in the gardens.

At the age of just 14, George himself had served an apprenticeship with his uncle James who'd been the head gardener at Sir John Stapleton's rather fine Georgian country house, Carlton Hall, Yorkshire. This is where his green thumbs were honed, a gene I definitely never inherited from these maternal forebears.

The surname Seymour is generally believed to derive from a Norman place name, introduced into England after the Norman Conquest. Most scholars trace it to Saint-Maur-des-Fossés, near Paris, whose name comes from the Latin Sanctus Maurus (Saint Maurus). Norman families bearing variants of the name de St Maur or de Sancto Mauro settled in England after 1066, and over time the name evolved in spelling through forms such as Seimor, Seymor, and eventually Seymour. By the medieval period the surname had become well established among the English gentry, most famously in the Wiltshire family that produced Jane Seymour, the third wife of Henry VIII.

While that aristocratic line is the best documented, the surname spread widely across southern and later northern England, including Yorkshire, through branches of lesser gentry, soldiers, clergy, and farmers. By the eighteenth and nineteenth centuries Seymours were well represented in parish registers across England, and many emigrated during the great waves of imperial migration to places such as South Africa, Australia, and North America. But we're getting ahead of ourselves ...

Most of Redbourne's nearly-4000 acre-spread was under crops, employing most of the local village folk who were not already employed in the local pubs (Redbourne was known as the 'Street of Inns' for years, because it was a stage-coach staging post and 25 pubs fed off the passing trade). It is a 'chocolate-box' English village, with rivers and old watermills.

England itself was enjoying the Victorian boom period, where it was the workshop of the world: around one fifth of everything produced in the world was made in Britain, and the Commonwealth countries especially had a boundless appetite for its goods.

Then one day word got out: the British government was advertising in newspapers and through parish networks for agricultural workers, artisans, and labourers, to emigrate to Natal and the Cape Colony, and boost the white settler population.

Just £10 to sail (a typical fare would've been nearly twice that). A good discount but still a lot of money, given it was about six months' work for the average farm worker to earn.

Work aplenty was on offer, apparently. George was an adventurous soul — he'd sailed to the west coast of the USA 20 years earlier, after the death of his father, George, snr. At the time cheap land grants and a sense of adventure had lured a few Englishmen and Irishmen to the western states. But hardship, disease, or economic frustration hastened many back to Britain, or its colonies.

Now at home in their gardener's cottage, the 48-year-old George mulled the move to South Africa over with his wife of over 20 years, Mary Ann. They had eight children to consider, although their eldest son was already 20, and daughter Sophia, 18, was soon to emigrate and marry in Napier, New Zealand.

Yes, they would do it. It was a big financial undertaking, but he had a friend or contact already in South Africa, a fellow Englishman from Kent called George Williamson, and he would stand surety for non-payment of the assisted passages.

The transport was the brigantine *Catherine*, a three-masted wooden vessel with square sails, that plied between Britain, Africa, and Asia. With five sons, including John (more about him later), and daughter Eliza almost 11, they boarded the *Catherine* on a dull, overcast

November day, with the fresh westerly wind whipping up the Thames into a chilly, choppy cauldron. Forty-six passengers headed downstairs to the steerage cabins — glorified straw-mattress bunks piled high — with only one couple, the Eridges, paying extra for cabin class.

Below decks, limited light crept through hatches, and poor ventilation often meant dampness and lingering smells of seasickness or whatever was being cooked (often by the passengers themselves, under direction of the ship's cook). The plain but filling meals included salt meat, ship's biscuits, oatmeal, peas, and tea, served at communal tables. Georges's Yorkshire humour — with a muttered joke or sardonic observation — might've given him and others a protective layer and lifted spirits even when the biscuits and salt meat were harder and tougher than the deck timbers.

After four months cramped up at sea, you can only imagine the relief of arriving in Durban on 8 March 1862. But on arrival most settlers were herded into immigration depots until such time as work or housing could be found.

Within a month, George was appointed to manage the coffee and sugarcane estate of one Mr Churchill, at Sydenham, less than half an hour by horse-drawn carriage north-west of Durban's docks. They would live here for the next 18 years until his retirement.

In 1863 the Durban Corporation was sourcing ideas for what was to become Durban Town Gardens. Gardener George couldn't help himself, threw his ideas into the competition, and was a co-winner! Durban Corporation wanted him on board to execute the winning plans. But bringing the lush ideas to reality was another thing altogether, because sand dunes seemed to be consuming the continent around Durban. Onshore winds and large sand deposits brought along by the Agulhas Current created this situation where roads and even railway tracks were often smothered in sand. This was a far cry from Lincolnshire.

He diligently set about taming the countryside and converting it into green turf studded with ornamental trees and bushes. Gradually the gardens took shape, and so impressed were the town authorities they wanted him to move on to another challenge: stopping the drifting sands in other parts of Durban, starting with the hallowed racetrack (which was not yet at Greyville, the current racetrack, but nearby).

So, the next phase of the Yorkshireman's career was dune stabilisation: planting of indigenous dune vegetation, and installation of sand fences and brushwood barriers. This seemed to do the job, with as many as 50 acres reclaimed from the sand in one year. The *Natal Mercury* hailed him as 'active, courageous, patient, and highly intelligent, he brought force to bear upon Mother Earth which almost compelled her to yield her best for the general good.'

But it wasn't all work. Clearly there was time for play, and this is where worlds started colliding.

George Williamson (who stood surety for them) was the father of Ann Rathbone, the second wife of Ephraim Rathbone. One of their daughters was Annie Chieftain, and next thing there was romantic interest between her and George Seymour's son, John, who was also working as a gardener. Perhaps her attraction is that — unlike her siblings — he had no middle name at all, let alone a silly one: he was simply John Seymour.

Within a few years, they'd be married on the Rathbone's farm in Utrecht.

George soon retired, moving to land in 295 Main Road, Escombe, which he called St Albans (after his former employer) and set about creating a landscaped residential environment, now known as La Manta Gardens.

Upon his passing, the *Mercury's* obituary noted him as 'a colonist of the highest stamp.'

5

EUREKA!

TRANSVAAL 1860s. Imagine you're a young boy, mucking about on the banks of the Orange River that runs through your family's farm in what is now the Northern Cape Province. Suddenly something catches your eye. It's a stone, but shiny; sparkly even. That's what happened to Erasmus Jacobs in Hopetown. He picked it up and was sufficiently excited to show it to his neighbour Schalk van Niekerk, who thought it might be something valuable. So, he in turn passed it on to a travelling Irish trader, John O'Reilly.

O'Reilly's first thought is that it might be a diamond, so sent it to Dr William Atherstone, a prominent geologist in Grahamstown.

Eureka! Yes, it was a diamond. In fact 21.25 carats worth. It became known as the Eureka Diamond, was sold for £500, and in 1867 triggered an El Dorado-like diamond rush that would change the course of South African history.

Within three years, 7000 diggers had descended on New Rush as they called the Barkly West (Pniel) area, 100km further up the Orange River. A further 30,000 hopefuls — blacks, whites, women, children — flooded into the Kimberley area adjacent to the Vaal River.

Into this seething morass on the dusty and barren stretch of Karoo *veldt* (open country), arrived many with little but stars in their eyes. One was a 19-year-old by the name of Cecil John Rhodes. Another was 16-year-old Caractacus 'Crack 'Rathbone, who gave up farming and headed with his new brother-in-law John Seymour to mine some claims at Heilbron. These proved fruitless, so they moved on to Dutoit's Pan, and then on to Kimberley, where they mined for a year before selling out their claims one year later, moving on to a short stint on a gold reef at Marabastad, before both returned to farming.

Caractacus headed to the South coast, where Ephraim would also soon acquire land in Lower Amanzimkulu in Pondoland — inland from Port

Shepstone. Ephraim passed away at 70, leaving no will, but left assets including his property at Amanzimkulu, two wagons, a herding pen, and some property ("or claim on some property") in the Transvaal. Half of all Zululand was not his apparently.

John returned to the mining-heavy area of Newcastle in Midlands, Natal, where Annie soon gave birth to their first child, George Frederick Seymour, and later two more sons and a daughter.

Yet another arrival to the rush was a young dark-haired boy-nearly-man, with a wide face, angular nose and strong jaw: Henry. Yes, another Henry Llewellyn Lloyd, the grandson of the orange merchant-settler Henry, and son of James who'd been working as a carpenter in Smithfield, a rural farming area.

We're not sure when exactly Henry arrived at New Rush but he probably set to work prospecting for diamonds. These were dry diggings, meaning decent-sized diamonds lay on the surface, or just below it. And if you dug down just a few more feet under the topsoil, even more riches were yielded.

Sounds glamorous. The reality was less so. Prospectors lived in anything from tents to huts … some even in holes in the ground. Anything to escape the wild winds that frequently lashed the *veldt*. But just like on the cramped settler ships, disease sniffed an opportunity. Many came down with 'camp fever', an unspecified condition but mostly an infection which comprised some or all of malaria, typhoid, dysentery, tuberculosis, chickenpox, smallpox, syphilis, and gonorrhoea. To get treatment, you went to yet another tent where there *might* be a doctor, but ...

Some 'medicos' were merely first-year dropout students. And they were the better ones! Quacks had a field day, offering miracle cures for prices depending on the depth of your pockets on the day.

But soon enough, real doctors arrived including Dr Leander Starr Jameson, who was recommended by the Dean of the University College Hospital, London. Tents became small wattle-and-daub clinic buildings, then a stone building, but that burnt down. Then finally in 1871 a 20-bed hospital. And so the number of hospitals and beds grew to cope with the amount of camp fever doing the rounds, as well as accidents and injuries from work and play. (Jameson would later befriend Rhodes, fall under his spell, and tarnish his reputation with involvement in the ill-fated Jameson Raid of Transvaal.)

Under Sister Henrietta Stockdale, the matron at Kimberley Hospital, a register of all qualified nurses in the area was proposed to manage their resources. Opposition to this register came from none other than Florence Nightingale in England. Nightingale feared that formal registers could become mere administrative tools, emphasising paperwork over actual competence and care, and colonial posts not meeting and replicating British standards and morals. But, as we now know, Registered Nurses are the bedrock of the hospital system globally.

The Kimberley area was considered the greatest honky-tonk town in history. Shopkeepers, barkeepers, traders all flocked to service the prospectors. As did practitioners of the world's oldest profession.

The Star of the West, Canard Hotel, the Globe Tavern, and the Halfway House — among many other less salubrious establishments — slaked the thirst of the hard-working and hard-living miners. Beer and biff were the order of the day.

The New Rush shanties were home to many red-light establishments, where for a few shillings a miner could lighten his load in the most basic of circumstances (see 'camp fever'). If someone had struck it rich, and were feeling a little fancier on the day, they might sidle off to the French Madame's Establishment, where a night's entertainment would set them back a couple of pounds.

And food-wise, apart from *biltong*, another local delicacy was introduced to the British, firstly in the Eastern Cape, then on the mine camps of the Witwatersrand, through intermarriage and cultural transfer: *boerewors*. This local farmer's sausage was a staple enjoyed widely at *braais* (BBQs) by the later 1800s and is a national signature dish to this day.

Rhodes had come to South Africa for 'health reasons' and was an active miner, befriending Charles Rudd, who'd arrived some years earlier. An astute schemer, Rhodes — with Rudd — started buying up claims of unsuccessful miners, and buying out others who'd had enough.

One area, a hill, was particularly fruitful. Resources were focused there: thousands of sweaty labourers using basic hand tools such as picks, shovels, and wheelbarrows. It soon became known as 'The Big Hole'. Heat, dust, and poor sanitation sapped the health of those lucky enough not to be involved in frequent collapses and accidents. Rugged stuff. (It was 60 years before the International Labour Organisation introduced safety standards for mines.)

In 1880 Rudd and Rhodes formed De Beers Mining Company. Within 20 years they would control 90 per cent of the world's diamond production.

Henry (grandson of Settler Henry) was working as a storekeeper and living at Pneil, a 19-hectare Lutheran Mission estate, originally established as a settlement for freed slaves, close to Barkly West. Anglo-Dutch buildings lent the area a distinctive feel, but mainly it was a makeshift enclave of tents and shanties for prospectors.

He'd taken a fancy to a young half-Spanish lass, Mary Emeline Rivas, who was living at Waldeck's Plant, an alluvial mine on the Vaal River, only 5km away. He was 26, she was 32 when they decided to marry in 1883. Her uncle gave consent to their union, and they got married at St Mary's church (the principal Anglican parish on the diamond fields, which replaced the original tent).

Oh, it's probably worth mentioning one small thing: they were first cousins! She was the daughter of his aunt Alicia, the first of Settler Henry's many children to be born in Grahamstown.

Mary's father was a Spaniard, Mariano Rivas (originally Ribas), who was shipwrecked off Cape Recife, the treacherous entrance to Algoa Bay known widely as a ship-eater, because it would be 1851 before a lighthouse was built on it. In total 2400 vessels had run afoul along the treacherous Cape coastline since the 1500s.

One night in August 1842, the low-lying cape and strong Cape Agulhas currents conspired to make the captain of the *Sabina* — a two-masted wooden brig en route from Manila in the Philippines to Cadiz, Spain — believe he was further out to shore than he was. Next thing at 4am they were locked in the death grip of its rocky reefs in heavy seas, and the ship broke up quickly. Of 62 on board, only 40 survived, washed ashore in battered shape.

Many such survivors either waited for onward passage to Spain, or, like Mariano — probably a humble colonial servant in the Philippines, or a trader — got on with life in the Cape and assimilated, marrying Alicia four years after his shipwreck. Mariano was 19 years older than Alicia, and already 45 when Mary was born.

When Henry and Mary gave birth to a daughter Marionetta, there was clearly great excitement, because — while baptisms were typically witnessed or sponsored by the parents only — no less than three other friends sponsored her baptism at St Mary's in Barkly West, where they'd married. Mary sadly passed away in 1888 at their home in Hebron (65km southwest of Barkly West) when Marionetta was just an 18-month-old toddler.

On top of that, Henry's father James (who'd also moved up to Barkly West and lived at Waldeck's Plant where daughter-in-law Mary Rivas used to live) had passed away the previous year.

Poor Henry struck rock bottom.

6

TURNING EMERALDS INTO GOLD

IRELAND 1879. Flicking through the *Dundalk Democrat* newspaper at this time made for dreary reading: economic distress, land agitation, and increasing support for nationalist movements.

And certainly the poor weather wasn't helping anybody's mood. Local harvests — oats, barley and potatoes — had failed. And everyone of a certain age still had The Potato Famine of the mid-1850s fresh in their minds. Crops were fetching less for farmers.

On top of this, the Irish National Land League was clamouring for land reform and a better deal for tenant farmers. Plus, the Home Rule movement was gaining serious steam, demanding self-governance for Ireland.

This was not *craic* (fun) as young Michael McGee knew it. Because he stood to lose a lot. You see, just a couple of years earlier he'd lost his mum and dad in short succession, and inherited the family farm, a rather lovely sprawl of 52 acres named Dee Farm, on which a few cows, cattle, and pigs enjoyed life, while the stock horses did all the hard yards, such as ploughing the fields. He lived at Charleville, a rather splendid Georgian-style pile, surrounded by a forest rich with game for hunting.

One day, a letter in the newspaper caught his eye. It was from a local lad who'd emigrated to South Africa and was having a fine time prospecting at Pilgrim's Rest, which was at the heart of the Transvaal gold rush after Alec 'Wheelbarrow' Patterson found massive deposits in the local creek a few years earlier. In less than a year some 1500 diggers were working 4000 claims.

The letter excited Michael. South Africa seemed like a vibrant place where good weather, an abundance of wild game hunting, and the chance to strike it really rich all came together. He shared this with his girlfriend, Bridget Sarsfield, the 19-year-old daughter of a publican who lived in Mullins Cross, about 9km away.

What if we ran away to South Africa, and made a fantastic life for ourselves there? A wildly romantic notion. *But* …

Michael's father had stipulated some very stern conditions in his will. Michael got the farm but was obliged to support his brother and sisters, including lodging and clothing, from the profits of it to the tune of £600 (more than the Eureka diamond was sold for!) at a rate of £70 per year. If he left his siblings or married a wife before the age of 28, that was it — the farm would go to his younger brother Patrick.

Michael was only 20.

Madly in love with Bridget, he decided to go for it: South Africa or bust. Or, South Africa *and* bust! They decided to elope, because his sisters Kate and Bridget (yes, another Bridget) weren't big fans of the idea of their brother marrying a publican's daughter. *How common! What would people think*?

He had to break the news to Father Joseph Healy, the local parish priest who also happened to be the co-executor of his dad's will. Because if he forfeited the farm, to his brother, the £600 (worth about £85,000 in today's money) would come to him. Hey, that'd get them some boat fares and get them started in Africa.

Father Healy tried his best to counsel them. He talked them into at least marrying before they sailed off. A quick ceremony took place at the Kilsaran Roman Catholic chapel, although curiously Bridget's father's occupation was listed as 'farmer' not publican as thought. But tellingly, the Sarsfield side of the family was clearly more supportive, with her siblings witnessing the marriage. (Ironically, the McGee sisters would both later marry publicans.)

The Union Steamship Company operated a regular mail and passenger service between Britain and South Africa from Southampton. Around three or four weeks later the iciness of Ireland's winter was replaced by the balmy blanket of Durban's humidity. They took a coach inland to Pietermaritzburg, the staging point for ox wagons to Pretoria and beyond.

It was only two or three days before they arrived in Lydenburg, then headed to Spekboom in the Limpopo region.

But by the time they arrived, Spekboom was more Spekbust, because the easily-accessible alluvial gold had been hoovered up by the hordes of gold rushers. They headed back to Lydenburg, where Michael found a job.

Rotten timing though. He thought they'd left reforms and uprising behind. The Boers of the Transvaal were sick of the domineering Brits telling them what's what. By the end the year, it was on, a full scale four-month conflict in the Transvaal called the First Freedom War. The Boers gave the Red Coats a bloody nose.

Amidst all this, Michael and Bridget had started their family, and would eventually produce 11 children, one of whom was Rosie, my maternal great-grandmother.

Michael had also set out his own business shingle, carting supplies to the goldfields at Barberton, about 50km away.

When the Pilgrim's Rest alluvial gold started to run out, some diggers went to nearby Barberton where more gold had been found, and some went to Johannesburg, where gold was first discovered in 1885. Michael's transportation business gained traction to the point he was able to buy a farm at Dullstroom, 60km or so outside Lydenburg.

With even bigger plans in mind, a couple of years later, he traded up to a larger farm and set up a grain mill on the river at Sterkspruit. Then another mill at Pilgrim's Rest.

Clearly Michael had a great nose for business and sniffing out marketing opportunities. A bit like Cecil Rhodes did.

7

CIRCLE THE WAGONS

KIMBERLEY, 1880s. As the expression goes, when you're at the bottom of a hole, stop digging. Henry Lloyd had only one way to go, and that was up. He made the switch from storekeeping to diamond prospecting at some point, and perhaps even sold out his modest claim — because claims around the Kimberley were typically drying up now — perhaps to that man Rhodes, who had consolidated most of the region's worthwhile claims. Much of this development and expansion was financed by the Rothschilds, possibly introduced by unassuming fellow German-Jewish magnate and diamond pioneer, Alfred Beit. They provided significant financial backing to Rhodes' ventures, and his consolidation of diamond mining operations under De Beers.

The Big Hole eventually went down to 240 metres, with 50,000 (mainly black) labourers toiling in it. It would yield over 14,000,000 carats of diamonds in its life.

All of this fueled Rhodes' ego and grand imperialistic plans. He was of the belief that the more 'red' of the British Empire across the globe, the better off the world would be. Dreams and schemes were two things he was not short of — a Cape-to-Cairo railway was one. And expanding the British empire northwards, another.

But even in his own backyard there were territorial tensions: the Cape Colony was red, as was the colony of Natal, and the protectorate of British Bechuanaland and Zululand by now. But the Transvaal was not. It was an independent Boer republic called the South African Republic after it regained independence in the very recent First Anglo-Boer War.

He was convinced by the intelligence received from adventurer and hunter Frederick Selous that the Portuguese had desires to push west from their territory on the east coast and annex the large swathe of land north of Transvaal known as Zambesia. Rhodes also keenly felt that the Boers were hungry to swallow up that land, and possibly the Germans had designs on it, too. The time to act on behalf of the Crown to secure Matabeleland and Mashonaland was now.

Known as the Rudd Concession, this 1888 agreement gave Rhodes's private companies exclusive charge over all minerals and metals in Matabeleland in return for £100 per month (about £14,000 today). Oh, plus 1000 Henri Martini rifles with ammo. And throw in a small fishing boat on the Zambezi. OK, OK, OK, said Matabele King Lobengula from his *kraal* (village) at Bulawayo, putting his signature to a deal allowing British gold mining on his peoples' land.

His people didn't understand white man's fascination for these glittering rocks. And Lobengula himself — ever-open to the advice of witchdoctors — was fearful of the myriad dramas that would unfold if he opened his territory to mining. (He already had the losing concessionaires in his ear, muttering darkly, that the contract actually allowed for more than just a bunch of prospectors digging holes; and another losing party had already gone to plead directly with Queen Victoria.) Also, any road construction would enable the Mashonalanders to move quicker into his fiefdom.

Nervous noises were being made by Britain's military advisers who estimated that a military force of at least 2500 (with a supporting budget of one million Pounds) was needed to conquer the Matabele kingdom. Perhaps a more peaceful method could be sought? Selous thought they could skirt Matabele country and aim for Mashonaland instead, which seemed more potentially lucrative.

Rhodes sent Dr Leander Jameson (you remember him from the Kimberley hospital) to have a chat with the physically-imposing Lobengula — he was nigh on six-feet and very portly — to soften him up to Rhodes' way of thinking. He also hinted that the British could protect Lobengula from those dastardly Portuguese and covetous Boers. Here're some Henri Martini rifles to get started with.

On the back of this, in 1889, master-manipulator Rhodes then obtained a Royal Charter mandate from Queen Victoria to explore and develop the entire area north of the Limpopo River. The British South Africa Company was formed. As sovereign as it sounds, it was pure private enterprise. And capital of £1,000,000 was allocated to this.

Of course, this was not all altruistic — the Rhodes pocket always had to benefit directly or indirectly.

With Lobengula now back in their corner again (sort of, he was still wavering, because he saw it as Rhodes' army and not the Queen's), it was time to make it happen. The king was expecting a few prospectors digging a hole in Tali; Rhodes was making plans for a whole column of hundreds of soldiers and prospectors and wagons to move onto the land, a place where previously only a handful of Europeans, mainly missionaries, had set foot.

The hawkish soldier and adventurer, Frank Johnson, said: 'You give me a cheque for £87,500 and supply me with field and machine guns, rifles and ammunition, and I will undertake to hand Mashonaland over to you, fit for civil government, within nine months.'

A contract was signed for him to create a road from Palapye to Mount Hampden, to be completed within six months. Johnson would also receive a land grant of 80,000 acres and 20 gold claims for each of his '12 apostles', key people nominated by him.

A Pioneer Corps needed to be raised, which Johnson would have to fund, to build the roads, and protect the worker parties. Lobengula was updated on this scope creep. Take it or leave it: if Matabele people resisted, they would feel the full fury of the British troops.

The 23-year-old Major Johnson started setting up recruiting agencies in the key centres of Cape Town, Johannesburg, Port Elizabeth, East London, Queenstown, and Kimberley. They needed people preferably with military experience and some sort of wealth behind them, so they could lobby Whitehall to bail them out if it all went pear-shaped.

Pioneers were each promised 3000 acres and 15 gold claims. Two thousand applications were immediately lodged. A mixture of skills and trades were required, shades of the 1820 Settlers parties, in order for them to establish self-sufficient communities at the other end.

One application was from a gentleman in Kimberley: the prospector Henry Lloyd, now 34, a widower. (His daughter Marionetta was probably left behind in Kimberley with grandma Mary. Marionetta became a nurse in Mafeking, never married, and sadly died at the Carnarvon Hospital in Kimberley aged just 28, with the most likely cause being TB or pneumonia picked up from a patient, both very prevalent in the crowded mining areas.)

Protection for the Pioneer Force was needed, on the dime of the BSA Company. And so, the BSA Company Police (BSACP) were formed, a mounted infantry unit along the lines of the much-respected Bechuanaland Border Police, with which Frank Johnson had served before. And so, in March 1890, Kimberley became the mustering and training point for the BSACP, with the first members attesting at the Central Hotel, Kimberley. A tent city of men, horses, and material spoiling for action.

Under overall command of Lt-Col EG Pennefather, they learned the fine art of layering the wagons in defensive formation; firing the water-cooled Maxim guns, which could rattle off 500 rounds of anger per minute; and using steam-engine-powered searchlights. Others specialised in artillery.

By June the force had moved up to Macloutsie (in modern day Botswana), and staged further north to build forts, such as Fort Tuli. Surreal scenes developed when a band of 'Matabele' warriors — bedecked in traditional ostrich plumes and crane feathers — strolled nonchalantly into their camp. Were they friend or foe? No one was entirely sure, but they turned out to be emissaries of Chief Khama the Third's from Bechuanaland, and he was on side with them. The end result was that a football match was played on the flat dry bed of the Shashe River, and the 'Matabele' left the following day, with the forces' gift of an ox to slaughter and eat.

And so the road building began in earnest, with the rest of the force giving them three cheers to the success of their journey. In all there were 350 troops plus artillery, with 47 wagons in support. Plus around 123 wagons of civilians, which included prospectors, government officials and the like. Plus a supporting cast of 300 of Khama's strong-bodied native Bamangwato men, under the command of Raditaladi, who did most of the 'road chopping'.

The intrepid Selous rode out front — having ridden this territory before on hunting expeditions — pointing out trees to be felled. Behind the advance party were the road makers. Large axes were wielded against the mopane trees and other obstacles in the Mashonaland bush. It was a hard slog, with only five miles made on the first day. Behind them came a carriage bearing a Maxim gun. Then the train of wagons. Then the rear-guard with yet another Maxim wagon. Flanking patrols were sent out looking for Matabele marauders on either side of the column.

Lobengula had made no assurances of being able to control his warriors should they decide their land had been infringed. It was estimated he had 20,000 men at his disposal, armed with anything from elephant guns to flintlock rifles, and of course Rhodes' own Martinis. But apparently, they feared the magical searchlights more than the Maxims.

That night the column slept fitfully in the surrounds of a thorn bush hedge *zareba* (enclosure) on guard against the many threats of Africa. They had tents but slept in the open beside their horses or under wagons. The circled wagons were interlocked, with the front wheel of each parked up beside the back wheel of the one in front. Cattle were tethered to the wagons, on the outside, forming another barrier against invasion. And quite a beefy barrier it would've been, with 16 oxen pulling each wagon, totalling over 3000 beasts. Horses were kept inside the *laager* (defensive camp).

Meanwhile, there was a young man with sharp features and piercing eyes who was making something of a nuisance of himself. George Frederick Seymour had just turned 17, and had not been selected for the force, but decided to tag along anyway, intermittently pleading to be accepted. Eventually an officer said something along the lines of, 'Alright, if you're so darned keen to join, we'll have you.' *If you don't ask, you don't get.*

And so Corporal George Frederick Seymour became Trooper #399 BSACP, assigned to E Troop who were, for now, staying put to form the rearguard from Macloutsie Camp. His weekly pay was a modest 7 shillings and 6 pence.

He cut quite a dashing sight in his uniform: a bandolier with hundreds of rounds of ammo for his Martini Henry rifle slung over his shoulder, and a Webley six-shooter revolver strapped to his belt. Plus an axe, which was both tool and weapon. Brown cord tunic over a grey flannel shirt, and grey cord riding breeches teamed with yellow leather leggings. A blue cavalry overcoat would protect against harsher elements.

Oh, did I mention yet that George F Seymour was the grandson of that entrepreneurial sugar farmer Ephraim Rathbone?

A rhythm was found where the road makers would leave camp just after breakfast, trying to clear 10 miles each day, and pinpointing a suitable *laager* site. The Pioneer Column would avoid the cloying heat and humidity of the day, marching from 3am to reach the *laager* site by breakfast time. The civilians would then rest through the day, until another evening march commenced around 5:30 till about 9pm. Conditions varied from sand to mud, from thick and tangled bushland to grassland, always looking over their shoulder for attacks from the fierce Matabele. The column straggled over five to eight miles when the going got hardest.

Fever struck men down. Crocodiles got others. Occasional nervy moments of *Matabele* groups shadowing the column filtered through the group.

While it was not yet the rainy season, flooded river crossings were arduous, and muddy sections threatened to suck the boots off a man's feet. Some crossings, like the Lundi River took four hours per wagon, accompanied by the cacophony of cracked whips and cracked jokes. Sandbags were often placed to smoothen rocky riverbeds, sweaty troopers working in nought but a slouch hat. Family folklore has it that Henry's wagon became bogged and traction could only be gained by placing objects under-wheel, such as a small wooden grandfather clock he had among his possessions. (That clock would become a family heirloom passed on to the first-born son of each generation.)

Other sections required rock-blasting to clear a way through. And the Providential Pass was heavily wooded, with over 300 metres in altitude to be climbed in short order. What a great place for the Matabele to ambush them! Conditions got easier as they thankfully reached the cooler highveld. So much so, that inter-troop cricket matches were sometimes played.

In mid-August they reached the site of the Great Zimbabwe ruins, presenting a blanket to the headman, with some party leaders enjoying a guided tour of the impressive granite edifices. Built by the Shona people sometime between the 11th and 15th centuries, they stand like the Pyramids and Machu Picchu as testament to great civilisations, tinged with a mystery to their origins, and how such an ancient engineering feat could be undertaken. Dry-masonry walls soar to over 11 metres, each stone selected to interlock perfectly with the next, without the need for cement, such is the precision.

Finally in early September, George Seymour and his E Troop comrades were on the move, marching from Macloutsie to Fort Tuli.

Conditions got drier and drier as the column headed further north and east. The oxen began to suffer dehydration, with successive rivers, such as the Gwebi River, offering insufficient flows to be viable. The course was amended on the fly. At times, two span of oxen (32 beasts) were needed to tow each wagon, such was the debilitation of the animals. Troopers' uniforms were threadbare, some even bootless by now.

Johnson's contract stated the end of the road to be Mount Hampden, because that was a known and easily found landmark. But just south of that, a great flat expanse across the Mukuvisi River, in the shadow of a *kopje* (hill), presented itself as a much more suitable place for settlement.

On September 12, after nearly three months of hard slog, the ragged column halted. There was nothing there, and nothing to see. The end of the road. Literally.

Elated at having completed his contracted scope of work, Frank Johnson and a few headed off into the nearby Hartley Hills, eager to do some prospecting, and stake their claims. First in, best dressed, right? And so Skipper Haste took command of the column. That night they relaxed, and their tents were used for the first time on the 400-mile trek, sleeping in the flat open area.

The next morning, they would plant the British flag and claim this bit of Africa for the Crown. Mashonaland, another bit of red on the empire's map.

Alas, no one had a flagpole. Nothing for it but for Lt Tyndale-Biscoe to find a straight trunk among the nearby msasa trees and cut it down to size. It was erected in the middle of what would become Fort Salisbury (named for the then-British Prime Minister, Lord Salisbury) and secured with a series of stays and halyards. Tyndale-Biscoe unfurled his Union Jack while all gathered around the square. The buglers struck up *The Royal Salute*, and the two seven-pound guns blasted a twenty-one-gun salute. BSACP troopers presented arms.

'Three cheers for her gracious majesty Queen Victoria!' Lt-Col Pennefather called out, and the three lusty cheers of the troopers blared out from Cecil Square — nothing more than an empty space with a few pole-and-*dagha* huts erected by the advance party — into the desolate African wilderness.

George Seymour missed all this pageantry because his troop only arrived a few days later.

When the Pioneer Corps was disbanded on October 1, as per the plan, all those involved were offered their 3000 acres of farmland and 15 gold mine stakes. But George apparently said, 'No thank you, I only came for the adventure.' So he took £5 in lieu, saluted, turned on his heels and headed back through the bush to South Africa.

The general mood was that piles of money were just waiting to be made; a great sense of anticipation pervaded the group.

Henry was only too happy to start a new life with some land and the tantalising prospects of possibly making his fortune in these gold fields. 'The settlers who came to the territory were adventurers, the kind of people who thrived on a challenge, and possessed a strong will to succeed,' wrote AS Hickman.

None of them appeared to know they were making history. 'The pioneers were men of deeds rather than men of words,' wrote Sir Robert Tredgold. 'Hardship and deprivation are accepted without complaint, and danger and death are faced with unassuming courage.'

Chances are George and Henry did not meet each other and certainly could not have known that — a couple of generations later — their respective offspring would meet, marry, and produce a few great-grandsons … including me.

And so the pioneers set about taming this flat area of African bushland.

Rhodes' friend, former medico Jameson, was running Mashonaland in a way that somewhat mirrored Rhodes' self-serving style. Interactions with local natives were minimal. The European settlers occupied separate worlds to the local Shona people.

The constantly whispering wind carried on it the clanking of hammers, the rasping of saws, the creaking of ox-wagons, the neighs and bellows of their harnessed beasts, and the calls of jackals, antelopes and hornbills — regularly reminding them that this was the domain of wild animals and predators.

Earthy aromas from the thousands of kilometres of bushland surrounding them mixed with the wood smoke of campfires, as simple meals were cooked, water was boiled, or heat was sought: many might've been surprised that the nights were as cool as they were, getting down to around 6 degrees Celsius.

Soon, business shingles were going up as the pioneers set about making a living, generally supplying what their fellows needed most — groceries, hardware, clothing — Meikle's, Haddon & Sly, and Bonsella Stores. Then came the Fuchs Brothers with their farming supplies. And of course, the Salisbury Hotel to slake thirsts and provide meals for locals, and beds for travellers.

From that humble beginning, business empires quickly bloomed, and the future national capital of Salisbury was born.

8

BULAWAYO BOOMTOWN

BULAWAYO, 1893. The land further to the west — the Ndebele kingdom under Lobengula — had always been of interest to the BSA Co, because it was thought to be rich in minerals, especially gold. Hence the original Rudd Concession. But relations with their king had soured considerably since he felt he was misled by their intentions.

Now that the hopes for 'a second Witwatersrand' (the gold reefs around Johannesburg) in Mashonaland were looking like a massive exaggeration, many disenchanted pioneers packed up and headed back south. Thoughts began turning back to Plan A: the potential riches of neighbouring Matabeleland.

Reports had been made as early as 1866 by Henry Hartley that Matabele people in the Umfuli River area hung cow skins in the river, took them out, dried them, and could simply shake the gold out of them. Unbelievable, easy riches!

Since before anyone could remember, the Matabele and Shona people had been at each others' throats, with the Matabele leading the points table. The more martial Matabele loved to raid cattle and maraud — killing all men and old women and kidnapping young maidens — from their eastern neighbours. *'Mazweti wia!'* would be the terrified alarm passed from *kraal* to *kraal* warning of their attacks. When confronted, Lobengula was unrepentant. His underlings were agitating to fight the white man, too, and were uncontrollable in any case. The BSAC positioned themselves as protectors of the Shona.

When a major cattle raid was staged by 5000 *impi* in mid-1893, the BSAC used it as a pretext and trigger for its own military actions. They went in all Maxim guns blazing and cut down thousands of Matabele around the Thabas-Induna *kopje*, at a cost of only a dozen or so BSAC troops. Lobengula fled north as they closed in on his Bulawayo HQ, which was overrun in November of that year, marking the fall of the Ndebele kingdom.

Jameson declared the town of Bulawayo — around 260 miles south of Salisbury — open.

And so new land became available to settlers and pioneers, for commercial enterprises, agriculture, or cattle ranching. Bulawayo had the benefit of a more strategic location, being more centrally located than Salisbury. It was on established trade routes, and the much-vaunted Cape to Cairo Railway was said to be passing through here when it took shape.

Pioneer Henry Lloyd was one of several who saw the opportunity and grabbed it.

We can only assume he sold his gold claims and/or land around Salisbury to raise some capital. Because the next we know for sure, 10 hotels had mushroomed in Bulawayo. And one of these was the Central Hotel, an impressively large single-story tin-roofed building, with a generously sized overhanging shaded walkway supported by several columns. Owned by Henry, it dominated the corner of Rhodes and 8th Street, in a strategic location opposite Market Square. Around it were wagon makers, auctioneers, stationers, a tobacconist, and other hotels.

The general area of Zambesia, covering the areas of Mashonaland and Matabeleland, officially became the country of Rhodesia in 1895.

But, wait ... more skin drums of war being beaten. With the Matabele having being subdued in 1893, the Shona rose in similar fashion, for identical reasons: land dispossession, forced labour, even taxes on their huts, and other stringent colonial policies handed down by the BSAC.

Enough! The Shona put great store in their spirit mediums and traditional leaders, so when Mbuya Nehanda and Sekuru Kaguvi called them to rise up and resist in 1896, the Mashona people did so. Isolated farms, mines and settlements signalled the start of the Mashona Rebellion, part of the broader First *Chimurenga* uprising, which involved the Matabele too.

Bulawayo was firmly in their sights, and the town was surrounded. Around 1000 settlers and 300 women and children dug in behind sandbags and ox wagons.

But the BSAC forces — supplemented by civilian volunteers and makeshift militia groups — managed to hold them off with superior weaponry. They bought enough time, a couple of months, for reinforcements to arrive from other forts in Salisbury, Bechuanaland, and even as far as Mafeking, South Africa.

The town was under siege but never taken. Safe to say Henry's poker games — a game he'd also enjoyed with fellow prospectors back in Kimberley — helped pass the time more pleasurably.

Once that skirmish was over, the good times slowly returned for the settlers.

The Central Hotel became a well-known landmark in Bulawayo's social and commercial life, as the town grew apace, especially on the back of the railroad which was completed in 1897. In later years the hotel was renamed Le Chalet and traded largely unchanged until the late 1960s, when it made way for Meikle's store. (Today Rhodes St is renamed Joshua Nkomo St, and a large statue of the nationalist leader stands opposite where the hotel entrance was.) What stands at that site today is a modest guesthouse, the Bulawayo Central Lodge.

Given their name and adjacent location on the corner of 8th Ave, it's safe to assume Henry also owned the colonial-era-styled Lloyd's Buildings at 181 Abercorn St (now Herbert Chitepo St, named for another liberation hero), behind Market Square, and Lloyd's Chambers (northwest corner of 8th and Main). The former was one of the key commercial properties in the city, housing offices, shops, and various businesses including Bulawayo Timber, Bulawayo Ice and Cold Storage, Bulawayo Brick and Tile, Bulawayo Gold Reefs Developing Co, and a few others. Many of these were businesses or enterprises operating under the British South Africa Company, and Henry presumably had a fairly tight relationship with Mr H (likely standing for Henry) Lamb, the company secretary for many of these entities.

Bulawayo was steaming ahead as a vibrant town, supporting agricultural, mining, and early industrial efforts. The African Banking Corporation, Bank of Africa, and Standard Bank of South Africa moved into the burgeoning town, as did churches of many obscure denominations, plus they had their own hospital. Then of course, that most British of institutions — The Club. The Bulawayo Club was a prestigious gentlemen's club for the British colonial elite: businessmen, administrators, and other prominent figures. The three-story club embodied the British colonial lifestyle and provided an exclusive space for networking and relaxation, forgetting one was in a frontier town for a while.

And like many frontier mining towns, Bulawayo had its 'wild west' air, attracting fortune hunters and those with a large appetite for risk and adventure. Gambling was the most preferred entertainment — poker and faro (a fast-actioned card game) mainly. Many lived for the day: if it was boom times, they wagered bigger sums. If things were desperate, they bet big sums anyway to improve their fortunes or recoup losses. Massive fortunes were made and lost in a single night's reckless activities.

Henry also owned the Exchange Bar at 81 Main St (now Jason Moyo St, named for a freedom fighter), a corner block with 7th Avenue, behind the Central Hotel. As one of only three bars in the town, it likely served as a popular social spot for drinks and gatherings, reflecting the growing town's bustling atmosphere.

It is easy to imagine long nights of convivial poker games, what with having your own pub, and tons of cash pouring in. And it might well have been here that he started brewing his own beer, Lloyd's Lager.

All of this was in place by 1896, so Henry had enjoyed a barnstorming few years in Bulawayo. He had made his fortune. Finally. But sadly, at the cost of losing a young wife and leaving his daughter behind.

Enter a young German lady, Marie Meyer. *Very young*: 16. She had come to Rhodesia via the Transvaal or possibly German South West Africa (now Namibia) it appears. At that time, there were thousands of Germans in South Africa, drawn by the economic opportunities of mining. Germans in large numbers trace back to Lutheran missionaries from Hamburg, Germany, who settled in Natal during the mid-19th century.

But less, perhaps only hundreds, were in Bulawayo. Family folklore has it that she was passing herself off as something to do with German aristocracy. All we really know is that she was born in Hamburg in 1874, and possibly came out by ship as teenager, then probably made her way to Rhodesia by ox-wagon. Gutsy lady. (All archive records from that period in Germany were destroyed so verification proved impossible.)

She caught Henry's eye, they fell in love and were married in 1897. She was a full 19 years younger than he. Things might've been a bit confusing because Henry's mum was Mary. His deceased wife was Mary. And now here was Marie.

9

WHITE MAN'S WAR

SOUTH AFRICA 1899. No sooner had peace broken out in Rhodesia, than South Africa was plunged back into more divisive warfare. This time it was white on white, proving how fractious and nuanced all these co-existences were. The Boers — who'd moved north to the Transvaal and Oranje Vrijstaat to escape the British — found they couldn't escape the damn interfering British after all. Especially not when the Transvaal was proving to be a, er, goldmine. Fiercely independent and suspicious by nature, the hardened Boers had a massive mistrust of British intentions, not helped by the ill-fated British-led Jameson Raid on the Transvaal a few years earlier.

Yes, the good doctor Jameson had been at it again, this time trying to overthrow the Boer government. Supported by his fan Cecil Rhodes and the British South Africa Company, the raid aimed to incite an uprising among British immigrant settlers — known as *Uitlanders* (outsiders) by the Boers — but no such rebellion resulted. Jameson's force of 500 men was quickly defeated. Rhodes' name was dragged through the mud, and he was forced to step down from direct leadership positions in his industry-dominating companies. The raid embarrassed the British government, heightened tensions between Britain and the Boer Republics, and led to this next saga which pitched the McGee and Seymour families into battle … on opposite sides of the stoush.

In October 1899 the Boers delivered an ultimatum to the Brits to withdraw their troops from Afrikaner territories and guarantee independence: back off or else! The Brits chose not to listen. So, the Boers besieged the key British towns of Ladysmith, Kimberley, and Mafeking, which lay just beyond their state borders.

Michael McGee sided with the Boers. After all, in Lydenburg (translated as 'the town of suffering' after the Boers' early struggles there), he was in their territory, and most whites there supported the notion of a '*boere staat*. But — more importantly — he was Irish, and the Boers were against the English: and anyone against the dreaded English must surely be his friend!

Initially he was active in taking provisions, most likely wheat meal, from Lydenburg to Ladysmith. By ox cart, this was at least a 20-day journey one-way through mountainous terrain.

Rhodesia sided with the British but was dependent on rail and telegraph lines (especially to areas such as Kimberley and Mafeking) which were disrupted by the Boer operations. Several areas were economically isolated and effectively under a wartime lockdown.

In Bulawayo, many businesses suspended trading, local gold mines went under, and insolvency soared. The Meikles barely pulled through, and the Standard Bank suffered a liquidity crisis. Many European merchants, mine managers, and the like headed for Salisbury, or the Cape, seeking sanctuary and steadier conditions.

In Natal, George F Seymour had fronted up in Pietermaritzburg to volunteer for a newly formed mounted unit, the Imperial Light Horse (ILH). Growing up on a farm around Newcastle — in the Drakensberg foothills — he was a competent horseman. And with prior BSACP experience in Mashonaland with the Pioneer column, the 27-year-old was now considered an experienced soldier. George was selected as one of 444 from 5000 volunteers. One of their founding officers was an Australian expat who left Johannesburg at the onset of war, Major Walter 'Karri' Davies — so nicknamed because he was a marketer of Aussie hard woods for mining and railways. He'd led the disastrous Jameson Raid and been jailed by the Boers as a result. Now seriously motivated by revenge, he and other founders financially underwrote the formation of the unit and served without pay. Sgt Seymour — replete with an ostrich-plumed slouch hat and sporting an enviable moustache to look the part — earned around 3 or 4 shillings per day (about £19 in today's money, for an annual salary around £8-9000).

Within a few weeks Sgt Seymour and the Imperial Light Horse were in the thick of it at Elandslaagte, where two of their number won Victoria Crosses. But the grim reality of losing their commanding officer Scott-

Chisolme, leading from the front, was a sobering start. From there, they charged on to Colenso, trying to reach Ladysmith, but were repelled by the Boers. In that one week alone — dubbed 'Black Week' — the stunned Brits lost 3000 men.

A great showing was also made by the Boers at the Battle of Spion Kop: it seemed the Red Coats were not so adept at tactics in rugged and rocky terrain. The Brits briefly occupied the summit but were driven off it. Perhaps this is where the derogatory term for Afrikaners — 'rock spiders' — came into being? The British suffered heavy losses, not just from battle though: they were falling like flies with typhoid fever too. But George's Light Horse captured Boer commandant Hendrik Prinsloo.

Then it was on to Tugela Heights, a series of engagements along the Tugela River, where the Brits were in a desperate struggle against Gen Louis Botha's troops who occupied the high ground. It took two weeks of artillery and infantry action to finally break through Boer defences. The road to Ladysmith was now open. Full speed ahead!

The garrison at Ladysmith had been surrounded by the Boers for nearly four months, along with civilians of the town, with disease and daily shelling taking its toll. George and the Light Horse took on the Boers ' six-inch 'Long Tom' artillery guns — which had effectively kept the Brits' heads beneath the parapets — and put two of the menacing guns out of action. They were then faced and challenged by a Boer picket around Wagon Hill. 'Fix bayonets and charge the bastards!' was Maj Davies' colourful cry. Although Davies was badly wounded in the buttocks, it was reported in the international newspapers as 'a flesh wound' (nearly a century before *Monty Python and the Holy Grail* made that line famous), although he never fully recovered from it. Thanks to the VC-winning heroics of Trooper Albrecht and others, the siege of Ladysmith was soon over. British morale shot up.

With the ILH's impressive siege-busting performances, Gen Redvers Buller next tasked them to press on to Mafeking, which had been under siege for six months and, by late April, had less than three weeks' supply of water, food, and ammunition left. This would lead to perhaps the most famous and fabled British action of the entire Boer War, because — on paper — the 1000 Brits and natives were completely outmanned and outgunned.

Inside Mafeking, Col Robert Baden-Powell had been holding out, keeping the Boers out of rifle range. To the dismay of the Boers he'd also armed the native Fingos (albeit with outdated muzzle-loaders) and encouraged them to go out on cattle raids to supplement their dwindling rations. The Boers accused him of violating the principle that this was 'a white man's war'.

And so, a combined column of nearly 1150 Brit reinforcements closed in on Mafeking. Artillery softened up the Boers, who suffered massive dispiriting casualties, and advance guards pinged rifle shots into their lines around the town. This went on for days. Boers could be seen deserting their lines amid clouds of dust. The Boer leader at one time spoke of surrender, but no one noticed his white flag in the darkness. Meanwhile, long-since used to the false hope of rescue, Mafeking civilians were deeply engrossed in the finals of a long-running billiards tournament.

Karri Davies asked for volunteers for an officers' patrol, and George Seymour was one of eight officers who put up his hand to join the mission to relieve the siege of Mafeking. Nervously, they mounted their steeds and rode toward the town by the light of a near full moon. They moved out carefully, skirting the outer line of Boer positions. Scrub, fences, and the low shapes of farm buildings half-swallowed by dark all promised danger. At one outlying farmhouse they almost rode straight into a picket. Rifles came up fast, voices snapping in Afrikaans and broken English, the moment poised on a thin wire. Then hesitation. In the wavering lantern light, someone on the Boer side recognised Davies. Australian Davies was well-known in the Transvaal, a reformist voice in the uneasy Uitlander vs Boer politics. 'Don't shoot, it's Davies!' went out their call. Rifles were lowered. No one quite committed to fire, and no one quite stepped forward to close the distance. The patrol did not linger. Whatever advantage there was lay in movement, not in explanation. They edged away, closing on Mafeking town proper. There was no further resistance. The posse entered the market square, reportedly to claps on the back from some, who helped them from their horses. Somewhat surreal and anti-climactic after the intense lead-up action. The main relief column entered the town the following morning.

It was a major British victory because Mafeking — though not much more than a railway siding and some tin shanties — was the birthplace of the Boers' rebellion. The Brits had avoided another embarrassing defeat, and the Afrikaners' spirit had been crushed ... for now. Baden-

Powell took the salute in a ceremonial march past, the townsfolk sang *God Save the Queen*, and fireworks lit up the sky. (Baden-Powell later turned his military profile, that of a leader who'd bunkered down and endured a siege, into founding the Boy Scout movement and developing skills such as self-reliance.)

Sgt George Seymour earned a fourth clasp on his Boer War medal for his involvement in Mafeking. Karri Davies refused all medals and calls for a VC, saying: 'I do not fight for medals, but for my Queen.' He did, however, later make a special presentation of a silver salver to each of his eight officers for their role in that historic occasion.

That same month the ILH took the major centres of Johannesburg and Pretoria, before heading further east in the Transvaal on guerrilla missions, mopping up pockets of resistance.

Michael McGee's trade routes had been severely disrupted as the war widened. Lydenburg became more isolated and impoverished as payment for mineral options expired and landowners were no longer receiving that rent. Cut off from commercial markets and cash, they eagerly watched as the war played out. But by September 1900, the war came to them: Redvers Buller's men — including George Seymour's ILH unit — reached Lydenburg.

Action around Paardesplaats, the strategic mountain overlooking the town, was intense, in contrast to Lydenburg town, which surrendered with a whimper.

The McGee's home on the outskirts, Pine Lodge, suffered some fragment and bullet damage. As a prominent citizen and owner of the M McGee & Son mill, Michael was in the British's sights, and arrested on charges of aiding and abetting the Boers' war effort. Along with the other burghers of the town, he was marched at bayonet point through the streets, then held briefly in a chicken run at Machadodorp — as though he didn't hate the English enough already — en route to *Artillerie Kazerne* (artillery barracks) in Pretoria, where he was held prisoner alongside other Lydenburgers and Boers for three months, then a further six months — most likely at the Simmer and Jack gold mine — in Germiston, Johannesburg.

A very dark side to the British behaviour in the Boer War were concentration camps where 28,000 Afrikaner women and children died, plus a further 20,000 native civilians. But, given that victors write history, not much was ever made of this atrocity.

Lydenburg was now surrounded with barbed wire entanglements, with forts and gun emplacements bristling at every turn. Tents sprung up like summer mushrooms on any open space, such as the market and church grounds. British soldiers, with their equipment and stores, now dominated the town.

Michael's wife Bridget was luckily not arrested, and — true to her enterprising nature — soon turned her hand to making biscuits and ginger beer, which she sold to the British soldiers. Much-needed funds, given she had nine mouths to feed (including daughter Rosie, just 16 then), with another on the way. She also sent money to Michael in prison.

Michael had some contacts in high places which he leveraged, and secured an early release, returning to Sterkspruit, where he continued his farming and milling operations. But the Boers then suspected him of supplying the British with meal and blew up his mill. And the British — who helped themselves to up to 800 bags of meal, and 130 cattle from his farm — also suspected him of being a double-dealer and blew up his other mill at Pilgrim's Rest just in case.

Undeterred by this classic shit sandwich, Michael returned to Lydenburg and opened a factory making hop beer, which the hot, sweaty, and bored Red Coats loved. A roaring trade was done there. And Michael and Bridget produced one last child, a grand total of 11.

George F Seymour survived, despite having ridden conservatively 4000km during the war, and possibly would've walked a bit bow-legged after that. He returned to Mooi River and soon married a German, Wilhelmina 'Minnie' Diffenthal, who also lived at Mooi River, at St John's Church, Weston.

Then finally in 1902 peace broke out. The battlefields held the bones of 22,000 British soldiers (about one third killed in action, the rest by disease), and up to 9000 Boers.

The economic hangover cured quickly, especially with the re-opening of the Cape-Bulawayo Railway. But many 'pioneer capitalists' had been wiped out, absorbed by corporates and BSAC-dominated enterprises with deeper pockets.

And with the signing of the Vereeniging Treaty, the British annexed all the Boer Republics, which became part of the British Empire, and the formation of the Union of South Africa followed in 1910. More red bits on the map. The new flag, the *'Oranje-Blanje-Blou'* (Orange/White/Blue) featured the Union Jack in the centre, flanked by the Orange Free State flag and the Transvaal *Vierkleur*, as a compromise between British imperial identity and Afrikaner traditions.

But what the 1910 treaty really did was to unify and galvanise the Afrikaners in their hatred for the Brits.

George F Seymour took up a position as mechanical engineer at Treasury Mines in Cleveland, looking after things underground and on the surface there for many years. That suburb mushroomed on the back of mining support and service industries. His parents had moved up to the Transvaal by now, his father John still a gardener as he'd always been. Appropriately John would pass away living in a suburb of Johannesburg named Turffontein (home of the famous racetrack).

Post-war, Michael moved his mill into town, opened a bakery, and ran a general dealership. He also moved into auctioneering and became a sworn appraiser. Then he sniffed opportunities in the new-fangled automotive caper, starting with a Dodge franchise in 1924, and a Ford dealership in 1926 (which the family still runs in Voortrekker St, Lydenburg, to this day day, with great-great grandson Clifford McGee at the wheel).

With irrepressible energy, Michael was mayor of the town for a couple of terms, chairman of the Turf Club, and founding member of the Agricultural Society and Golf Club. Bridget, not to be outshone, repaid Father Healy's faith in them as a couple, and gave generously of her time and efforts to the local church. Not everybody gets a Papal recognition: in the 1950s Pope Pius XII bestowed on her the *Cross Pro Ecclesia et Pontifice* medal, among the highest awards made to laypersons for dedication to the church and Pope.

With such full dance cards, Michael lived to the ripe old age of 80, and Bridget just one year short of her 100th birthday; a longevity which runs on their side of the family. The town of Lydenburg is still reminded of their legacy by the presence of the McGee Ford dealership and even electric lights, which Michael championed.

There had been widespread unrest on the mines by white miners for a while, but in 1913 their black co-workers joined them. The tension had been building between the Afrikaner workers and returning WW1 veterans (mostly of British descent) and local workers, which had developed into strikes and riots, reaching boiling point with the Rand Revolt in 1922.

One cold wet evening, George Seymour was working in his offices at the Reef Gold Mines on the Witwatersrand. Suddenly rioters surrounded the mine offices. George was with the mine secretary. Startled, he noticed a rioter was about to club him. George — turning on his best Afrikaner accent — shouted in Afrikaans: *'Nee, stop, ek is een van julle!'* (No, stop, I am one of you!). That saved him a belting over the head. Just then a taxi drew up, and one of the ringleaders told the mines secretary to get in. As he did, *BANG*! One of the rioters shot the secretary clean through the back of the head, killing him instantly.

10

A HOUSE OF CARDS

BULAWAYO, 1902. With the Boer War nearing its end, a massive economic hangover gripped the town. Trade routes and investments had been disrupted. Imperial confidence shaken. The mood was weary and wary. But the poker games continued. The stakes ever-rising, no doubt much to Henry's young wife's consternation, we can only imagine. Put yourself in the head of a compulsive gambler: 'Damn! Maybe I'll win some back on the next hand. Or the *next* one. Or the *next next* one …'

Henry and Marie had a boy in 1902 and was named — you guessed it! — Henry Llewellyn Lloyd. The new baby was nicknamed 'Dick'. Then over the years, at lengthy intervals of three or four years each, came three more siblings: Dudley, Phyllis, and Marie.

Possibly Henry sold off Lloyd's Lager to finance his gambling debt, because Castle Breweries had moved into Rhodesia, and took over the brewing of Lloyd's Lager. Possibly he also sold off the Central Hotel to the Meikles brothers — an enterprising trio of Scottish brothers who got involved in hotels, stores, and trading. (One story goes that he might've lost that hotel in poker to Thomas Meikles, but Thomas seemed to have been of a sober and restrained nature, unlikely to be wagering those sorts of bets.)

The poker continued. Until one day Henry the Pioneer woke up totally broke. He'd lost the lot.

No farmland. No gold claims. No hotel. No bar. No buildings. No brewery.

Meanwhile in the early 1920s, the British South Africa Company lost its grip on Southern Africa, with Northern Rhodesia becoming a protectorate of Britain, and Southern Rhodesia becoming a self-governing British colony in 1923.

■ □ ■

Dick was a lively youngster, keen on music, and could blow up a storm on the bugle, as well as play the piano. Having finished school at Chaplin, he worked in the HR department of a local mine.

He was a man of many talents, but none more so than his bushcraft skills, understanding the lay of the land.

One night at a local social dance, Dick met a tall and strong-minded Transvaal-born Irish lass, Eileen McFarlane. Being musical, dancing the latest styles came easy to him, and this is possibly what gave her a great first impression of him. They married a week before his 24th birthday and soon started a family.

A daughter first: Patricia ('Paddy'). Then a son, George Llewellyn ('Buster'). Dick desperately wanted two sons. Then came another two daughters — Dorothy ('Dot') and Kathleen ('Kay'). And another, Beryl. And finally another son: Henry Llewellyn Lloyd. This Henry was nicknamed 'Little Micky' — probably because of the Irish in the bloodline, and then simply 'Mick' which was the name he went by for aye.

While the 1930 Land Apportionment Act restricted blacks access to land, Britishers of all stripes — especially farmers and ex-military types — came to Rhodesia, often incentivised by the government to settle and take up land. Some exuded eccentricity of the type that British expats in the 'tropics' the world over were famous for. The town of Gwelo was not spared, especially in the form of the Boggie family. Major James Boggie was a pioneer and his Scottish wife, Jeannie, was as feisty and colourful as they came. (He would later become a member of parliament and — due to his passion for wildlife — bring in the act of parliament which saw the establishment of the Wankie Game Reserve.)

Jeannie could be seen riding side-saddle into Gwelo town on a regular basis to collect the mail and run errands. When her husband passed away and was buried, she had him exhumed, and reportedly re-assembled his skeleton, which she kept under her bed.

Meanwhile, Rosie — the daughter of Michael McGee — found herself attracted to a tallish, broad-shouldered man, four or five years her senior. Thomas Tait was keen on anything with a ball involved, especially tennis, cricket and soccer.

As he played soccer for Old Natalians, he had possibly attended Martizburg College (previously known as Natal High School) before moving up to Lydenburg, Transvaal.

Known for his even temperament, he was a popular guy, but his sporting prowess was where he really stood out. In 1905, he was selected for the Transvaal Currie Cup soccer team.

They lived in Pretoria, and had two daughters, Alys and Kathleen, and another child who died in infancy, described presciently as 'too beautiful to live'.

Tragically, Thomas himself was cut down in the prime of his life, aged just 40, when the Spanish Influenza epidemic swept the globe. Despite his elite fitness, the flu led to double pneumonia. His father-in-law Michael McGee dashed from Lydenburg to his bedside at General Hospital, Pretoria, but — despite the best medical attention being procured — Thomas passed away.

Henry the Pioneer continued scraping out a living, literally, working as a diamond digger and prospector on his arid cattle farm at Willoughby's Siding — also known as Willoughby's Halt, named for Major Sir John Christopher Willoughby, a member of Rhodes' inner circle who played a prominent role in the Pioneer Column — outside of Gwelo.

The tiny town of Gwelo was 100 miles to the north of Bulawayo. The area was hot but fertile, and importantly it sat along the main railway line between Bulawayo and Salisbury, important markets for their product and livestock. It was becoming a strategic agricultural centre.

Here they had 3600 acres, and another additional bush lot on the main road, with a different name to the main property, Forest Vale Farm. There were no vehicles on the farm at that stage, with milk taken to

Willoughby's Siding in large churns, probably carried by the farm labourers, possibly in a wheelbarrow.

Their house was two pole-and-*dagha* rondawels — one for sleeping, the other for living/cooking etc — joined by a passageway.

It was growing into something of a commune. About 100 metres away was a brick house, which Pioneer Henry and Granny Meyer moved into, with Dick and Eileen moving into the main *rondawels* under the gum trees (after Dick retired from the mine with a lung problem), and Granny and Grandpa Macfarlane in another *rondawel*, and Uncle Clem (Eileen's brother) and his pointer dogs down in another pole-and-*dagha* house by the river the other side of the property.

Life at Forest Vale Farm was hard going, because of the annoying silica sand which dominated the area, making it difficult to grow anything viably.

At the venerable age of 75, Pioneer Henry was feeling rather poorly and was taken off to the Gwelo European Hospital on Selukwe Road. Dr Vickers diagnosed cardiac degeneration, and after one week, with his son Dick at his bedside, he passed away from cardiac syncope.

He left no will, and Marie — who grand-daughter Kay remembers as 'a very small, very slim, very strong, very gentle, lovely lady' — signed the death notice noting that, in any case, he left "no movable or immovable property" and the value of the estate was less than $200. He'd passed the farm onto Dick already.

At some point, possibly in swapping from the *rondawels*, Henry had also passed the grandfather clock — that one that survived those muddy moments on the Pioneer trek — to Dick.

An L-shaped headstone in the Gwelo Cemetery — inscribed 'In Loving memory Henry L Lloyd 1890 Pioneer-1931. Cherished Memories of a Dear Father and Granddad' — with a large iron cross at the feet, commemorates his colourful journey.

All we have left to show for his one-time African empire is a battered tin mug, with the spidery inscription of 'Lloyd's Lager' on the side.

11

A GENTLEMAN NAMED BUSTER

SOUTHERN RHODESIA, 1929. George Llewellyn Lloyd was born right into the eye of the Great Depression, and Rhodesia was hit hard with agricultural and mining commodity prices tanking due to its reliance on global export markets.

His father Dick was initially employed in HR at Shabani Mine. Rhodesia by now was one of the world's leading producers of asbestos, with Gwelo at its epicentre. The Shabani mines were a major employer and contributor to the economy, exporting chrysotile (white asbestos) to the world.

The mine was something of a community hub with residential areas, administrative buildings, and a hospital, apart from the mine workings which were both open-pit and underground. The Shabani Mine Club was the social epicentre for whites.

Their whole house — sitting atop a hill, with terraced staircases running down the slope from the house — was covered in fine mesh. Every day, Eileen would be out vacuuming the mesh to remove the filtered asbestos, which got into and onto everything in the district.

While they were quite self-sufficient growing veggies at home, Meikle's was where the grocery shopping was done, once a month. 'Cheeses, and luxuries, if you like,' says daughter Kay. 'We'd order it and it would come by rail to Shabani. Our gardener Bonzo had a big basket on the back of his bike. We lived a funny life,' she reflects.

As a mother, Dick's wife Eileen was 'very serious, and made sure we behaved ourselves,' says Kay.

At first, all the kids attended the local junior school at Shabani. George — nicknamed Buster — used to ride his bike to school each day with some of his older siblings, a matter of 3km there, and 3km back (and any stories involving walking backwards through the snow in Rhodesia should be taken with a pinch of asbestos). They'd have to cross a quarry and a railway line in the process.

'On the way was a small gully,' recalled Dot. 'This was where the *tokoloshe* lived, and we would run like blazes to get through this dangerous patch.' *Tokoloshe* are the mischievous and sometimes malevolent spirits of Zulu/Xhosa folkloric belief.

A Bata tanning and shoe-making factory was also a big local concern, and good shoes were needed for the conditions and distances covered.

Buster wanted to be bigger and stronger and was told by his dad or kids at school, the only way to grow was to put cow shit in his shoes! This he did religiously, daily, for about two to three weeks before being told they were pulling his leg.

The garden was full of chickens scuttling about. And young George once saw a mouse scuttle up a tree and called out: 'Look — a monty!' And immediately his nickname changed from Buster to Monty! (But would revert in later years back to Buster.) He was a natural left-hander but back in his day, everyone 'had' to be a right-hander, whether they were or not.

Adventure never seemed far from him growing up.

Their father used to take them on picnics, which invariably involved prospecting for gold. They were often successful in finding small gleaming morsels. The area was littered with the five-stamp timber-based presses used by early-stage prospectors, with heavy iron rods that were raised by a pulley wheel then dropped down to crush the ore.

They had two English Springer Spaniels which, bred as gun dogs, were excellent for flushing out game in the fields, and a popular breed in Rhodesia in the day. An early memory involved playing with these dogs near a river (several cut through the lower Gwelo area). One minute they were running carefree along the river bank, the next moment a large croc burst out of the water, snatched one yelping spaniel, wrenched it back to the river, and the death rolls commenced. Traumatic. But at least it took the dog and not the boy. Such is the frailty of life in Africa.

Snakes were also a constant presence and threat. Dick one day had been bitten by a snake, and turned to his boss boy Sixpence [all African males were then called 'boy' regardless of age], giving him his knife, and holding out the affected finger because the go-to treatment was to cut across the wound and bleed out or suck out the venom: 'Cut it out! Cut it out!' Sixpence promptly but inexplicably proceeded to cut his own finger!

The kids were all introduced to guns early, because shooting was the main leisure activity. 'It was an African way of life,' says Kay, whose favourite gun was a .22. 'I was hopeless — I could only hit noticeboards, but I didn't always hit them,' she laughs.

Later Dick became the facilities manager at Gath's Mine — JW Gath had originally pegged that claim in 1907 — looking after the housing for thousands of native workers in the compound. Housing and facilities were segregated along race and occupational rank, reflecting the colonial practices of the day. Daughter Dot recalls the kitchens: 'I remember seeing huge pots of *nyimo* beans cooking ... delicious! '

After primary school, all the kids went off to board at Chaplin, founded as Trinity Church School in 1902. After the government took it over seven years later, it was named in honour of Lt-Col Charles Chaplin, a pioneer-settler who'd done much to further the local community and education.

Chaplin's colonial-revival-style buildings are imposing, standing proud with their arches and portico. The students wear smart green blazers and ties and aspire to the motto of *'Pro Honore'* (Do it with Honour).

'We had to be well dressed,' remembers Kay. 'Very British lines, we used to dress like British girls.' She is quick to point out that 'we were British Rhodesians' and did see England as the motherland. She recalls conversations around the dinner table about Henry being a pioneer, an obvious point of family pride.

Their rival schools were Plumtree and Milton, who they often managed to beat at rugby, perhaps the best measure of any school's prowess. The girls played hockey. They also produced a number of international cricketers over the years such as Steve Elworthy, Richard Kaschula, and Robert Ullyet (also a hockey Olympian). On the more academic side, they produced the Africa Editor of *Financial Times*, Michael Holman.

In town, they might have noticed Jeannie Boggie riding her horse around town. She continued this until she was 80. She gained even greater prominence in the late 1930s when she funded and built the Boggie Clock as a memorial to her late husband and to the Pioneers in general. The 10-metre-ish structure is located at the intersection of Main Street (now renamed Robert Mugabe Way) and 8th Street, where late on busy weekend nights it managed to jump out at more than a few drivers. Such news stories often made the pages of the town's very own newspaper, *Gwelo Times*.

The clock's wildly expensive imported Westminster bells would ring out on the hour, and peeled 12 bells to mark midnight, much to the annoyance of guests at the Midlands Hotel just metres away. The council soon had it silenced. But the Boggie Clock continued to be the town's centrepiece for New Year's Eve parties and gatherings, waiting for it to strike midnight.

The tiny but growing town now boasted a Meikle's store, Ainsworth Chemist, and Duly & Co motor dealership. It was also boosted by creation of the Empire Air Training Scheme (EATS), a scheme to develop pilots in and from the Commonwealth colonies — which Southern Rhodesia was at that stage — to bolster Britain's RAF.

Royal Air Force Station Thornhill was built on parts of two commandeered farms, and soon trains began arriving with dashing young British pilots (a pattern that continued till the end of the Second World War).

While Rhodesia was the last to join EATS, in 1940 it became the first to present pilots qualified to go up against the Luftwaffe and other adversaries. Later, Canberra bombers and Hawker Hunters only added to the displeasing din. And Boggie was most annoyed when they practiced bombing runs with toilet rolls on her beloved clock!

One of the pilots that possibly annoyed Boggie was a young Rhodesian hell-bent on flying Spitfires: He gave up his university studies at Rhodes to attend flying lessons at Thornhill. He was also an old boy of Chaplin School, where he'd been head boy, victor ludorum, and captain of rugby, cricket, athletics, tennis, and boxing. Ian Smith was something of a leader, it seems.

In 1942, the same year Buster started as a boarder at Chaplin, Smith earned his wings. But the following year, posted to Egypt, Smith's

Hurricane throttle malfunctioned on takeoff, making a right mess of him. After several reconstructive and pioneering plastic surgeries, he was offered a training position but took another combat role flying Spitfires in the Mediterranean instead. So, clearly determined too.

Dick Lloyd had taken on Forest Vale Farm from grandfather Henry the Pioneer, and turned his hand to agriculture after retirement from the mines due to a lung problem. Wife Eileen would spend a lot of time contentedly doing crochet. Dot remembers the jackals always getting into the chickens.

They'd all pile into Dick's green 'vanette', and make the roughly 20km drive to Gwelo: 'It was big enough to fit everyone and everything in.' Although Kay does recall it breaking down at least once and having to be ferried by another passing car to school.

Like teenagers anywhere music was an important part of life. They had a record player, 'a big construction', Kay remembers. The small community around Shabani was such that everybody knew everybody else, and there were lots of socials, usually staged at the Shabani Mine Club. Dick would invariably be on the piano, getting the party moving. 'We danced the quickstep, everybody could do that, and the waltz,' recalls Kay fondly. 'A lovely life.' Dick also played the mouth organ.

Sport was important as a social and physical diversion to those in such colonial outposts. And Gwelo Sporting Club filled that role, offering tennis, rugby, cricket, and golf. Socially, it played host to dinner dances and war-effort fundraisers. Southern Rhodesia was unique in the British Empire and Commonwealth at that time: it held extensive autonomous powers (including defence, but not foreign affairs) yet lacked dominion status. But it is ironic that Rhodesia adhered to Imperial British social norms on the playing field, while trying so desperately to assert itself as an independent entity with anti-British national identity.

Sometimes those who leave Britain are more British than the British themselves. Witness place names around Gwelo such as Hereford, Clydesdale, Shamrock Park, Staffordshire, and Shropshire.

The education system was along British lines, and Buster threw himself into all and any activities going: sports, drama and debating. In 1945 he won the Harriers Cup (cross-country running), made the 1st XV rugby team, and enjoyed boxing, which was popular and considered a great way to build discipline, physical fitness, and character.

That same year he also gained his Cambridge School Leaving Certificate. The following year he repeated to gain a Matric Exemption, was a house prefect, and was awarded his rugby colours. The headmaster, Mr Farrell, described him as being 'of cheerful disposition and straightforward.'

Buster went back to help his father on the farm during the difficult post-war years, getting his hands dirty and gaining valuable practical experience on the land for a couple of years. One of the tasks was mowing grass fields to make dried thatching to roof the workers' houses.

He and brother Mick — who was showing promise as a cricketer, playing in the Nuffield cricket trials for selection in a Rhodesian Schools team — at some point apparently invented a rudimentary solar-heating system for their pool (something which only became commercialised in the late 60s — they should've patented it).

George also did shifts in the asbestos mines, with barely even a basic face mask for protection, laughing at their dust-covered faces with only eyes poking through the sediment. (If only they knew the dangers — although as early as 1924 asbestosis was first diagnosed, and the link with mesothelioma cancer established in the 40s.)

On top of that, George was also running out for the Mashonaland rugby team, with rugby spirits in Rhodesia at a high given the national side, the Sables, had given the All Blacks a 10-8 hiding at the Hartsfield rugby ground in Bulawayo in 1949, in front of 10,000 fervent fans. They remain the only non-Test nation to beat them. The locals put it down to the 'Shangani mermaids', mythical chimera who opposed anyone crossing the Shangani River (although they hadn't totally stopped the Red Coats in 1893).

Well-toned by his physical exertions, Buster signed on to do a Bachelor of Science degree at the University of Natal, Pietermaritzburg. He immediately got involved in more boxing and rugby, playing front-row prop because he was a physical specimen to be reckoned with. A fact not lost on the ladies on campus, apparently.

At least half the students lived on campus, creating a lively community vibe. Buster moved into Oribi Residence, where freshers' initiation and orientation programs were important parts of the early student experience (like it or not).

Sprogs, as freshers were called at Oribi, were subjected to various indignities, such as having to crawl along corridors on their hands and knees at night. They also had to wear red bow ties — symbolising raw meat! — and attend song practices in the Student Union building as preparation for the Rag event and annual inter-campus sports competitions. The centrepiece of Rag Day was often a parade of costumes, floats, and other shenanigans, with the aim of raising money for local charities.

A few years behind, Buster's brother Mick would take advantage of his seniority as a 3rd year student. 'Seniors used to send juniors off to march on the oval during socials, so they could get first crack at the junior girls,' laughs former student Paddy (nee Edwards), who Mick successfully made a bee-line for.

Wednesday dinners at Oribi were extra-formal, marked by meals such as pork with apple sauce and ice cream for dessert (pretty elaborate compared to post-war privations in Britain). Some seniors mischievously smuggled wine into these events using the large pockets of obsolete academic gowns. This was not condoned by Oswald Black, PhD, the warden of the residence, but he was generally tolerant of high jinks.

Off campus, the nearby bar of the fin de siècle Imperial Hotel got a regular workout. Billing itself as 'South Africa's best hotel' it boasted amenities such as hot and cold water and a telephone in every room. Heady stuff!

Buster got around in a little MG sports car. (British cars like Austin Healey 100s and Triumph Roadsters were also quite common.)

His rugby prowess continued to develop, making the combined Natal University team in 1950, and earning his half-blue the following year (allowing him to gad about in a striking white blazer with blue/green/black stripes).

His consistently strong performances soon led to selection in the Natal provincial side. Unfortunately, his very first match proved a baptism of fire. Or ire.

Against Eastern Province, he came up against Amos du Plooy, who would earn over 100 caps for his province, become captain, and earn a Springbok cap aged 34. Amos, 29 years of age to Buster's 21, was well-versed in the dark arts of scrummaging. Before the teams took the field, he glowered at Buster: 'Lloyd, I am going to brrreak your back today!' he growled in his heavily-accented English.

Match starts. First scrum down. *SNAP*! Amos's formidable strength and scrummaging skills broke George's back. And that was the end of Buster's rugby career. Say one thing for Amos: he was a man of his word!

With playing rugby now out of his system, Buster could now concentrate a little more on his studies and other stuff at Oribi. He was already on the House committee, and in his final year he was made House president. (Fellow committee member Peter Booysen would go on to become a professor and principal at Natal University.)

'I could not wish for a better head student, as I found him ever-willing to co-operate with me in running a hall of residence comprising 250 students,' wrote Oswald Black of Buster. 'He is endowed with a happy, cheerful disposition, and fine character traits. Moreover, he is a born leader and it would not surprise me if he soon attained a position of leadership in his chosen field of agriculture. His conduct has always been that of a gentleman.'

So much so, Buster once found a guy sitting on his car bonnet when he came out of the club one time.

'That's my car, do you mind getting off it please,' he said.

The cocky guy just looked at Buster dismissively.

'Would you please get off my car?' Buster repeated.

Another dismissive look.

'Well, then … sorry.'

'Sorry? What for?' the guy said.

BAM! Buster laid him out cold with one of his handy right hooks. A couple of other stories underscore his modus operandi — an apology upfront, followed by a singular knockout punch. *That's a gentleman.*

Growing up, Kay Lloyd dreamed of becoming a nurse. 'The other choice was a typist, and I didn't like that.' She went off to train as a full-grade nurse at Salisbury General Hospital.

Men were often admitted with broken bones 'because they couldn't drive properly' she says, while women mostly came in with issues like appendicitis. One night on shift, a cheeky young blond man named Mick Flint was wheeled into her ward. 'He was in hospital after an accident, he had a broken arm or leg.' There was a bit of banter between them. 'But when he asked what he should do with his shoes, I told him to throw them away, and that upset him terribly.'

'But they're my best shoes,' Mick protested.

'After he was discharged, he dragged up the courage to ask me out, ' recalls Kay of the Crown servant she married in Salisbury soon after, and they'd be husband and wife for the next six decades or so. (Mick's family had a rather tragic story in which his siblings — twin boys Geoffrey and Richard — both died at the same time shortly after birth, following circumcision. In honour of them, Mick and Kay named their first-born Geoffrey Richard Flint.)

Kay's father Dick retained an intense interest in fossicking and gemstones, which proved his undoing. Attending a gem industry expo in Johannesburg with daughter Dot, an exhibitor was extolling the virtues of silica in glassmaking and other industries, because of its purity, hardness, and heat-resistance. Dick said, 'Oh, our place is full of that stuff, it's everywhere!' The exhibitor enquired of the whereabouts of this farm, and Dick casually gave him the details, thinking nothing of it.

Soon, a gang of men arrived at Forest Vale Farm and began banging pegs into the ground. 'What's going on here, then?'

Under the Mines and Minerals Act, mineral rights were vested in the state, not the landowner, and prospecting licenses could be pegged over privately-owned farms. In practical terms, this meant that anyone with the correct paperwork could legally enter another man's land, drive in pegs, and claim mineral rights irrespective of crops, livestock, or tenure. Dick still owned the surface, but the subsoil — valuable silica — now belonged to Consolidated Mining.

With conditions becoming unbearable, Dick and Eileen moved into a house at 8 Strand St, Gwelo, leaving the farm behind.

The family's once-winning hand had turned into a handful of dust.

12

A LADY NAMED JEN

SOUTH AFRICA, 1954. Meanwhile a tall, young, sporty, brown-haired lass from Zululand started 'varsity' at the University of Pietermaritzburg. Jennifer Seymour turned up from Empangeni to study a Bachelor of Arts degree.

She was the granddaughter of the war hero, George Frederick Seymour, and the middle child of mechanical engineer George Edgar Seymour and schoolteacher Alys (daughter of footballer Thomas Tait, and granddaughter of Michael and Bridget McGee) who lived in Darnall, northern Natal. Sugar cane country.

Darnall, in the Lower Tugela region inland from Zinkwazi, was named by the farm's original owner, David Brown, after his hometown in Yorkshire. He was one of the first to introduce cane to this part of the coast and set up a sugar mill in 1904. But his mill proved unviable and he sold it to Liege Hulett, another Englishman, who'd left home with just £5 in his pocket, but now had a 600-acre farm, a grand homestead, and a company — JL Hulett & Sons headquartered in Kearsney, near Stanger — with capital of £50,000.

A couple of years after buying the Darnall mill, Hulett (in the style of Cecil Rhodes) would acquire other mills in Amatikulu and Felixton and ultimately become synonymous with South Africa's sugar industry.

◻ ◻ ◻

George Seymour was a mechanical engineer who had moved down from Lydenburg to run the mill on the Walter Kramer farm, just outside Gingindlovu (said to mean "swallower of the elephant", a reference to King Cetshwayo's military strength, before his trouncing at the hands of the British here in 1879). The area — halfway between Eshowe and Richards Bay — was heavily malarial, and both George and Alys were afflicted by it.

When Kramer's mill closed, George was head-hunted across to work for Hulett's at their Darnall mill.

First son David was born at the Queen Victoria Hospital, Eshowe, in 1931. He remembers their Darnall house as a brick-and-tile affair. 'Our father was a manager, so we had a pretty big place,' he tells me. 'Single story, one of the better ones in town, and the servants had their own little quarters at the back.'

Around the age of four he remembers one episode in the garden. 'I was with the garden "boy" and we were loading soil outside the property. I absentmindedly had my foot through the spoke of the wheelbarrow. And this Zulu picked up this barrow and pulled back, hard. And there was my bloody leg in there.' Infection later set in, resulting in a tennis ball of pus on the ankle. 'I've still got a bit of a bend in it,' he points to his lower foot.

His younger sister Jennifer was born in 1936 at the Westminster Nursing Home in Overport, Durban, a residence-turned-medical facility, highlighting the community-driven approach of the day, especially in matters of maternity.

In something of a *Tom and Jerry* pattern between older brother and younger sister over the years, he was clowning around one day. *THUMP*! 'Jennifer fell out of the cot, because I did something stupid. Landed on her head!'

There were other headaches. Father George's car was constantly breaking down. 'He bought it second-hand; it was only about £50 or something. He got so bloody sick of this thing breaking down, that it broke down once more, and he just left it on the road … that's where it stayed.'

Fortunately, his career was on the up-and-up, so finances (and transport) improved. Engineer George was promoted to manager and transferred to Felixton, a small milling town about 120km north.

Their home was set on a hill, amid five acres, with a double garage. They even had an Indian chauffeur, Mardhu. Sometimes he'd let a very young David coast down the last bit of the driveway into the garage. Once or twice, this was slightly misjudged, resulting in dents to both the garage and the car (and possibly David's ego). There were also nannies, Indian rather than African, which David can't explain as the latter were far more common at the time.

Felixton was very much a company town, centred around a company swimming pool and hall. 'Everything in Felixton happened at the hall ... movies, functions, etc … movies every Saturday night,' says Jennifer. 'Doctor MacDonald and family lived near the pool, and we had to pass by their house to get to the pool. He and his wife were very English, with a couple of kids.' More about him later.

The company always put on a Christmas party for the kids each year. 'Some chap from the company was always Father Christmas — we never called him Santa back then — but I never knew he was just someone from the company.'

Her playmates included John Carr and John Clapham, as well as Paddy Saunders, whose father also worked at the mill. 'We were the same age, in the same class, so we just did everything together,' said Jen. The Seymours now had a black dog called Timmy, 'a big thing who preferred to be left alone.' When they were about four, they were playing ball games and the ball rolled under table where Timmy was sleeping. 'Paddy crawled under to get it, roused Timmy and *SNAP*! It bit Paddy square on her nose! '

Despite that, they (meaning Jen and Paddy, not Timmy and Paddy) would be lifelong best friends.

Which is more than can be said for Paddy's twin brothers Ian and Keith and Jen's brother David. 'They were the worst bastards I know,' recalls David. 'They used to beat the shit out of us every day. And if they weren't beating us, they were beating each other.' David would co-opt his mate Richard Grantham, but they were no match. 'So, the only time we could get them was when we were on the farm — we'd get the Africans to help us keep these buggers under control.'

Someone whom he could control was Jen. The pond in the garden was full of frogs which were annoying their mum, Alys. She asked David to collect them all. He put them in a bucket but needed Jen to sit on top and stop them jumping out while he fetched the next lot. 'These things jumped and jumped and bumped up against my bum,' she laughs.

David was boarding at St Charles, a Marist Brothers school in Pietermaritzburg, where his younger sibling Roger would also later attend. David became firm friends with a French Mauritian guy, Michel 'Micky' Ray, whose sugar-farming family had moved to South Africa.

David remembers as a 10-year-old catching the night train home to Zululand for holidays with him and other friends. 'We left Pietermaritzburg for Durban at 1pm, then hung around the Durban station until 11pm at night.' He remembers blackouts being enforced 'to stop Jerry's ships and subs shooting us up in Durban.' Then they'd hop on the next train to Zululand. 'And the old conductor used to rattle on the clacker, "Amatikulu next stop!" And you had to jump out at 6am with your toothbrush in your hand.' Helicopter parenting was still far in the future.

Back in Zululand, school holidays meant time for David to practice his bird-shooting skills. Rule number one his father had always drummed into him was never point your gun at anyone. Once as a teenager, he'd gone out shooting birds for the day with a friend his age. In the evening, they were walking back home. David opened the rifle and felt in the breach where there was no bullet. He then aimed the rifle at a tree and pulled the trigger. *Click* — no bullet came out. He then playfully aimed the rifle at the back of his friend's head in front of him and pulled the trigger. *Click* — no bullet, of course. He then aimed the rifle at a tree again, pulled the trigger, *BANG*! The gun discharged.

They'd quite often travel up to the Transvaal to see their relatives, the McGees. 'We used to run around on the farm there,' recalls David. 'It was on a river, where the trout hatchery was. Michael was a character and he was running a successful garage. Often you were held up because bridges over rivers were flooded, and you'd have to wait on the side of the road, waiting for the river to go down.'

The Second World War even reached these inland rural communities of South Africa. British sailors and airmen were billeted with local families. Jen remembers them as being 'easygoing on the way in, shell-shocked on the way out — withdrawn, staring, murmuring.' On one memorable occasion, she was sitting behind a serviceman at home as he was drawing a chart. She was drinking water and managed to spill a few drops on it. He exploded, then slapped her on the face. She sat stunned, then went off to bed, cheek glowing red. But overall, there was mutual appreciation, with all signing the family's blue autograph book, leaving messages of goodwill and thanks; sketches, watercolours and cartoons; and future addresses in England.

The Second World War also touched the Tait family directly. Rosie's other daughter, Alys' sister Kathleen ('Kay'), grew up in Lydenburg with a keen interest in playing music, and tennis. She trained in nursing at the Sanatorium, Durban (originally the McCord Zulu Hospital, a medical missionary institution, focused on care for the under-served). She then moved on to the Mothers' Hospital, a maternity hospital in Johannesburg. With the advent of WW2, Kay answered the call, becoming Captain Kathleen Tait, South African Military Nursing Service (SAMNS).

Together with their British nursing counterparts, they were deeply involved in the North African campaigns, particularly in the Western Desert and Egypt. They played a crucial role in providing medical care under unimaginably challenging conditions. They served in mobile hospitals, often dangerously near the front lines, treating soldiers injured in famous battles like El Alamein and Tobruk. In the former battle, around 13,500 Allied soldiers died, and the same number again were injured. Working in harsh desert environments, these nurses had to deal with intense heat, dust, and frequent bombing raids.

She probably served at some point in the infamous 'Fig Tree' Dressing Station, a series of subterranean caves on the Gallipoli used by the Australians and South Africans. The fig tree marking its entrance amid the otherwise barren landscape became a beacon for frequent German artillery attacks.

Kay married a Mr Phillips (of whom details remain obscure, but seems to have been in the legal field, and possibly a magistrate in Lesotho for a while) and they had a couple of daughters, Rosanne and Patricia. In circumstances similarly obscure, Kay then remarried a Mr Clayton, a farmer in the Albany/Bathurst area, and continued nursing till the day she died aged just 51 in 1966. She also enjoyed a creative sideline as a floral arranger of some note in the Grahamstown area — a skill perhaps inherited from her Irish great-grandfather James Sarsfield.

Around this time, Engineer George went away on business for about one month. Alys —'who'd done nothing hard in her life' according to Jen — couldn't deal with their newly born younger brother, Roger. They put Jen in boarding school at Port Shepstone, and Alys and the baby stayed at grandfather War Hero George's house there. Port Shepstone on the South coast of Natal was popular for its beachside vibe and vibrant community life and had attracted a lot of European migrants (notably Norwegians) in the latter part of the 19th century.

David recalls his grandfather George, who they used to visit a lot. 'I remember him very clearly, when we were still little tackers. Married to a German lady who settled in South Africa, Grandma Willy.' Wilhelmina was also known as Minnie.

■ □ ■

'I was sooo homesick,' Jen said of her first taste of boarding school. 'I'd wait until lights out, then, when everyone was asleep in this huge dormitory, bawl my eyes out.' The first night, the five-year-old didn't know where the toilet was and was too shy to ask. She woke up, busting. Nothing for it but to pee in her felt slipper. 'Next morning, the Sister Superior was very understanding, but asked me what was wrong with my slipper?' Perhaps the Sister had noticed something odd. The homesickness never abated.

Another time, the Sister had pointed out a room full of hats. All identical. 'This is your hat.' Then they had to go to church. 'They all looked the same, we grabbed our hats, I grabbed the first one. We hadn't even reached the church when we were all lined up: "Girls, someone's taken the wrong hat." Straight away I knew. It was so humiliating in front of others.'

A longer-term solution was found by Alys, who'd attended the Loreto Convent in Pretoria as a young girl: Jen was sent to Oakford Priory boarding school at Verulam, an imposing collection of Gothic buildings a little north of Durban. 'All the nuns were German, and a couple English. They did everything around the place, meaning hard manual work, handyman sort of stuff.' Germans generally were not rounded up nor interned in South Africa, unless they were Nazi sympathisers or members of the Afrikaner ultra-nationalist *Ossebrandwag*, which had a paramilitary wing, the *stormjaers* (storm troopers). There is no suggestion that Grandma Willy was involved with them.

This was a school of tough love. The nuns did not nurture the boarders with love and affection to make up for their wrench from their parental bosom. Rather, they dispensed leather straps and wooden rulers for the most minor infraction, to inculcate obedience to the Lord. It bordered on emotional and physical cruelty.

The nuns attended mass every day. But for some reason one day no service was held — perhaps the priest couldn't attend — so it was fortunately empty when the whole chapel came crumbling down.

Even home was not an overly affectionate environment. Jen rarely received a hug from her father; it's just how parenting was done then. In quieter moments back home on holiday, she would enjoy reading Enid Blyton's brand-new series *The Famous Five,* featuring the adventures of Julian, Dick, Anne, George, and their dog Timmy. Or she would go for a ride on her second-hand bike.

'It was during the war and new things were hard to come by,' Jen explains. Coming from the little shop at the top of the hill, as she headed downwards, she realised she had no brakes. At the bottom of this slope was a brick wall, the back of her parents' house. 'What I remember as this bike gathered speed was this Indian *dhobi* (laundry) guy by the side of the road looking up, seeing me, and — with eyes and jaw wide open — watching me whizz by to a certain disastrous finish.' Sure enough: *SMACK*! She hit the wall head-first, leaving clear teeth marks in the bricks. Her chin was split open. And she lay unconscious in the hospital for three days. 'After I woke up I had to spend the next few days pulling my teeth down bit by bit out of my gums.' Sometime later, these were replaced by a plate of two false front teeth.

Another time she was not feeling well in the middle of the night. It was decided that the company doctor should be called. At the mention of Dr MacDonald's name, she cried: 'No, no, he might be drunk.' MacDonald was alcoholic. And there was one triggering memory: One day at the club, Paddy and Jen bumped into him. 'We screamed and ran out on the verandah which skirted around the whole club. We ran and ran and ran, then finally stopped, figuring we were far enough away. Then we looked up and saw his face staring at us from out of the round porthole-like window of the club door behind us. More screaming!'

Undaunted by her bicycle accident, Jen loved the idea of having a horse, so her father bought her one. Only in South Africa could a horse come with its own 'Basuto pony boy 'to look after it. Samuel, had moved into Zululand from neighbouring Basutoland (now Lesotho), where ponies were a vital form of transport in the rugged terrain, and also a symbol of wealth and masculinity — 'so he was a bit of a foreigner, 'explains David of the horseman.

Bibi the horse had endured an arduous trip up from beyond Durban. 'The horse was in a terrible state ... it was just going wild and I thought it was going to kill itself,' remembers David. 'Bibi was quite hyper,' recalls Jen. But when she got on, it quietened down: 'It must have felt a little gentle person was on board.'

Often David and Samuel would head out into the field to bring Bibi in from grazing in the afternoon. 'With just a bridle. And we would both jump on the horse bareback. And I'd hang on to Samuel. If he didn't have a bridle, he'd just tie a rope around the bottom lip of the horse.'

Quite often David had to bring the horse back on his own. 'And the horse was galloping home for its evening feed. There was no stopping him!' He had to duck under the trees at the back of the house to the stable — a corrugated iron affair with a swing door. 'And I was petrified that if the door was open, Bibi would rush in and then stop dead, and then I might amputate my leg on the sharp corrugated iron. But if it was closed, it also rushed up and it stopped on the side of the stable, and I'd go hurtling off into the bananas.'

Despite all this, fun moments were had, and Jen convinced Paddy she should also get a horse, which she did, perhaps just to join in. But this came to a rather sticky end: Samuel was murdered,' recalls David. 'Samuel was getting off (romancing), I presume, with a Zulu maiden. And they found his body, stabbed to death.'

Other disasters happened around this time. David recalls one unusually cold night in Felixton, 'and the five African servants were in a little place built on the property next door for the workers. They had a coal fire going in a tin. There was no ventilation. And you probably don't even know you're dying, and they never woke up next morning.'

Empangeni — just nine miles away — was the big smoke relative to the small town of Felixton, where the big attraction was a sizeable tennis centre. Alys loved her tennis and golf. Being a Tait, those sporting genes were prominent and she played avidly.

So, she might've been disappointed when husband George was promoted yet again to look after the Huletts' other mill at Amatikulu, a good hour's drive south.

Like Felixton, it was a company village, where dances on a Saturday night at the company hall were the social highlight. Vinyl records were played. But George was not much of a party boy, especially given his position in the company, and he was respected as such, and behaved accordingly.

The dentist would pass through town from Empangeni once a year. And Jen would make up feeble excuses each time. Until it was inescapable. This resulted in a mouthful of silver fillings.

While the war cramped their travel plans, they still enjoyed local holidays. When growing up, Jen's favourite spot was Richards Bay. 'It was during the war, so we didn't go very far. About 45 minutes or so. Mum and Dad would play tennis and fish.' David and Roger were also avid anglers.

Back home they also enjoyed the regular gymkhanas, often held at KwaMbonambi. David's favourite memories were of the race-fixing among the old guard. He'd stand behind them, 'so we could see who would win, and then go put money on the horse,' he laughs.

■ □ ■

By the end of the Second World War, South Africa was tugged in two directions. On one side stood Jan Smuts — wartime statesman, global hero, loyal to Britain and the Commonwealth. On the other stood an increasingly confident and resentful Afrikaner nationalism, nursing the old wounds of Boer defeat and dreaming of a republic free from English influence. Behind this rising tide was a secretive, disciplined brotherhood: the *Broederbond.* Its members quietly infiltrated pulpits, classrooms, civil service desks and party rooms — shaping minds, placing their men, tightening the cultural ligature.

The war had pulled the country into the Allied camp, but many Afrikaners saw Hitler's fight with Britain as poetic justice. 'The more extremist *Ossewabrandwag* marched in protest, sabotage flared, and

Smuts' loyalty to London only deepened the nationalist grievance. When peace arrived, the old Field Marshal suddenly looked from another age: tired and irrelevant. The National Party — reorganised, ruthless, and backed by the Dutch Reformed Church, farmers' unions, and those *Broederbond* cadres — offered something simpler: Afrikaner power for Afrikaner people.

In 1948 the Nationals swept to victory under Dr DF Malan on the promise of apartheid — a word packaged as "separate development" but understood as white supremacy made bureaucratic. For the first time in the Union's history, all cabinet members were Afrikaners. 'Today,' Prime Minister Malan gloated, 'South Africa belongs to us once more. For the first time since Union, South Africa is our own. May God grant that it always remains so.'

Their aim was to put South Africa out of Britain's grasp entirely. Preferably outside of the Commonwealth entirely. Within a year, they'd rewound Smuts' plan to recruit British immigrants and passed a bill to make it harder for Britons in the country already to gain citizenship, and thus the vote.

In 1951 Ernest George Jansen became Governor-General of South Africa, still formally a British dominion.

In the Nationalist government, he was most recently Minister of Native Affairs but was thought to be too soft on the new policy of apartheid, for which his department was primarily responsible. He was subsequently given this 'sideways promotion' to the politically neutral post, and was replaced by the hardliner Hendrik Verwoerd.

Jansen and his wife Martha were keen proponents of Afrikaner cultural life, calling for the reinstatement of the Boer States. He had been the Master of Ceremonies at the laying of the foundation stone of the Voortrekker Monument in 1938, and at its dedication in 1949, in front of a crowd of 250,000.

In his new role as Governor-General, the office represented the Crown. But the square-jawed thin-lipped Jansen deliberately broke with tradition — he refused to wear the Governor-General's ceremonial uniform, choosing instead to appear in plain civilian dress. He also declined to swear a personal oath of allegiance to the monarch, opting for a version that emphasised service to South Africa rather than loyalty to the Crown.

This was done quietly and without theatrical confrontation. Afrikaner republicanism expressed itself through restraint, not rebellion. Jansen was signaling that the symbolic centre of power had shifted, foreshadowing the more dramatic political events that lay ahead.

Ideology hardened into law: racial classification books, Pass Laws, the Group Areas Act, Bantu Education. A machinery of control, tightening bolt by bolt. Globally, apartheid was to become perhaps the most famous, or infamous, of all words in the Afrikaans language.

Jansen would die in office in 1959 and was buried in Heroes' Acre at Church Street Cemetery, Pretoria. We'll find out a bit later how he ties into the Seymour family.

▣ ▣ ▣

Jen always did well at school, but the *Tom and Jerry* relationship with David continued: 'You might come first in class,' he once said to her, 'but you are the stupidest person I know.'

For high school she moved from Oakford to Collegiate in Pietermaritzburg, which had been running since 1878. The girls wore pretty floral-patterned school dresses. Jen dived into tennis and hockey with zeal.

And with David, Jennifer, and Roger all in private schools, it was financially fortunate that again their father was promoted, this time to consulting engineer and general manager of the Hulett sugar mill group, who by now had mills and operations in South Africa, Rhodesia, and Swaziland, while gearing up for a JSE stock exchange listing in Johannesburg in 1952.

The family moved to a home with lush and spacious gardens at 6 Palmiet Drive, Westville, outside of Durban. George would soon be on the committee of the South African Sugar Technology Association, which held its meetings at the experimental station at Mt Edgecombe.

'My father had responsibility for those early developments and flew regularly to those mill sites,' recalls David. 'He had the responsibility of purchasing the machinery required, which involved flying overseas to Britain, Europe, and the Americas.'

Many of those flights were on BOAC Comets, the world's first commercial jetliners. Flying in those days didn't enjoy the safety record it does today. Within months of launching, three Comets had fallen from the sky due to metal fatigue.

One trip was to New Orleans, aboard a Clipper with a bar for first-class passengers. 'At the bar, a man introduced himself to my father,' says David.

'My name is Tony Curtis.'

'Pleased to meet you,' my father replied, 'I am George Seymour.'

He had no idea who Tony Curtis — soon to star in *Some Like It Hot* with Marilyn Monroe — was! 'They subsequently ended up in the same hotel, but the idol seemed more interested in the hotel's resident Spanish dancer.'

In his spare time at home, George nurtured a love and skill for oil painting, doing impressive small canvases of landscapes and homes. This enjoyment of art was also passed onto Jen, who enjoyed painting in a similar vein.

◼ ◻ ◼

Meanwhile David had finished high school. He spent a fair bit of time with his grandparents down in Port Shepstone because, on leaving school and starting work, David had an extreme growth spurt and literally outgrew his spine, growing six inches in that year. Doctor's orders: rest in bed for 10 months.

'And Grandma Willy comes in polishing the bloody floor in the morning. And I'm lying in bed. She used to crap on me: "Young man, you need to get up now. Yes, you should be up and about." She was the fiery one, kicking me up the arse.'

One thing Willy loved was her Sunday drives. She'd put on her large bonnet-like hat and David was volunteered as their chauffeur. 'And she'd get her husband, George, the pioneer in the car. "David's going to drive us this afternoon."' David was 19 and had only just started driving: 'They didn't know how bloody endangered their lives were!'

But David used to also sneak out on his own, and head to social dances in Kokstad — an almost two-hour drive each way — and make a night of it. 'I had the odd girlfriend here and there. Got back at about one in the morning. 'Then lie in bed all day to recover, earning Willy's wrath. You can almost hear it: '*Raus*! *Raus*!'

Jen remembers her as 'very German, very outspoken: "Jah, jah, I told you so",' she laughs.

While Willy was rather stern in nature, her husband George was rather subdued and more distant, spending a lot of time in the garden by that stage. 'Probably to stay away from Willy,' David jokes. They then moved inland to Kokstad, spending their time at home at 56 Coulter St. George would soon pass away, aged 77 — after a coronary thrombosis at home, with Wilhelmina at his bedside for four hours — having lived a very full and adventurous life, which — as a wide-eyed youngster — David relished talking to him about. Granny Willy would live to a ripe old 85, passing away in Matatiele nearby, in the foothills of the Drakensberg.

Fifteen years after the National Party's triumph in 1948, South Africa had become a hardened, divided fortress of ideology. What began as Afrikaner political victory had ossified into a rigorous system of domination. Nelson Mandela describes in *Long Walk to Freedom* how apartheid was 'not so much a policy as a creed,' enforced with laws that reached into every corner of personal life: where one lived, studied, worked, even loved. Samson, in his biography *Mandela*, charts how the *Broederbond's* invisible hand directed a disciplined nationalist project — binding Afrikaners together through language, Calvinist faith, and a shared history of grievance against British rule.

English-speaking whites, meanwhile, found themselves caught awkwardly between power and conscience. Beneficiaries of privilege, yet often uneasy with its cruelty, they formed the core of the liberal opposition — speaking out in newspapers and universities but rarely risking their comfort for change.

For black South Africans, patience was running out. Mandela and others met in the *shebeens* (township bars), excited, even intoxicated by the cool scene — fuelled by jazz and *marabi* music — flourishing in

Orlando, outside Johannesburg. They were dreaming and scheming: This is what an enlightened South Africa might look and feel like.

In 1954, Jen was at university, studying all this Political Science stuff that was evolving in real-time around her. She was paying her way as a magician's assistant. 'She came down from Pietermaritzburg Uni with one of her friends and the magician for whom they used to act as assistants,' says younger brother Roger Seymour. 'We would always go out on the *Sarie Marais* boat on Durban harbour, and the magician would, inter alia, make preselected cards appear from a pack of cards — whilst he stood metres away. *Voila*! What magic, especially for an 11-year-old, and such fun for big sister, too!'

Later, Jen would drive Roger and his good friend Chris Mellor back to boarding school in Pietermaritzburg after school holidays. Then after Chris moved to Durban High, they fell into an agreeable holiday routine as young teens. 'We had a set routine in summer,' recalls Roger fondly of his friend who lived on Durban's South Beach. 'Morning spent on the beach, then his mum used to make us lunch, then off we went down West Street to Joe's Snooker Saloon for a few games, then off to the afternoon movies in Smith Street!'

Around this time, Jen had gone down the south coast on a trip with her mum and dad to Port Shepstone. 'There was nothing there but one big hotel.' (Actually, a rather unassuming single-story affair overlooking the beach.) She'd gone out with a group of friends and met this gent who was a married doctor. (Dr MacDonald from Amatikulu it seems.) She describes him as 'a good-looking chap with blond hair, blue eyes — his wife was the same. And their three children. Sue Newton (a friend of Jen's) had a fling with him because she was naughty like that, but had moved on.' Now he was clearly trying to line up Jen. They had dinner at the big dining room of the hotel. 'He kept ordering more drinks, probably gin and tonics or whatever. I've never been a drinker. We'd have a couple of drinks at varsity, but I was never sloshed. In any case I was never going to go out with him — he was an alcoholic and I hated people who were drunk. I was trying my best to act mature and sophisticated but felt sicker and sicker and incredibly tired. He drove me home to my grand-parents' house where we were staying. I literally fell out of his car and ran to the door.'

Having heard all about this chap George Lloyd from her girlfriends, one day he came driving up through the university in his sports car and said

'Hello' to some of her friends. Jen was rather underwhelmed, given his reputation as a 'mover and shaker' with the girls: 'Is that him?'

However, they both went to social dances on campus, and things picked up pace from there. 'Dances were the big thing every Saturday,' Jen tells me. 'We jived. I was pretty hot stuff, oh yes!' she laughs. 'George was a good dancer too, very rhythmic.' But she was clearly impressed: 'He was head of residence … George got to the head of everything.'

Two rivers were now running toward the same sea. But what lay downstream, nobody knew.

13

THOSE WERE THE DAYS

ZULULAND, LATE 1950s. Having qualified as a chartered accountant in Durban, David Seymour decided to move back up to Empangeni, Zululand — where relatives the Rathbone family had pioneered the sugar industry — to pursue his career. Also, it was where all his mates were.

He would open an accountancy practice with Peter 'Puck' Addison who was also a keen cricketer and would become local mayor.

Mauritian Micky Rey, a couple of years older than David, by now had a girlfriend, 16-year-old Penelope Coelen, from Durban Girls' High School. 'She was a lovely person. I have a photo of us fooling around having a kiss. All in good fun,' laughs David. After school, she went on to work as a secretary, entered the Miss World contest aged 18, and became the first South African to win the title. She left the glitz of Hollywood where she was trying to break into film, and married Micky, took the name Penny Rey, and raised five sons on their sugar farm around Ballito.

David was active in all the sports going at the Empangeni Sports Club, even becoming captain the golf club. Younger brother Roger was also making a name for himself at St Charles College, captaining the 1st XI. He went on to play 16 seasons of 1st League cricket in Durban, a few 'unofficial games for Natal provincial elevens', against teams like SA Defence Forces, as well as playing 'one official game for Natal B.' His highest score was 120 plus a couple of other centuries and a 97. 'I remember Barry Richards saying to me once, "You are a 50 man", so I did score a lot of half centuries. I was a bit of a dasher as a batsman,' he understates.

'In this day and age he would have been a legend in the T20, 'David reckons of the prolific and stylish left-handed big hitter. Roger was rather keen on rugby, too, as we'll see.

‘It was very much a hunting, shooting, fishing existence,’ David says fondly of his Zululand decades. David’s eyes light up at the mention of fishing, especially the Trout Bungalow in Mooi River, in the pristine Drakensberg foothills. Originally built as an officers’ mess for British officers stationed at Harrismith in the Boer War, it was the first stream in South Africa to be stocked with trout, those coveted Scottish brown specimens arriving in 1893.

Happily, the Trout Bungalow was owned by Dr Gordon Johnstone, a director of the WF Johnstone building conglomerate (who would later be David’s best man at his wedding).

Most of David’s fishing pals were schoolmates, descending from Maritzburg, Durban, and all parts of Zululand for lads’ fishing trips. The ringleader was often Ronnie Theunissen, whose family had a big house right on the beach at Zinkwazi, an hour north of Durban. ‘The Theunissens were well known, and they married the Rattrays, who had a bit of money and farms … they were all pretty wealthy, these guys.’

The beach was ringed with dunes, and sea eagles patrolled the lagoon that fed into the ocean. Nomadic *strandlopers* (beach walkers) favoured this stretch of coast for a couple of thousand years. In 1903 Bernard Theunissen acquired the first two-acre plot on the south bank of the lagoon, and a big two-story home was built.

Ronnie was a born organiser and, years before the term ‘glamping’ was invented, the whole camp would be set up for five-star camping. Having a household staff of at least four on hand probably helped.

Cape Vidal, in the greater Bhangazi area in Northern Natal, was another happy hunting ground where he’d go every year with Ossie Tedder, Brian Batchelor, Norman Cheeseman (who played wing for Natal), Norman’s brother Ron, and others. Ossie was a very keen fisherman: ‘So keen, I don't think he ever got married!’ laughs David.

Ossie owned one of the first Willy’s Jeeps to come into the country post-war. Just as well, because the road access was atrocious. The track mostly wound around lily-covered water pans for 22 miles from St Lucia, taking a full two tortoise-like hours. With no signs, they’d occasionally get lost — so landmarks such as mdoni trees would be used to navigate. One dark and stormy night they got lost, the Jeep got stuck on its belly on a hump, necessitating sleeping in the Jeep (and opening the windows only led to an invasion of mozzies). Fed up, one of the guys had gone off on foot to find the camp, and in turn had to be rescued: 'It was a good thing he did not bump into a hippo or croc,' said Ossie. 'There was no place to put a pin between the mosquito bites on his face and neck.'

They'd then have to take a punt across the estuary to reach the sand-swept beach. If the Mozambique current was running close to shore, the water would be a deep purple.

Previously local hotelier Harry Morton and Dr Maurice Hulett (grandson of Sir Liege Hulett) would winch their Jeeps up and down onto the beach in this area, which would take them six hours to do. Now, thankfully, there was a ramp down to the beach.

Here they'd set up camp in a hollow (for protection against the wind, because there were no casuarina trees along the beach then). A 44-gallon drum of water would have to be carted in for drinking and cooking. But the fishing proved fruitful:' Brian got the world record for bonefish,' says David proudly. 'Nineteen pounds, eight ounces.' That record stands unbroken to this day, over six decades later. Kingfish were also a good regular catch, as well as stumpies and pompano.

To underline how seriously all this fishing was taken, a typical diary entry of a catch would be along the following lines: 'Cape Vidal. Hooked at 12:30, incoming tide. Bait: moonfish. 15 kg line. Time to the beach: one and a half hours. Wind: northeast.'

With the steep ledge just off the beach, crayfish were there for the taking, washed down by copious amounts of beer. 'We used to frolic in the nude because we never saw another living soul on the beach,' said Ossie.

So Bhangazi became a regular annual trip. Ossie's Jeep would sometimes be loaded with as many as 13 souls — with multiples more cans of beer — and they'd drive for miles and miles along unfettered stretches of beach.

To keep the beers cold, they started bringing a huge block of ice, which they'd have to pre-order from Durban and collect on the way up.

One year, Ernie Getkate (one of several of the Getkate clan in this group) brought his Indian cook Harry along. On the first morning, a howling gale was blowing, so Harry was installed in a makeshift kitchen on the beach surrounded by a couple of sacks tied to sticks, to prepare a joint of cold venison for lunch. 'If there is one grain of sand in the meat, you are fired,' joked-warned Ernie.

Harry's hair and face were covered in sand as he nervously presented the venison, but amazingly there was not one grain of sand in the dish.

Tired of striking camp after their usual 10-day trips, Ernie and Colin Foxon floated the notion of building some sort of shack on the beach. Colin was a cum laude graduate of the 'it's easier to get forgiveness than to get permission' school.

They started casting around for materials. Treated timber poles were bought, and timber and ceiling boards acquired from the old Amatikulu Private Hotel. Colin pre-fabricated the 36' x 18' hut at his home, and transported the components to the beach on the back of his truck. The guys then assembled it all on the beach, and — just like that — the Bhangazi Fishing Club had its headquarters.

Further up the coast, an Italian vessel the *Tomavo* had floundered on the coast in 1920. The lads looted the wreck, relieving it of its cargo of wine. A bathtub also caught their eye, which was duly loaded on the back of their truck. They now had a water tank for their HQ! A portable toilet was added. Next came an old-fashioned ice chest to keep the butter cool and a deep-freeze which would be taken in and out of Bhangazi on each trip. Ossie rigged a 32-volt lighting plant, until the sand destroyed its inner workings.

But, sure enough, all of this illegal development came to the attention of the Forestry Department officials. They insisted a lease for the land be taken out, and an annual rental paid. They also wanted a list of members of the Bhangazi Fishing Club and to sight its constitution! This was duly drawn up.

'Those were the days,' David says.

Then of course there was hunting: Birds … of *all* types. 'We used to go to the local dances, and target nurses and teachers.' he grins, possibly forgetting his mum was once a teacher. In his later 20s, he shared a house opposite the cricket ground with a friend, the local chemist, Chris Edwards. After a match, and several beers, David had fallen asleep in his bed with a cigarette. Chris had arrived home to a house full of smoke and found David asleep on his burning coir mattress. 'We carried it outside, put it under the tap,' says David. 'If I'd left the window closed, I would have died.' The next morning, the doused mattress was still burning away in the garden. It would not be his last house fire.

One evening he bumped into a tall and elegant blonde lass, Jill Scott from Pietermaritzburg, a teacher nine years younger then he, who'd just finished her training and was on her first assignment. 'Her first and last teaching post,' David laughs, because they were soon married, and went on to have three children (including a daughter Josie and grand-daughter Catherine who became teachers), and they remained married for 63 years till he passed just as this book went to print.

Meanwhile Jen was still toiling away at her degree. And Buster was keeping busy on his father's farm in Gwelo, where — as an innately keen student of languages — he became fluent in any number of dialects such as Shona, Ndebele, and Zezuru through his daily interactions, enabling him to communicate easily and affably with the locals in several areas. Later, he'd add Zulu and Xhosa to this mix.

He was also pulling late-night shifts as a proofreader on the *Gwelo Times*. Several times he'd jump on his 'jammy iron' motorcycle — most likely a BSA Gold Star or a Triumph Thunderbird — and make the ride down from Gwelo to Pietermaritzburg, a 1200km ride, which would take a good 20 hours. The things we do for love.

Jen was never a fan of motorcycles, and Buster certainly lost his nerve when, on a trip with a group of friends, they were riding behind a lorry loaded with construction materials. As they were flying along, a gust of wind suddenly ripped a sheet of corrugated iron off the truck which came scything through the air and clinically removed the head of his friend riding point. The bike and body ended up in a ditch roadside, the head and helmet on the other side of the road.

He shelved the bike and took to hitch-hiking instead. This almost ended in disaster: one fellow picked him up just outside Gwelo. But as Buster got into the car, the fellow pulled out a pistol from under the seat. 'Right, you drive.' What the hell? The driver, probably already a few cans in, then proceeded to open another can of beer. Every town they came to, he'd order Buster to stop at the pub. And they'd go in for a beer or two. Then back on the road. Somewhere, either still in Rhodesia (the Beit Bridge border was about one third the distance to Durban), or in South Africa, they stopped for fuel. By now this guy was getting a bit sloppy and possibly sleepy with it. Buster stopped the car, and bolted for it, as fast as a front-row forward can run, in the general direction of away from that crazy bugger.

And yet another small disaster was about to happen to Buster. Working on the farm one day, he was operating an auger grain-feeder machine, when he put his hand in to clear a blockage, and lost the top knuckle of his right middle finger, clean off.

Jen always had a determined sporty streak in her, and climbing up the face of Table Mountain — nearly 1100m high — was good evidence of that. Its near-vertical faces on the final summit approach attract many technical climbers, and rightly so according to Jen, who found it a real challenge, but worth it taking in the vistas of Table Bay and Robben Island way down below.

Robben Island was off the coast of Cape Town and had been used as a penitentiary by the Dutch since the late 17th century. Over the years it became a leper colony, and a military base, and was about to be repurposed as a maximum security prison for political prisoners ... and soon attain worldwide notoriety.

On graduation, there was an overseas trip to Switzerland arranged for Jen and her classmates. She promptly signed up for her first international adventure, stocking up on warm winter woolies and boots for the Alps. She loved skiing so much that, when her tour group moved on to other places, she told them, 'No, I want to ski some more. You go on ahead, and I'll catch up with you,' which she did. Pristine Switzerland would always remain one of her favourite, if not absolute favourite places, in the world.

Brave for a young first-time female traveller, and an inkling into her strong inherited nature, which was about to be tested even further.

14

ALL ROADS LEAD TO RHODESIA

FEDERATION OF RHODESIA AND NYASALAND, 1957. South Africa's economy was growing on gold and industry. But socially things were tightening under apartheid — Pass Laws expanded, political freedoms shrank, racial segregation hardened, and the increasing cultural chauvinism under the Afrikaner-dominated state. Perhaps acknowledging the need for greater homeland defence, the Defence Act 1957 introduced compulsory military service for white South African males over 18. All had to serve three months.

Rhodesia projected a tempting alternative: strong post-war economic growth, rapid expansion in agriculture, mining, and tobacco, and a more relaxed racial climate (at least in comparison to Pretoria's legal iron fist).

Having worked as a librarian and letting agent after finishing university, Jen decided she'd move up to Rhodesia to be closer to Buster in 1957, with discussions of engagement in the air. She chatted excitedly with her friend Marigold who also had a fiancé-to-be, 'Rip' Ripley-Evans in Salisbury, so she was keen to move up there, too. A Girls Own adventure in the making. Marigold was a talented artist and would make her name with her landscapes.

Jen hitched a ride with good friends Stuart Ingham and Joan Brown (later Ingham), overnighting in Johannesburg, with the plan being that Buster would meet them further north once they'd crossed the border into Rhodesia.

'Everyone was clamouring to get into Rhodesia in those days,' recalls Jen, 'so there was a clampdown at the border.' The immigration official asked her purpose of visit.

'I have a job,' fibbed Jen, '... um, with ... Unilever.'

She was not a great fibber. She knew someone — Jean Beach — whose husband actually headed up Unilever. That scanty information was apparently good enough to earn the entry stamp in her passport, and it turned out to be closer to the truth than even she realised. 'There was not much work in Gwelo so I got a job with Unilever as touring promotions girl for margarine, which was the next big thing. Demonstrating it in supermarkets and shopping centres.'

She would soon be granted a Residence Permit in the Federation of Rhodesia and Nyasaland on condition she practiced her occupation of 'commercial demonstrator'.

She and Marigold moved into a flat together in Salisbury. Not that Jen spent much time there, because she was mostly on the road. On one trip to Northern Rhodesia (later Zambia), she went into the restaurant at her hotel. It was full of men: 'Miners from all over the world, looking at me, passing comment, and so on,' she recalls. 'And I did the stupidest thing … I ordered spaghetti. All these things were new to us, and I didn't know how to eat it properly, so had these strands hanging from my mouth with all these male eyes on me,' laughs the suddenly not-so-glamorous promo girl.

Despite this, Buster's marriage proposal soon eventuated, with a yellow gold engagement ring topped with an impressive 0.72 carat yellow diamond, which came from Dick Lloyd's farm outside Gwelo. 'Sometimes they would find diamonds in the fields,' says Jen.

Together with friends they'd travel to different parts of Rhodesia, sometimes Nyanga in the cooler Eastern Highlands — where many English-style lodges and cottages had sprouted — and generally explore the beautiful countryside.

Buster meantime had applied to the Federal Ministry of Agriculture for a position as a lecturer in poultry at the Gwebi Agricultural College. He got accepted based on his BSc and two years of relevant experience, with a starting salary of £1100 per annum (about £32,000 these days). And so he moved to Gwebi, about an hour's drive northwest from the capital, and took up his position in the Animal Husbandry faculty of the small college. There were not much more than 50 students and staff at the college.

In March 1959 a state of emergency was declared in Nyasaland, and the BSA Police and troops were mobilised to stabilise the situation. Dr

Hastings Banda became the primary voice of anti-colonial resistance and was duly arrested and jailed without trial, along with several other activist leaders. Which only served to steel resolve, of course.

Perhaps triggered by this, in May, Buster applied to the BSA Police Reserve and was assigned to the Field Reserve Salisbury Urban station, with rank of Police Reservist #7425. The force had grown out of the original BSA Company Police, with the Latin motto *'Pro Rege, Pro Patria, Pro Lege'* ('For the King, For the Country, For the Law'). He was duly issued a set of blue overalls emblazoned with 'BSA POLICE', and a British WW2-style tin helmet. They were given training in riot control, use of truncheons — 'minimum pressure' — and tear gas.

In June 1959 George and Jenny got married at Holy Trinity Church, Musgrave Rd, in Durban. Long-tailed suits and top hats for the gents, lovely sapphire gowns for the bridesmaids. They left the church in a two-tone cream 1956 Chevrolet Bel Air with white-walled tyres.

And in that moment, the confluence of colourful characters we've been tracking in this story since the early 1800s — the Lloyds and the Seymours — truly coalesced. Two rivers had become one.

■ ■ ■

They knuckled down to start married life in Gwebi. There was almost no town to speak of, just the college as the epicentre of this rural agricultural area. They lived in a modest 'nothing fancy' tin-roofed house with a pretty garden.

To Buster's surprise, Jen could not cook! She had grown up always with cooks, nannies, or boarding school kitchen staff doing the cooking. He took it upon himself to get her up to speed in the kitchen. Meantime, it was pretty much eggs on toast! One imagines there would've been occasional dining out at local haunts like the Blue Gardenia at Greencroft or the Yellow Orchard a bit further out: a spaghetti bolognese could be had for 3/6d (less than £2 in today's money). Jen was a fast learner and would become a keen and passionate cook.

The tennis courts attached to the college were where Jen met everybody worth knowing socially, and there was also a swimming pool. Mainly it was farmers and their wives who came in to play tennis. 'Lord and Lady Such-and-Such farmed in the area,' she said of the Scottish cattle farmer James Angus Graham, the 7th Duke of Montrose. 'Their type really formed Rhodesia; there were a lot of them there. They were part of us — frightfully proper, but not standoffish because they couldn't afford to be.'

And social mores were clear in some areas, not as clear in others. 'You would've been frowned on, tossed out, if you'd mucked around with the blacks,' she says. 'We lived a very pure existence.' But others perhaps not: 'One guy was a bachelor and there was another couple … but the two guys were on as a couple. It was hard to tell who the couple was,' she laughs. They started a poultry farm near Gwebi, which Buster helped them set up.

In February 1960, Macmillan, then British Prime Minister, was on a tour of Africa and delivered a seminal address to parliament in South Africa. He declared that 'a wind of change is blowing through this continent,' referring to the rise of African nationalism and the irreversible tide of decolonisation.

South Africa and Rhodesia saw it as betrayal and reacted in hostile fashion to the notion that white minority rule was not desirable and sustainable. African nationalist leaders on the other hand saw it as a rubber-stamping validation of their independence movements.

The African National Congress (ANC) had grown sharper, more urgent. Mandela's generation pressed for mass mobilisation, defiance campaigns and ultimately — when the state responded with banning, bullets, and the treason trial against Mandela and 156 of his comrades — armed struggle.

A song which had been kicking around since 1897 got banned from public performance in 1960 after the shocking Sharpeville Massacre. Though its lyrics were mild it had become a stirring symbolic element, galvanising the blacks. It was *Nkosi Sikelel iAfrica.*

South Africa was a political crucible: three powerful identities — Afrikaner nationalism, English liberalism, and rising African nationalism — clashing over ownership of the land and the future of its people. It was a country standing on a *panga-edge* between repression and revolution.

South Africa became a republic and left the Commonwealth in 1961. Interestingly the orange, white, and blue flag didn't change.

In the July 1960 Mutiny Riots, Congo's military had mutinied against their white officers, leading to widespread violence and riots. European settlers and Congolese civilians became targets, evacuees hitting the road south. Buster and Jen billeted a French couple. 'They had just been married the day before and ran out the door basically with the huge bedspread that her grandmother had given them. And her wedding shoes,' recalls Jen. The couples played Cluedo every night, and then, after three weeks, Congo was deemed safe to return to (although the crisis went on till 1965). 'They went back and had a car crash and were quite seriously injured.'

With security becoming an issue, Buster bought a Czech-made Česká Zbrojovka (CZ) semi-automatic pistol, and told Jen she must have a lesson, but she always had a flimsy excuse not to do some target practice. She just was not a gun person.

Eventually Buster said, 'No more postponing, tomorrow lunchtime I will give you a lesson.' He pinned a target to a gum tree at the bottom of the garden, and taught Jen how to load the eight-round magazine and aim. Jen's first shot she pulled the trigger ... and burst into tears. The lesson was over.

A little later, Buster had gone into Salisbury for a meeting. Jen was at home alone, with the pocket-sized pistol next to her bed. She heard some noises in the spare bedroom and crept down the hall to investigate. Sure enough, someone was trying to get in through the screen on the window. She brought a wavering hand up to aim. Just then Buster casually said, 'Hello, it's me.' Jen, shaking violently, lowered the weapon.

'I nearly shot him,' says Jen. 'Whether I would've hit him or not was another matter.'

But generally, Gwebi was peaceful and it was here that Buster and Jen started their family, firstly with a corgi Zeta, and then with a son, Glendon Llewellyn, born at the Lady Chancellor in early 1961. 'Everybody had their babies there, and all went into one ward together, all next to each other,' Jen explained. It was quite a social scene, and many lifelong friendships were born here too, such as Peter and Faith Glavovic, of Croatian descent, speaking to the cultural melting pot Rhodesia had become.

Glendon was a sixth-generation African Lloyd. Buster often said Llewellyn-Lloyd was originally a hyphenated surname that proved too cumbersome so we all just got saddled with the Llewellyn as a middle name and Lloyd as a surname.

Its roots are Welsh and Welsh-border, joining two old Welsh currents, one meaning 'leader' and the other 'the steady grey of age', as if someone long ago decided to stitch courage to endurance with a hyphen. The name Llewellyn was worn by the 13th century ruler Llywelyn ap Gruffudd (one family tree seen online links us directly), before crossing into common usage in the 17th century.

And now Rhodesia and Nyasaland added one more South African, with margarine demonstrator-turned-mother Jenny becoming a citizen in May, 1961, giving up her South African citizenship in the process. Unlike her grandfather, trooper George Frederick Seymour in 1890, she was here to stay.

15

CALIFORNIA DREAMING

CALIFORNIA, USA, 1961. The Ford Motor Company Rhodesia was set up in the Salisbury suburb of Willowvale in 1961, and the first car — the roomy and robust Ford Zephyr Mark 11 — rolled off the assembly line that July. Soon, one car would be rolling off its lines every 20 minutes. With six cylinders it could burst from 0-60mph in just 17 seconds, making it popular within the British South Africa Police.

They announced a Ford International Fellowship bursary scheme, and Buster won the first scholarship. He was accepted by the University of California, Davis, to do his Master of Science degree in Poultry Science.

He planned to undertake advanced study of poultry genetics. 'Indirectly it should bring down the price of eggs in Rhodesia,' Buster — who was guest of honour at a lunch with Ford's MD Ralph Fawcett — told the *Rhodesian Tobacco Journal* reporter with a smile.

The Rhodesian government loaded him up with colour slides in the event he had the opportunity to talk-up Rhodesia over there. There were scenes of Kariba Dam, tobacco fields and processing, the Zimbabwe Ruins, Victoria Falls, and Salisbury skyscrapers such as the Pearl Assurance, Grants, and Norwich Union buildings.

And so, they packed up for this international sojourn, a year in California, with baby Glendon aged just seven months. Not ideal when your 36-hour flight in Boeing 707s and DC-8s goes from Salisbury to Nairobi to London (on BOAC) then on to New York and San Francisco (on Pan Am).

The Lloyd family had first set foot in America long before. Settler Henry had a brother Thomas who'd arrived there with other family members around the same time Henry had settled in South Africa. Same intrepid spirit. And Thomas's son had been one of the pioneers of Salt Lake City.

■ ■ ■

Davis, California, was a small rural town in transition, tapping into a progressive future through its university. The Amtrak rail system ran through the town, and new highways (a recent national fixation) connected it with Sacramento and San Francisco. Initially they lived downtown. 'Glendon and I loved it, but Buster had to walk a long way to uni.' recalls Jen. En route he would pass fields of tomatoes, almonds, and walnuts, and barns for the farm animals. Not for nothing is the university nicknamed Aggies, a nod to its agricultural college roots.

Tired of this daily walk, they soon moved into on-campus housing. 'Just a two-story up and down wooden affair,' says Jen. The campus itself offered no Ivy League splendour: more modern functionalism.

They were determined to see as much of America as they could while there. You would think Ford could've thrown in some wheels as part of the scholarship, but they spent about $600 to buy an early-50 cream-white Pontiac Chieftain, resplendent in chrome strips and stripes. On one trip they arranged a house swap in Aptos, near the scenic Monterey Bay. As they approached the address they'd been given, Buster slowed down. They were to collect the keys from the neighbours next door. Jen studied the people at that address: 'It can't be here, they're black!' she said. Turns out they were Mexican. In return the Mexican neighbours said: 'We saw you pulling up, and said, "It can't be them — we were expecting some black people from Africa!"' A good laugh was exchanged.

Jen revelled in the beauty of the Ocean View Boulevard along the Pacific Grove coastline of the Monterey Peninsula, looking hip in her cat's eye sunglasses. Pink ice plants carpeted entire towns and headlands. Blissful days were spent on Seacliff Beach at Aptos, where the long wooden jetty and wreck of SS *Palo Alto* provided a uniquely Californian backdrop. The Beach Boys had just scored their first hits — *Surfin 'USA* and *Surfin' Safari* — which captured the era's languid, carefree zeitgeist.

They visited Lassen Peak and experienced snow — Glendon delighting in snowball fights and carrot-nosed snowmen, which traumatised him when they melted — and drove through the Sequoia National Forest (including the amazing hollowed-out Wawona tree which their gas guzzler could easily pass through.) They also visited the brand-new Disneyland at Anaheim where Pluto caused Glendon to melt down.

The highways and freeways were mind-blowing compared to the goat-tracks of Rhodesia. Jen particularly remembered them being pulled over for going too slowly! Minimum speed limits were in place on some highways.

They marvelled at the Grand Canyon, a good 14-hour drive away, en route to New York City, where the Statue of Liberty, Brooklyn Bridge, Empire State and Chrysler Buildings awed them. A long way from the back blocks of Gwelo!

Jen didn't take to the Americans: too much hyperbole for her. But overall, America was a thoroughly enjoyable and rewarding experience.

In the meantime, Buster aced his academic work, scoring A's in all five subjects, with a perfect grade point average of 4. And Jen was pregnant again, her bump showing quite obviously by now, the tenant inside kicking and carrying on. Which would not have made the long flight home any easier.

Glendon was by now fully mobile, in his little red *tackies* (sneakers), and wandered up the aisle into the first-class section where the rich and famous were sleeping off their champagne. He went up to one reclined figure whose face was covered by a hat. He lifted the hat, went 'Peekaboo!' and walked off, much to the chagrin of the awakened passenger.

By the time the plane had landed in Rome, a popular variant of the itinerary in those days, the new baby was desperate to get out. 'No, no, please,' Jen said. 'Please hang on till we get home to Rhodesia.'

Being the obedient soul I was destined to be, I listened. Instead of Rome, I was born in Salisbury at the Lady Chancellor that November, 1962, soon after their return. Mum haemorrhaged badly during this birth, a harbinger of a rare bleeding condition that would plague us both in later years.

And Buster MSc returned to work at Gwebi College to share his new-found international knowledge on chicken and eggs. But even he never found out which came first.

16

BATMAN VS UDI

SOUTHERN RHODESIA, 1962. Arbor Acres Farms was originated in Connecticut, by the Italian-American Saglio brothers. By 1939 they expanded into poultry production, constructing their first chicken house from a discarded piano crate, and began poultry breeding, notably developing the Arbor Acres female line broiler. This innovation achieved significant success in both US and international markets.

Poultry was a good cheap source of protein for the local population. When they decided to enter the Rhodesian market, they head-hunted Buster to set up and run it. Irvines — a large family-run poultry company — might have had a small holding in Arbor Acres 'operations. Crest Breeders (in the same area) was also a major player.

The Arbor Acres farm was about 10km via the Main Salisbury Road (now Masvingo Rd) south of Salisbury. The land was previously called Langford Farm, believed to be owned by Tim Henwood's parents before (more about him later in the show).

I believe the land was then owned by Ben Bellingham, a dark-haired Rhodesian cattle farmer of English heritage, with a rather bellicose nature, compared to his very meek wife. The red soil-lined Barrington Road (now Mbuya Nehanda Rd) was planted with Virginia tobacco and maize, and lined with massive msasa and mopane trees.

Everybody smoked in those days. Pops — as we all called Grandpa Dick — always had a pipe in his mouth. Granny Eileen smoked 60 Benson & Hedges a day, as did Uncle Mick Flint. Mum smoked, Gran and Grandpa Seymour smoked. Dad enjoyed cigarettes, cigars, and pipes (though not necessarily at the same time). His pipes — a fashionable collection of straight ones and curved ones — were ceremoniously stuffed with Amphora tobacco, much of it sourced from Rhodesia, which was blended and produced by the Douwe Egberts company in Holland, and then re-exported to Rhodesia. No one had yet heard of carbon footprints. Nor, seemingly, lung cancer.

Tobacco represented 10 per cent of Rhodesia's GDP and a full one third of its total export earnings, even outshining the mining sector.

And in the middle of these fields was a small simple house: single-story, white-painted, with a red-tiled roof. Blazing bougainvillea bushes fringed the house, and a scrubby lawned area of several acres surrounded it, separating it from the endless African wilderness. The house belonged to the farm, but Mum and Dad (who either rented it, or enjoyed it as a perk of the job) added a bedroom to it — with a growing family in mind — as well as renovating it. The money shot was a covered verandah area, with a slate floor and slate feature walls, the perfect place for evening chats over sundowners. This would be the only home in Rhodesia I knew.

My earliest memories of life seem to date back to when I was two, date stamped because I remember having measles, confined to bed (I shared a bunk bed with Glendon) and hearing our car coming up the driveway, and opening the curtains to have a peek outside.

Occasionally a fire would break out in the surrounding fields — possibly caused by a lightning strike or a carelessly flicked cigarette butt — and the whole sky would burn a sinister crimson, as teams of beaters took to the fires flailing wet sacks. Some would burn for days, burning right up to the back of our house on a few occasions. Terrifying nights.

There was a small, old pastel yellow Ford Anglia body stranded wheel-less beside the long dirt driveway with a roundabout full of prickly pear bushes. It was as much a plaything for us, as a home for the region's many mambas, adders and cobras.

Adjacent to that was a thatched *rondawel*, a general storage room, used much like a shed, where Dad played alchemist with home-brewed beer bubbling and fermenting away, and large galvanised tin tubs full of seasoned meat marinating away, soon to be hung and dried into biltong.

There were so many distractions in our garden and surrounding area. You could wander down a bush track to a small river or stream. There we'd watch the local ladies pounding peanuts on the rocks, producing the richest, freshest peanut butter you've ever tasted in your life. (Peanuts grew wild in the red soil around here.)

Then there was the red Battlewagon, a four-wheeled cart. Dad would sometimes pull us around in this thing, or we'd improvise and put Zeta in there ... the other dogs were too big for us to manhandle (or dog-handle), and give her a ride to remember. And, as a daily reminder of the hazards of farming life, Zeta only had one eye, after chasing a rabbit under a barbed wire fence. We now added a huge black dog Zimba, who seemed half Labrador-half Rottweiler, and Peter, an Alsatian-cross.

Then they constructed a tennis court at the side of our house. A team of labourers hand-made all the clay bricks. To do this, there were a series of holes dug, around four or five-feet deep, in which one worker would stand, up to his armpits in clay all day, scooping out the clay from around him, and deposit this into wooden moulds, which sat on the ground around him. These were then carried off by another worker, to be laid in the sun to dry. They must've made thousands of bricks all told. Then they surfaced the court with sand. Lines pinned down. Net up. Fences installed. And, cue the tinkle of ice in the silver ice bucket, as tennis parties broke out. This meant Cokes for us kids, probably gins and tonic for the big kids. *Happy days*!

All milk jugs and food plates served outside came with a lace-and-bead-doily covering to keep the ravenous flies at bay.

My aunt Paddy Lloyd — who used to brew sensational homemade ginger beer, always with raisins floating in it — tells the story of an afternoon tea with the ladies in the garden one day, when a workman was sent around to fix something. He surveyed this leisurely scene and announced, 'When I die I want to be reincarnated as a Rhodesian housewife! 'Paddy laughs. More about Paddy later.

Mum would soon have the gardens looking prettier, with all manner of posies, agapanthus, and a flourishing rose garden, overlooked by large picture-windows from the living room of the house.

The art on the walls was eclectic to say the least. One framed work was a Japanese geisha figure painted on silk. There were two works of Japanese painted tiles, bamboo in gold and black ink. How, when, and why these Japanese pieces were acquired, remains a cultural mystery. Another was a bold graphic screen print of the moon over a lake. Another was a print redolent of Van Gogh's Parisian cafe scenes. Others were more in the western classic renaissance mould. All the frames were in the style of the day: gold, ornate, and chunky.

We had a couple of house 'boys': Goliat — a young, pleasant-faced man, with a ready smile who helped with anything and everything in and around the house, and another, London, was always out in the gardens.

As for communicating with our domestic servants like Goliat, Mum told me, 'We just expected them to speak English, but it's a pity that we didn't learn to speak Zulu fully and properly.' Instead, *fanagalo* or more crudely 'kitchen kaffir' was the pidgin hybrid we used. *Fanagalo* was a Zulu-based language that evolved in the mines, often blending English, Zulu, and Afrikaans into a single sentence to make it readily understandable to all. For the longest time I thought it was called 'funny galore'.

In our homes in Rhodesia and South Africa, shoes were never shoes — always *skatoels* (from Zulu *izicathulo*), meat was always *nyama*, medicine was always *muti*, cups were always *inkomishi*, snakes were always *inyoka*, hot was always *shisa.* And you never tied anything, you *bopa'd* it.

It was always exciting when Mum and Dad had friends over for a dinner party. The silver — cutlery, salt and pepper dispensers, gravy boat, drink coasters, coffee pot, candlesticks, all hallmarked silver — would be duly polished with Silvo till they were positively gleaming. Then we'd be up the next morning while they enjoyed a slower start to the day and go through to find the coffee tray still on the lounge room table. Jackpot! There'd be the beautiful, ornate blue-and-gold coffee cups, with equally ornate silver teaspoons. A small jug of super-creamy milk, and the cold remains of a pot of Douwe Egberts coffee. We'd drain all the leftovers, tasting like some heaven-sent concotion.

There was one dinner-related ritual which played out nearly daily: Goliat preparing to cook a chicken.

With a lightning-swift grab of his hand, Goliat had a choke-hold around the neck of a huge black chicken. It squawked for mercy, as the other hens clucked and ducked and scurried away.

Moments later, as it continued its vain pleas for mercy, Goliat wrestled it into position on a circular tree stump, about one metre high. It had a smooth top, like a cutting board, which in fact it now was. One hand holding its head, he reached for the *panga* and, with a short backswing, brought it down sharply across its neck.

As its eye turned accusingly upwards with a final look of 'you bastards', the headless body scrambled in a higgledy-piggledy zig zag pattern along the dusty path, before finally keeling over about 20 metres away. Goliat, dressed in his red-trimmed white cotton uniform, would then amble down the track, scoop up his main ingredient, and head off up to the kitchen to prepare dinner.

The novelty of this phenomenon never wore off. (Fun fact: In USA in 1945, Mike the Headless Chicken survived headless for 18 months because the axe missed his brain stem, and he was fed with a dropper down his neck.)

Dad would usually arrive home around that time, the large dark grey 'Vroop Vroom 'car (most likely a late-1950s Dodge) rumbling up the laterite driveway.

We – my brothers and dogs – would race towards his car, us hitching a ride by standing on the spacious running boards, the dogs yelping with excitement.

Then sitting on the slate-paved patio, came one of the best parts of the day … Dad selecting a huge dry stick of homemade biltong, pulling out his trusty Swiss Army knife, and slicing it into generous strips.

Then he'd pop the gold cap off a longneck bottle of homemade beer or Lion Lager. We'd all queue up for a slurp of the bitter tang of the foam.

Soon, the steam would be gone from the day, long orange shadows from the soaring forest surrounding our garden, raking across the vast lawn. This was usually the cue for a flock of guinea fowl to start pecking their way across the garden — like a catwalk show for the season's latest polka dot fashions. We also had a pet chicken, a large white leghorn called Mary, who later would meet an untimely end when hitching a ride with Glendon on the wheelbarrow in the garden, and tipping off the front, ending up under the front wheel. (I can't be certain she didn't end up in Goliat's pot.)

Occasionally a leopard tortoise might saunter casually by. (And 'saunter 'was only when it reached top gear.) These black-and-yellow shelled beasts often stood at over two-feet tall, weighed as much as a large Labrador, and could be ridden by us kids in some sort of slow-motion rodeo! They were friendly enough and would stick around on the verandah if there were lettuce leaves going. Our cousins — Mick and Paddy's sons, Bruce and Hal (real name Henry Llewellyn!) — around the same age as us, would delight in seeing these things up close when they visited.

There was even a great big pink pig who just free-ranged round the garden, scoffing whatever he could. Fate unknown.

Further down the back of the garden, we had a small cage full of chinchillas and guinea pigs. I don't know how many, but less after a mongoose would get in at night and treat the coop like an all-you-can-eat buffet.

Thirst sated by a couple of homemade draughts, Dad would then turn his attention to the dogs. They needed checking for ticks daily, and Dad would duly find four, five, six or more of these bulging parasitic buggers in their fur. A dull grey balloon, filled to bursting, with pathetic little legs and faces lost in their newly inflated form. Soon, a box of Lion matches would be produced, and the ticks were torched where they lay, bobbing and hissing hopelessly in the copper ashtray.

In the background would usually be some Louis Armstrong blowing away, his trumpet piercing the quieting evening, amid the chitter-chatter of the birds settling down for the night.

Mum doesn't remember the music being much different from what they were listening to in America: 'So we were pretty much up-to-date.' Chubby Checker and Herb Alpert albums sat next to the turntable. *Spanish Flea* was an uplifting favourite which got a regular workout, as did Perez Prado's mambos. Bert Kampfaert's chart-topping *Tijuana Taxi* and *A Swingin' Safari* also added that slightly Afro-Latin flavour to the air. We even had original Elvis Presley 78s. I assume most of these eclectic discs came over with them from the States. One of my most early and enduring musical memories was *There's a Kind of Hush (All Over the World)* by Herman's Hermits.

It gave me a feeling of permanence, and that all was right with the world. Surely, nothing could ever rock this Rhodesian idyll …

Then, it was dinner time.

We'd file excitedly into the dining room to sit around the large circular hardwood dining table, with ornate metal lions' claws decorating the end of each foot. It seemed as large as a circus ring to me back then.

And in would come Goliat, dressed in whites for dinner, with a large red-lipped white enamel bowl. And sitting in the middle would be a golden-roasted glistening whole chicken. The headless victim from earlier that afternoon.

Dad would go through the sharpening ritual with his bone-handled carving knife.

"Drumstick please, Dad!"

"Drumstick please, Dad!"

There'd be at least four requests for drumsticks around the table.

We'd tuck into a succulent, farm-fresh free-range (before that was a thing) roast chicken. With pumpkin, mashed potato, peas, and tomato. Always tomato, which I promised I would start eating when I turned five.

An incredible pile of peas would find their way 'accidentally' onto the Persian rug beneath the table, oddly usually in the area directly surrounding my chair. One great thing about Persian rugs – their ornate woven patterns do disguise a lot of things.

These rugs were all bought from Henri Lidchi's carpet company, an international art and rug operation, which was operated out of Pearl Assurance House in First Street, Salisbury. Dad spent nearly £500 on four pieces (around £10,000 today) and these adorn my living rooms to this day.

But tomatoes were not so easily flicked surreptitiously from the plate. And so there'd always be a couple of quarters of tomato to contend with.

'But I've already eaten lots, look there's only two pieces left,' I'd claim.

'Rubbish, I only gave you two pieces,' Mum would say.

At which Dad would come around, lift the sleeve of my T-shirt and feel my feeble not-yet-formed bicep.

'No, see, I can see your tomato hole.' He'd prod his pork sausage-like forefinger into my muscle. 'See that … *tomato hole*!'

Indeed there was a hole – in the absence of any muscle – and I grew up fully believing each vegetable had its own allocated space within our anatomy.

'But I'm full.'

'Ok, no pudding then.'

Disapproving glowers across the table from Mum and Dad. And so, with much grimacing and groaning, tomatoes would be consumed. Because you wouldn't want to miss the pudding. Often a hot Bird's custard over Lyons Maid vanilla ice-cream (both British brands).

Mum would ring the little ornately patterned brass bell, which sat in its circular cradle on the table, and Goliat would come and clear the plates. Then momentarily re-appear bearing the desserts on a tray.

Dinner finished, Mum would tinkle the bell again, and Goliat would appear to spirit the mess away.

At which point, we'd sometimes retire to the large rectangular living room and watch TV. Mum and Dad would occupy large wood-framed armchairs, while we either coveted a leather Moroccan pouf or a spot on yet another Persian rug on the carpeted floor.

Rhodesia was the first country in Southern Africa to get TV, in late 1960. Programming kicked off at 4pm, to the strains of the British national anthem (which would also close proceedings at the end of transmission after the late news.)

The black-and-white set would flicker to life with a crackle, and we'd laugh along to the *Beverly Hillbillies.*

Then sometime after the news, would come the theme song of *Downtown.* It was Petula Clark singing her hit of the same name. And that was bad news. Not because there's anything wrong with Petula Clark, but because that was my bedtime.

So a big hug and a kiss for Dad, who would grind his five 'o clock-shadow whiskers into us, with painful but pleasurable results.

Mum would more often than not give us a bedtime story, something from the large library of books in our house. It might be *Noddy and Big Ears Go to Toyland, Black Beauty, Tootles the Taxi*, or something from Robert Louis Stevenson or some such.

We'd delight in it, sometimes distracted by a lizard scurrying across the floor. At which we'd leap out of bed and try to stomp on its tail, leaving it wriggling sidewinder-style in the middle of the parquet floor, while the hapless owner scuttled off to safety up the wall.

Lights out. All around was pitch black.

Then you'd hear the "hoot-hoot" of a friendly owl perched on the roof with his night-vision goggles ready to rain ruinous hell on an oblivious passing mouse.

And so, another perfect day passed for us in Rhodesia.

■ ■ ■

Our nearest neighbours, further along and across Barrington Road — in reality just two parallel concrete strips one wheel span apart (shared when a car or Land Rover came the other way) — were Ben Bellingham and Granny Tommy. I don't know who's grandma she was, but she was a dear old thing who seemed about 150 years old to me. She got around in a Morris Minor Traveller, with indicators that were on stalks that popped out on the side when activated. We marvelled at this technology! The wooden frame at the back made it look like a shipping crate on wheels, albeit a very smart shipping crate. All proudly assembled from knocked-down kits in Rhodesia at the BMC (British Motor Corporation) assembly plant in Umtali. They also made Morris Oxfords and Austin Cambridge.

One hot afternoon, Dad got a call from Granny Tommy: 'Buster please come over, I've got a snake in the house.' Dad grabbed his gun (a

Winchester .22/.410 combination shotgun-rifle). He corralled Glendon and I into the back of the Vroop Vroom car. We raced off in a cloud of dust, arriving momentarily outside Tommy's house. Dad leapt out, shouting to us to remain in the car. Er, so why did you bring us? My heart was pounding … what kind of snake, how big was it, would it attack Dad? Just then I noticed a large rusted-through hole in the floor of our car. Clear daylight shining in through the floor. Shit, what if the snake got in here?!? There was nothing around to cover the hole with, so Glendon and I took turns in covering it with our feet (we didn't wear shoes anywhere except to school at that time).

'OK, time's up, your turn.'

'No, you counted too fast.'

'Your turn!'

'No, your turn!'

As always Glen pulled rank.

After what seemed like a few sweat-stained hours, Dad emerged triumphant, with a large dark snake draped over a stick. Granny Tommy was beaming, relieved. We were relieved.

We believed Dad was invincible with his gun. Until the time an Egyptian Cobra slithered across the lawn near our verandah. Dad set off to confront it, and the damn thing chased Dad around a small tree … round and round and round until perhaps the snake got dizzy, or Dad shot its hooded head off. I forget how that one ended. One snake sort of blurred into another in the Rhodesian bush.

Often times, I'd be sitting on the steps out the back of the kitchen, enjoying the warmth of the sun on my back, and something would catch my eye: a black mamba, or a cobra, or 'just' a house snake. Or go to pick up a ball in the garden: snake. Behind the bathroom door: snake.

Paddy Lloyd recalls one trip she made with Mick from Durban to Salisbury, and they stopped at a motel en route. 'Separate rooms of course because we weren't married yet,' she stresses. 'I went to open the door of my room, but it wouldn't budge. It turned out there was this huge python sleeping up against the inside of the door!' She ended being moved to another room with five beds, which she had to share with another woman. Morality aside, Paddy recently shared with me: 'I hate my middle name, Mabel. Mick used to tease me terribly by singing *'Roll over Mabel, your navel's on the other side!*'" which is an old rugby club song.

Guns were a way of life on a farm. Dad would head off many Saturday afternoons for a spot of hunting. Might be birds. Often monkeys or buck. In his younger days, bigger game was fair game: and they didn't come much bigger than elephants.

After he was done, he'd come home, then sometimes take us to the killing fields, where you'd see trees draped with lifeless monkeys like some absurdist art installation. We'd marvel at how he'd drilled them at such great distances with a .22 rifle.

Then would come the gun cleaning ritual. Dad was always meticulous about maintaining everything well. Out would come the bore brushes — long bendy rods with bristles on the end — the Singer 3-in-1 Oil, and the polishing rags with a strong metallic solvent smell. The beautiful wooden butt of his gun would get the treatment till it gleamed, and the bore brushes were threaded into the barrels in turn. Then Dad would hold them up into the light to check his handiwork. We'd all cluster round to have a look into the rifled barrel. Such precision engineering, screwing its way from one end to the other.

If he'd bagged some antelope, these would be strung up and skinned and cleaned. Then transformed magically into biltong in the *rondawel.* It was like a macabre laundry in there, with all these bits of drying meat — in various stages of desiccation — hooked in serried rows on washing lines.

There are two kinds of people in this world: those who get biltong, and those who don't.

Mind you, a close second was sweets. Saturday was officially Suckerday (suckers being what we called lollipops). Mum and Dad would go into Salisbury to do the grocery shopping once a month, usually at the OK Bazaar on First Street. 'I don't know how I managed to keep all of us fed without running out of things, because we lived a long way out on the farm,' Jen said. What they couldn't get at OK, they'd get at a small grocery/fruit 'n' veg place on the corner nearby.

The answer was we were pretty self-sufficient with our huge veggie patch. Corn. Radishes. Eggplants. Strawberries. Carrots.

If we were lucky, we got to go with them into town, and then there would be some serious politicking, badgering and cajoling to get them to go to Sweet Corner or Arenel Sweets. We preferred the latter because one of their signatures was candy cigarettes, a white musk-flavoured stick with a red tip, resembling a lighted cigarette.

If it was a particularly hot day, then we'd be treated to a Zoom, a rocket-shaped ice lolly with red, yellow, and green stripes — strawberry, banana, and raspberry flavours, ie all the food groups — recently introduced by Lyons Maid.

One memorable Suckerday, we three kids were fighting over sweets. 'But you've already had three!' Mum sat us down and force-fed us every last sweet she could find, in the hope of making us sick. No such luck … we were match-hardened veterans when it came to sugar tolerance.

Apart from Suckerday, Saturdays were also the day the beer tanker came to the farm to deliver the workers' supplies for their party night. Picture a petrol tanker truck-trailer backing up and pumping its load of fresh *utshwala*, traditional African beer made from fermented sorghum millet and water. We'd help wrangle the massive hoses into a gathering of 44-gallon drums. The creamy beer would foam and froth, sending our noses into overdrive. Earthy, malty, with grainy top-notes, a sommelier might say. And then, the payoff, Dad would scoop some up in a plastic cup, which we'd pass around, savouring each precious drop. It paired very well with suckers.

Whilst on pairing, I once got into the medicine cabinet in the bathroom enticed by the many bright coloured pills and tablets I saw there, and hoovered the lot. Mum found me hiding behind the sofa in the lounge room, shoving some yellow pills down my throat. A quick phone call later, and I was bundled into the car, and driven at great speed — something Mum was very fond of, I realised — to a clinic where a vacuum was put down my throat and my stomach pumped. I seem to remember being rewarded with a bag of jelly beans, which made me think it was all worth it.

The usual medication if we got sick was Vicks Vaporub. It was the best feeling in the world when Mum asked, 'Do you want a chest rub?' Every known disease known to mankind would evaporate at the very touch of it.

Anything to do with the tummy was immediately dealt with by Phillips' Milk of Magnesium.

Another medical episode eventuated as a result of a tsetse fly bite that turned septic. The bite is searingly painful because the fly sticks its nose into your skin and then activates an injection and suction mechanism. But two or three days later, the bottom of my right shin started to get angry. A nasty red swelling. Then things turned nasty fast. Next thing I had this massive pus volcano going on. Doctor time. Injections, far more painful and scary than the tsetse fly bite. And then I was sent home, Dad carrying a bag of syringes and antibiotics to deal with the secondary bacterial infection that had set into my leg. Every day for a week or so, Dad jabbed my leg, obviously concerned about sepsis setting in. I screamed the whole house down each and every day. To this day I have a dent in my lower shin as a souvenir.

Another souvenir I picked up was one afternoon playing with Glendon. The garden 'boys' had been slashing the long grass down our driveway to Barrington Rd. We came across these slashers which had been left there for them to continue tomorrow … long bits of flat steel, perhaps a metre long, with a curved end. We start slashing the grass, the weeds, the flowers, whatever we could find. And next thing: *SWISH*! Glendon connected me right on the forehead. A torrent of claret. He hightailed it, leaving me to find my way, by braille, back to the house. Mum nearly faints at the sight. Out comes the basin and the mercurochrome. Once all the blood is washed away, I just have a neat one-inch flap of skin hanging from my forehead. Out came the Elastoplasts and I was ready to fight another day.

Yet another souvenir was gained one afternoon when we found a length of black rubber pipe lying around. Glendon found some matches and lit the end of this piping, which seemed happy to be alight and turn molten. He dripped some on the ground as we watched in fascination. Then as usual he decided to take this game up a level. He started swinging the piping around above his head. Flaming molten splotches of this stuff was flying everywhere. All great fun till it landed on my left forearm, sizzling and searing into my flesh like Napalm. Screams and many tears ensued.

On yet another day, I was cutting oranges in the kitchen. For kids parties they'd do this thing where the oranges would be cut in quarters, the orange pulp eaten, and then red jelly set in its place. Yummy, refreshing. There I was, just able to reach up to the kitchen counter, with one of Goliat's very sharp small knives, trying to slice this orange. *SLIP*! The blade slid off the side of the moist orange, carving into the bone below my left forefinger. More screaming and carrying on. Rushed to doctor. Five or six stitches. Scarred to this day.

And yet another, another, *another* day, we were riding our bikes along the driveway. I had this big blue tricycle, with this plastic noise-making machine mounted on the handlebars. Simply by pulling its red lever, I could dial up sirens, guns, engines, and all kinds of cheap sound effects. I was doing laps of the roundabout — probably being chased by Glendon — when I took the corner too sharply, caught my tyre on the rockery, and went flying face-first into the forest of prickly pear plants. These are a cactus with flat rounded pads for leaves, and spines which grow up to 2.5 inches long, the punk rockers of flora. Now on top of the wailing sirens, guns and engines, was the wailing of some white kid whose head was full of spikes. Again, a tear-riven walk to the kitchen, where Dad sat me on the counter and painstakingly — read: painfully — dug these out with a sharp knife. I had a new respect for the plant after that and always gave it a wide berth.

I was to become an avid motorcyclist later in my twenties, but my very first experience on a real motorcycle was at the Thorne's farm. Tony and Maryanne lived not too far from us. She was a fun, artsy lady, who bred chinchillas, and often had several scuttling around on the back seat of her car. We'd be around at their place for sundowners, and we kids would be waiting to hear the buzz of Tony's motorbike, probably a medium-sized BSA, coming down from the fields. When we'd hear it, all three of us, plus one or two Thornes, would race down the dirt road to meet him. Then we'd clamber aboard this bike, balanced in all sorts of precarious positions, some standing, me often straddling the front handlebars — being careful not to get the key caught up in my undercarriage — and we'd all ride triumphantly back to their farmhouse.

The 'Melsetter Murders' on 4 July 1964 marked one of the earliest violent flashpoints of Rhodesia's liberation struggle. Near Melsetter, in the Eastern Highlands, African nationalist guerrillas crossed from Mozambique and attacked the South African-born missionary Pieter

Nel, his wife Janet, and their two young children on their farm. All four were brutally killed, shocking the white community. The murders intensified settler fears of insurgency, hardened white resistance to political change, and fuelled Ian Smith's later justification for Rhodesia's Unilateral Declaration of Independence (UDI) in 1965. UDI severed the apron strings from Britain, to preserve white minority rule against pressure for majority African governance

'Ya, I though Smith was quite good,' Aunty Kay Flint told me recently, 'because there was truth in what he said.' Kay's son Geoff has memories of grandfather 'Pops' Dick Lloyd around this time. 'His job was to watch the news every night and everyone had to keep quiet and he used to cheer on Ian Smith.'

Dot was more in favour of the moderate, less-resistant ideas of Allen Savory, who would come to more prominence later proposing faster advancement of the black population, but she voted for Smith in this election anyway. Cousin Ian Daniel (Dot's son) remembers the result as being big news at school that day, but no real sentiments attached to it.

The UDI move led to international isolation, sanctions, and a long guerrilla war. Some see Melsetter as being the start of 'The Bush War ' which raged until Independence in 1980, and would involve Pop's grandsons, Kay and Dot's sons directly, and everyone else in our family less directly.

■ ■ ■

But UDI meant nothing to me, because in 1966 *Batman* came on TV. It ran once or twice a week, and — despite its cheap production values and not-so-special- effects — enthralled us with its cityscapes and storylines. Loveable rogues like The Joker, The Penguin, Catwoman. But mainly it was the Batmobile racing them to the next crime scene that captivated us. Way cooler than the Vroop Vroom car. I mean with a jet engine tailpipe, Batphone, and double-canopy cockpit, what was not to like?

Glendon and I got Batman and Robin suits (you can guess who was who). I spent an unhealthy amount of my childhood playing Glendon's sidekick. And that Christmas I got a toy Corgi Batmobile, with flaming exhaust, rocket launcher, and a chainsaw which came out of the front bumper. Our imaginations were fully fired!

You pretty much had to make your own entertainment, because other forms of entertainment were a bit thin on the ground. One weekend, there was some kind of circus at a field near the centre of town, where this hairy elephant covered in red dust, swung a big hammer, driving pegs into the ground. Mum and Dad headed off to the next attraction, and I was following a little way behind, when suddenly this little monkey — dressed in a bright yellow vest with a little red fez — chased me. I took off, startled by this weird near-human, lucky not to drop my Zoom ice-cream, and made it safely to where Mum and Dad were, who of course just laughed at this surreal sight. Oddly, over the years, I've had recurring dreams about that damn yellow-suited monkey.

And then there were three of us. In mid-1966 our younger brother Roger was born at the Lady Chancellor Hospital. At this time, Jen met and befriended Margie Phear, a widow who was in to see her new grandkid. She was a South African art teacher and ethnobotanist, who published books on food plants and wildflowers of Rhodesia. Margie's work would soon attract the eye of Sir Robert Tredgold KCMG PC, a prominent legal chap and former acting-Governor of Southern Rhodesia, and acting-Governor General of the Federation of Rhodesia and Nyasaland. He was a strong champion of individual human rights and resigned his Governor-General position in protest when he felt the government was suppressing nationalism with the Law and Order (Maintenance) Bill. After re-marrying, Margie went by the name of Lady Tredgold, and remained very active with her art. She and Jen would remain firm friends over the years.

When Rog first came home, it was decided we needed a nursery table on which to change him. Mum and Dad went out shopping, and I remember them coming up the driveway in their white station wagon (maybe an Opel or Peugeot). Strapped to the roof racks was this white table, with its four legs facing upwards. All very exciting. Just then the car pulled into the carport, and all I heard was *CRUNCH*!!! The legs were sheared off by the beam across the garage roof. I can still imagine Dad's alarmed voice now: 'Oh, *gats*. Bugger!!!' But being the handyman he was, the legs were soon restored.

One good thing came from that: they built us a new bedroom at the end of the house. It had a tin roof, and it was heavenly to go to sleep with the thundering of the rain on the tin at night.

Of course, we couldn't wait for Roger to join us on bike rides and other adventures. Why was he so useless, just lying there all day?

Dad got on the tools and built this amazing wooden Wendy house, a toy house big enough we could all walk upright in it, with a few open windows, and V-shaped roof to top it off. Beautifully carpentered. One hot afternoon, perhaps tired of chasing the chicken and pig around, Glendon and I were in Dad's biltong shed. We found a hammer. Nice! What can we do with a hammer? I looked around … There in front of me was the Wendy house. Yes, never mind Dad's craftsmanship, we could do some real damage with that hammer. In a thought process that still sounds odd as I type this, Glendon thought we should ask for permission first.

So off I went, vaguely in the direction of the house, and returned shortly after, having spoken to exactly no one. 'Yes, Mum said that would be fine, but only a few planks.' And we set about knocking a few planks out of the back wall. Hey this is fun! Then a few more. This is really fun! Then a few out of the side wall. Then I grabbed the hammer and smacked a few more planks out, and with that the whole darn thing came tumbling down with a'creaking and a'cracking. I recall us clambering free of the debris, both lost in our separate thoughts of 'Geez, we've really done it now'. Though I can't remember that specific belting, I am sure one was surely dealt to us. (Just like with snakes, good thrashings blurred into one another after a while.)

At the back of our house, reached via a long pathway through the bush — or a short-ish drive around it — was a grass airstrip. Dad's favourite game was to drive us there in the Vroop Vroom car, and taxi down to the end of the runway. Then he'd go through the pre-takeoff routine:

'Fasten seatbelts.' We fastened our seatbelts.

He tuned the engine. 'Ready for takeoff?'

'Ready!' He'd release the brake and we'd go thundering down the runway at absolutely full bottle, expecting to become airborne any moment. The world outside was a blur. We imagined our cheeks were stretched fully back against our ears, such was the velocity. And then just as we should surely be airborne, we'd run out of runway, and Dad would veer off to avoid the trees at the end, looking as disappointed as us that we didn't take off.

'Next time!' he'd say, and we fully believed him.

After all, we'd seen Dad flying before. Mostly in gliders. There was an active glider club there, and some weekends it was abuzz with a tow aircraft or two, and several gliders. Other times would be small planes with parachutists. What a thrill to look up at the sky and see these figures free-falling, then see the parachutes darting and diving across the sky (they were still the old-school round ones, but with more control vents by then) and then the parachutists land with a run and a tumble on the grass near us.

Dad flew into Kitwe, Zambia, around this time. The Cessna 172 was a rugged workhorse and quickly became the world's most produced civilian aircraft, popular with farmers and bush pilots. They flew this thing into Kitwe, a good three or so hours' flight away. Upon landing, something was deemed amiss with their papers. Since UDI, Rhodesian citizens required a visa to enter Zambia — because the newly independent Zambia did not recognise the legitimacy of the Rhodesian government anymore — and they scrutinised Rhodesian papers more than most, looking for any excuse to delay or derail your visit completely.

I'd hazard a guess and say Dad and pilot had not pre-applied for a visa and had just landed there. Next thing they were refused entry, detained in a cell overnight, and allowed to fly back the next day, with a notice to the effect that he was a 'prohibited immigrant'.

'He wasn't your traditional grandfather,' says Dick Lloyd's grandson, my cousin Geoff Flint. 'Quite friendly, quite jovial, you could sit on his lap. He was very kind, he was always there for us. Was he the guy who was gonna go and play with you in the garden and all that sort of stuff? No.' But he did make up for it with his vivid stories. 'I remember we used to go to bed every night and wait for his story — he told us a story every night about his life … about hunting, animals, his dogs, crocodiles, all sorts of stuff. We used to love it.'

Grand-daughter Wendy has strong memories of 'Pops' when she was a young teenager. 'And Pop would sit and write and write and write. He was writing his diaries.' So clearly, he was a keen storyteller. And in Rhodesia — like Somerset Maugham's Malaya — there was no shortage of colourful raw material to draw on.

For a few years Dick was feeling the ill-effects of his degenerative coronary artery disease. They had moved off the farm to 8 Strand St, Gwelo, but were by now spending more time in Salisbury with relatives, such as Kay (a nurse) and Mick Flint at 3 Houghton Close, Mandara. (Their 'boy' bore the wonderful name Bandit.) One night just before Christmas 1966 Dick had a thrombosis and died en route to Salisbury Central Hospital. He passed away, regretting ever mentioning that silica sand on his farm.

Forest Vale Farm was left to all his children, but none showed an interest, apart from daughter Dot and her husband Shaun, who looked after it for several years before giving it up.

In the meantime, while waiting for Roger to grow up, I was going to kindergarten at Waterfalls Nursery School. There was a little mini-bus that picked me up some days and drove the short distance to the house with a playground and sandpit. Nursery school was mainly good for one thing: jam sandwiches at break time. Always soft white bread. Always strawberry jam. And if you got a sandwich made of all crust, that was a day to celebrate. The other good thing was afternoon naps. We'd all settle down in this darkened room after lunch, where sun-lounger pool chairs lay in rows, and we'd collapse on these things for a siesta. On reflection, those were the good old days!

My report card from Waterfalls was rather prescient. 'Stuart loves stories, 'Mrs Godsmark wrote. Also 'Likes singing in general' and 'Vocabulary: *quite good*' (italics mine), which I'm sure anyone who's ever read any of my books would think is a bit of a stretch!

One event which was hopefully expunged from my record involved some little girl who used to sit opposite me on the table. I'm not sure exactly how this unfolded, but — at her invitation — I put my hand down the front of her pretty little panties and was caught red-handed (pardon the pun) by Mrs Godsmark and summarily sent to Siberia, or at least the sandpit outside, to cool my jets and have a long, hard look at myself.

Fortunately, this event didn't make news at home, as far I can tell, and no more was mentioned of it. Plus, I got to be first in the queue for jam sandwiches that day, scoring a crust. So, a good result overall!

Next stop was Frank Johnson Junior School, named for the man who had pulled together the Pioneer Column, Lt-Col Sir Frank Johnson KBE DSO, no less. The school logo was a golden wagon wheel. I knew none of this back-story then. What was exciting was the uniform: khaki shirt with double button-down pockets, khaki shorts which reached below my knees, green cap, green tie with gold and silver stripes, and a belt which was green, gold, and silver fabric and fastened with a silver snake-shaped buckle. How proud I was to be in big school and wear that uniform like my big brother.

Of course, it was soon time for school photos. The night before I pulled out Mum's pinking shears and set to work on my fringe. Just tidy things up a bit. Net result: a jagged zig-zag across the front of my head, preserved for posterity in the official black and white portrait.

Frank Johnson looked like every other school you've ever been to — a couple of rows of red-brick buildings, joined at one end, with a hall where school plays and speech days were held. I think my teacher was Mrs Vermaak, though others seem to think it was a Mrs Smith, and the main thing I remember was Tiger Milk. Credit to some marketing genius, every school had Tiger Milk as part of the government's nutrition program. There were two components; one was the fortified powder — a very synthetic strawberry flavour, although it came in chocolate and vanilla too — which Mum scooped into our drink bottle at home. Then, armed with coupons, we'd line up at break time and the teachers and/or milk monitors would fill up your drink bottle with Tiger Milk. (I suspect our mate 'Fatty' Kruger was somehow double-dipping on the coupon scheme!)

1967 signalled a turning point. In August, a combined force of Zimbabwe People's Revolutionary Army (ZIPRA) — which was the Zimbabwe African People's Union's (ZAPU) military wing — and *Umkhonto we Sizwe* (African National Congress's (ANC) armed wing — infiltrated Rhodesia via Wankie, the game park near the Zambezi River, from Zambia. Known rather unfortunately as the Wankie Campaign, this was the first joint Zimbabwean-South African guerrilla operation. The Rhodesian security forces won that particular battle, but it was just one battle within what was now a protracted guerrilla war.

Initially much of the unrest was in the eastern and north-eastern sectors, along the Mozambique border.

And sanctions meant that Rhodesia was running out friends for trading, too, with two-thirds of Rhodesian exports now finding a market in South Africa.

■ ■ ■

Around this time we attended a demonstration by the security forces at the school. A couple of highlights were K9 units setting German Shepard dogs upon a 'suspect' whose arms were bound with what looked like baby mattresses and given a 50-metre start. Of course the dogs got them every time, followed by a bit of ceremonial roughing up by the handler for good measure.

The other display was an army chopper coming into a landing zone, with red flare smoke, and teams dismounting. All very impressive stuff. I loved the Allouette 111's ability to take off and land vertically (first time I'd seen a chopper) with the roar of its rotors. While above a Dakota C-47 circled, disgorging its payload of paratroopers, who seemed to be floating in the sky hanging desperately onto large mushrooms, such were the colour and shape of their primitive chutes. In my child's mind, I never connected it to anything that was unfolding in the real world around us.

Dad, aka British South Africa Police (BSAP) Reservist #7425, was often called out in this tense post-UDI time. He'd be gone for the evening, a whole night, or the weekend. Quelling riots or skirmishing pockets of locals pushing back against the increasing repression of political organisations, imposition of curfews, and detention of activists. Often a grey BSAP Mini Moke would turn up — with a few black and white occupants — and off Dad would go with his BSAP overalls and tin hat and truncheon.

Sometimes it would be a grey Land Rover, with mesh screens over its lights, windows, and anything else that might be smashed up. They'd use pepper spray and truncheons where ordered. Dad recalled one time when one of his fellow reservists had not used the requisite restraint, cleaving one poor rioter's head. 'Ja, ja, as per training, sir … minimum pressure,' he'd claimed as they climbed back into the Land Rover to the consternation and rebuke of his officer.

For now, we were able to travel safely around the country as we wished.

Well, not entirely safely. One time we'd stopped at a petrol station. (These were mainly the red-and-yellow Shell, and the green shield logo of British Petroleum before UDI, but after UDI both brands withdrew reluctantly and slowly from the market.) I'd gone for a pee and was skipping back to the car and tripped just as Dad was manoeuvring the car away from the bowser. *SPLAT*! Next thing I was flat on the forecourt, arms extended to break my fall, and the car tyre reversed over my hand. I looked at my hand in disbelief — completely pancaked, about ten times the size of a normal hand, like one of those big joke plastic jobs you see people wearing in a football crowd. Lots of screams and squeals, mainly from Mum, as she rushed me to the bathroom to run this great elephantine limb under the cold water.

Which probably prompted Dad to tell one of his favourite Dad jokes:

'Doctor, will I be able to play the trumpet after my hand heals?'

'Yes, of course.'

'That's good, because I couldn't play the trumpet before!'

What was most amazing about those drives is that it was just on 1000 miles to our favourite destination: Umhlanga Rocks in South Africa. That's a big distance with three brats in the back.

Aunt Paddy Lloyd remembers that on similar long trips, she and Mick would put the back seats of their station wagon down, install a mattress, and their two boys plus nanny would be happily bouncing around at the back, playing with their toys, napping when they wanted.

We kept ourselves busy with playing 'Car Cricket'. How that worked was certain types and colours of cars were worth a certain amount of 'runs' ie, every car you passed, the designated batsman scored one run. If the car was, say, yellow, you scored two, green was a four, and a Mercedes was a six. Red was out. Then the next person had their turn to bat. Endless hours and miles were happily passed in this fashion.

We'd also have comic books to read. *Superman* and *Batman* and *Archie* comics. This introduced us to a range of characters whose adventures we avidly lapped up: Archie, Betty, Veronica, and Jughead. Between those, and car cricket, suddenly we'd arrived at the Natal coast. Of course, being from land-locked Rhodesia, we'd have our necks craned to see who could spot the ocean first.

The magic of seeing the vastness of the Indian Ocean for the first time was quite something. It was so … big … and so … blue. Who would've thought?

Umhlanga Rocks was a carefree enclave, just north of Durban, with wide leafy streets — vivid flame trees, sprawling milkwoods, and strangler figs dominated the coastline along with the red-and-white banded lighthouse — and Umhlanga was becoming the 'happening' spot. The Umhlanga Rocks Hotel had been there since anyone could remember, then came the Oyster Box with its tea garden, and now came the glitz in the form of Sol Kerzner's The Beverly Hills Hotel. It was considered Natal's first five-star luxury hotel, priced for the international jet set at the unthinkable price of R20 per night (USD28 then), including breakfast, for a luxury sea-view suite. Cabana Beach Resort would come a few years later.

We stayed at a beach house down Lagoon Drive, with a lush green lawn, copper leaf hedges, and scraggly frangipani trees. It was separated from the beach only by a short path and some shrubbery.

What glorious, blissful days of summer were enjoyed there. We were up early and spent all day frolicking on the beach, me in my little tartan-accented swimmers. Of course no sunscreen on. I was getting a real head start on developing my melanoma condition which would come to bite me on the arse, like the dog in the Coppertone ads, much later in life.

Apart from the sound of seagulls, the most exciting sound was the ring of the Clover ice-cream boy's bell. They used to saunter up and down the beach with an ice-box slung across one shoulder, held by a wide leather strap. That was our cue to find Mum and Dad, who were probably relaxing under their beach umbrella, or on the patio of the beach house. Either way, we'd hotfoot it — literally, because the sand was blazing hot by afternoon — to find them, and more importantly, their coins.

As I recall there was a choice of cups and cones. Limited flavours, only vanilla and a choc-top variety. Maybe an Eskimo Pie. That was heaven on a stick right there. Life never got better than that. Ever.

Then, suitably re-sugared, it was back into the water for a cooling swim. We'd all been taught to swim the old-fashioned way … by being thrown unsuspectingly into the backyard pool of whoever it was in Salisbury claiming themselves to be a swimming coach. That was always Lesson One. You figured it out pretty quickly, trust me.

At night we'd be totally exhausted. With no TV in South Africa yet, we headed to bed early so we could do it all again the next day. And the next. And the next.

Each night, I'd slide in between the sheets. The worst nightmare was a grain or three of sand on the sheets, because that would scratch your sunburn, sending sharp slivers of pain up into your brain.

Of course, after a few days of this, your nose, ears, shoulders, and back would be as red as the lighthouse's top. Then start blistering. Then start peeling. At first, little specks of skin. Later, large sheets. That in itself was hours of entertainment, seeing who could get the largest tract of intact skin off your brothers' backs.

It wasn't summer unless you'd shed your skin like a python.

One day we'd been to the shops and got soft drinks, which came in an unbranded squeezy plastic bottle shaped like a teddy bear. They might even have been called 'animal squeezy bottles'. They came in the colours which contained the most added sugar possible: green, red, orange.

Once again re-sugared, someone (not me surely, because my Waterfalls Kindergarten report — signed off by the principal AM Davey — certified me as 'a good boy') had the bright idea of re-filling the bottles with water, and ambushing cars along Lagoon Drive. Eventually a black Morris came along, Glen and I sprung out from behind the copper leaf hedge and gave the car a good squirting. Some splashed off the windscreen, most of it ran harmlessly down the side, or nowhere near the car. Haha — great fun! The brake lights came on, and the car pulled over. This old bloke got out of the car, mad as hell.

We did the honourable thing and scarpered inside. Not so smart, because he just followed us into the house, and confronted my Dad, telling him what these Animal Squeezy Bottle miscreants had done to his car. We watched from behind the safety of some large furniture. But Dad was soon onto us. He went out into the garden, found a decent bougainvillea branch, cut off a length with his Swiss Army knife — what the hell, did he keep that down the front of his bathers? — and came after us.

In a lifetime of thrashings, that is the one I remember the best. Or worst. Remember the *most*, let's say. The thorns were still on this branch, but luckily my little white bum was not sunburned because that would've been too much to bear. The more I yelled and shrieked and pleaded the more Dad laid into me. Then it was Glendon's turn.

I guess that serves us right for spoiling his afternoon nap. I'd probably do the same these days (er, if it were still legal, that is).

But even that couldn't diminish the pleasure of those wonderful endless beach holidays at Umhlanga Rocks.

Then we'd reluctantly climb back into the car to make the journey back north again. A playful trend at this time was plastic oranges used as car aerial ornaments. These were promotional fruit juice containers and, simply flipped over with the little spout upside down, they happily sat on your aerial.

By now Roger was old enough to be taught how to ride. He could not have been more than eighteen months old by now. Outside the kitchen door was a slope in the grass. Quite gentle, we thought. And there was a large rock, surrounded by some bullrushes. A perfect launching spot, we thought. We hauled up the big blue trike, got Rog to stand on the rock, and position himself on the saddle. He couldn't reach the pedals let alone work the brakes. Never mind. We held it steady. 'On the count of three! One, two, three …' We propelled him down the slope, faster and faster he went, straight at first, crooked at second, wobbly at third, spectacular face-plant at fourth. And so he was baptised into our world of bike riding.

Next was my turn for a very public face-plant. A show on Rhodesian TV at the time was called *Small Talk*. It was hosted by a grandfatherly looking character called Paddy, who wore a suit, bow-tie, and thick rimmed glasses. Most of the show seemed to be given over to shout-outs to kids whose birthday it was. I got on this show somehow, my first television appearance. No doubt I would have been dressed to the nines in my Sunday best.

We were all sitting in serried rows, like you might for a school photo. Paddy was in the middle, and I was on his immediate right. He asked all the kids what they wanted to be when they grew up. 'A fireman,' said little Tommy. And all the other boys and possibly girls too. My turn came: I confidently said 'Fireman', surprising myself and my parents who looked on. Of the twenty or so other kids on the show, they all wanted to be a fireman. Rhodesia's future was safe from pyromaniacs. Then Paddy started reading out all the greeting and birthday cards, passing them to me as he finished each one. But at one point, the stack got too big and unwieldy, and whole lot went — *WHOOSH*! — live on national television, scattered across the studio floor. I'm sure body language experts would have detected a nano-eye roll from Paddy, before he gave a grudging half-smile as if to say, 'It could've happened to anyone, little boy.' Cut. Thus ended my first TV appearance, perhaps the highlight of my broadcasting career in retrospect.

Back in the car, Mum said, 'A fireman???' (I've often wanted to add a slogan to my homepage: 'Stuart Lloyd: Disappointing my mother since 1962'.)

Talking of jobs, an occasional visitor to home was an Irish priest. Dad never joined us at church, the Cathedral of the Sacred Heart, at the corner of Fourth Street and Selous Avenue. (He always said he was Anglican, but he was actually baptised and made his first holy communion at St Cuthbert's Catholic Church in Gwelo in 1929.)

The Irish priest looked as though he'd come straight out of seminary, according to Mum, because he was so youthful looking, but had nine years based in South Africa prior to his posting to Rhodesia. 'What I like about Rhodesia is that not everything has an opposite,' he opined. 'In South Africa, black is opposite white, Afrikaner is opposite English, Dutch Reform is opposite Catholics.'

His point was well made, and Mum was in agreement with his sentiment. She loved, they loved, we all loved Rhodesia. Leaving was not on the agenda, despite the deepening sanctions and privations in the country. But largely, workarounds were in place, via third-party countries, with the ports of Mozambique benefitting greatly from the trans-shipment of goods bound for Rhodesia.

■ ■ ■

However, in South Africa the Tongaat sugar empire was thinking of expansion into the 'foods and feeds' sectors. Eggs, mushrooms, animal feeds, etc. *Who can we get to set this up and run it?*

Buster Lloyd's name was in the hat. 'Chris Saunders hired Dad to come down and start up the poultry business,' Jen told me. Chris Saunders was the chairman of the Tongaat Group and well known to Mum because he was part of her Zululand crowd. 'You virtually knew everybody in Zululand, so yes, we knew him from before. And of course, everyone knew my father because he was chief engineer with Hulett's.'

Buster was headhunted to set up and run the new division. It was too good a career step-up to ignore.

'I was always available for the next move,' Jen would later tell me. 'I was very agreeable to go back to South Africa. I was never "I don't want to go there" or "I don't want to do that".' They were, after all, going back to nearly where she was originally from. 'It was like going back home, a very happy time.'

I don't remember too much fuss or fanfare. I'm sure there were rounds of leaving parties held because we had a lot of uncles, aunts, cousins, on Dad's side of the family, apart from their friends. Mum had become very dear friends with her sister-in-law Paddy, another life-long friendship.

All I knew was this big green Stuttafords Van Lines truck arrived one day. All our stuff was loaded into it. Peter and Zeta were taken off separately and put into wooden containers with mesh windows.

We were taking the train to Beira, Mozambique and then going to sail down to South Africa from there. Just as we waved goodbye to Arbor Acres, and drove down the driveway for the last time, I remembered, 'Hey, I left my Crunchie bar on the window sill.' I'd eaten half, kept the other half hidden behind the curtain for later. But there would be no later. I probably sulked all the way to the train station.

From Salisbury we caught a train to the border at Umtali (now Mutare), in the Manicaland region bordering Mozambique. It had been an important gold mining and trading centre for the Portuguese and British for centuries.

The station at Umtali was a smallish two-story brick affair, and the kiosk was doing brisk business as passengers ferried to and fro between Rhodesia and Mozambique, passports and papers checked. Mum bought a pack of Marie biscuits and other snacks for the 200-mile 12-hour trip ahead. We boarded a small train — occupying the rear-most carriage which offered a large panorama window and headed into Mozambique.

I wonder if Mum and Dad had any sense of leaving the country their grandfathers had pioneered?

For us kids, there was a palpable air of adventure and excitement. Mum opened the Marie biscuits only to find them crumbly and infested with weevils. We busied ourselves with our comic books. I was re-reading *Richie Rich* for the umpteenth time. At Machipanda, the Portuguese border post, a swarthy officer — with an elaborate peaked cap, epaulettes the size of aircraft carriers, and an air of authority that entered the cabin several minutes before he did — checked our passports and papers again.

Then it was back to *Richie Rich* as the countryside passed. At one point, the train jolted sharply to a stop. We curiously looked around, surprised to see the train driver walking back down the track. After a hundred metres or so, he bent over, and with a gold-toothed grin, held aloft a dead rabbit. 'Dinner!' Well, perhaps it was better than weevilled Marie biscuits.

Clickety-clack, we passed through Chimoio, then some deeply wooded, steeper sections of track around Amatongas Forest. This was hard going for the little train, but not as hard going as for the gangs who built this railway.

The history of the line goes back to 1898 when Cecil Rhodes got his good friend Frank Johnson to set up yet another company to create a viable trade route. Of course, Rhodes would be the managing director of the Frank Johnson Company. Johnson in turn sent his old mate Selous to reconnoitre the Beira to Umtali route. The report came back very unfavourably … the road trip took three weeks and was riddled with tsetse flies. The only viable way through would be by rail.

They set about building this, at the massive cost of 400 European workers, nearly all of the 500 Indian workforce, and innumerable Africans. Most succumbed to fever, as did the 500 donkeys which were employed because they were thought to be tsetse resistant.

Their hard work is still evident in the form of the raised viaduct over the Pungwe River. And all too soon, we arrived in Beira. The Indian Ocean. Glittering almost purple-blue.

■ □ ■

In one of the weirdest naval blockades ever, The Royal Navy and Air Force monitored shipping in the Mozambique Channel for nine years after UDI in an attempt to ensure that no oil reached landlocked Southern Rhodesia via Beira port. They deployed HMS *Ark Royal*, plus dozens of other frigates and destroyers. Although the refinery at Umtali was closed, and petrol rationing was introduced, the country continued to function. Petrol seeped in through side doors — via Portuguese East Africa, South African goodwill, and a shadowy trade in paperwork and deniability. Thus the country never quite ran dry. Britain's overall oil embargo against Rhodesia failed, an exercise that cost Britain an estimated £100 million.

But you couldn't see the British ships because they had to be over the horizon in international waters, otherwise, the Portuguese might've had something to say. Weird and half-arsed in the style of great government decisions everywhere. *It's not going well but we can't be seen to be changing our minds.*

Back on land, the Praia Nova, the beachfront, was a hustling promenade, with cream Mercedes 190D taxis on the prowl, all elegant curves, and round headlights, some with whitewall tyres. Billboards for Manica Beer shouted from the forest of medium-rise buildings. At one end was the four-story Grande Hotel — considered the 'pride of Beira' when built by the colonial government, boasting an Olympic-sized pool, but already needing a lick of paint in the face of a raft of newer, shinier establishments like the Hotel Dom Carlos and Hotel Avenida. At the other end of the beachfront was the Macuti Lighthouse, with the rusted hulk of a large vessel washed partially up onto the beach.

We had an enjoyable afternoon when Dad hired a speedboat to take him waterskiing. We rode in the boat, marvelling at the fact that Dad could ski. Of course, we worried about sharks when he came a cropper and was just bobbing in the ocean for a few minutes while we circled back.

Overall, there was a different texture to this place thanks to the Portuguese influence. The music was different. The architecture was different (decades later I'd recognise the similarity with the 'shophouse' architecture of Singapore, Melaka, and Penang). There were a few gypsy caravans here and there near where we were staying. And then there was *peri peri* chicken …

This spicy revelation speaks to the exotic mash-mash which Mozambique was. The name actually means 'pepper-pepper' in Swahili, and the Portuguese delighted in the local herbs and spices they encountered here, especially African bird's eye chilli. It kicked like a donkey.

But it wasn't native to Africa — it had arrived thanks to Christopher Columbus' voyages to the Americas — and spread via Portuguese sailors in the Great Age of Discovery. They added this chilli to their marinade of lemon juice, garlic, oil, paprika, and vinegar. *BAM*! It was wildly popular in the local *tascas* (taverns) because it went so well with beer.

I imagine my five-year-old taste buds would've gone into overdrive at that first taste. And I remain addicted.

There was definitely something in the drinking water of Mozambique that resonated in my young soul.

And all too soon it was time to leave for the port. In a white Mercedes 190D taxi of course. We arrived at the dockside, revelling in the sight of a massive smart white ship, the Lloyd Triestino liner MV *Africa*. 'Hey that ship has got our name on it! 'It was an Italian liner which plied a route from Trieste, down through the Suez Canal, along the east coast of Africa, and round up the other side of the west coast of Africa.

MV *Africa*'s towering yellow funnel billowed smoke in preparation for its next 1850km leg to Durban. I gazed in awe at the rows of orange lifeboats strung along each side, and the colourful flags fluttering in the gathering wind. At least our family was not pioneering by ox wagons anymore — we'd moved up in the world!

The Italian design was typically elegant, with air-conditioned lounges, dining rooms, and large outdoor promenade decks. And off we sailed south along the Mozambique coast amid the groan and toots of the attendant tugs.

In my memory this voyage lasted weeks, although it was just two or three days. The highlight was a playroom set aside for us little kids. All was smooth sailing until we hit the Agulhas current, where the southerly winds whipped the sea into huge, steep waves which buffeted the ship in quick succession. This corridor of the Mozambique Channel is also prone to tropical cyclones.

Suddenly that morning's breakfast resurfaced. I barfed all over the floor of this playroom and was promptly sin-binned to get some fresh air on a bench on the deck outside.

As I sat there reflecting on my misfortune, I heard a sudden shout. 'Pull!' And *BANG*! An explosion. What the hell? Again: 'Pull!' *BANG*! I edged towards the railing and on the deck below I saw passengers doing some clay pigeon shooting, these discs being flung across the ocean, and disintegrating into a million fragments when the shot struck them. That took my mind off my seasickness.

That evening the storm grew increasingly angry. Mum got called. Rog had decided to feed the fish with his lunch projected proudly through the railings. We regrouped in the cabin. I was sick. Rog was sick. Then Glen. Then Dad. Everyone except Mum.

She wasn't hanging around, and headed up to the dining room for dinner, only to find — out of 864 passengers — it was only her, two other passengers, and the captain who had not succumbed to the green gills of seasickness.

The storm passed overnight, the next day dawning beautifully. And, after a replenishing mountain of breakfast, we played some fun games of deck quoits. Then in the distance we saw the Umhlanga lighthouse — memories of Clover ice creams, third-degree sunburn, and animal squeezy drink bottles! — and the Durban Bluff rose up beyond the crowded skyline of the beachfront.

17

SMALL VILLAGE CHARM

SOUTH AFRICA, 1968. Our new home in South Africa was Maidstone Village. En route past Umhlanga was sugar cane, sugar cane, and more sugar cane. The very land where Rathbone had first experimented with sugar cane a century before. The North Coast Road crossed the odd estuary, then we turned inland, through the town of Tongaat. On the left was a massive series of silos and smoking towers: the Maidstone Sugar Mill. Large Bedford trucks — painted in Tongaat's distinctive maroon and cream colour scheme — queued up in the roadway outside, laden with cut cane, waiting to offload their stash. Then through the ornate whitewashed village gates of Maidstone village.

Maidstone had a distinctly unforgettable smell. Smoky-sweet. Molasses. Somewhere between caramelising sugar in the pan and the yeasty tones of beer brewing. All pervasive, it stuck to your skin as much as to your sinuses. You could smell the mill long before you could see it.

In 1936 Douglas Saunders asked his friend, artist Robert Gwelo Goodman, to redesign the Saunders family home, Amanzimnyama, and its gardens near Tongaat. Soon after, as part of a broader anti-malaria effort and a desire to improve estate living conditions, Saunders commissioned him to rethink worker housing across the sugar estate. Drawing on the Cape Dutch style he loved most, Goodman set out to create a distinctive Cape Dutch Revival settlement. Maidstone and Tongaat were the result.

Indians generally lived in the Tongaat township area, and Africans in compounds distributed around the area. Goodman's plans for the nearby 'native village' of Hambanati convinced officials to relax rigid town-planning rules — an ambitious experiment that left a lasting imprint on South African urban design. (Goodman's paintings, especially those featuring his beloved Cape Dutch architecture, still sell strongly for unto USD$20,000.)

Towering palm trees lined wide streets. We pulled up outside a 'little village house' as Mum described it, at 16 Main Avenue. At the back was an avocado tree which cast shade over nearly the whole back yard, and a lychee tree on the side of the garage.

So this was home. For now. My first international move (I've made 10 international moves at the time of writing).

I had no idea of this at the time, but by the early 1970s, South Africa would be a country running on political fumes, held together by fear, legislation, and the increasing paranoia of the National Party that their domination was under threat. Prime Minister BJ Vorster, successor to Verwoerd, ruled through a tightening lattice of security laws. His Terrorism Act of 1967 gave the police even more draconian powers — extending the long shadow of contentious detention without trial — and gave little hope for optimism. Parallel to the uniformed police, the dreaded Bureau for State Security (BOSS) entrenched itself as the covert fist of white supremacy. Security forces became extremely efficient, with the aid of an extensive informer network. Legal and political opposition was effectively suffocated since Mandela's Rivonia Trial, and those not in jail were forced into exile.

Maidstone was very civilised — for example the Clover man delivered milk to your door overnight. You just left the empties out, and next day they were magically replenished. Yummy milk with a layer of thick rich cream just beneath the golden foil cap.

First came the bad news. Glendon went off to school up the road at Maidstone Primary School, and I was told that because I was not six before the start of the year, I'd have to sit on the sidelines for the rest of the year, and start Standard 1 all over again. Not impressed! Mum went in to see the principal Mr Harrison to fight my case, but the answer still came back as no.

Then came the good news. Just a few doors down lived Austin Schubert. And he had a great big sandpit and a great collection of toy cars, notably one orange Willy's jeep and one blue one. Happy days!

It was a while before that Stuttafords van turned up with all our stuff. Then there were a million boxes to be unpacked, like Christmas all over again, as we were reunited with long-lost possessions and prized toys (mostly Fisher Price, or made in Formosa — now Taiwan — in those days). Alas, no Crunchie bar turned up.

For six months I hung out with Austin and we played cars all day. I've got no idea why he wasn't at school, but that wasn't my problem — I was getting a colourful education at the School of Schubert. He was street-wise way beyond his six or seven years. I learned all the good swear words from him in English, Afrikaans, and Zulu! And when I think of some of conversations we had … one a very clear, graphic description of gay sex. 'If you can't get a girlfriend, this is what they do …' he explained. I made a note to myself: get a girlfriend, sooner rather than later.

In the afternoon, games of cowboys and Indians with Glendon and schoolmates would always break out, or some kind of war game in the garden. Another great discovery was that our house had this coal-fired water heater out the back … a big industrial steel contraption set into the back wall. It was perfect for melting crayons: you'd hold the crayons against its furnace and watch Jackson Pollock-like masterpieces materialise before your eyes. God knows how many innocent Crayolas were sacrificed in the name of abstract art.

Great excitement the day our dogs Peter and Zeta arrived from Rhodesia, after quarantining. Said Jen of Peter: 'I was quite nervous, thinking, I hope he remembers me, which of course he did.' Then they had to take them to the vet for their various injections. Peter was leaping about the car in excitement at the reunion and just being out of that damn wooden cage. Propping himself up to look out of the windows, his bum in Mum's face. When they arrived at the vet's, he started snarling. 'I was scared. He was growling at the vet and his African assistant, and would have nothing to do with them. He had his mouth all *bopa'd* (tied) up, and I had to sit on him while they gave him his *jovas* (injections).'

Some days we'd head off down to the Tongaat Reservoir, which was right behind our house. Skimming stones across the water. Walking out along the water gates, marked clearly 'Danger! Stay Out! No Trespassing' in four different languages. Lots of fun walking and balancing on the massive pipelines which snaked their way around the reservoir. And of course, we'd never wear shoes, always barefoot.

One afternoon at the reservoir, this 'houseboy' was walking this big ugly bulldog. Peter and the bulldog took an instant dislike to each other. The barks, and growls, and yelps reached a sickening crescendo as Glendon and the other guy tried to seperate the savage mutts. In the end, the referee declared it a draw, the bulldog dripping blood from his throat, Peter minus bits of fur and flesh here and there, and we all retired to our respective corners. I was shaking for ages after.

Another dog in the neighbourhood was Prince, a big Alsatian that belonged to the Hart family. It kept coming into our garden, where obviously big scraps would break out with our dogs. Dad got sick of this, and one time — around Guy Fawkes time — he hurled a large thunderbolt cracker towards Prince who got the fright of his life, turned and bolted … snout-first straight into our mango tree. We never saw that canine — the Dog Formerly Known as Prince — in our yard again.

Guy Fawkes nights became legendary. Piles and piles of wood would be built up, often with an effigy figure. And then it was on with rockets, and Catherine wheels, and many big things which went *BANG*! We graduated from sparklers and squibs to larger ordnance over the years, blowing the shit out of everything we could.

Other days we'd go wandering across the golf course looking for lost golf balls. Based on how many we found, the standard of golf there was not very high! I remember running down the fairway one day, and as I leapt across a dip in it, I noticed this greyish shape lying prone. Shit! *Pofadder*! Mid-flight I'm sure I levitated an extra 10 metres; unofficially the world record for long jump was shattered that day (and I quite possibly shattered in my pants too). You didn't mess with *pofadders*, one of the most venomous of all snakes.

Just outside the village gate was the tiny post office. And outside it had benches. Benches marked with bold signs I couldn't read: 'SLEGS *BLANKES*' and '*SLEGS NIE-BLANKES*'. I looked at the signs again, trying to make sense of it. Afrikaans I guess. And then I saw the translations: 'Whites Only' and 'Non whites Only'. And inside the post office, the signs were repeated, with strictly segregated queues. Even though the non-whites queue was long, and only one or two were in the whites queue, there was no thought of hopping across to get served in the other one. That was different from Rhodesia, and the first time I guess I saw or felt apartheid in action. (Later of course I noticed these signs were all over the place: beaches, hotel entrances, everywhere.)

Also outside the village gates was the Maidstone Shopping Centre, another gracious whitewashed Cape Dutch architectural affair, decorated with bucolic friezes in the upper gable part. A butchery sat on the lower right side. And in through the doors to the Spar supermarket, which was airy and spacious, with huge windows out the back overlooking the greenery of the golf course and gardens.

By evening the air would start cooling, and the smuts from the cane fires or the mill would start to settle. Little — and not so little — flecks of burned black cane leaves. And millions of Indian mynahs would descend on the trees for the night, with an unholy chorus of shrieking, gossiping, and carrying on. Until everyone was settled. Then the bats would start their nocturnal migration, clouds of them squeaking and beeping their way through the gathering darkness overhead.

Breakfast was the most memorable meal of the day. It had nothing to do with the Kellogg's Corn Flakes or the Rice Krispies or the Honey Smacks. It was the little toy giveaways in the pack. Always a single piece of single-coloured moulded Taiwanese plastic crap, like a racing car, a ring, or an astronaut. Choking hazards weren't invented yet.

While those cereals were British or American, South Africa had its own breakfast superfoods in the form of ProNutro and Maltabella. The marketing boffins at Bokomo had us believe ProNutro was this scientifically formulated high-protein breakfast of champions. Yeah, but where's the crappy plastic toy? On top of that, it tasted boring, and — worst of all — if you didn't get the right amount of milk in it, and stir it like crazy, it ended up setting harder than concrete. In fact, it could've been better used for brick-building and providing low-cost housing solutions. Or perhaps the army could use it to build air-raid bunkers.

Sometimes, maybe in winter with warm milk, there was Jungle Oats. Ditto, no fun plastic toys, so what was the point? Dad's breakfast was always a couple of fried eggs and toast. 'Eggs give you everything except

Vitamin C,' he'd say, 'so if you have eggs with a glass of orange juice you get everything you need.'

He would then jump into his exciting new wheels: a white Ford Zephyr Mk IV, a muscular car that billowed blue smoke (only leaded petrol in those days of course). Each morning he'd drive to his office, which was in the Tongaat Group headquarters, a very stylish Cape Dutch building just on the other side of the golf course.

One morning was slightly different: I don't know if he was hung over or tired, but he went to his car and mistakenly got into the back seat, briefly wondering where the steering wheel was!

At work he was hatching plans on how to dominate the egg world. Dad just went to work and came home as far as I knew. But the big strategic picture which they'd discuss in the board room, as they all sat around smoking their Rothmans King Size cigarettes, was to produce enough eggs to feed Africa with this, the cheapest form of high-class protein. And to do it in a vertically-integrated way, by producing their own feed, then grading, packing, and marketing the consistent end product to supermarkets. Words like 'economy of scale' and 'efficiency' were highlighted with new-fangled marker pens in neon colours.

Somebody in marketing came up with the differentiating brand name: Tongaat Big Brown Eggs.

This set them against all others — mainly ma and pa producers — who were producing smaller, whiter eggs. Anaemic in comparison. And that's where Dad's geneticist skills came in: tweaking chickens to lay more eggs, more often.

We'd always stop at the Shell garage adjacent to fill up the thirsty Zephyr. One of the attractions — once again, kudos to the marketing folks — they always seemed to have some sort of collectable thing going on, ie fill up your tank, get a plastic badge or sticker for your collection (and you got an album to keep them in). It might be the logos of airlines that flew into South Africa (seeing names like KLM or Sabena or PanAm fostered curiosity of the wider world). Another one might be the badges of the world's major rugby teams. The Springboks of course (who were about to tour the UK and Australia in 1970), all the British teams, New Zealand, etc. Another promotion was the 'See Your Country' series, featuring landmarks and scenic highlights: Blyde River

Canyon, Durban's beaches, Table Mountain, and even the Voortrekker Monument.

Tank filled, it was thrilling to drive out with Dad through the cane fields, and suddenly come across this clearing where massive yellow diggers and trucks were hard at work, flattening and clearing the earth so the chicken runs (more like warehouses) could be built. This was like a Tonka Toy fantasy come to life! We couldn't get enough of it.

Mum was busy with her tennis, just up the road at the Maidstone Sports Club. How great it was to live in a village where everything was on your doorstep. The club was an imposing double-story block in — you guessed it! — Cape Dutch style. A massive open area upstairs allowed members and guests to enjoy drinks and meals overlooking the tennis courts, 9-hole golf course, bowling green, and the swimming pool.

Inside the club, downstairs, was a buffet hutch, where you could buy sweets, snacks and soft drinks. Cokes were ubiquitous but Appletiser was my favourite, a home-grown sparkling apple drink.

The waiters and club staff — mostly Indians and a few Africans — dressed smartly in black pants, white shirts, even black bow-ties. Inside, apart from the restaurant, was a large theatre where they showed movies on Saturday nights and staged all the school productions, and various community events, such as Christmas parties. Dad loved the restaurant because the curries were the real deal. He would literally pour sweat over a particularly good vindaloo, which the Indian chefs had dished up. He also enjoyed the sports bar area at the back, where he'd imbibe a few beers after an afternoon of golf. Downstairs was the Maidstone Library. I became addicted to the *Hardy Boys* adventure and detective stories. I also borrowed *Paddington Bear*, but it didn't grab my imagination and I had it sitting around for years, amassing a huge overdue fine.

The bustling playground adjacent the tennis courts had a few of the usual merry-go-rounds, swings, slides, etc. Naturally, the challenge was to spin the merry-go-round so hard and fast that whoever was on it went flying off due to the centrifugal force. Or if any of my brothers were on the swings, to try and swing them high enough to do a full loop over the bar (I don't think this was ever achieved, except for some kid saying 'You should've been here yesterday — I did a full loop-the-loop').

But the star attraction was a decommissioned Avonside cane train locomotive. We'd clamber aboard this green thing and spend hours pretending to stoke the boilers with coal, twiddle various knobs for full steam ahead, apply the brakes, struggling to look out of its two porthole windows. We climbed all over it, on the roof, up around its smoke stack. No hovering parents in sight, no one to say 'Careful, Johnny.'

And next to that was the swimming pool, lined by copper leaf hedge. It felt Olympic-sized … in fact the lengths felt more like the Panama Canal. At this stage I was happy to swim widths.

Overall the club was the epicentre of village life, more like Club Med.

But then came 1969, and the spell of this magical interlude was broken by me having to start school all over again. Class 1, revisited. (It was officially called Sub A, and second year Sub B, before you started Standard 1, but we all called it Class 1 and Class 2.)

Maidstone Primary School started life as an outlying private school in 1881, catering to the kids of local farmers and those in the milling industry.

There was a short walk up (max 1.5 km) Main Avenue, past the club, and then cut across to the imaginatively named School Road. A walk we did both ways, unaccompanied, each day, and the only time I remember wearing shoes as a kid.

The uniform was just plain khaki, with a green blazer worn only for school photos I'd imagine — it was warm year-round. The logo on the pocket was the Maidstone slave bell. This reflected the heritage of the area, the bell design being based on the bell that stood in Maidstone Barracks (near the Tongaat sugar mill) since the 1860s. It was rung to signal work shifts and mark breaks or prayers for indentured Indian labourers, and was ironically a symbol of community for them, because it was associated with their ability to stop work and gather together.

A full-scale replica of this bell stood in the grounds of the school, which was a long L-shaped brick block, with open verandahs running its entire length. Big sash windows ran down both sides of each classroom. Separately, sat a scout hall, and a couple of pre-fab classrooms, including the music room, lower down the slope. Beautiful jacaranda trees gave it a pleasant bucolic feeling. Except one afternoon when we were told to go read outside. Yay! Sitting under the tree, *SPLAT!* A bird pooped on me. I ran to the bathrooms to rinse this disgusting mess from my hair. Job done, I came back and moved to sit under a different tree. Two minutes later, *SPLAT!* The giggles and guffaws from my so-called friends could be heard in Cairo, I'm sure.

My 'gang' included Wayne Glover and Lance Gold. The Glovers had a bunch of boys our age and our families became firm friends. Ditto, the de Riquebourg family who had a bunch of boys — Greg, Bradley, and Steven — and a daughter Michelle. Their glamorous mum Jean was a teacher at the school.

Their father was called Peter, which gave rise to a funny incident at church one Sunday because he used to do a lot of the readings: at the end he'd say 'Thanks be to God' to which the audience would respond 'Thanks be to God.'

Glendon turned to Mum and whispered: 'Is Mr de Riquebourg God?

'No, I don't think so, darling, why?'

'Because all the people in the church said "Thanks Peter God" after he finished reading!'

Brendan Collins' father spent all his spare time and money building a huge concrete yacht in their garden in Havana Rd, just behind the school. Mostly I was surprised that concrete could float, and once I got over that, was wildly impressed as they described its self-righting technology.

The Collins, with their four kids aboard, eventually set off several years later. 'We were heading either to Canada or Australia which ever country accepted us first,' Brendan's sister Lindy told me recently. 'We found out it was Australia when we got to St Helena, and sailed to Brazil and up to the Caribbean through the canal and across the Pacific.' They arrived in Australia in 1977. 'It was a mammoth task with no self-steering, no computers, just charts, sextant, and tables. Hurricanes and all sorts of adventures!'

There was a lot of romanticism around sailing at the time, with the exploits of 18-year-old Robin Lee Graham fresh in people's minds. In his sloop *Dove*, he'd become the youngest person to circumnavigate the world.

Apart from Mrs De Riq, the staff included Kit Veitch (whose kids Ross and Lynn were both around my age), Elizabeth 'Bun' Bird, Mrs Meulemans, with Pam Baptie in the admin office at the end. The headmaster was Mr Harrison, a tall rather pasty-faced man who wore grey safari suits and thick-rimmed spectacles, as I remember.

We were divided into two houses for sport: Lions and Tigers, red and blue. We'd have swimming and athletics tournaments.

Morning break and lunchtime the whole school played stingers. This involved throwing a tennis ball as hard as you could at somebody — anybody! — hence the name, because a direct hit would really sting. Our defensive superpower was a handkerchief wrapped around one fist ... you were allowed to punch the ball away.

One day some kids were playing on the field with what I thought was a soccer ball. I was walking past, and this thing came sailing through the air, so I just instinctively went to give it a header. *THUNK*! It was a medicine ball, full of sand and steel shot. I thought I'd broken my neck, and saw the proverbial stars, slinking away as though everything was OK, thinking, What the hell happened there?

Yo-yos were also a great fad. Sponsored by Coke (Red, or gold in limited edition), Fanta (blue or orange), and Sprite (green). Many fingers and knuckles were shattered in the name of mastering that game, along with tricks such as 'Walking the Dog', 'The Eiffel Tower', and 'Around the World' (the latter accounting for many shattered light-fittings too).

Another fun thing was tok-toks. These were a wooden cotton reel with a rubber band threaded through the centre, a toothpick as an axle, and a slice of candle used as a bearing for the toothpick. You wound the axle up, tightening the rubber band, then it would judder along the ground. Races were popular, people pimping their models with the thickest rubber bands they could find.

Cotton reels were also used in French knitting. Four nails were tapped into the top, with wool threaded down through the centre of the reel. Then the yarn was threaded around the nails, and a long tail emerged from this tiny primitive knitting loom. Pretty pointless.

One day I'd gone to David Uppington's house, across the road from school. Afterwards, I'd walked back through the village to home. The next morning getting ready for school after a big bowl of Corn Flakes, I couldn't find my shoes. Searched everywhere. Then it dawned on me — I'd left them at David's house. Damn! 'Well, you'll just have to go to school barefoot then,' Mum said.

So off I trotted, but by the time I arrived at school, assembly had started, which was always held on the flat asphalted area in front of the classrooms. I tried to slink down the path invisibly but that was never going to be possible with 100 sets of eyes on me, *kaalvoet* (barefoot). Lesson learned! I never forgot my shoes again.

But there was bigger news: We would not be walking to school anymore, because we were now to move into our real house, a long long way from the village ...

When not looking for my shoes, Mum had been busy with designing our new house. 'It was wonderful,' said Jen. 'You just chose your spot and designed it, and Tongaat paid for your house!' The spot was to be at Klipfontein, closer to the site of where the chicken farm was taking shape, on the southern side of Tongaat.

Arrival in Africa: The Lloyd family arrived in Algoa Bay on the *Belle Alliance* as settlers in 1820, surfing into shore in these whalers. The Seymour family arrived in Durban on the *Catherine* as settlers in 1862.

Wagons of the Pioneer Column into Mashonaland cross the Nuanetsi River in 1890. Henry Lloyd and Trooper George Seymour both participate. The Union Jack raised in Cecil Square, Salisbury, 13 September 1890.

The larger than life figure of Ephraim Rathbone, who introduced commercial sugarcane farming to South Africa from Mauritius. After the First Zulu War in 1879, he claimed (and won) half of Zululand in damages.

Sgt George F Seymour of the Imperial Light Horse,
one of just 8 officers to relieve the famous long siege of
Mafeking in the Boer War, May 1900.

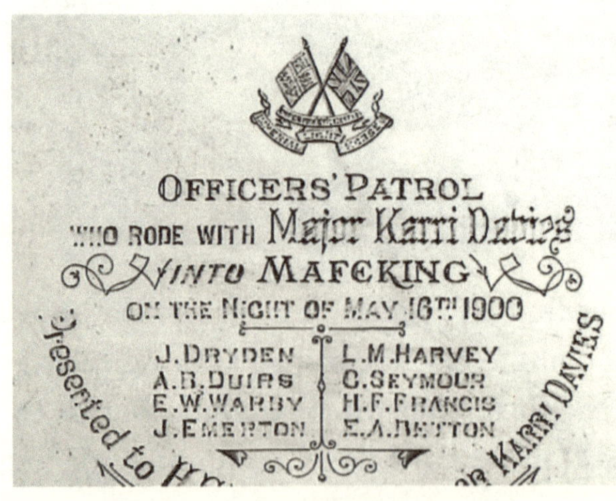

Pioneer Henry Lloyd in 1893, after the full occupation of Bulawayo. He built a property and mining empire (including the Central Hotel below) then lost the lot.

Dick Lloyd with a five-stamp mill typical of that used by small-scale miners, and the main farm house in Gwelo on father Pioneer Henry Lloyd's farm.

Dick and Eileen Lloyd, with the first two of their six children, Paddy and Buster. Four more followed.

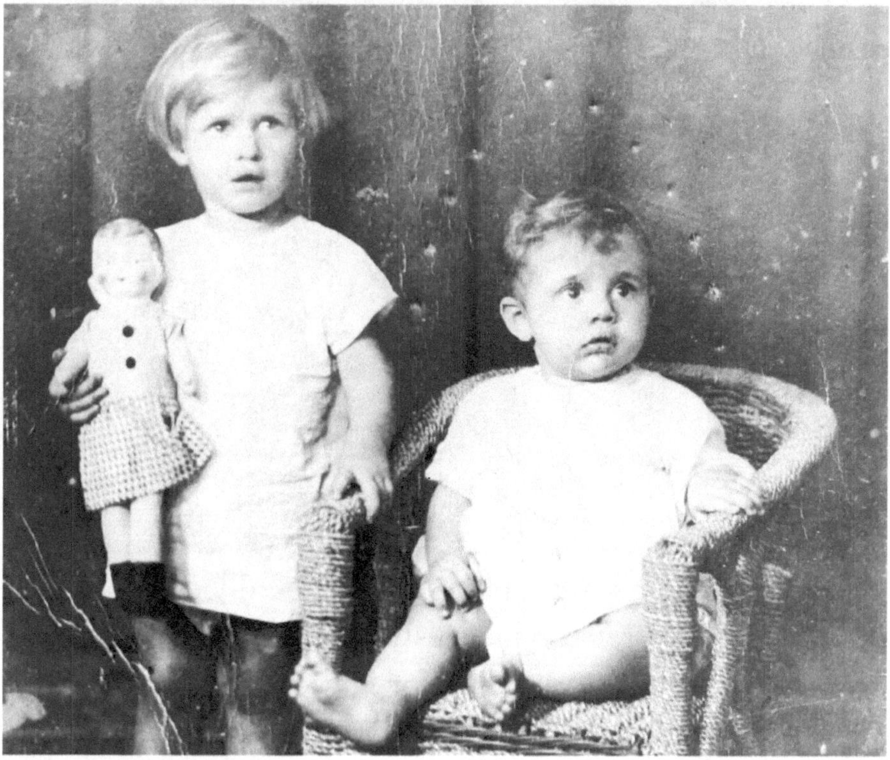

By putting cow shit in his shoes (he really did that!) Buster Lloyd grew up into a strapping lad who enjoyed boxing and rugby, playing for Natal – then his back was broken by a Springbok front-rower.

Record-breaking swimmer Mick Flint and nurse Kay.
Dick and Eileen Lloyd with offspring (plus Mike Avery, front) at home at Shabani mine, Rhodesia c 1952.

George Seymour (second from left) who would marry keen sportswoman and teacher, Alys Tait.

George Edgar Seymour with first son David in Darnall, Zululand, circa 1932. George went on to become chief engineer with the Hulett's Group.

David Seymour riding Bibi, with Samuel the Basuto 'pony boy'. Samuel would later be murdered after a tryst with a Zulu maiden.

The wedding of George 'Buster' Lloyd and Jennifer Seymour, in Durban 1959. This moment brought together the two amazingly colourful and accomplished family trees — the Lloyds and Seymours — that form the basis of this whole story.

Keen fisherman and accountant David Seymour marries Jill Scott, a school teacher on her first 'and last' assignment in Empangeni, Zululand.

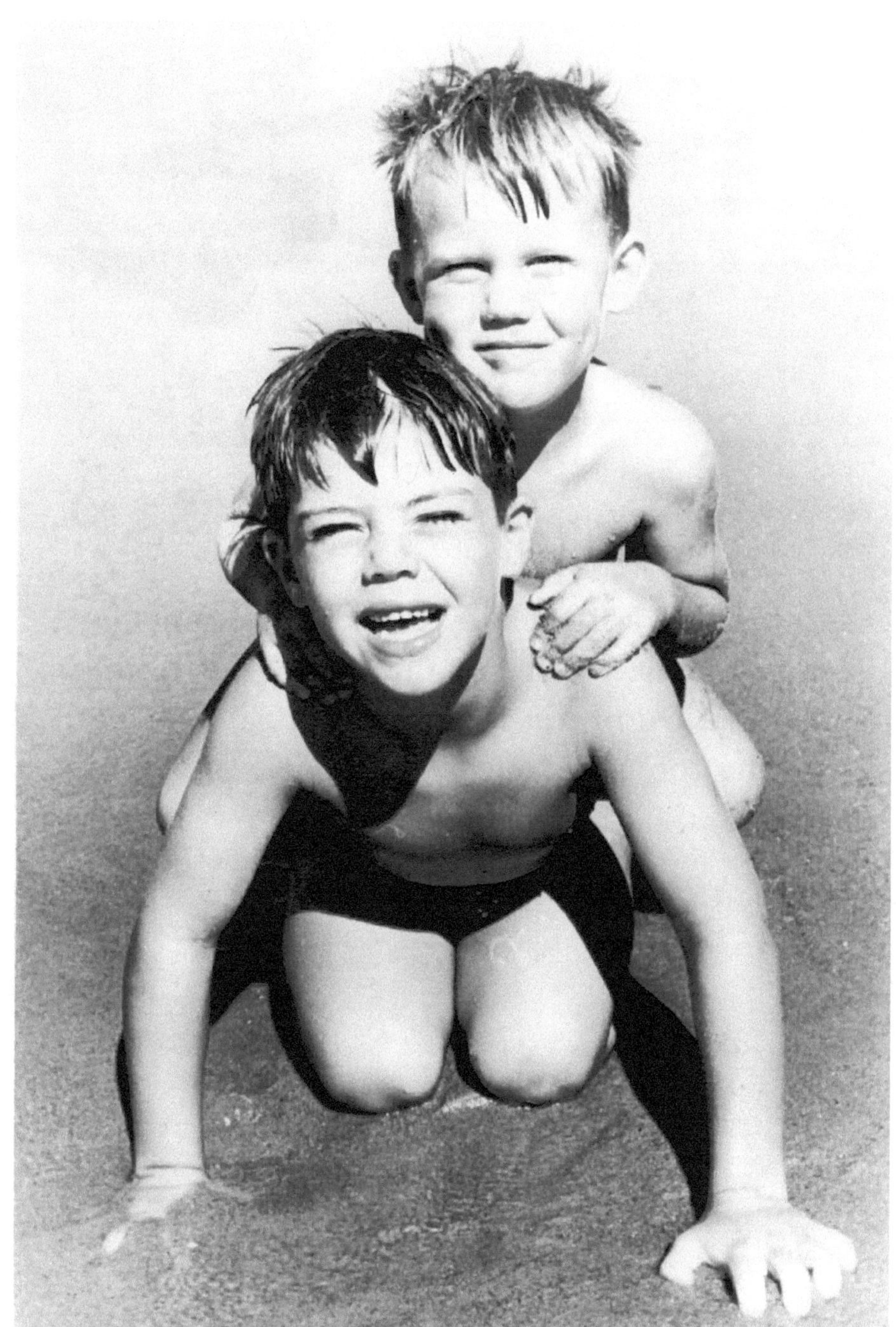

Glendon and Stuart enjoying Umhlanga Rocks c 1967.

Best friends for life: Paddy Shuker and Jenny Lloyd.
Jenny and Buster sailed on the liner MV *Africa* from Beira to Durban in 1968 to start their new life with the booming Tongaat Group in South Africa.

Brother Roger after one of his many mishaps,
this one involving a cricket ball, others involving
sea urchins and plate glass windows.
Glendon enjoying our garden in Klipfontein, 1970.

Roger Seymour in full flight. He played for Northern Transvaal and Natal, facing off against the mighty All Blacks and British Lions, and was nominated for the Springbok trials in 1970.

Four-generation photographs: Michael & Bridget McGee (above seated), with daughter Rosie (top left; bottom seated), and Rosie's daughter Alys (top right; bottom 2nd left back row). Jen with kids below.

London and Goliat at Arbor Acres, Rhodesia.
Beatrice and Mabel at Klipfontein. Mabel was stabbed at our home one night, Beatrice later murdered.

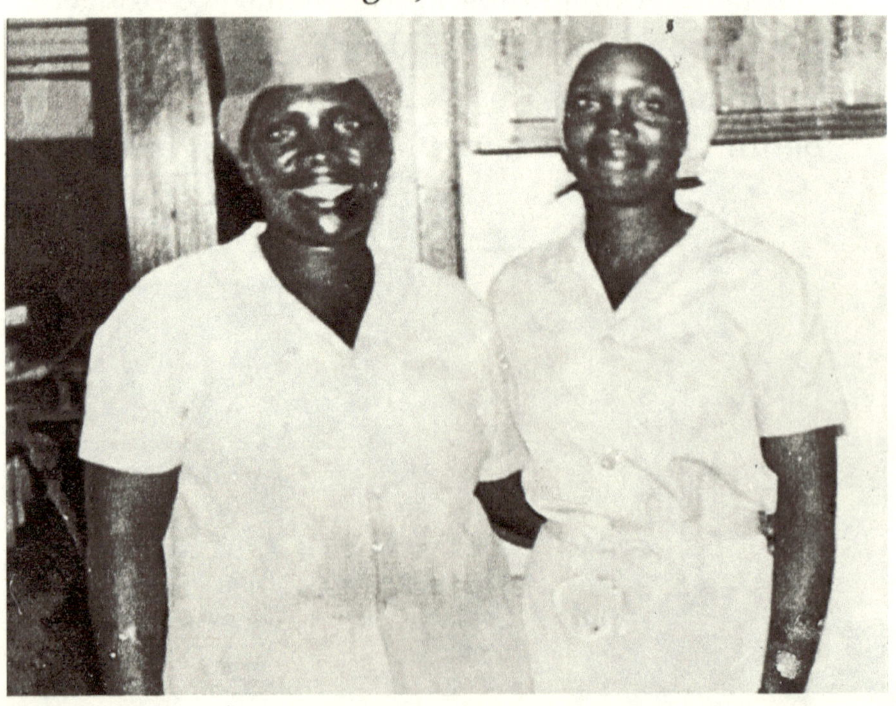

BSA Police Section Officer 8868 Ian Daniel. His varied career saw his Land Rover blown up by a landmine in the Matibi Tribal Lands area, airlifted to hospital in Triangle, Rhodesia, and medicated with free beer.

2nd Lt Lloyd Flint was assigned to an independent infantry company, and saw brutal action around Mutare and Nyanga along the Mozambique border.

The only family photo that shows all of us. Glendon, Roger, and Stuart at home in Klipfontein, South Africa, 1970, with parents Buster and Jen. Photo taken with Dad's Voigtlander camera on tripod with timer mode. In this lounge room we danced to songs like Miriam Makeba's *The Click Song* and Margaret Singana's *Mama Tembu's Wedding*. *Tie a Yellow Ribbon* would soon take on a life of its own thanks to Mum's lead-foot driving.

Glendon, Stuart, and Roger in Tongaat 1972,
with re-enactment done in Kiama, Australia, 2020.
Seems unfair to have such good looks in one gene pool.

18

THE CHIMNEY IN THE CANEFIELDS

KLIPFONTEIN, 1969. Jen presented her idea of this H-shaped house to chairman Chris Saunders. He looked at her H-shape and said, 'Are you sure that's what you want?' Yes, she was. Two wings of the house — one for living spaces, the other for sleeping spaces — were joined by a corridor, with a covered verandah in the front area, and a courtyard out the back. 'Then they got an architect in to do the building drawings, pipes, etc.'

The house was just a few kilometres past Chris and Pam Saunders' own stately mansion Herrwood (half way between Tongaat town and the beach). A perfectly-laid brick road led to their house from the main road into town (now called Ushukela Rd), and Pam's Mercedes sports car glided along it and up their endless driveway, lined with soaring pine trees. Beyond their turnoff was just a dirt road leading to a cane siding, turn right up and over a small hill on the way to Clairbrooke, as the poultry farm was originally named, changing soon after to Carisbrooke.

Through the cane fields, on the left, a driveway had been graded, with clay banks on either side. About all you could see from the road was a looming white chimney, earning our house the nickname of *Ishimula* (chimney). As you drove up the driveway, the house announced itself. A smart white structure, grey-tiled roof, double garage. And that chimney, which could probably be seen from the moon. The garden (although not landscaped yet) was a massive sprawl carved out of the cane, sloping down to even more garden area. 'That's where the pool's going to be,' Dad pointed.

A blue and yellow awning jutted out from the large picture-frame window of the lounge room, from where we could see cane fields, cane fields, and more cane fields, rippling green waves in the wind. It was a view Mum never got tired of.

We immediately loved it. Glendon and I were in the room at the back of H. Roger was in next to us. Then Mum and Dad's master bedroom and ensuite looked over the front garden. In the 'crossbar' section of the H was the study, where our bakelite phone sat. It was on a shared party line, so always jangling with other people's morse code-like ring tones. Our 'number' was loooooong-short-loooooong, which you dialled with a hand crank on the side.

In the other wing of the H, was a large lounge room overlooking the garden and cane fields, with a dining room next to the entrance, then a kitchen with a breakfast counter. Behind the garage, were some small rooms which were the servants' quarters.

We soon had Mabel Nkomo and Beatrice Mapamulo join our family. Cooking and babysitting. Mabel was young, lighter-skinned, sassy, and cute. Beatrice clearly enjoyed her own cooking a lot, the buttons on her large tunic often straining under the workload. Both had ever-ready beaming smiles. Beatrice often wore berets, while Mabel preferred a *doekie* (headscarf). At the time Mum hired Beatrice she didn't know her husband was in jail.

'What for?'

'Rape, madam.'

'Oh, lovely.'

Years later, after her husband was released from jail, Beatrice would be stabbed to death by him after he found her in bed with a lover.

In the servants quarters, I was fascinated by their sleeping arrangements: both had their steel bed frames propped up a few inches off the floor with bricks and tin cans. Why, I asked. 'The *tokoloshe*,' they explained. Some local belief that this little bad guy stalked bedrooms to frighten or even attack those he could reach up to.

Our dogs loved the new house, because they had acres and acres of space. Actually unlimited because there were no fences anywhere. Just beautiful rolling fields of sugar cane. Green gold.

Mum set to work landscaping, and miraculously in the fertile tropical climate, we soon had acres of landscaped lawns and flower beds, hibiscus trees, plus a turquoise jade vine growing on the pergola outside the dining room. This seemed to attract really gaudy yellow/red/blue grasshoppers called pyrgomorphids (but we called them totoviaans). There were also plenty of yellow slugs attracted to it, climbing up the wall. My favourite trick was to get some salt and pour it on them, and watch them liquify in front of your very eyes, dripping down the wall.

Silkworms were a popular fad. You could find them in mulberry trees, which grew everywhere. You simply grabbed some fresh leaves off the tree, popped them in a shoebox, poked some holes in the lid, and you were in business, literally, because you could on-sell worms to your classmates. It was endlessly fascinating to watch them eat the leaves, poop tiny black cannonballs, growing rapidly, until one day you'd find them huddled in a corner, spinning a cocoon of fine yellow silk. They'd be completely covered over. And then two weeks later, a white moth would emerge. Fun fact: the moths don't have a mouth. They only have a few days in which to breed and lay eggs, then they die. Talk about a narrow job description! Then the worms hatch from the eggs.

Swallows also appeared, building elaborate mud nests under cover of the eaves and verandah. They would appear for a few months, then migrate to the other side of the world, then magically reappear for summer again.

The vivid red hibiscus were fun to play with: we had an elaborate story-game where you pulled the flower off the tree (I'm sure Mum would've been thrilled), and it was something about the Queen going to the toilet. First you snapped off the golden crown of the flower. Then you disrobed the queen by peeling off the petals, leaving just the stem, which you gave a squeeze to, and out popped a little white thing — the pistil, part of its reproductive system. *PLOP*! Much hilarity for those who'd never seen it before.

Of course, in went a veggie patch. And grove of banana and papaya trees. Passionfruit vines grew wild everywhere, and blackberry bushes came alive with their purple fruit in the clearing behind.

All fruit and veggies, especially that bought from the market, was washed in a big bowl of Condy's Crystals because it was the purple promise of safety. It stripped all the chemical nasties and bacteria after its questionable supply chain journey.

At the back were a few big established trees. We eyed one up for a treehouse. Dad got busy — God knows how he hauled all the wood up there, a good 20 or so feet in the air — but before long we had our own little Boys' Own headquarters, a platform reached by a ladder.

Apart from the treehouse, Dad later built us a very cool 'man cave'. Having gotten over the trauma of the Wendy house in Arbor Acres, he ordered in a load of beautiful pine wood and we set about building this hut, big enough for several kids to sleep in. When it was completed, I set up a plastic sheet at the entrance to stop the wind and rain, fixed on the roof with a few bricks to hold it down. First time we used it, I pushed the plastic sheet aside to get in, and *DONK*! I copped a full-sized house brick on the noggin for my troubles.

We took to kite flying, creating small kites from bamboo struts and brown craft paper. We attached these to fishing rods, and up they went. Up, up, up until you could barely see them as a speck in the distance, with several rolls of fishing line under full strain.

We also found that the sloping grass banks down to the bottom of the garden were perfect for rolling down, inside of car tyres. A great way to break your neck, which we never quite achieved.

We all had a bike, and could and would ride as far as the eye could see. And further sometimes. The stables were a popular stop-off, in a little company enclave of houses and workshops a few kilometres away. Here we would pat the company horses, and sometimes catch and milk the goats for the sheer fun of it. And find a stray *panga* (machete) and cut some cane. All the dirt roads were littered with the bleached-white pulp, the fibrous stuff you'd spit out once you'd sucked all the juice out of the cane. Groups of African workers (mostly Pondos from the Transkei) would shuffle along the roads, their food and drink canteens dangling and jangling from their belts, *panga* in one hand, and stick of cane in the other. Laughing, joking, spitting out cane pulp.

Many days we'd just stop and sit in the guava trees that lined the road past our house to the chicken farm. Sit on a branch and just gorge ourselves on guavas. Unlike our settler ancestors we were at no risk of suffering scurvy.

Dad had a killer Hornby train set which he mounted on a large plywood base in the garage, and we raced the Pullman and little green steam engine through the English countryside setting, red-lining them for such long durations that transformer boxes often spontaneously combusted.

Amid all these fun and games, we were actually going to school. Each morning a little Toyota *bakkie* (utility vehicle) with a canvas-covered tray at the back would arrive at the bottom of our long drive to take us to school. And now we meet one of my childhood heroes — Louis. He was a big, strong, good-looking African, with a great smile, and a sense of humour that really engaged us kids.

We talked about movies, because every day we drove past the cinema at Tongaat which had big lettering out the front such as *Midnight Cowboy*, with Dustin Hoffman, and often a rudimentary hand-painted poster. *The Cross and the Switchblade* was also a huge movie around this time, the compelling story of Nicky Cruz (played by Erik Estrada of CHIPS fame) and the violent Mau Mau gangs in New York being tamed by a preacher.

American culture in the form of stuntman Evil Knievel was also front and centre. He captured our imaginations with his All-America get up and his bikes, such as the steam-powered 'Skycycle' rocket. Ironically he made his name with epic fails at Caesars Palace and Snake River, and had more broken bones in his body than unbroken ones.

We talked about Cassius Clay (whom Louis strongly resembled) who was now making a comeback as Mohamed Ali, and the upcoming fights with Joe Frazier and George Foreman were headline news. We also talked about Louis Armstrong, one of Dad's favourite musicians, as he died around that time.

And Louis the Driver himself came close to meeting his maker. He was off for a few days once. And then when he returned to work, his head was all swollen and round and bruised. He'd been bashed up at the weekend, his jaw broken. It was wired shut for weeks, so he could barely whisper out the side of his mouth.

We looked up to Louis in many ways. We loved him. He was a really skilful driver, best demonstrated in the wet season, summer, November through to March.

The dusty red clay road that led past our house would turn into a sticky, sucky quagmire. Slippery as hell. The Toyota slid all over the place, but Louis kept it on the road. We may have got bogged once or twice, at which farm workers might lend their muscle to push us out, with co-ordinated rhythmic sing-shouting. They knew teamwork instinctively and music was the backbone of their lives.

Each evening the drums would start up and the singing and the chanting, coming from the compound beyond the stables. It was the soundtrack of my youth, and perhaps why Zulu music is very much deeply imprinted in me to this day.

Once we'd moved to Klipfontein we were going to church at Tongaat less, instead heading down to Gennazano, just south of Tongaat Beach. Here the congregation was largely blacks. Often we were the only white family in attendance, and everyone was in their Sunday best, literally, but it was the singing that took the service to the next level. Multi-layered harmonies that came not from choir practice, but instinctively from within. Beautiful and heartwarming, life-affirming sounds that raised the rafters with belief. Not like the half-hearted warbling that most white congregations typically muster.

Dad always had great sound systems. Now we got a hi-fi system with speakers the size of bar fridges. And a TEAC reel-to-reel player. I remember him bringing home a 45 single one time. He put it on. The song started with a rich, solo a cappella voice. With Xhosa clicks. Then a driving bass line came in for a few bars. Then the whole band jumped in. And life somehow changed. Mum and Dad danced right there in the living room, on a Sunday morning (generally we just weren't that sort of expressive family). We played it over and over. Dad showed me the label: *Qongqothwane* (*'The Click Song'*) by Miriam Makeba. What I didn't realise then was Makeba was already in political exile in the UK, and her music was banned by the SABC, and her records not distributed in South Africa. How Dad came by that recording I'm not sure.

Music was really getting on my radar. The SABC ran the Springbok Top 20 or Springbok Hit Parade each week. 'Hi there pop fans, this is David Gresham … welcome to the Springbok Radio Top 20!' Every time we drove along Berea Road in Durban where the towering radio mast and dishes were, I'd look up to see if I could spot David Gresham or the other announcers and performers up there. Strangely, I never did. This radio thing was pure black magic.

Gresham's show was sponsored by Chappies Bubblegum, which came in yellow/blue/red striped wrappers, and had trivia and fun facts often tied to music, printed inside its wrappers. Then would come the big songs of the day: *Pretty Belinda, Venus, In the Summertime,* and *Chirpie Chirp Cheep Cheep.* A very innocent time for music. But there were some edgier songs creeping in on the back of the American War in Vietnam (of which I heard nor knew nothing at the time), such as *Yellow River* and Creedence Clearwater Revival's *Have you Ever Seen the Rain*?

I read lots of comics which dealt with the Korean War and, in my over-active imagination, pictured us being invaded by the Chinese, and how I might repel them by pointing out, 'See, we're friends, because it says "vitreous china" right here on our toilet bowl.' I'm not sure it was a water-tight defence strategy.

One of the first real pop hit tunes I knew was *Burning Bridges*, the theme song from the movie *Kelly's Heroes*, starring Donald Sutherland as the loveable Oddball character, who drove a tank. Clint Eastwood also starred, and he would figure large in many of the movies in my formative years. In that movie, someone held up a sign which read 'POW' and I wondered what that meant. 'Prisoner of War,' Mum explained. I didn't realise at the time I'd one day go on to write several books about WW2 and POWs.

We watched movies at the Ballito Bay Drive-in. It was a big night out for the family, armed with picnic rugs, a basket of chips and goodies, and a thermos flask of steaming hot cocoa. We'd drive into the paved area, trying to find a good central spot to watch from. Then pull up next to one of the hundreds of little posts, from which a box-like speaker hung, joined by a large coiled cable. This would be suspended from the driver's-side window, and hopefully you got a speaker which didn't crackle and hiss and pop all the way through the show. These were really enjoyable family outings, and we saw some great movies there: *Swiss Family Robinson, Paint Your Wagon, Hello Dolly*, and one or two in the *Carry On* … series. The line about being born under a wandering star always resonated with me, and Dad could carry off Lee Marvin's deep bass with aplomb (he might've even been one octave lower than Marvin).

Carry On at Your Convenience starred English comedian Sid James, and a budgie that correctly predicted winners of horse races. Horse racing was huge in South Africa, although we weren't a gambling family (apart from that high-stakes poker-playing great-grandfather of ours!). As we now had a pet budgie in our menagerie, a blue-grey one called Georgie, we joked: Wouldn't it be funny if he knew the winners?

The next day, we pulled out the weekend race guide, and read out all the names from the main race. Georgie chirped at a couple of names, horses we'd never heard of. We laughed. How funny. How silly. How exciting. Mum went and put a couple of Rand on both of them. Well, guess what? They ran first and second, and Mum collected 38 Rand! We are made, we thought! Wild riches on tap. The next week we repeated the process. Georgie cheeped at one or two. Mum backed them. And they're still running. So that was the end of Georgie's forecasting career.

While not a big gambler, Dad enjoyed regular poker nights. One guest was Ben Gunn, a rather corpulent chap, who took a seat around the circular table, and *CRASH*! His chair splintered and there he lay sprawled inelegantly on the floor amid a pile of fractured matchwood. Roger was wildly unpopular one night, as he stood watching the poker game in progress (not really encouraged, because kids were not part of their parents' world in that generation). He snuck in behind one of the other players, and was whispering in Dad's ear 'He's got a three of clubs, a six of diamonds, a Jack of …' You could almost hear pistols being cocked under the table, as he was politely ushered from the dining room.

Back to the movies: Our recurring favourite movies were *Herbie the Love Bug* series. The little cream-coloured VW Beetle with race number 53 on it. Beetles were popular on the road at that time, as were the VW Combi vans. (They'd feature highly in our Car Cricket games).

Other times we'd watch movies at the Maidstone Club. *Tarzan* movies with Johnny Weissmuller were evergreens, never mind they were at least 20 years old by that stage. We could all relate to that rugged man of the jungle, and all secretly aspired to at least emulate his feats, if we couldn't actually be him. *Follow Me Boys* was another popular one, which played to the cub-scout morality of small-town America. Movies always started with a *Tom and Jerry* short first, and black-and-white *Movietone News* with those quaint clipped BBC accents.

The SABC was our sole source of broadcast entertainment. Some wags nicknamed it 'Some Assholes Believe this Crap', others 'Soul And Brain Crusher' and yet others 'South African Broadcasting Castration'. But it was what we had.

Sarel Marais hosted the breakfast show on Radio Port Natal. At night they ran radio dramas: *Pick a Box* (a quiz show with Bob Courtney), *Consider Your Verdict* (a court room drama in which you then played judge, jury and executioner), and *Squad Car* (a police procedural). *The Avengers* was their highest rating adaptation.

Our favourite was *Squad Car* which happened to be on Friday or Saturday nights when Mum and Dad were often out. All three of us boys would crawl into their empty bed, and tune in to the radio. 'This is *Squad Car*. They prowl the empty streets at night ...' Cue the sound of a big engine revving, tyres squealing etc. Then they'd get into some true-life crime, which would have us both riveted and scared as hell. The tension would be broken by the commercials, a jaunty Chevvy commercial singalong jingle which tapped into stereotypical white South African life: 'Braaivleis, rugby, sunny skies, and Chevrolet.' Maybe an ad for General Tyres. By the time the story ended, we'd be cowering under the sheets, wondering what time Mum and Dad would come home. Our imaginations worked overtime, thanks to the power of radio, the theatre of the mind.

Squad Car even had a board game, which I got as a present one year.

A little later, thankfully, we got a 'police boy'. Poisa, we called him, which literally means policeman. He was a short old bloke, who'd turn up just before sunset each evening, wearing his woollen cap and carrying a *knobkerrie* (a wooden club with a bulbous end). His first order of business was to have a chat with the maids, then fill up his canteen with hot tea, then position himself under the treehouse. And promptly settle in for a good night's kip.

We had burglar bars on all the openable windows, but we never fixated on security or insecurity. Besides we had Peter the dog. Zeta offered nothing in the guard-dog stakes.

One Friday night Mum was home but Dad was away on business. We were all in the living room watching the radio — because that's what we used to do before there was TV, kids. Some nights we'd play Monopoly or Cluedo. Next thing out of the darkness outside loomed a dark face, pressed up against our window. The surprise and shock! We were after all miles from our nearest neighbours. And tens of miles from a police station. Mum shouted at him: 'Buzz off! Buzz off!' Probably added some Zulu: '*Hamba khona*!' (Go away!). The face was unmoved. She gesticulated: Away, away! Still nothing. What did he want with us? Mum went off to the bedroom to get Dad's gun. We kids sat there, frozen, hearts thumping. Slowly, ever so slowly, he turned and disappeared into the gloom again. Mum reappeared with the shotgun/rifle, 'Where is he?' We pointed, indicating he'd moved off into the garden.

She peered out, saw nothing, opened the window a crack, shouting '*Hamba khona*!' She raised the gun to the window sill, the barrel waving all over the show she was so nervous. She could not have hit the side of a barn! But thankfully, the mystery visitor sidled off into the night. And Poisa peacefully slept through it all.

But Poisa was in the thick of the action one time when we were all away for the weekend. We returned home on the Sunday to find he and Mabel in a very excited state. Poisa's hand was bandaged, as was Mabel's shoulder. Someone, I believe Mabel's boyfriend or would-be suitor, had turned up drunk one night to our house. Entreaties for him to leave had escalated, at which he pulled out his knife and lunged at Mabel. She turned away and Poisa thrust his hand out to protect her, the knife going through his hand and into her shoulder, narrowly missing important bits. She was patched up but still shaken.

One telling incident was Mum coming home one day, with Mabel sitting on the sofa reading us a story. As soon as Mum came in, Mabel darted down and sat on the floor. 'I knew it was not the done thing,' Mum would tell me later. 'Certainly not acceptable to many of my friends. But I said nothing and she moved and sat on the floor anyway. We were both seeing it from the other's point of view. To me that full gap of apartheid behaviour was never the right thing.'

Mabel sadly left us some time after, to be replaced by Lakshmi. Lakshmi was Indian who looked after us very caringly, and gave us some exposure to the exotic Indian culture with her gold nose rings, wailing pitch-bending Indian music, and — when she was going out on Sundays — saris in rich purples, yellows, and golds. But her biggest hits were the savoury samosas, and *koeksisters* she'd fry up around Diwali time. *Koeksisters* are deep-fried plaited pastries that are immediately dipped into cold sugar-syrup. A dietician's nightmare, but paradise for hungry young boys. We ate our body-weight in these, willing to convert to Hinduism. It was only recently I learned these were not Indian at all, rather an Afrikaner recipe as the name suggests.

The musical tapestry was rich: around Tongaat, high-pitched ululations and sitars dominated the soundscape emanating from the tailor shops and markets. Around Maidstone it was more the *masqanda* style of Mahlatini and the Mahotella Queens. And always the boom-boom-boom of drums coming from the cane-cutters' quarters at sunset.

One end-of-year school party with Kit Veitch, we pushed back the chairs and tables, and danced with abandon to *Sweet Caroline.* And on our radio at home songs like Lynn Anderson's *(I Beg Your Pardon) I Never Promised You a Rose Garden*, and Mungo Jerry's *The Pushbike Song* dominated. But Jimmy Osmond's *Long Haired Lover from Liverpool* seemed to capture the zeitgeist best. Long hair was making an entry, and fashions began changing. I think the first person I knew with longish hair was Bernie Ryall — who drove a pale green VW Beetle and was an extra in *Zulu* — and his cute sister Belinda was in my class. The big hit *Pretty Belinda* did nothing to quell my crush on her.

Pink hot pants were everywhere (but thankfully not on the big and bulky Bernie) leaving very little to over-active imaginations. And peace signs began popping up here and there: One library book I borrowed had 'Make Love Not War' penned inside it. I had no idea what that meant. But the hippy-era had arrived, which no doubt would've alarmed the rather conservative authorities. And my parents (the ultimate conservative authorities!).

Meantime, I was committing fashion crimes of my own. Or rather I was complicit in them, because Mum did the actual decision making and purchasing. The worst perhaps was at my first Holy Communion, after a few Sunday school classes with the bespectacled Mrs Pascale. For the big day at Tongaat Church, everyone was in virginal white outfits. And here comes Stuart in a mustard safari suit. *Mustard*! And not a subdued Dijon mustard colour, we're talking French's Yellow Mustard. I think I wore that only once.

One of the funny asides to that, we were sitting in a circle with Mrs Pascale one session, and she was asking if there was anyone that Father Duffy, the Irish priest, could pray for. Yes, I said: 'My father is going in for an operation.' Now I think I might've oversold it in order to get a prayer for Dad mentioned: he was going for a knee cartilage operation, but how it came across in the church service was more like he was going for a double amputation. I do remember clinging to his leg in the lounge room, crying, because I did genuinely believe they were going to chop his leg off.

He'd crocked it playing golf (on top of all the rugby he'd played earlier in life). It was a huge soccer-ball swelling that caused him major pain. He went to every kind of specialist and quack. His last resort was a blind naturopath, who said, essentially, stop drinking coffee. And that did the trick in terms of reducing the swelling and pain. But the operation was unavoidable.

Around this time, Mum got a phone call at home, someone organising a cricket match, and would Buster like to play? 'No,' said Mum, uttering a wonderful spoonerism: 'He can't at the moment because he's got a nonky wee!' Silence at the other end of the line. Mum could hardly compose herself at the gaffe: 'Er, wonky knee.'

Dad was a frustrated doctor in his own way, with a great understanding of the human body. One anecdote reflects his dry humour: 'You can't cure a cold. So if you get a cold, stand in the rain, then you will get pneumonia. You can cure pneumonia.'

We were busy with swimming lessons. Terry Gulliver was our swimming coach, an Aussie who drove a bright yellow and green VW Kombi. It seemed most of the village was learning to swim with him, and then a Friday night competition started. Glendon was a strong swimmer, and Rog would become a good swimmer. But I was more in the submarine class. Wrong bone density, I guess?

Perhaps as a result of my non-progress, Terry returned to the Gold Coast in Australia, where he set up (and is still involved in) a swim school that boasts several national champions, and techniques for teaching babies to swim that have been adopted internationally. Perhaps it's time I went back for a refresher.

We took up sailing around this time, at the company's WeWe Dam, just outside Maidstone village on the road past the Fairbreeze Hotel, with its prominent signage for Mainstay Cane Spirits. We took to the water in a little green bathtub-like dinghy. It was probably an Optimist, but it was hard to be optimistic because this thing used to take on half the dam's water with the net result we were half-submerged and making next to zero headway, struggling to make it back to shore before it got dark.

Even with our generous handicap, we'd usually win a prize like a bailing bucket for finishing stone last.

Sailing and waterskiing became really popular, and it was a wonderful social setup, with a small clubhouse, colourful pennants flying atop its mast. On the banks of the dam, picnic blankets would be set up, *braais* would be blazing, and beers would be flowing. Golden days.

There were yacht races. Power boat races. Ski races. Even greasy pole contests, in which contestants try and wrestle each other off a horizontal highly lubricated telephone pole into the water.

Soon, everyone who was anyone in the Tongaat area had some kind of boat or was there with someone who had one.

Brian Bentley sailed a Laser and a Paper Tiger, which we envied. His father John had a Hamilton Jet boat, which could spin on its own axis, and travel in super-shallow water. Alan Hankinson had *In Full Flight*, an aerodynamic boat which went like the clappers. Local scuttlebutt often had it that 'he was on' with Margaret Rycroft, the matron at the hospital. Thanks Peter God built his own ski boat called *Ricci*, which he steered around with a nautical captain's peaked cap on his head. Then we got a little motorboat called *Daisy* and learned to ski.

That was magic, because we'd go down early in the morning, passing the smartly uniformed *poisa* at the dam gate, who'd snap off an equally smart salute, and as the dam would come into sight, Dad would declare, 'Millpond!' Sure enough, in the still of the morning the water would be smooth as glass. Perfect for skiing. We'd ski for a few hours. Then the wind would get up. We'd pull the ski boat out of the water and rig up the sailing dinghy and enjoy the windy conditions. Then late afternoon, millpond again, so finish off with a few more laps of skiing until the sun went down around 7pm in summer.

Brad de Riquebourg became really passionate about his skiing, competing seriously further afield in South Africa. And introduced us to barefoot skiing and ramps. A couple of decent ramps had now been installed in the dam.

The de Riquebourgs also featured heavily in another annual event, a go-kart race down Tongaat Hill (behind the David Whitehead & Sons factory). The long and winding road, layered in teeth-grinding bumpy gravel, undid all but the hardiest of contenders and karts. Chassis would snap, wheels would be off, karts would be off into the cane. But the De Riq's always fronted with something far more robust than everyone else, with big pneumatic tyres, and manic grins on their faces.

Now it's probably a good thing that this was the days before video cameras, because — whether it was skiing or karting — there were some wipeouts and face-plants that were world-class. But worse than thudding into the water at full-speed, legs and limbs flailing akimbo, was waiting for the boat to circle round to pick you up. Because the dam was home to a very fine colony of leguaans … that'd be Nile monitor lizards to you; four or five feet of muscular grey reptile swimming next you, flicking its forked tongue like a snake.

'C'mon, hurry up, Dad!' I'd gurgle, lifejacket riding up around my neck. 'C'mon!'

One time Glendon and I were skiing two-up, which was always fun, because you could introduce a bit of synchronisation, such as swapping positions from left to right, crossing under each other's tow ropes. Sometimes we'd get tangled up, or hit the boat's wake too hard, and into the drink you'd go. The rule was if one fell off, the other had to drop off, so we could both be collected together and take off again.

One day Glendon and I were flying along. Suddenly he went down sharply, as though shot by a sniper. I dropped off, waiting for Dad to circle round. And waited. And waited. I cast my eyes around for leguaans. Of course, every stick in the water looked like one. So far none. Good. But then I looked back to where the boat was. Why the hell was he taking so long with Glendon? 'C'mon Dad!' Still, he was hovering some distance away, then I see him hauling Glendon back on board. Huh? Eventually they pulled up next to me in the water.

'Get in!' Dad shouted.

'But I want to ski some more …'

'Get in, quickly!'

And that's when I saw Glendon lying across the back of the boat, covered in blood. The keel of the ski had come down and cracked him across the top of his skull, causing a nasty gash. An open head wound with dirty dam water pouring into it — what could possibly go wrong, other than bilharzia, giardiasis, cryptosporidiosis, typhoid, E.coli, leptospirosis, and whole lot of other nasties that I can't spell, which are commonly found in Natal's waterways. In short: this was not good.

We whizzed Glendon up to the Tongaat Hospital, where Dr Willie Mukhuiber was the doctor. I sat outside in near panic. Soon they emerged. Glendon was alive with his crown shaven to make way for a latticed network of sutures.

The wipeouts kept piling up. One day, John Bentley asked if I'd like to ski behind his jet boat. 'Yes, sure, I'd love to!' I suited up, awaiting my tow. He gave me the thumbs up request: Ready? I gave the thumbs up response. With that came the mighty roar of a V8 engine mixed with the roaring hiss of jets expelling water under high-pressure. My arms were almost jolted out of my sockets. But I was up and running. Damn this was so fast I was barely touching the water surface. Skimming rather than skiing. At the first turn I whipped across so fast I swear I heard the 'crack' of Mach 1 as I broke the sound barrier. Geez, maybe this is too fast? I tried to free one hand from the tow bar to give a 'slow down' hand signal. He acknowledged it, and next thing the roar grew louder as he floored it. Hoooooooly shit! And then my world became a tumble of sky-water-sky-water-sky-water-water-more water-cough-choke-splutter-water. John circled around to get tow me again.

I reached down to count my limbs. All present. 'Uh … I think that's enough.' I gurgled, surrendering all pride and dignity for self-preservation.

Another time, when I was finishing off a run behind Dad's boat, I whipped off across the wake to make an impressive finish, where you gracefully glide in, and then gradually sink down into the water just near the beaching spot. But this time I carried a bit too much speed into the finish … and saw the land approaching very quickly, too quickly, still coming at me quickly. There was a lip of earth, a bank perhaps 6-12 inches high on the edge of the dam. Too fast and late to stop, I went careening straight into it. Eyes closed, sphincter braced for impact. To my surprise, I cleared it, and kept going along on the grass for a good five or ten metres before coming to a stop. Still standing, still alive, and held my hands aloft, in my best Olympian gymnastic 'Tadaah!' dismount pose. A smattering of applause — mainly relief I'd say — rose up from those lucky enough to witness my narrow survival.

One time when cousin Wendy was visiting us from Rhodesia, we took her out on the boat, and she was watching us do our thing. She was keen to have a ski, so Dad told her to put on a lifejacket and jump in. She proceeded to stand up on the side of the boat and dived in headfirst … only to find that the dam in that part was only about one metre deep, and she re-emerged with a face full of mud, weeds, and assorted muck from the bottom of the dam.

Later we upgraded the ski boat to a faster one called *Ghoti*. We scratched our heads at the name until Dad explained it was based on George Bernard Shaw's spelling of 'fish': 'Gh' as in rou*gh*, 'o' as in w*o*men, and 'ti' as in ra*ti*on. F.I.S.H.

The dam was later renamed the Dudley Pringle Dam, in honour of Dudley who was a farmer further up towards Compensation. His wife Rosemary, who was a very gracious lady, had an amazing story. She'd lost her wedding ring and was distraught. She imagined it lost or stolen, gone forever. In desperation she visited a fortune teller. He mumbled something about a rose garden. 'Do you have a rose garden?' he asked her. Yes, the keen gardener did. 'It is there, I see it lying in the grass next the rose garden.' She drove home, went straight out to the large rose garden and there, glittering in the sun, was her diamond ring!

Roses featured in our garden too, which was coming along beautifully, with carefully landscaped rockeries, and slate-lined flower beds. And then came the fateful day Dad arrived home from the farm with this tiny week-old Merino lamb, which had been neglected by its mother. We fell in love with this wretched ball of fluff with its white coat and black head, and long tail (which had been left on because it was too weak to be docked like the others in the herd).

We named it Lamby, originally enough, and enjoyed feeding it baby bottles of warm milk. On about day two or three, there was a heck of a thunderstorm. Lightning crashing, absolute downpour. And no sign of Lamby. We looked everywhere in the house and garage, nothing. Panic. Mum and Dad and Poisa all grabbed torches and headed off into the storm outside, while we added our pleading yelps of 'Lamby! Lamby!' from inside. After a while down at the bottom of the garden, Mum saw something moving. It was Peter, our Alsatian-cross, carrying Lamby in his jaws. She negotiated gently with the dog to give up its prospective feast, which he did. She snatched it up in her arms, and raced back to the house, Peter on her heels showing intense interest.

We nursed it back to strength and the dogs got used to it. More than that, Lamby got fully imprinted into thinking it was a dog. He moved in their pack. Ran with them, ate with them, slept with them. It was cute to see them all asleep together in the sun, Lamby chewing his grass cud. And he was getting bigger now, and developing stumpy horns, which he was happy to show off at short notice, and we were all the subjects of head-butts from him.

He also grew very fond of eating anything and everything in the garden. Mum's prize spring blooms were all mown down by the marauding mutton's mandibles. She was so annoyed she got a rope and a wooden stake, and everyday Lamby would be assigned a different area of lawn to graze on, with the stake driven into the centre of it, giving him about a 20-metre radius to roam and eat. At the end of each day we'd see him tightly up against the stake, having wound himself around and around and around until he'd run out of rope. Smart, he was not.

Klipfontein was the scene of many great extended family Christmases. The magic of Christmas kicked off when Mum would bring out the nativity set, and we'd all 'help' her set it up. It invoked such wonder in us. Then June Clarkson's Christmas card would arrive in the mail, always hand-made by our brilliantly talented friend and artist, and every year unique. Hundreds of cards from friends far and wide would be strung up in the lounge room.

The pool was always the centrepiece for hanging out, with its slate surrounds and tiled wall of fountains.

Even visiting priest Father Duffy would come round for a swim sometimes. But one afternoon put the fear of God into Mum. Her friend Judy Nye had come round for some tea, and they were having a wonderful chit-chat. At some point Mum said, 'Oh, where's Christopher?' referring to Judy's young son, perhaps only three years old at that time.

They called out inside the house. Nothing. Went out into the garden and called. Nothing. Mum looked down at the slope, but no one was in the pool. Until she took a few steps further down and saw this small figure on the bottom of the pool. She dived in fully clothed, and retrieved this body, blue in the face, and he soon vomited all this water out, started coughing and spluttering, and was back in the land of the living.

A funny thing about the pool. Several months after it went in, a huge storm came through and the pressure from the underground water table popped the whole pool up out of the ground. It looked like the *Titanic* with the deep end lifted into the air. There was a crack running along the middle of it, but somehow it was all repaired and sorted like it had never happened.

Meanwhile in Rhodesia, cousin Ian Towel had become Ian Daniel following Dot's re-marriage to Shaun Daniel, and because there were now five young mouths to be fed in the household, he was wearing second-hand school shoes 'at least three sizes too big for my feet, with a fancy woven leather top to them, much to the amusement of my classmates' when he moved to Gwelo and started at Thornhill High School.

It was a childhood of considerable freedom, with weekends full of adventure: 'Mum had only one rule ... don't be late for school on Monday.' Sometimes he'd go hiking, other times even thumb a lift to Salisbury.

At 17 Ian finished school. 'I wasn't a crap student,' he says, 'I was an idle student.' With 28 per cent for maths, that was clearly not as interesting to him as rugby and weightlifting. 'I did art. And the poor art teacher must have been the most frustrated woman ever because for two years I had one painting which I never finished.'

He went off and joined the British South Africa Police cadets, meeting the physical requirements easily, and satisfying the minimum need for O Levels English. There were a couple of other 17-year-old cadets at the Salisbury Depot. 'On your 18th birthday you were called out from the squad in the morning parade and told to march yourself down to the HQ building. There you reaffirmed that you wished to continue in the force, took the oath, signed on, then marched yourself back. Prior to marching up the road you had a cadet number and when you came back you had a patrol officer number.' Salary: around R$123 per month.

It was drummed into him that as a policeman you were part of the community. The language to be used was English, because — unless you were qualified in Shona or other languages — your versions and statements could be easily challenged in court. Interpreters were always to be used.

His instructors were generally British migrants with war and/or police experience. No Rhodesian-born men had made it to officer-level in the police yet (that'd take a few more years). As it happened there was one former London Metro police officer, around 30, who left the force after his initial three-year stint, and was driving to Johannesburg when his car broke down. He started walking to the nearest phone box, when a truck went past, a box fell off the back of it, and killed him on the spot. 'If it's your day, it's your day,' says Ian, who quickly adopted a fatalistic attitude. 'I'm not going to be able to change anything.'

He fell on his feet. 'After grooming the horses on some days, we were taken to the riding school. By the time we passed out, we were going on regular morning rides into the countryside, over the hills into the Botanical Gardens, and had a lot of fun with the horses sliding on their bums down the sides of the hills. Great days.'

Instruction on weightlifting and assessments for physical strength were done at the depot gym. He once went to the University of Rhodesia gym with two of his instructors who were serious weightlifters. Despite his very slight build they were impressed with his strength, encouraging him to strive for competition-level weightlifting.

One of the Drill Sergeants was his gym instructor. Ian remembers one parade inspection with a woman warrant officer on parade.

Drill Sergeant: 'WO, are you wearing knickers?"

'Sir, yes, sir!' she replied.

'Then why is there dandruff on your shoes?'

It was all the whole squad could do to avoid cracking up laughing.

Soon after, Patrol Officer Daniel was ready for his first station assignment. His instructors came to him: 'You've asked to go to a country district station.' they said. 'We'll get you into the gym and keep you in town.' was their scheming proposal.

'No thanks, I don't want to stay in town, I want to go to the bush,' replied Ian, upsetting them.

Even though he was raised in the town, he preferred bush life. 'As kids we'd go to the farm in Gwelo every week.' Cattle dipping was done weekly, casting and dehorning once a year as needed, with irons heated on coals used for branding and dehorning. 'Very fulfilling days with lots of laughter and joking around with the farm labourers and us, with the mishaps that happened. It was great running around the paddock, grabbing a cow, and throwing it on the ground, the cow shit squeezing up between your toes as you did it. Absolute fun!'

And so he headed to his first bush posting at Gutu, a tribal area in the high veldt, 260km south-east of Salisbury.

'At 18 years of age, I was investigating murders and shit,' Ian says. 'I remember my first murder. I was on call at 8 o'clock at night, and the phone rang, someone saying a murder's been reported. I had no idea what to do.'

He rang his boss. 'He said, "You get hold of Sergeant Major Muginiwa and take him with you".' Muginiwa directed him on what to do, and they headed out to this *kraal* in the middle of nowhere, arriving in the early hours of the morning.

'Found the dead guy, put him in the body box.' Rounded up witnesses, got statements. Who stabbed who? What did he stab him with?

'Well, where's the knife?' Ian asked.

'Granny's got it.'

'Granny?'

They were led across to an elderly lady, clearly traumatised but also clearly suffering dementia — she'd hidden the knife for safekeeping but could not remember where she'd hidden it.

'We spent about four hours, sun's come up, it's getting a bit warm, everybody's searching, still can't find the knife. We eventually found it stashed in a little food store inside a hut.'

That was the easy stuff compared to other cases, he reckons. 'I had a missing person reported. And then he was found drowned in the river. And we went to get him, and his body was waterlogged. And I never knew, but you touch a body like that, and all the outer layer of skin comes off and sticks to you.' They got the body out of the river, all covered in sticky skin. 'And he was so waterlogged we literally draped him over a bush to drain.'

They then got statements, put the body in the metal box, put it on top of the Land Rover. 'Driving back, he was still draining, and every time we went down a slight hill all his body fluid and water would come floating over the windscreen, and we had to turn the windscreen wipers on to keep going.'

Did he become hardened? 'I don't recall ever being afraid or put off in any way against dead bodies and handling murders and suicides, and whatever else rolled along. There were no fears or phobias. There was no apprehension, there was nothing to get over — it was just life ... and death. It was just part of the job.'

Before he knew it, he'd spent two years in the bush of Gutu.

Then, a couple of fateful meetings in bars.

On ordinary patrols they'd normally stay out in a local district commissioner's house, which were dotted around the countryside. Ian drove back a couple of kilometres to a bottle shop in the local township. 'It couldn't have been more than about two metres wide by a couple of metres deep. Beautiful ice-cold beer. I bought a few beers and was standing there, and the black guy sitting at the bar turns around and says, "You speak Shona?" No, I don't sorry.'

They got into a very lengthy and wide-ranging conversation over many beers. 'He was a smart guy, and we spoke about everything from playing chess to the French Renaissance.'

Turns out he was based in France. Towards the end of the evening, he introduced himself.

'Leo Mugabe,' the man said.

'Oh, that's a very prominent name,' Ian said.

'He's my uncle.'

After more friendly conversation, they parted and went off separately into the night. 'I had no issue with him,' says Ian.

'It turned out that Leo was actually one of the Nationalists I was supposed to check on if he was in the country,' Ian tells me of the man that the best intelligence seemed to indicate had left the country. He followed up by submitting a report saying he'd chatted with him in-person in that bar: he's back in-country.

Robert Mugabe was Jesuit-educated and studied at Fort Hare University in South Africa, where'd he'd been exposed to Pan-African ideas and early nationalist thinking. After graduating he'd gone teaching in Ghana, Northern Rhodesia (now Zambia), and Southern Rhodesia. On his return home he joined Joshua Nkomo's National Democratic Party (NDP), emerging as an organiser and speaker of note.

The NDP was banned, and Nkomo formed its successor, the Zimbabwe African People's Union. Mugabe was at odds with Nkomo's perceived moderation and co-operation with white liberals, and so it was that by the end of 1962 the British South Africa Police (BSAP) had listed Mugabe as an 'intellectual subversive 'and he was being monitored.

When the rift with Nkomo came to a head the following year Mugabe broke away to form the Zimbabwe African National Union, with a decidedly more Marxist and militant stance. Special Branch flagged him now as 'a dangerous and articulate propagandist'.

When he started espousing violent resistance and overthrow of the white minority in 1964, the police stepped in, arresting him and detaining him under the Emergency Powers regulations. He'd officially crossed the line and become a 'problem element' to the Rhodesian government. He would spend the next 11 years behind bars.

And bars was often where you'd find Ian when he was off duty, having concluded his posting at Gutu. One night he met a policeman who was stationed in Vila Salazar — on the railway line near the junction of the Mozambique, Rhodesia, South African borders.

Turned out he was looking for a replacement and had not found anyone yet: 'Vila Salazar at that time was a dead-end post,' says Ian, who volunteered for it anyway, and was one of only two white senior officers there when he arrived in March 1975.

The modest station was the only building on the Rhodesian side, isolated in the Gonarezhou National Park. A few kilometres away was a recently closed detention centre for nationalists apprehended under Emergency powers. Long-term inmates had included that man Mugabe and Joshua Nkomo, both released in 1974 after pressure from the South African government following FRELIMO's takeover.

FRELIMO, the Mozambique Liberation Front under Samora Machel, led the nationalist struggle that culminated in Mozambican independence following Portugal's 1974 revolution. The detention centre was closed with 24 hours' notice soon afterwards, although tensions in the region remained palpable.

A little to the south-east was Crook's Corner. 'It was called Crook's Corner because crooks used to move the border post depending on which police were coming looking for them ... never a dull moment, ' laughs Ian, whose typical call-outs included assaults (one guy slit from ear to chin), and cross-border cattle-rustling.

'For me Vila Salazar was a fantastic posting because I was there six or eight months and I was out game viewing in the government Land Rover.' Marauding lions, herds of 500-plus buffalo, and bull elephants provided wonderful distractions. 'Fishing, and having a ball, and they called it work. I loved the posting.' Perhaps apart from the time their Land Rover bogged more than halfway across the dried-up Nuanetsi River. Totally stuck. In Mozambique territory. 'We did not want to be there if a patrol came along.' So he slogged off about 6km to a road workers' camp. They had a good time around the campfire that night, and next morning returned to the scene with a bulldozer, checking for fresh tracks. None. Opened the bonnet. 'It didn't blow up.' They were safely towed backwards into Rhodesia. 'And the boss didn't find out,' he laughs.

The train to/from Mozambique would pass through once a week, and Ian would jump on at the border, about 65km away, with the customs and immigration guys. Often, they'd grab a roast chicken over the border at Chico's bar, then they'd ride the train back to Vila Salazar, 'drinking and misbehaving', then get off and wander back to the police base.

The pranks continued when a junior troop arrived at the station. Senior colleagues convinced — 'and he needed a lot of convincing' — this gullible young policeman that part of his duties was to masturbate the station's dog, which was kept in a cage and never had contact with the outside world, weekly. This he did, coming inside to report his success. 'At which everyone killed themselves laughing. Policemen can be very cruel sometimes. When you're bored in the bush, you create stuff.'

The social hub was the Gona Stagga Inn, a pub built by locals, mainly police. The punters were generally from Customs, Support Unit, Tsetse Fly Department, and Police. 'To get enough ceiling height for the dart board, they actually dug a ramp downwards,' laughs Ian. Behind the bar was a propellor from a Red Cross flight which had crashed on the airstrip nearby. Charlie Pride's *Greatest Hits* was always on high rotation, and card games like 'black bitch' (referring to the queen of spades) were always popular.

Often ladies from Malvernia were brought in for socials. Mostly they were school-going daughters of Rhodesian Railways workers stationed on that side of the Mozambique border. One night, with a dance party in full swing, an officer mischievously grabbed his FN and fired off an entire magazine on automatic, with an almighty racket. Only one officer did the right thing and hit the ground. The rest were too pissed to care and laughed it off with wry amusement.

One evening they were enjoying a social gathering on the riverbank, and someone had flown some nurses in from Fort Victoria. The plan was to spend the night sleeping out under the stars. One guy paired off with a nurse whom he was interested in, perhaps not fully reciprocal, and they disappeared off into the night. Soon they heard her voice: 'No, Jesus wouldn't like it! Jesus wouldn't like it! Jesus wouldn't like it!' Then a male voice: 'Well, Jesus is not getting it!'

Soon after, a big modern building replaced the old police station, replete with new pub. 'They made us pull the old pub down, a sad day.'

Another time, Ian had made a trip to Fort Victoria and was coming back in his Land Rover. He stopped off at the Rhino Hotel for a beer. There were a couple of tourists there — 'Swiss or Swedish' — and Ian got chatting with them. 'After a few beers, common sense went out the window, and I said come and spend the night with us at Vila Salazar. It was great for them — we saw some cheetah in the headlights on the road on the way back. 'A good party was had but the next morning Ian was called onto the mat by his boss.

'What the hell do you think you're doing?' the officer berated him.

'Um, look, they're visitors,' Ian stammered.

'You don't bring bloody strangers here! We've got border tensions!'

'Yes, sir.'

The next morning the tourists wandered down to the border post with their cameras, happily snapping off some photos. 'And FRELIMO objected,' says Ian a tad sheepishly. Luckily the objection was only verbal this time.

'Strangely big, fat, jovial Peter, the mess cook, lived in Mozambique. Every morning he would walk back to Mozambique, and every afternoon he'd walk back to us, then in the evening before sunset, having cooked our meal, he'd walk back to Mozambique.'

So Peter passed on the message about the tourists. 'I have no doubt he was a spy of some sort,' admits Ian, who says they were always cautious about their conversations in the mess when he was present, but much freer in the evenings when he'd clocked off. 'His one redeeming factor was that he made an amazing impala venison roast.'

Soon, locked boom gates were put in place at the border. After Ian left this posting, FRELIMO would show their ongoing affection by lobbing rockets onto the new police station building, which proved a sitting duck. Rhodesia moved artillery units into the area. Streams of refugees also began pouring into Rhodesia from Mozambique.

With these regional conflicts deepening, and South Africa increasingly engaged, national service in South Africa was extended to 12 months.

We used to love visiting Gran and Grandpa Seymour's place in Westville. They had a huge garden to explore, with a massive African tulip or flamboyant tree in the back yard which was so laden with bright orange flowers it looked like it was ablaze. Gran would entertain us with a music box, or a little plastic smoking monkey — she'd light little straw-like cigarettes and this thing would blow smoke rings. She also had these little plastic terriers that were a promo giveaway from Black and White Scotch Whisky. And a bottle of Cinzano was always a staple in her bar cabinet.

Later we gave Gran a present … a real poodle named Suzy. It grew into this huge hyperactive ball of fluff, which would bowl Gran over, and jump on her playfully, ripping her forearms to pieces. Poor old Gran was a patchwork of plasters as a result.

Memorable lunch parties and Christmas gatherings were had on their verandah, overlooking their wonderfully landscaped rockeries, with the whole extended Seymour clan in attendance.

Granny Rose Tait was living there at this time. She lay in her room with the curtains drawn against the heat and light outside, and always had a very kindly smile for us. We'd make a bee line for her room because, after a sufficient amount of chat, she'd reach for her bedside drawer, grab an envelope and peel off a Rand or two each for us. Wild riches!

Roger Seymour was living there too, now that he was back from his UK and European travels. He came back with a longish mane of shaggy hair and a bushy moustache, very un-accountant like. The world was loosening up in that hippy era, but it was promptly shaved off before the next family get-together. He had a bizarre story of how he was supposed to meet cousin Patricia Philips who was working in an admin/secretarial role at a USA military establishment in Wiesbaden, Germany. 'But bizarrely the authorities said she had passed away from a brain tumour three weeks before I arrived!'

Roger's room was at the end of the house. One evening, despite the burglar bars on the window, some thieves had managed to literally fish his clothes from out of his room using a pole with fishing hooks on the end. One afternoon he was practicing his golf on the front lawn, and I walked across in front of him. He drilled this ball and smacked me square on the temple. Fortunately, it was only one of those light plastic practice balls, but to this day I'm not sure if he meant to do it or not.

■ ■ ■

For my eighth birthday, I woke to find a beautiful wooden upright piano in the study. A brass inlay declared it was made by Grotrian Steinway, the brother of the iconic piano manufacturer. I fell in love with the instrument immediately, and with that grew a love of music composition that lasts to this day. After I mastered *Three Blind Mice*, I figured I was ready for Carnegie Hall.

Mum found a piano teacher in Maidstone, Betsy McPhee. Glendon and I went for lessons in their home, near the Maidstone Club. She was a stickler for flat, smooth hand movements. Anything more pronounced and she'd declare you 'porcupine fingers' and a wooden ruler would smack down on the offending digits. A further degree of difficulty was introduced by the fact that she was a smoker, and would sit beside me puffing away, exhaling large clouds of blue smoke. Sometimes I could barely see the keys or the music sheet in front of me. 'Porcupine fingers!' *WHACK*!

After that Sue Brown came into the picture as the music teacher at school. Swiss by birth, and steeped in all the classics, she and husband Justin lived on a small farm near Stanger and were family friends of ours (with three kids around our age). Her choir lessons were always enjoyable, and she had us singing in rounds — *Frere Jacques* was a timeless favourite with its lyric line of 'Ding Dong Dang' — and doing lots of exciting things musically. Sue nurtured my playing, steering me towards classical pieces. We worked and worked and worked on Beethoven's *Minuet in G* until she was ready to unleash me on my unsuspecting classmates one day. She built me up with this gushing introduction, putting me forward as some kind of wunderkind, a latter-day Mozart-like prodigy.

I started to play, but the nerves were so much that what notes my eyes were seeing and what my fingers were playing bore no resemblance to any artist, living or dead. I got about eight bars in, completely tripping over myself, blushing bright red, and even welling up. She assured me it was OK to take a deep breath and start again. Which I did, this time making it all the way through the piece. Nothing like falling flat on your face in front of all your classmates!

Mind you we had a good laugh shortly afterwards when Sue asked one of the boys to tell her about Mozart. 'Mozart was born at a very young age,' he said, not entirely incorrectly.

Under Sue I made great strides because she was a fabulously inspirational player herself, as was her daughter Heidi, and very patient. Her husband Justin was a different matter altogether — he had rather large hands, with broad fingers, and asked Sue if it was OK if he could file down the black keys so his fingers could fit better. They also had a drum kit at home, which their son Nicky played. That was always fun to bash away on when we visited them. As were games of croquet on their lawn. What I didn't like was they always had pet snakes in the house, probably courtesy of eldest son Chris, who — as Dr Chris Brown — went on to establish the Directorate of Environmental Affairs in Namibia and is currently the CEO of the Namibian Chamber of Environment.

Another happy result of our friendship with the Browns was that they had an Old English Sheepdog, this massive fluffy thing. It mated with their other dog, a smaller brown dog with short hair, resulting in a large litter. They offered us a pup … but only after they had first pick. We took second pick, delighted to add Eliza to our fold. To their amusement, their pup turned out to have mainly short hair but with these random straggly tufts of long sheepdog hair everywhere.

Every year the class choirs would perform at the annual prize-giving days in the Maidstone Club. A grand stage, with red velvet curtains. And all the expectant eyes of the proud parents on you. I was to sing a solo verse one year and came down with a cracking cold a few days before the big event. The show had to go on of course, and Sue had a sneaky solution: she changed the key down a few tones for my solo, to make the range easier for my croaky throat. I'm pretty sure I sang it in the original key anyway and couldn't wait to get off stage.

Somehow after that, I was requested to sing solo at a wedding in the Maidstone church a few weeks later.

We also competed in district music eisteddfods. One night as I sat in the front row with Dad, a youngster from Stanger was playing along with his band to *Greensleeves* on an electric guitar. He was way out of tune (hey, I was a Mozart-like prodigy, I knew these things), but the twang of those strings had me mesmerised, and I would migrate across to the guitar a few years later and mis-spend much of my late-teens/early 20s playing guitar in bands.

Around 1972 Mum and Dad headed off on a trip to Europe: Austria and Spain. We were all sent off to various friends' houses to be looked after while they were away. Lamby was sadly sent back to his herd on the farm.

I was assigned to Ron and Wendy Glover, who lived up the road at Umdloti. Ron managed that section for Tongaat, and they had four sons with shockingly white bleached-blonde hair: Gavin, Wayne, Sean, and Calvin. They were a really nice family, with a large garden, some horses, papaya trees, a tennis court, and we hung out there a lot. We played toy cars on a sand track out the back, me with my pride and joy, a pine-green Jim Clarke racing car, emblazoned with #4.

Funnily, they had a little terrier called Buster, who was not allowed inside the house. One night Mum and Dad had gone there for dinner and were enjoying some pre-dinner drinks. Suddenly Wendy shouted: 'No Buster — *outside*!!!' Everyone looked at my Dad — Buster — before realising she was referring to their dog.

They had a workers compound just across the road and up the hill from their house. Quite often on a Saturday night, movies were shown. An old projector would whirr away, with large white sheets strung up for the screening. It was always cowboy movies: Roy Rogers (and Trigger), Gene Autry, Wyatt Earp, Billy the Kid. We loved the movies, and Mrs Glover made us all coloured cowboy scarves. We had the hats and holsters, too. And, of course, we would try to emulate their feats on horseback on every possible occasion. We were fully immersed in the Wild West.

Mum and Dad were away for a month but it felt like years to us. Their postcards from Seville (featuring oranges, naturally) and Austria (featuring a statue of the waltz king Johan Strauss) were read and re-read.

As much fun as it was at the Glovers, I wanted them home. Then came the big day we were all going out to meet them at the airport. 'They'll be the ones with all the big presents in their arms,' I optimistically claimed.

I'm ashamed to say that as I glimpsed them coming through the airport, I was immediately disappointed — no sign of any gifts at all. But they did have gifts in their cases … a goat-skin leather water bottle from Spain, a music box Swiss House which doubled as a barometer, and a few little games and things. Plus, a couple of oil paintings from Spain, one sepia-coloured street scene, and another rustic river scene (both adorn the walls of my living room to this day). We also hung on their exotic stories from afar, and of course there was slide night.

We loved slide nights. Dad would set up his Kodak projector, unfurl the foldaway screen, and spend all afternoon sorting the slides into the correct order, and most importantly, the correct orientation. Then we'd settle in to watch the pics from their trip. One that made us howl with laughter was one of Mum and Dad in a horse-drawn carriage, and a pigeon has perched itself squarely atop Dad's shiny pate. Mum told us of the beauty of the classical music in the streets and houses of Vienna.

Later Dad had a conference in Madrid, and Mum tagged along. 'He was great at languages,' recalled Jen, 'and within a week he was speaking to the locals in Spanish.' They then crossed the border to Germany. 'Dad said, "Over to you" because I'd studied German in school 20 years before. First meal I ordered a mixed grill-type thing, and this dish arrived with a big silver dome cover. Dad lifted it to find boiled vegetables! He went out and bought me a German dictionary the next day,' she laughs.

All of these exotic episodes embedded themselves in me; gave me an incurable wanderlust and curiosity for the wider world.

One of the most impactful books on their shelves was *Around the World in 2000 Pictures* by Milton Runyon. This doorstop volume featured black-and-white pictures from just about every country in the world. The pages I kept turning back to time and again were those from Japan. The carefully curated gardens, steppingstones over rivers, the temples with raked-sand yards, everything seemingly with a place and a purpose in the overall scheme. And of course, that squiggly but tidy writing. To this day I love Japan, to which I've travelled several times and can't get enough of. That book sits on my bookshelf.

We also had a subscription to *National Geographic*, and these magazines were absolutely entrancing to my young mind. Photos from all ends of the earth, showing pyramids and dhows on the Nile, Machu Picchu and ancient Inca culture, eskimos (who, it turned out didn't invent the Eskimo Pie), lost tribes from Papua and New Guinea, and so on. What a wonderful world we lived in! And it was possibly the only publication in the conservative climate of South African media where you could see topless women, albeit they were hill tribe grandmothers from the Golden Triangle (a place I'd one day live near).

Not all our reading was highbrow. We had subscriptions to English magazines such as *Beano* and *Dandy*. This introduced us to the world of colourful characters such as Dennis the Menace, Minnie the Minx, The Bash Street Kids, Desperate Dan, Korky the Cat, Billy the Whizz, and

Martin's Marvellous Mini, which we devoured as soon as the mags arrived. An illustration of the newly opened Sydney Opera House really impressed me. One of the magazines had a 'pen pals' section at the back, and Glendon struck up correspondence with a Canadian, Mark Frantzen.

We'd have to go down to the Maidstone Shopping Village to collect these magazines. One Saturday heading to the pool, I was casually walking the aisles. The jingle *I'd Like To Buy the World a Coke* was often playing (and proved such a success, that the New Seekers adapted the lyrics to *I'd Like to Teach the World to Sing (in Perfect Harmony)* and hit #1 in the UK and #10 on the Springbok chart with it.

On this morning, the jingle *Feeling Groovy* was playing (Groovy was a faddish strawberry soda soft drink at the time). I thought, Oh I'd like some of that, so grabbed a couple of cans from the fridge, and rolled them up into my swimming towel. Then I casually looked at the record racks, because the album cover art was always scantily clad women, sometimes in hot pants, feather boas, and/or in skimpy cammo holding machine guns. Then I went to the front desk to collect my magazines and headed out.

As I went to leave, the manager cleared his throat, and said, 'Where are you going?' I felt an instant hot flush of guilt and embarrassment. Busted! He made me unwrap the towel, and you can imagine my feigned surprise at how two cans of Groovy had possibly got tangled up in there. I handed them over, then slunk away to find my parents as the butchery next door, knowing that if they found out about my side-hustle shoplifting career, my arse would be belted beyond recognition.

Another soft drink incident involved driving home from church with Mum one time. We'd bought a big bottle of Coke — glass in those days — and were bouncing along up the dirt road to home. I was resting the precious bottle between my legs, and the Coke over-fizzed. *BANG*! The bottle exploded, sending two jagged shards into the top of my inner thigh. That came very close to doing some serious damage, and I still have a scar that resembles a snakebite in that delicate place.

One afternoon we'd gone to a section of the farm with Dad, where the sheep were grazing on a distant mound. We wondered if Lamby would remember us after all this time. We all called out 'Lamby! Lamby!' From the top of this hillock, one sheep raised its black head, then came bounding down, leapfrogging the herd in its way. He came down to us, and enjoyed bounteous head-rubs, and I'm sure his un-docked tail was wagging.

■ □ ■

Roger meantime had started school at Oakford (the same convent school Mum had gone to), probably because he was too young to start at Maidstone — and she'd drive him out to Verulam, a 20-minute drive each way every day.

Once he'd started at Maidstone he said to Mum, who was head of the Maidstone PTA and tasked with handing out the various class and school prizes: 'Mum, if I win a prize tomorrow, will you kiss me?'

'Yes, I guess so, if you want me to.'

'No, that would be embarrassing,' said my younger brother, confidently expecting a podium finish.

Next day, he did win a prize, and Mum handed over the prize (always a book!), and backed away. Then Rog reached up and kissed Mum. 'I was so touched, it was so special,' she'd later say.

Another time, Mum asked Roger what he wanted to do when he grew up. He gave this a moment of careful thought before replying, 'What do you mean? I want to retire!'

Speaking of retirement, it was time for Mr Harrison, our school principal, to retire. And the news came that the new head would be Digby Stanley. Digby — a barrel-chested man with a deep suntan and generous sideburns — could not be more polar-opposite to Harrison. He came with a reputation for being very sports oriented.

The Stanley clan moved into the principal's residence on the path just below the main sports field, which had a verandah opening onto the front. They had three daughters, Lynn (at university already), Lois, Calda, and a son Logan, at our school.

Digby used to do weightlifting in his skimpy leopard-skin speedos on his front verandah, in full view of everyone. I'm not sure what the school mums made of this.

One of our extra-curricular activities was cubs, which was held in the little hall below the main school buildings. It was adorned with large photos of founder Baden-Powell (yes, that same guy who sat-out the siege in Mafeking), and various posters of skills and clever things you could do to earn a sleeve-full of extra badges. Our khaki uniforms were super-smart with '1st Maidstone' badges, and green-and-yellow scarves, tied with brown leather woggles. It was a different world, with its own sub-cultural lexicon. Mrs Whoever became Akela the leader (named after the wolf leader in *The Jungle Book* by Rudyard Kipling). And we stood in a Howl Circle and solemnly promised we'd do our best for her in a call-and-response: 'Dyb, Dyb, Dyb, Dob, Dob, Dob.' (Do Your Best, Do Our Best.)

We recited the cub scout promise:

"I promise to do my best,

To do my duty to God and the Queen,

To help other people,

And to keep the Cub Scout Law." Whatever the Cub Scout Law was!

Cubs gave rise to a number of great outings, mainly set around great big bonfires, with resulting singalongs. *Kumbaya* anyone? *Oh My Darling Clementine*, *Campfire's Burning*, and *Bring Back My Bonnie to Me* were other favourites.

There was a South African flag on a stand inside the scout hall, the first time I'd been really up close to the standard, and looked at all the various little flags that made up the central insignia of it, thinking in my own way, *Gee, that's a complicated mess*, not knowing half the story or checkered history of how South Africa had come about. Naturally we belted out the national anthem *Die Stem* (in Afrikaans) at cubs and at assembly. I loved that melody, very rousing, but wasn't quite sure how the cliffs gave us answers ('*waar die kraanse antwoord gee*') — certainly, the cliffs around WeWe Dam gave me no answers on the afternoon when we had to cook a damper-like flour-and-water concoction. It was a complete culinary catastrophe. I didn't get my Cook's Badge, but at least I got my Fire Badge for the raging fire which reduced it to a rock-like block of carbon in the pot.

One afternoon after school, a group of kids was killing time before cubs, kicking a soccer ball around on the top field. And along strides Mr Stanley with his great pet big shaggy pet Alsatian. Great, Glendon thinks, he's going to teach us how to play soccer.

'OK, you kids, all down to my office.'

'Great, maybe he's going to show us some moves on the blackboard.'

'OK, you kids, line up outside my office.'

'Uh-oh.'

Each of them was given two strokes of the cane for playing soccer. 'It's a sissy's game,' he explained to them.

That wasn't Glendon's or my last visit to his office for a flogging. Mr Stanley could certainly dish it out, using the heft of his Popeye-like forearms. You got bent over his comfy chair and could hear the cane whistling through the humid air on its way to ruining your afternoon. Getting sent to Mr Stanley's office was a thing we dreaded and kept most of us in line. If you were lucky, you were told to go and see Mr Stanley the next day. That meant you could come well prepared the next day with several pairs of underpants on. But it still bloody hurt! And then you'd walk out of his office, body buzzing with adrenaline, force a smile at Mrs Baptie in her admin office, then you'd turn a sharp right and sprint to the toilets and soak your bum in cold water.

Every Thursday we had woodwork, and Digby was our teacher. It took me all year to not complete some kind of small wooden rectangle thing, meant to display prowess of chiseling dovetail joints. I didn't get that gene. Digby was onto me, with the result that every Thursday that year I'd wake up with a mysterious stomach ailment. I missed 31 days of school that year (but still got the coveted 1st Prize at prize-giving). By Friday mornings I was miraculously fine again.

'I only had one run-in with Digby,' says Roger, 'and it was bad. I bent over the Chesterfield, and got smacked, and then you had to say "thank you" after each one. Thank you, sir, could I have another?' he laughs.

But you didn't have to be sent to his office to feel the wrath of his cane. He took it just about everywhere with him. Especially to sports training, like rugby practice. In the middle of one practice session, I was scrambling towards the ruck, when the ball suddenly appeared out the back, I picked it up and charged forward with it. Stanley blew his whistle: 'Lloyd, what are you doing? That's the scrum half's job.' With that one of two things would happen … but both of them involved you bending over and touching your toes. The first option was he'd get the scrum half (in our case Etienne Erasmus) to run up and give you a kick up the arse with his rugby boot. Or the second option, Mr Stanley would whack you one or two on the arse with his cane.

He graduated to using a sawn-off cricket bat, a lethal weapon, wielded with disastrous results for any minor transgression. These days you could sue for millions of dollars for this sort of corporal abuse, but that was what we knew at the time, all completely normal in the context of South African schools.

Frightened of the consequences of displeasing our coach, we did our best in rugby, in our smart new rugby kit of pine green jerseys (with slave bell logo on the left chest), white shorts, and pine green socks. This matched the new livery of the Tongaat Group, and all its vehicles including *bakkies* and cane trucks were a smart white with green trim, logo, and lettering.

The big thing was Gola rugby boots, a streamlined English design with two vertical stripes and one horizontal strip. Quite a departure from the hobnail-boots of the previous generations. If you didn't have Gola, you weren't Springbok material. But Adidas was also popular, in their smart blue box, with three white stripes. A couple of years later, they were the brand to have, because their new day-glow green stripes guaranteed you could run 25 per cent faster. At least!

One afternoon Mum was driving past the sports field, where a match was in progress. She looked and thought, That looks a lot like Stuart … hold on, it *is* Stuart! She screeched to a halt, ran onto the pitch mid-game, and brass-hooked me off the field.

Why? Well, I'd just come out of hospital from a tonsillectomy which went horribly wrong. We all looked forward to having our tonsils done because all we'd heard is you get to eat jelly and ice-cream for a couple of weeks. What's not to love about that? My turn came, and in I went to Addington Hospital, near Marine Parade, overlooking Durban harbour. Usually a straightforward op, I nearly bled-out on the operating table. This is when they discovered I had a haemophiliac-like condition. I woke up feeling very groggy and sorry for myself, to see my parents looking rather relieved and happy. 'Ice cream and jelly' I croaked.

'No, darling, you can't eat anything yet,' Mum said, 'because you have all those tubes in your mouth.' Sure enough, there was enough piping, tubing, and hosing to start a plumbing business protruding from various orifices of my little body.

'Ice cream and jelly,' I repeated before passing out.

The next day I was awoken by a cannon blast. Then another. Then several others. At close range. What the hell??? It turned out to to be the Queen's birthday, and a 21-gun salute was in progress from naval ships across the road in the harbour.

Then I was propped in a wheelchair and taken to the operating theatre again, pipes still protruding from my nose and throat. Half-way down the corridor, a doctor stopped us and asked for my charts. 'Is this the boy who had his nose cut off?' he asked. I reached for my nose, phew, it was still there. No, this was the boy who bled during the tonsillectomy, they told him. Anyway, things were cauterised and after a few days I was sent home with strict instructions to rest.

Which is why Mum was somewhat shocked to find me playing a rugby match just a few days later. Because, well, rugby. It's not a matter of life and death ... it's far more important than that.

19

RUCKS, MAULS, AND RELIGION

DURBAN, 1965. Rugby was religion in South Africa. Correction: *Is* religion (the Springboks were rampant back-to-back world champions in 2019 and 2023). Rugby came to South Africa a full century before I was born, with a game played in Cape Town between British soldiers from the garrison and local civilians in 1862. Its popularity spread among the British expats before jumping across — like a runaway bushfire — into the Afrikaner population.

Some of my fondest memories were of watching my uncle Roger Seymour (Mum's brother) in full flight at the legendary King's Park Stadium in Durban. I'm not ashamed to admit a bit of hero worship. If he'd had a poster, I would've had it on my wall.

After all, there in the middle of the stadium packed with 40,000 fans, he was often the central figure for Natal, being their fly half. No 10. Pivotal.

He was blessed with the Seymour/Tait sporting genes, and played every sport at school level reasonably well, but had not particularly shone at rugby according to his own high standards: 'I had not played for Natal Schools or Natal Under 20s,' he tells me from home in Somerset West, near Cape Town.

However, he'd played 1st League rugby for Durban University, and met a couple of players who'd played in the Carlton Cup in Pretoria over post-match beers.

'Dennis de Klerk had played for Natal at scrum half with Keith Oxlee, the Springbok fly half. I clearly remembered Dennis's words (he had a slight stutter, making the words even more memorable): "Rog, every Saturday in the Carlton League is like a t-t-test match. When you finish the game after 80 minutes, sometimes you f-f-feel as if you have been through a m-m-mincing machine because the rugby is physically very hard!"'

The Carlton League featured the heavy-hitting Transvaal clubs of the day, such as the Diggers, Wanderers, Pirates, Police, and Defence.

When Roger got his call-up for compulsory military training in 1965, he was sent to Potchefstroom for six weeks for basics, then posted to Pretoria. The last thing on his mind was to ever play rugby there.

But word got around the camp that Roger had played some rugby before, so it wasn't long before he was asked to play for the Engineering division vs Infantry in an inter-regimental mid-week game.

'With Dennis's words still ringing in my ears, I immediately said no, ' said Roger. 'He would not accept my answer and — after telling me I would get off work early, etc — I eventually agreed. I played well, nothing special, and was walking to my transport when two guys came walking towards me. One was a short portly guy (who happened to be the Defence rugby coach) and the other was none other than Frik du Preez, a legendary Springbok and one of my rugby heroes.'

Iconic lock Du Preez was voted the South African Rugby Player of the 20th Century in a 2000 poll.

'They asked me to come and play rugby for the Defence club. I was still in a negative mindset explaining to the coach about transport problems and not being a permanent military member, when the coach firmly said: "Roger be ready at the security gate of your division and I will send a military jeep twice a week to pick you up for practices".'

He was soon selected for the Defence 1st team, and shortly after selected at fly half for Northern Transvaal, playing four games for the province. 'I enjoyed my rugby in Pretoria; the added bonus was that I got out of camps and drills on weekends.'

Defence also flew to Rhodesia in September 1965 and played against all the Rhodesian forces in four matches. 'Politically it was interesting times and I remember being introduced to Ian Smith before the main game in Salisbury. In our leisure time we also flew to Vic Falls and saw Kariba dam from the air … a wonderful experience.'

The Defence and Police teams comprised some supremely tough buggers. I remember watching Defence playing Police at King's Park. This one player had given all he could give on the field and had gotten at least as much as he had given. Near the end of the match, he was virtually minus two arms and a leg, and limped toward the touch line, his head bleeding profusely. The coach strode up to him and barked: '*Veldt of grens toe*! '(Back on the field, or I'll send you back to the border!) He forlornly soldiered back onto the field and put his fractured face into a few more rucks.

In 1966, Roger had returned to Natal and made his debut at fullback, given that the Springbok incumbent Keith Oxlee wore the #10 jersey. Fortunately, Oxlee retired the following year, and Roger played 30 games for Natal over the next six years.

Afternoons at King's Park were exciting events, usually with curtain raisers featuring the U20s, then the B teams, then, before the main event, always a bit of slapstick theatre. Ever since WW1 when soldiers from Durban were referred to as 'banana boys', the Natal team had unofficially adopted this nickname. Playing up to it, some guy in a white lab coat — let's call him Banana Boy — would run out onto the field to a massive roar and plant a huge banana tree branch in the centre spot. Other times, he and the opposition's mascot might take it a bit further, with the Banana Boy diving over for a try down one end of the field. The Castle-filled stadium would erupt. Then for many it was time to light up a Lexington ("for after action satisfaction" as they advertised in the rugby programs of the day) and watch the gladiators go at it.

■ □ ■

Roger met Renee Rossler at a party around this time, a nurse who'd attended Pietermaritzburg Girls High, worked at Grey's Hospital, and was doing a midwifery course at Addington Hospital. A protracted courtship ensued.

Renee comes from a fascinating family whose family's South African roots trace back to Lutheran missionaries. Her father Walter Rossler's father served as the Native Commissioner on the South coast of Natal, responsible for administering native affairs and maintaining order in that district. Their homestead, Morgenzon at Shelly Beach on the South Coast, later became the site of the Metropole Hotel, a popular local spot for eating, drinking and dancing.

The family left their mark on local geography around Shelly Beach: Rossler's Point was named after the family, and Wally's Channel after Walter, presumably a keen fisherman as well as a legal eagle.

As a magistrate Walter Rossler moved around the country during his career. His postings included Eshowe (where Renee was born), established as the capital of Zululand in 1887 and the administrative centre for the region.

The Residency where they lived was a grand Victorian-era British colonial style house adapted with large verandahs and decorative woodwork to suit the sub-tropics better. Built in 1894, it was declared a national monument in 1986.

When Renee was just two years old, during the visit of King George VI in March 1947, The Residency was used overnight by the king's party — which included Princesses Elizabeth and Margaret chaperoned by RAF Wing Commander Peter Townsend (later known because of his scandalous romantic relationship with Princess Margaret). A rare case of gamekeeper turned poacher!

Renee's mum was Corrie de Waal (nee Jansen). The de Waal family had farming interests in Natal, including farms called Brandkraal and Strathurn. Clearly strong-minded, Corrie studied history and art at Stellenbosch University in the 1920s. She was also accomplished on the harp.

Corrie's uncle was Ernest George Jansen, Governor-General of South Africa, yes, that guy who refused to swear allegiance to the monarchy — the very same royal family who'd stayed under the roof of Renee's father's house.

■ □ ■

Rugby tours to South Africa by the British Lions date back to 1891, and in 1968 they toured again. 'I was fortunate to play against the British Lions and faced the greatest Welsh half back pairing in history of Gareth Edwards and Barry John, as well as the British Barbarians in '69,' says Roger. Sadly, he missed playing against the Wallabies in that same year due to an ankle injury and was on the bench for the England match in 1972.

But the All Blacks tour in 1970 was a highlight, even though the home side was beaten 29-8. Roger lined up against the likes of Colin Meades, Brian Lochore, Graham Thorne, Sid Going, and Chris Laidlaw. Gran Seymour (Alys) was always there, as a super-fan of the game and her son. She knew all the players' names on both sides, and would always be talking about Morne Du Plessis (or 'two plus three' as she called him), Frik du Preez, Jan Ellis, Piston Van Wyk, Hannes Marais, etc, delighting in the pronunciation of the more guttural Afrikaner names like Labuschagne ('Lah-boo-SKUK-knee'), and analysing their skills and form.

Ironically there were two Kiwis in the Natal team: fullback Terry Mehrtens (whose father was an All Black and whose son Andrew — born in Durban — would become an All Black). The other was winger Peter Hatchwell.

The match was also something of a flashpoint in international rugby relations, thanks to Natal and Springbok captain Tommy Bedford, an architect whose time as a Rhodes Scholar in Oxford had given him a very broadminded perspective on apartheid. Post-game he was asked why the All Blacks were only playing one match in Durban despite how much they professed loving playing in that city. 'Because Natal is seen by the Afrikaner government as the last outpost of the British empire,' was the gist of his response.

Bedford — whose socks were always around his ankles from the moment he ran on the field — was immediately and controversially dropped from the Boks squad and would become an agitator for racially-inclusive rugby as a way forward to an apartheid-free society.

Roger's star, however, was rising and newspaper articles championed him. 'After playing a very good game against the 1970 All Blacks, I was nominated by my union to attend the Springbok trials. I never went as the Springbok selectors did not agree to it.'

Our routine on match days was always for Dad to park at the Durban Country Club — with its Cape Dutch clubhouse nestled amid lush greens and fairways — then stroll across the fields to King's Park, near the Lion Match factory. Post-game, there might've been a Castle Lager to be had in the car park with a friendly face, then back to the Country Club, often for drinks and dinner. Gran and Grandad Seymour were always there, but of course there was a separate ladies' bar area where Gran and Mum would adjourn.

If Natal had won, the evenings would stretch out longer, to the screech of a million mynah birds in the trees along Marine Parade, as the lights on the Bluff and the hotels along the waterfront twinkled in the twilight.

But at the age of 28, Roger called time on his rugby days. 'I thoroughly enjoyed my Natal rugby days, but it was a labour of love and two free beers after each game. It was also difficult for me in particular, working all day, lectures in the evenings, and then qualifying as a chartered accountant in between. How different to the professional era of today with all its money and added perks.'

He kept fit, super-fit actually, and often ran the Comrades' Marathon (Durban to Maritzburg or vice versa) a 90km steep-sloped slog. In 1973, he and Renee — who'd just returned from nearly three years of travelling in the UK, Europe, and Israel — got married, on the day of the marathon! 'Now I'm your real aunt,' she said to me at their wedding.

Rugby-wise he took to coaching the Marist club side, taking them from 3rd division to 1st division in two seasons.

In 1977 he was approached by the Natal Rugby Union to coach the Natal under-20 side. 'I really enjoyed this stint. However, rugby did not pay the bills plus I wanted to spend more time with a young, growing family and stopped after season two.'

He also kept his hand in as a player, with the Natal 'Old Crocks' side. 'We had one or two fixtures each year — one of which was against Kearsney College 1st XV, and then later Michaelhouse.

In 1980 the British Lions side toured SA. 'The British Lions Supporters Club had a team and they had asked for a game against our Old Crocks side on the Friday before the Natal match. I was asked a week before the game to play and — thinking this was a side of beer-swigging old farts from the UK – I said, "Sure of course I want to play!"'

So Roger duly pitched up on the Friday for the game. 'A couple of Old Crocks came up to me and said, "Rog you won't believe this … this team is not a bunch of piss-cats — they have two ex-Lions players and a host of not-so-old rather serious players as well, and now, Rog — sit down before we tell you this — you are marking Phil Bennett today!"

Bennett — 'The Welsh Wizard' who'd played with the 1974 Lions dubbed 'The Invincibles' — had retired from international rugby only two seasons before, with two Five Nations grand slams and an OBE to his name. His try against Scotland in 1977 was voted the greatest Wales try of all time. *World Rugby* called him 'one of the greatest to have ever played the game' and he would later be inducted into the World Rugby Hall of Fame. So fairly handy, then.

'To cut a long story short: we got smashed by the Lions Supporters on the day!' Roger chuckles about the experience.

But for his achievements in the rugby world, one of Roger's most colourful memories happened not at an international level, rather — while working during the holidays for brother Dave's business — when he played rugby for the Empangeni 2nd XV team.

'There was a chap called Koen — a big fellow who played in the second row. After a rugby game on a Saturday evening, he would eat a whole large roast chicken on his own!' This left an indelible impression on Roger, as large as the impression the second rower had left on his many opponents those afternoons.

20

MEANWHILE, BACK IN ZULULAND

ZULULAND, 1960s. Meanwhile, life in Zululand — even for an accountant like David — refused to be dull for even one minute. One of his clients was Derek Heaton Nichols, who trained at RAF Cranwell, the same base as flying ace Douglas Bader. But that's where the similarities end, because Nichols — son of Senator George Heaton Nichols, the post-war South African High Commissioner in London — was shot down on the first day of the war and spent the duration in the bag at German POW camps.

This didn't dampen his enthusiasm for flying, and he took David up a few times. 'All the farmers in Zululand were learning to fly,' says David. 'And many had narrow escapes. Some of them are lucky to be alive!' His great friend Richard Grantham was flying with Cyril Johnson one time in Johnson's brand-new plane from Matubatuba (near Richards Bay), and coming in to land, the aircraft was making a noise Johnson didn't recognise. Faulty gadget, he thought. He put the plane down on the grass strip to find out, the hard way, that he had just landed without the landing gear down. 'A big mistake in his new bloody aircraft!'

Another time some friends flew to Bazaruto Island, a pristine paradise off the mainland of Mozambique. 'Only about a 15-minute flight.' Two aircraft took off to fly from the island back to the mainland, weather closed in, and there was no visibility. Cyril Johnson found a small gap in the cloud, went through and landed quickly.' Mick Kelly and Batstone, not so lucky, they crashed in the sea and both were killed. Mick's trousers were found.'

In the 1960s and 1970s, the *Natal Mercury* newspaper organised competitions offering flying bursaries, providing aspiring pilots with opportunities to receive flight training, usually in a De Havilland DHC-1 Chipmunk, a single-engine, two-seat aircraft (replacing the earlier Tiger Moths).

David put in his application and was accepted as a candidate for full pilot instruction and told to report to the Wings Club at Stamford Hill Aerodrome in central Durban. Excited but nervous as hell as he talked to his instructor, Pablo.

'What do you do when pilots freeze on a plane?' asks David, in preparation for that possibility.

'Well, I pull out the spare joystick and hit him on the head.'

Once airborne, Pablo handed David the joystick. 'And now I'm flying. And he said, "Now left rudder, head for the Country Club in Durban, and we're going to land." So, I'm following his instructions, and he said, "Right, just let the aircraft down a bit ... yeah, a bit higher." I didn't know how hard to pull the thing to get a reaction.'

Pablo was just sitting there with his arms folded. 'I said, "Hey, look, I'm not that keen to fly!" He said, "Hang on, careful, you're going into the fence. Pull the rudder back up!" And this bugger's still just sitting there with his arms crossed. Now the airstrip's coming up. He said, "Let her down, let her down." And then as we landed, he grabbed the stick, shouting "Stick in!" We landed, and that was my bloody flight.' David was back on solid ground, and that got flying out of his system.

Not that solid ground was accident-free. One day in his office, his wife Jill rang and casually said: 'I think you should come home. The house is on fire. 'At the side of the house, they had a coal-fired slow combustion system to heat the water attached, and she'd noticed flames burning about half a metre above the roofline.

Bertha, their cook, sprang into action. 'She was a big strong Zulu lady and got water in a bucket and caught it before it got over the other side of the brickwork.' Their slate roof had a four or five-feet overhang, the chimney had furred up and cracked, and the escaping heat set the rafters on fire. The fire engine was just a Land Rover with a pump, so it was not much good, but able to extinguish the rest of the blaze. 'Thank goodness for Bertha!'

As mentioned, Roger was spending university mid-year holidays working for Dave's business. Fishing remained a high priority, going out on Commander Heyns' boat from Richards Bay to try and deplete the world's stocks of salmon and kob. 'Richards Bay was then a small hotel and about 40 seaside cottages; now of course it is a large coal exporting port and a large bustling town,' says Roger.

When not crash-landing planes or putting out house fires or dealing with Jill's frequent bingles reversing their Mercedes out the driveway, occasionally normalcy would break out … like tennis every Sunday at Bruce and Sheila Am's, followed naturally by a few drinks and lots of increasingly tall stories.

21

IN DEEP (CHICKEN) SHIT

KLIPFONTEIN, EARLY 1970s. Great excitement: we now had near-neighbours at Klipfontein! Two houses had been built on the slope behind us. One was for the mild-mannered English accountant Dick Thorn, and the other for the far more garrulous Scottish family, the Leiths. They had three sons our age — an instant playgroup, or tribal warfare, depending on the day.

There was also lots of construction happening further down the road towards Tongaat Beach, where the new estate of Westbrook was taking shape. Tons of heavy equipment was left there. One day Dad came across some kids who looked like they were up to no good with the Caterpillar earthmovers, putting sand in the diesel tanks. He shouted out to them. One of them was our schoolmate Gary, whose family were recent immigrants from Yorkshire or somewhere 'oop north'.

He stared down Dad: 'If ya don't shut your bleedin' cakehole, I'll get me dad's 'ammer and bash your bloody 'ead in!' Needless to say, Dad — The Boxer Formerly Known as Buster — would've been well impressed by that.

One afternoon after school we were mucking around with the Leith boys, as we did most days. But this day was different because we'd found a box of Lion matches lying in the grass beside the road.

We then did what most curious schoolboys would do: see what happens when you set fire to the nearest thing.

Unfortunately, the nearest thing to us was a sugar-cane field. It was that time of year where the cane was fully-grown (probably two-metres tall or more) and the leaves brown and dry.

I struck a match and held it to the nearest leaf. It sparked and crackled and was soon aflame. Nice! We stomped out the little flame. Now everyone wanted a turn. Matches were lit, leaves caught fire. We stomped them out. Great fun!

And then came my turn again. I held the match to a bunch of leaves, and suddenly the next leaves caught fire, and the ones next to those. We slapped, and stamped, and swiped at the leaves. But all it did was send sparks into the neighbouring stalks.

Shit!

Some of the boys pulled off their shirts and swatted the flames with them, but this just fanned them further. The hissing, crackling and popping of the flames in the cane grew louder, like turning up the volume of white-noise radio static full blast.

Brainwave: 'You guys go run for some water!' The nearest tap was down near our house over 100 metres away. We all ferried cups and dishes and buckets from the tap to the fire, which was by now rampaging angrily across the field, which stretched further than the eye could see. Smoke and sparks clouded the sky.

By the time a farm truck arrived, full of workers with damp hessian sacks to beat the flames, and some hoses and pumps that sucked water out of our swimming pool, nearly a whole football field's worth of valuable sugar cane had been burned, with thousands more acres at risk.

And the troubles only got bigger when a looming figure stepped out of a pick-up truck which roared to a halt next to us.

It was Mr Potgieter. 'Potty' to his friends, which at that moment I wasn't. All diplomatic relations had been severed. Mr Potgieter was a big, muscular man with a big bushy moustache, a World War 2 veteran no less, with a stern manner at the best of times. In his hand was a rattan cane.

'OK, who started this fire?' he barked, waving his cane around menacingly.

The sound of crickets. We all studied our toes and the ground with sudden amazing interest.

Then a little high-pitched voice stuttered from the back of the pack.

'M-m-m-me, sir.'

It was my voice.

'Step forward, Lloyd.'

This can only mean the beating from hell, I thought, as I stepped through past my brothers towards him. Then suddenly his angry face turned to a big beaming grin. 'See that? This boy is honest. He has owned up.'

By now my eyes were watery. Not from the smoke as much as being overcome with emotion.

'Well done, that's a good thing you've done in owning up there,' Mr Potgieter said, patting me on the shoulder. *Phew*! I couldn't believe I wasn't going to be receiving a thrashing. Instead, I was being praised for my bravery and honesty.

I didn't cop a thrashing from Potty, but I'm sure that was one of the many occasions when Dad (and sometimes Mum) would wield a wooden spoon from the kitchen with such devastating effect, the damn things would sometimes break across our bums, to often comical effect.

The burned-out field sat like a silent witness to our misadventure for months after. But the rainy season soon took our mind off it, because the drainage ditch running alongside that field along our garden boundary become a gushing torrent that we could jump into and get washed along to the bottom of the garden. Muddy good fun.

Which led to the time when we rigged up a trailer on the back of the trike. I was riding, and Roger or one of the Leith boys was in the back of this cart. I came screaming down the Leith's garden, hit a boggy patch of mud, and was sent cartwheeling over the handlebars into the mud. My passenger was dangling from the handlebars. But lying in the mud, my problems weren't over. Next thing I let out a blood curdling yell — my toe was on fire and a massive black scorpion with tail curled in anger emerged from the mud, not happy.

Around the same time, another 'only in Africa' tale emerged. Dad, brother Uncle Mick, and family friend from Rhodesia, Stuart Ingham, had teed up a fishing trip at Lake St Lucia, about a three-hour drive north of us, beyond Richards Bay.

Our new car, a deep-blue Mercedes 230-4, motored along comfortably, and behind that, our little fishing boat, *Imvubu* (hippopotamus) swayed around on its trailer, like the tail of a happy dog, bristling with rods like alien antennae.

Dad came from a long line of very unsuccessful fishermen, but that didn't dampen his enthusiasm. I had inherited his enthusiasm, but that graph dipped sharply if we hadn't landed a record-weight Marlin within, say, ten or fifteen minutes. Tops.

In the basic cottage we rented for the weekend, an old enamel stove dominated, and the first order of business was to get some tea brewing. A huge tin kettle was found, with capacity enough to serve an entire army. But try as we might, the stove didn't seem to want to play. Everyone had an opinion of course. Or a special technique — flick the switch this way, then light, or light then flick. No, press it in.

Eventually, exasperated, someone went in search of some help. The 'boy' arrived and fielded our question: How to light the stove? He looked at it, threw an arm behind his head and gave it a good old scratch, before opening the lower door panel, and pointing: 'There! The firewood goes in there!' Wasn't it obvious to us? Problem solved, he walked out nonchalantly, probably thinking, *Gee, these white guys sure are dumb*. Only problem is it was a gas stove!

Time for some late-afternoon fishing. Although it is an estuarine lake, St Lucia looks like the open sea because its waters cover 350 square kilometres. We motored our way towards the centre of the lake, admiring the lush and luminous wetlands, spotting the odd croc, and relishing the birdlife, which was coming home to roost for the evening, in full squawk. Pelicans patrolled the shallows, curious and hungry. Fish eagles ran aerial surveillance from above.

Soon enough, we dropped anchor, a job I enjoyed, throwing out the curved iron hook and feeding out the multi-coloured nylon cord until it was firmly on the bottom, then securing it round a fitting on the bow, utilising exactly none of the knots I'd learned in Cubs.

Then came the baiting of the hooks. High science, mixed with a dash of philosophy, and a large helping of hope, from lessons lived and learnt the hard way. Soon we all had a rod and a line in the water. Immediately: *BANG*! Fish on. Up came a tilapia. Then another. Someone hooked a catfish, which lay forlornly on the floor of the boat, like an unshaven hobo, with its funny whiskered face. OK, this was my kind of fishing! Soon I had a tilapia on, Dad deeming it small enough we could use it for live bait to catch something far grander. Into the bucket it went.

Dad was that excited, he rigged up an extra rod, a short metallic red number, cast out, then propped it up inside the gunwales of the boat.

It was one of those days the fish were virtually jumping into the boat. Then suddenly zzzeeeeeeeeeeeeeeeeeeeee, the reel of the unattended red rod screamed, the tip bent, and *SPLASH*! It went flying overboard, dragged into the water. Gone.

Never mind, we still had some fishing to do before the twilight dropped its black velvet curtain on the day.

The 'boy' gutted and cleaned the best fish, and we gave him one for his family, too. And straight onto the *braai* outside they went, washed down with a few Castles or Lions.

Soon it was lights-out, with an early morning start planned. But the quiet of the night was disturbed by the roaring of a nearby pride of lions. No wait, that's just Dad snoring. Plus, maybe Mick and Stuart Ingham too.

Three o'clock wake-up alarms are not usually a good thing. Except when there's a day on the lake to be had. And when it saves you from suffering through more sleepless hours of point-blank range snoring.

Having finally worked out the gas stove, coffees were dispensed … Ricoffy instant which could defibrillate a dead elephant in an emergency.

As we opened the door to head off, an airstrike was called in, the air alive with squadrons of those damned Apache mosquitoes. Launching *Imvubu* we could barely make out the moon, the clouds of mozzies were so thick.

Guided only by our bulky yellow Eveready Dolphin torch, we nosed out, spotting the tell-tale red dots of crocodile eyes along the banks. The plan this morning was to head down through what is known as 'The Narrows' down to the estuary, which leads out to the sea.

Eventually we reached a spot where the collected wisdom had it the fish should be biting. They were!

No sooner did the lines go in, than the bottom of the boat was a seething, flapping morass of slimy and scaly captives. One poor bugger was a grunter, which lay there doing its best imitation of Dad's notorious snoring. We hauled in fish after fish, hoping for kingfish but usually hooking tilapia.

As the distant horizon glowed with the faintest glimmer of light, I casually looked around. 'Hippo!' I shouted excitedly. Everyone turned to look. 'There,' I said. 'About twenty metres away.' They craned to see it, basically a big black round rock poking above the water. Or was it a rock? They went back to their fishing.

The dimmer of dawn was cranked up. 'Er, hippo!' I said again. 'And another one!' They all gawked. Then a silence dawned on the group. An inaudible collective thought bubble of *Oh shit*!

Imvubu sat in the water perfectly ringed, ironically given the meaning of the boat's name, by a circle of 29 hippos. All submerged bar their massive heads, with stupidly small ears twitching lazily in the morning light.

Dad had done his fair share of big game hunting and was not one to panic usually. But here we were truly up Shit Creek, albeit with a paddle. But that was all. One paddle was not going to defeat a platoon of Africa's most fiercely territorial beasts. That they are responsible for more human deaths in Africa than many other large animals, including lions and elephants, was probably zapping across the synapses in all of our minds.

Dad quickly reached for the starter rope handle on the Mercury 9.8 horsepower outboard. His biceps bulged as he yanked it. Nothing. Yanked again, more urgently. He glanced over his shoulder, sweat on his considerable brow.

He gave the fuel primer a couple of desperate pumps. Yank. *Brruuuummmmm*!!! The Mercury kicked into life. Hippo ears twitched. Hippo heads swayed. I pointed out a discernible gap in the Hippo circle. It was a space almost dead-ahead. Dad gunned for it. I just remember the hippo heads and ears and the eyes getting bigger and bigger as the Mercury belched blue smoke, we picked up speed … then suddenly we were through.

As we emerged back into the lake proper, Dad had a thought. 'I'm going to go find my rod.' He wanted to see if he could retrieve his lost red rod from yesterday.

We aimed *Imvubu* towards the spot we'd fished yesterday. No GPS in those days, of course. Just an approximate feeling of where we'd weighed anchor. Someone took over the steering as Dad busied himself with tying several multi-hooked lures along his line. 'I'm going to trawl for it,' he said, as we scratched our heads at the improbability and futility of this exercise. I just wanted dry land and breakfast now.

Dad cast his line, as we zig-zagged our way around the area, dragging it along the bottom. Snagging on this, snagging on that, triggering false hopes. Eventually, *ZAP*! 'I've got something!' he shouted. Sure enough, the tip of his road was bending. Maybe a fish. Or just a root on the floor of the lake. The tip of the rod bent more. Some line went out. We stopped the boat. Dad reeled, and reeled, and reeled. Eventually up came a few of his empty lures and, as we craned over the side, we spotted the red rod on the end of the line. He'd actually hooked his rod, through one of the eyes.

We were all laughing incredulously at this. But as he reached to haul the red rod in, he said, 'Hold on, there's something on the line.' He put the second rod to the side, grabbed the red rod, and started reeling. And fighting, and reeling. And fighting, and reeling. Finally, he landed a good-sized kingfish. This thing had been swimming around with his red rod since yesterday!

Had I not seen it with my own orbs, I would have discounted this fishy story in its entirety.

Summer school holidays. Which meant about five or six weeks mucking around on the farm … our playground was as far as the eye could see in every direction. And the instructions were clear: do whatever you want, as long as you're home by dinner.

Dad had grown Tongaat's fledgling Carisbrooke farm division into a million-head of chicken operation. Fortunately, we were upwind, mostly, because a million chickens produce a lot of chicken shit, as it turns out.

The chickens were kept in an ever-expanding compound of massive tin sheds, like aircraft hangars, sprawled across a huge acreage. Between the sheds were roads, grass, and sheep to keep the lawns 'mowed'. Inside, were rows and rows of cages. Almost like aisles of a jam-packed supermarket. This was the bad old days of factory farming, in which hens were jammed in several to a small cage, jostling for room to turn around and peck at the feed tray, or peck the water trickler. Enough to induce paroxysms in animal rights activists, which fortunately had not yet been invented yet (but were soon to be spawned in Oxford, UK).

But Africa it seemed could not get enough of Tongaat Big Brown Eggs.

One day I'd hopped a ride with Dad to the chicken farm. Off Dad went into the office building, while I was left to my own devices, to find whatever mischief I could, or to help/hinder the staff in whatever way. The choices were many. The packing shed was always fun: all the eggs came along on a conveyor belt, to be sorted into small, medium and large. They'd roll down a stainless-steel plate according to size, where they were stacked in serried rows like dumpy little soldiers, and an automated sucker machine with rubber nozzles would swing around and lift 36 at a time to stack into an egg tray, or 12 for a dozen box. Sheer industrial magic!

But before this, they passed over a strong ultraviolet light which would show up cracks, dirt, or defects like blood spots. These were then weeded out by hand.

Among the defects were soft-shelled eggs, which I guessed missed out on their dose of calcium, and so were translucent. You could clearly see the yolk inside of them. I picked one of these novelty items off the line and was somewhat mesmerised by its squishiness. Like Play Dough. As I played with it, probably showboating to the other production workers — who unlike me were putting in a real day's work — I lost my grip and ... *SPLAT*!!! All over the smooth concrete floor. Just as the manager Erik happened by. A trendy young Indian, he sported some sharp sideburns, ludicrous flared brown slacks, and a wide-collared neon-pink body shirt. And a trademark smile.

But his smile disappeared. Boss's son or not, I had cost the company money. I was trembling in my Bata *takkies* (ubiquitous canvas sports shoes). "Breakage!" He declared. "Five cents fine."

I banished myself outside. There was no activity at the loading docks (usually refrigerated trucks and forklifts buzzing around), so I wandered through the security gate with a hearty '*Sawubona*' into the farm area. *Sawubona* is the Zulu greeting, but as I later learned, it's more than just 'hello'. It more literally means 'I see you, I acknowledge you' as a person and is part of the often intricate and elongated greeting process among many Africans.

Turned out the operation underway was clearing the tons of accumulated chicken shit from the concrete troughs which ran beneath all the cages. The acrid stench was eye-watering. The African workers on the job all had scarves tied across their faces. I raised my T-shirt over my nose. It was being pumped out, into the back of a deep trailer — like an open square tank — which was hooked to a tractor.

With the tank near full of the septic sludge, a signal was given, the pump whirred to a silent halt. And the tractor started up. It was one of the cool new Same Leone Corasaro 70s, a bright orange low-profile Italian contraption, with the front wheels almost the same size as the rear ones.

'Can I ride with you?' I asked the driver Samuel and clambered up behind his seat. 'Er, where are you going?'

'Westbrook, *umfaan*,' he said, addressing me as little boy. Not far, perhaps eight kilometres down the road. Perhaps they were fertilising the fields around there, or the gardens of some new house. One of my teachers Kit Veitch had just moved into the area, and other friends, the Greefs, too.

He put it in gear, and we lurched forward. Slowly. And a little further down the farm's rutted driveway, I'm still not sure what caused it, the tractor lurched. The load sloshed around. I tightened my grip on the back of Samuel's seat. It lurched again. And I looked around at the trailer, just in time to see a tsunami of green-black slurry crest over the lip of the trailer's front wall, basting me in a thick coating of chicken shit.

Samuel copped a minor splashing, too, so he reflexively slammed on the brakes. With that came the second wave, the aftershock, and now I was fully marinated in the ungodly malodorous muck.

'*AAAAARGGGHHH!*' I screamed, tasting the waste on my lips as I opened my mouth, wiping my eyes clear.

'*Haibo*!' exclaimed Samuel, whipping around. Wow! I'm sure he wanted to laugh but suppressed it enough to show a facade of concern at this turn of misfortune. White boy's not so white anymore.

Failing to spit out and wipe the foul muck from my lips and eyes, I decided to cut my losses and started the slog down the road back to the farm, scraping the vile stuff from my stinging eyes as I went.

The howl that went up as I arrived at the factory office was a mixture of surprise and sympathy and shock. Which morphed quickly into raucous hoots of laughter. Nothing's funnier than bad shit happening to some else, right?

Not only was I five cents in debt, but I was also now suffering six senses in deep distress.

I'm only guessing, but my episode might have played a part in fast-tracking the search for solutions to one of the poultry industry's biggest problems. At an animal science symposium, just a couple of years later, the managing director of the Tongaat Group, Dr Geoff Cleasby said: 'Egg producers … have a manure disposal problem.' No shit, Sherlock! I could've been wheeled out as Exhibit A.

And soon Tongaat set about working with an innovation firm in Switzerland, and imported a dryer machine which could turn chicken poop into a dried waste product, which in turn was fed back to the chickens as part of their rations. Alas, too late to save me a day of distress, but I feel like I put my body on the line and played key role in a very important scientific experiment.

■ ■ ■

Mostly, our holidays were far more pleasant though. Holidays to the Drakensberg, passing roadside fields of red, yellow, and orange red-hot pokers. We'd stay at places like Dargle in the Midlands. Simple place with *rondawel* accommodation, lots of fruit trees to gorge on. They had donkeys just wandering around. It didn't take us long to think we should try riding those. No sooner had I hopped on the back of this thing — no saddle or reins — than it sprung into full bucking bronco mode, and I was lying bruised on the gravel road, with my brothers howling with laughter.

Hikes were the usual activity in the Drakensberg, and we'd reach beautiful streams and caves, with one memorable overhang being Eagle's Cave. Bushman paintings in red, brown, and ochre decorated the cave walls and told stories of a previous time. On one bush walk, there was a couple with us. The lady had a slip and fell. The husband immediately called out: 'How's the camera?'

The Amphitheatre is an imposing wall of basalt, fully five kilometres across, which glowed yellow and red at twilight, with the rocky Tugela River in the foreground. And Giant's Castle soars to 10,000 feet near the Lesotho border. In the Bushman's River below, we'd delight at finding huge agates, zebra stones, and purple sugilite stones and crystals.

Just to the west of it was the imposing Mont-aux-Sources, where the headwaters of the Tugela River begin.

The real attraction was body surfing down the rapids. Especially after a bit of rain, the water would surge over rock walls and through massive boulders. And we — Dad and us three boys — would throw ourselves at the mercy of this. Down you'd go, over the big wall of water, hoping you'd sucked enough breath in to last until the eddies decided to let you go, then you'd be bouncing off rocks. So many ways to kill yourself, but endless summer fun. We'd do this over and over again. I'm sure Mum was doing her best not to watch any of this.

Our favourite, which became an annual pilgrimage, was to the Sani Pass Hotel, near the Lesotho border. It nestled among beautiful soaring mountains and was an absolute wonderland for us kids and parents alike. They'd be golfing or playing tennis or trout fishing or hiking. We'd be on the trampolines (they had several in-ground versions) and it was a wonder that no one broke their neck. Maybe they did but, hey, that was just the price of fun in those days. Or swimming (they had a pool with two serious high-level diving boards).

Or we'd go horse riding. The feeling of galloping those horses at full tilt across miles of grassland over the hills was freedom personified. Of course it was always Glendon vs Me in competition, and of course he'd always win. The Basuto lads who looked after the horses were master riders and great fun to ride with, and shared great tips on how to stay on your horse no matter what. And there was a lot of no matter what! Each horse had a different temperament and different reaction to your instructions and encouragement. Dig your heels in and hold on for dear life!

All this energy expenditure meant lots of food intake, and we gorged ourselves on fine food at every meal. The kids were in a separate dining room. Hands down our favourite menu item was the chocolate eclairs. One evening we'd ordered some. They didn't arrive, so we ordered some more. Still nothing. We called another waiter across, ordered more. Eventually they all arrived at the same time, and we sat there surrounded by this massive mountain of chocolicious calories and scoffed the lot down.

After dinner, there was always entertainment put on by the hotel. It might be a movie, or a dance (Mum would teach me all her moves from the 60s, which I still bust out to this very day). Or it might be mini 'horse' races, which were held amid great fanfare. These were little wood models, operated by strings, complete with bets and colourful commentary.

Back home, we had bought a horse, Rusty, a beautiful gingerish ex-polo pony. We stabled him opposite the Dudley Pringle Dam. He was a lovely horse to ride because he had a soft mouth, easy to turn, and we used to clean up in all the slalom races, weaving around a course of poles. His weak point was jumps — he was phobic about hurdles. All of us went head-over-arse several times in events trying to get Rusty to jump. Slightly worse was when he was galloping across an open field and came across a ditch, because that was a fifty-fifty … you either both went flying gloriously across, or he slammed on his brakes, and you joined the airborne brigade, ending up hopefully on a nice soft patch of grass.

He had a strong homing instinct if you were out in the fields somewhere, and as soon as he sensed home, he'd make a bolt for the stables, unaware that his beeline beneath low-hanging branches was endangering the rider.

One of our family friends, about my age, was killed in this manner on their farm near Stanger. He'd fallen from his horse one afternoon, with his foot still stuck in the stirrup, and his horse bolted home, dragging him helplessly along across the rocky road.

When we went to Mooi River to stay at friends' farms, like the Throssels or Hendersons, we'd also do lots of riding, and watching gymkhanas and polo games, a big social thing in farming communities.

We were very close with the Hendersons; Mum went to school with Lynne. Breakfast was always *putu* and *maas*, a coarse-textured maize porridge with thick, sour fermented milk. Then we'd head off with the shotguns to go and bag something, often ducks. It was my first experience with a shotgun — this a side-by-side double-barrelled model — and their son Joe told me to tuck it into my shoulder and aim for the front of the formation. A squadron of ducks soon flew over, I aimed, squeezed the trigger, and it recoiled like a donkey's kick into my shoulder. Then I squeezed the other trigger which damn near ripped my shoulder clean off my torso. The ducks flew on their merry way, unhindered. Lesson learned: tuck barrel snugly into shoulder. You don't make that mistake twice! Although it appears I did.

Apart from Sani Pass, another regular holiday spot for us was on the Wild Coast, where the sociable Glass family ran a hotel. The highlight of their location was the sand dunes which soared up from the beach to incredible heights, like snow skiing slopes, but pure hot sand. We'd go surfing down these things at breakneck speed all day on pieces of cardboard, or a body board.

There was a beautiful estuary which we had to cross to get there, always teeming with fish and sting rays and skates. The Glass family were keen on flying and the father and at least one of their sons was tragically killed in a light plane crash after one of our stays there.

This being Africa, safaris were a popular pastime, taking in parks such as Hluhluwe, the oldest game reserve in Africa, dating back to 1895. Always on the morning of Day 1, there was great excitement: 'Stop, Dad, there's an impala! There! There! There!' By the afternoon of Day 1, you'd suffered an overdose of impala and drove blithely past sweeping great herds of them. But the 'Big Five' were always keenly awaited, and hiding out at sunset around a watering hole was always exciting, not knowing what you might spot. Sometimes you'd know there was a croc in the water, but the thirsty animals wouldn't. You waited for that drama to unfold in living 3-D in front of your eyes.

One day we almost didn't make it through to sunset. We were driving along and spotted a pride of lions ahead. Dad stopped in the middle of the road. A hushed silence fell over us, as though we were in nature's library. All of a sudden one of us kids looked sideways and saw a huge white rhino charging from the left.

'Rhino!'

All: '*Aargh — RHINO*!!!'

Dust was being kicked up as he built up speed, thundering in a beeline for us. Dad started the car, slammed it into reverse, and burned rubber backwards. This great prehistoric blur of grey went flying past the nose of our car, and we got the hell out of there in the nick of time.

But perhaps the most memorable holiday was a family road trip we did to the Cape Province one summer. Cue games of 'car cricket' as we headed down towards Cape Town, through the great Karoo desert, with its endless hot dry orange stretches.

We stopped at Matjiesfontein, an unlikely oasis of preserved colonial village charm in the middle of nowhere. It felt like you were driving into a Boer War movie set, with the Union Jack fluttering from quaint vintage buildings. The hotelier David Rawdon had renovated the Victorian-vibe Lord Milner Hotel. The menu featured 'chicken and peaches' alongside the more usual duck l'orange.

After dinner, they were screening a movie in the courtyard under the stars. Chairs had been set out, and the guests were settled into the storyline with the projector whirring, when I trotted along the corridor — possibly been for a pee — and tripped on the extension cord. The projector ground to a halt, and a cry of dismay went up from the crowd. I slunk to a seat at the back, while the manager scurried around looking for the cause of this disruption.

We'd always keep our eyes peeled for the big orange and green Holiday Inn signs. That meant a night of unimagined luxury to us. We'd always have a decent punch-up deciding who got to sleep in which bed of course!

With very few cars on this road, car cricket was a bit like watching Geoff Boycott batting. Dour. By the time we reached the Klein Karoo area, huge bags of dried apricots were for sale everywhere. It's a surprise we didn't turn orange with the amount we consumed. Bag after bag. And fresh peaches and plums. We'd smash a piece of fruit then came the call, 'Planting a peach tree!' and the pip would be hurled out the open window. I imagine that highway now to be lined with fully grown stone-fruit trees. We delighted to the sight of ostrich riding at Oudtshoorn, but less to ostrich biltong, which was richly seasoned with coriander seeds.

If Dad had a long day of driving and another driver did something to annoy him, he'd eyeball him and mutter, 'I'll drill you for tuppence!'

Cape Town history and architecture was fascinating. Maybe it was all the large cannons. We enjoyed the New Year Minstrel Carnival (*Kaapse Klopse*) with its colourful satin costumes and the exaggerated face paint of the performers … kind of like an early incarnation of Kiss. It was also our first encounter with 'coloured' mix-race folks, many of imported Malay heritage, who had a very distinct look and language. They were great entertainers, especially small kids, dancing and strumming their fast-paced *ghoema* tunes for the crowd's amusement.

We were introduced to the concept of *Tweede Nuwe Jaar*, a second New Year's Day where most businesses were closed because the locals were still giving it plenty on the celebration front.

Table Mountain remains timelessly majestic, which I'm sure would've reflected how our ancestors felt upon their first sighting 150 years earlier. Sadly, we had no idea about our own family's early involvement in settling South Africa.

We went up the cable car to the top of Table Mountain, which was bad news because I just don't do heights. As we ascended Mum regaled us with how she'd climbed the face of this very mountain, which made me feel a bit wimpy with my white knuckles gripping the railing. The views of the bays and beaches far below through banks of cloud were simply stunning.

More dramatic though was the view from the Cape of Good Hope where the oceans begin an embrace which is fully consummated at Cape Agulhas. One side emerald green, the other midnight blue. And you felt all the danger and excitement of the Great Age of Discovery right there.

From there it was up the Garden Route, and car cricket became very lively with more vehicles on the popular road. We decided to spend a few nights in breathtaking Knysna. We befriended some people there and we were to join them for a BBQ on the beach at night. One of them was a keen stargazer and pointed out all the formations in the crystal-clear heavens above us. Meanwhile our seafood dinner was cooking underground in a pit they dug in the beach sand (similar to Hawaiian *imu* or Māori *hangi* techniques). Absolutely sumptuous and we all agreed it was the best fish *braai* in the history of ever.

Next stop, Plettenberg Bay where we got to stay at the Beacon Isle Hotel, a new resort on the rocks overlooking the amazing beach, developed by Sol Kerzner's Southern Sun hotel group.

We went out and bought a bright orange Banzai belly board, brilliant for bodyboarding. You could set your watch to the rhythmic arrival of perfectly formed waves which took you right onto to the beach. The odd fight would break out over whose turn it was to use the board. Dad preferred to body surf, and the sight of his bald head poking through the front of a wave with a huge grin on his face said it all. But the feel of kelp brushing against my legs freaked me out (luckily, the movie *Jaws* would only come out the following year otherwise I might not've ventured into the water at all).

We went exploring the area and spent some time at a lagoon. Glendon and I found this rowing boat on the side of the water. Next thing we were rowing happily across this lagoon, getting the hang of the rowlocks. Then we saw a four-wheel drive coming down on the sand on the other side. A middle-aged guy got out and shouted: 'Hey what are you doing with my boat?' Glen and I exchanged glances. *Shit*! 'Bring my boat back here now!' the man shouted. Glendon did the honourable thing — abandoned ship … jumped overboard and swam to shore in the opposite direction, leaving me no option but to climb out, grab the rope at the front, and do the walk of shame across the shallow lagoon, dragging this boat behind me. I eventually reached the shouting man.

'What the hell are you doing with my boat?'

'Um, we saw it there, and didn't know it belonged to anyone,' I mumbled. My cheeks warmed red; perhaps one of the most embarrassing moments of my life.

I handed him the rope, and he unleashed a torrent of unprintable Afrikaans in my direction. I slunk away.

My success with boats was not yet over. Because the next day we went to the Keurbooms River and hired some canoes. We had a crash course in paddling, and then set off up the black tea-coloured river. Easy! We glided past beautiful Afromontane forests, which rose up on both sides around us. In the water were endless squadrons of jellyfish the size of human heads. We eventually reached a little beach and pulled over for a break and a drink of water. It was deemed we had gone far enough, so should turn back now.

As I went to get back into my canoe, it tipped over, upending me into the water. With the jellyfish, I freaked out. Everybody laughing at me of course. And the more I tried to steady the boat and climb back in, the worse my panic became. I totally lost my shit! I finally got back in. Then we started paddling back, and it was hard going. How come, what's going on? I put my back into it, increased the depth and rates of my strokes but, when I looked up again, I was still opposite the same tree. What the hell? 'The tide's coming in now!' Dad yelled across. What had been a leisurely row up the river was proving a gargantuan struggle to get back. We eventually made it, all completely spent.

Then it was on to Port Elizabeth. Mum and Dad announced we were going to watch a show. It turned out to be some guy with a goatee called Rolf Harris, playing in this huge theatre. I knew him from my comic books with Coogee the Bear. He had us in stitches as he did his signature tunes like *Jake the Peg* but I had no idea what he meant by *Tie Me Kangaroo Down Sport.*

Oddly enough Australia was in our consciousness quite strongly then. Apart from Sydney Opera House, I'd seen Wave Rock — a geological formation in Western Australia — in a magazine. Shane Gould had scooped the pool with three world records and five medals at the 1972 Olympics. Margaret Court had also recently won a calendar-year Grand Slam, amid winning more titles than any other player in history, and up-and-comer Yvonne Goolagong — Gran Seymour loved joking about her name — had just won Wimbledon.

Then one day in Durban we had gone to watch a surf lifesaving tournament, which pitted South Africa against Australia and New Zealand. I remember staring at the two foreign flags, planted in the sand at the beach, wondering why they were near-identical.

On the way home from our Cape road trip, it was a stinking hot day by Australian or South African standards. We couldn't wait to get home and take a dip in the pool. As soon as we pulled up, Roger ran inside and changed into his swimming cossie. He ran up the hall, and through Mum and Dad's bedroom. They had double-doors facing the garden and pool, with huge panes of floor-to-ceiling glass either side of the door. In his excitement, he went running right through the window. *CRASH*!

We were on the lawn in front and Rog came flying through the air, leaving behind a cartoon-cutout of his body shape in the glass. Blood spurting from his leg, blood streaming down his face. He screamed. I screamed. Everybody screamed. Glendon and I legged it down the garden, just running. Dad scooped Roger up, wrapped a towel around his leg, put him in the car and sped off to the hospital. We were still running like headless chickens around the garden screaming, not knowing what else to do.

Hours later, Dad and Rog returned. He'd severed an artery in his leg, so Dad's quick action saved more than the day there. He'd also broken his nose and had a black eye that bulged like a purple balloon. Lots of stitches. An ugly end to a wonderful summer holiday.

Roger would be a frequent flyer at the Tongaat Hospital. One time, he'd stood on a sea urchin down at Sheffield Beach and had to get the countless toxic spikes removed from his foot.

Another time, our school team had gone to Umdloti to play cricket. We were one player short, so pointed to Rog and said, 'You fill in fielding for us, but just stay deep in that far corner, no one will ever hit it there.' In came this batsman who started dispatching balls to all parts of the park. One was looping in Roger's direction. He ran to position himself under it. 'Leave it! Leave it!' we're shouting. But he was moving closer, his hands up like an alligator snout to catch it. 'Leave it, Rog, get out of there!' Still, he was adjusting his position under the ball — which whistled clean through his outstretched hands, and snotted him in the right eye. A bloody mess. Off to Tongaat Hospital again, more stitches, more big black eyes, more stories to tell.

Glendon also featured in the casualty list. On his birthday, we had a game of cricket in the garden, he ran back to catch a high ball, and in the process tripped on the rockery, slamming his chin into the sharp slate edges. That pretty much put the dampener on the party, to which he returned all stitched up.

But none of this was anywhere as bad as what happened to Mr Hall, whose son Philip was at school with us. He'd been helping launch a boat in the sea at Tongaat Beach one day when a large wave hit the boat, the propellor was engaged, and it ran over him, slashing his torso in neat curvy lines, requiring major surgery. Luckily, he didn't attract the sharks and lived to tell the tale.

But the worst episode was when we'd been away one weekend, and returned to hear the terrible news that David, the eldest son of our friends Dave and June Clarkson, had been killed in a shooting accident. He was out hunting rabbits with a friend, and they had to clamber under a fence, when the wire snagged his friend's trigger, discharging the rifle and killing him instantly.

The beachfront at Durban was a paradise of playgrounds and theme parks. The Tropicale where you could pull up in your car, and waitresses on roller-skates would serve you milkshakes and burgers complete with trays affixed to your wound-down window. Nearby, dodgem cars, water slides, cable car rides, plus a Wimpy burger bar. It was the all-in-one go-to for just about every birthday party. Other times it might be ice skating at the ice rink at Kingsmead, or watching one of the shows they put on, such as *Disney on Parade on Ice.*

One time we went to see the HMS *Albion*, a British commando carrier which was doing a world tour. (The US Navy had stopped making port calls in South Africa by the end of the 60s, because the US Navy was 'racially integrated' by then and didn't like the racist SA approach). A little later we went to watch the majestic *QE2* steaming out of the harbour as part of its maiden world tour.

We'd often watch the cricket at Kingsmead in Durban. A beautiful cricket ground, with low grassy slopes where'd we'd spread out our blankets and enjoy the day's play. The Natal team was formidable, with players like Barry Richards, Vincent van de Bijl, Pat Trimborn, Henry Fotheringham, and Mike Procter in the side. The latter was a true all-rounder with a first-class high score of 254 and bowling best of 9-71 to his name. As a test bowler he averaged 15, which puts him right up there. The fact that he was Rhodesian and a Hiltonian made him a legend in my mind!

Alongside stylish lefty Graham Pollock (who once stroked 274 off the Australians), Barry Richards was probably my hero, with 28,000 first class runs at an average of nearly 55. Don Bradman would later include him in his 'all-time best X1'. His test average (based on just a handful of matches against Australia before the sanction sidelining) was 72. I took to turning up my collar after I saw how Barry wore his cricket shirts.

Clover Ice Cream had a 'Rands for Richards' program running, where he pocketed R1 for each run he scored (and I think $6 for every four, and $10 for every six he hit). Needless to say, we were eating ice creams like crazy for his charitable cause!

One summer, the chance came up to have cricket coaching with Barry Richards. Mum signed me up and drove me to the Durban Country Club. Gran Seymour turned up too. A big day. Then we got into the drills, starting with fielding. Barry asked me to demonstrate. Just Barry and me.

'Where's the inside of your foot pointing?' he asked me.

Well … it's pointing there … forward.

'No.'

It was but, now confused, I changed my answer … er, backwards.

'No,' he says, a tad exasperated, implying I was a bit of a dummy. The other kids laughed. 'The inside of your foot is pointing there, to me.'

I was so embarrassed, flushed red, that I immediately decided I didn't like this guy after all. Never meet your heroes, they say.

By contrast, my tennis coach Peter Waters at the Maidstone Club was patient, pleasant, and inspiring. (He'd coached champions like Kevin Ullyet and Wayne Ferreira in a 55-year coaching career.) And when I'd lost my teeth, he'd always make sure to sing, '*All I want for Christmas is my two front teeth, my two front teeth* …' when I was in earshot, with a cheeky grin on his face.

But overall, in South Africa, storm clouds were gathering. Inside the townships another energy was rising. Blacks struggled more than ever with the apartheid economy's wage suppression and job reservation, while factories demanded more from underpaid black labour. By 1973, Durban's wildcat strikes signalled that something had broken loose. 'The seventies had stirred up black workers to demand higher wages, and strikes erupted unpredictably,' journalist Anthony Sampson noted. Young people, meanwhile, were gripped by the ideas of Black Consciousness, an assertion of worth in the face of a system geared to crush dignity.

The National Party's answer was, as always, to push back even harder: Bantu Education, pass laws, and the mad architecture of apartheid's 'independent homelands' designed to deny citizenship to millions. Divide and conquer. It was politics of containment.

Censorship was another tool the conservative government wielded heavily. In the 1960s and 70s, South Africa banned not just revolutionary tracts but novels, memoirs, love stories, even children's books — anything that unsettled the racial order or the moral certainty of the state. *Lady Chatterley's Lover, Lolita*, and *The Catcher in the Rye* all fell foul of the censor, as did *Black Beauty*.

In October 1974 widespread industrial unrest erupted. The workers at the Maidstone mill had come out in force, angry. They'd taken up position outside the main building, chanting and dancing, waving their sticks in the air. We'd passed them on the way into school that morning. The situation was volatile. Mum got a call to come and collect Rog and I (Glendon had already headed off to board at Cordwalles in Pietermaritzburg). Mum said to Beatrice: 'But we treat these people, people like you, very well … you are part of the family. They wouldn't kill children, would they?'

'Madam,' Beatrice replied, 'when they get into this, they will kill anyone.' Mum aka Leadfoot Lloyd might've set a new speed record in her little white Peugeot 304 to pick us up.

Was the storm about to break?

Part 2

THE STORM BREAKS

22

THE BUSH WAR

RHODESIA 1970s. Tim Henwood was born in Salisbury, the son of a former Natal Midlands man who had wandered north as a very young man. While Tim grew up through the 50s on a farm just outside the capital, his father owned service stations and dealt in cars — being the original Jeep dealer, then the BMC dealer (the merger of Austin and Morris) — and later during UDI sanctions, whatever could be smuggled over the border.

His father would sometimes travel to Germany and then return, bringing in 'heavy vehicles and trucks in the middle of the night,' Tim laughs, though he never found out exactly how. 'If he told me, he said he'd have to kill me.'

Tim schooled at Prince Edward (formerly Salisbury Grammar), which had a proud heritage dating back to 1898. Known for strong academics, sports, and military cadet tradition, it educated many Rhodesian leaders. 'All through school we used to sing *God Save the Queen*, but our identity was definitely Rhodesian.'

After school he headed to Gwebi Agricultural College where, he says, my dad Buster was still well-known and remembered. One night there was a party which is where he met a beautiful young blonde nurse, Wendy Avery. 'Well, Wendy met me,' he clarifies. 'I wasn't in a fit state to meet anyone!'

Wendy — the daughter of my uncle, policeman Mike Avery and aunt Paddy (Buster's sister) — had grown up in the capital, a Queen Elizabeth School girl, and very much a city girl. But she fell for this farmer.

Once Tim finished at college, they were soon married and headed off to farm at Mvuma — 'just a petrol station and a hotel' — about 200km from the capital. Theirs was a 35,000-acre cattle ranch, much of it bushland, reached by a rough gravel road which petered out into dirt roads, making it a good three-hour drive to the city. In good weather.

Low-lying bridges would be washed out. 'So a few times you couldn't go anywhere — you just sat and looked at the bridge for a few hours while the water went down.' And, without basics like electricity, it was a hard landing for Wendy.

'Wendy went from city girl to bush girl,' Tim grins. 'She got clever quick — or hungry, depending on how well she planned those shopping trips.'

The only social life was at the town's club, about an hour's drive each way. Tim had other outlets, such as fellow members of the Commercial Farmers Union, which was something of an old boys' club that advocated for the 5000-odd farmers.

After a few years, Tim and Wendy did a swap with someone who preferred to do it tough on a ranch: 35,000 acres at Mvuma for 3500 acres of cropping farm at Banket. 'Value for value,' says Tim. While it was mainly cropping — maize, soya bean wheat, barley — they also ran about 200 head of cattle. Around 90km from the capital, it was an easier drive in their Mazda *bakkie* 'and seatbelts were a thing you only saw in movies.' Their family was growing and they bought a VW Kombi, which they used for holidays: They used to have a big playroom in the back of the Kombi.

Social life improved because their farm backed onto the local social club. The club was self-financed by the community and offered rugby, bowls, tennis, polo, squash, golf. In addition, there were garden clubs and flower shows, and the community theatre also put on shows and pantomimes. The 200-or-so members were virtually all neighbours. Friday nights meant children running feral outside while parents held court at the bar. 'Many of the world's problems were "solved" late at night,' Tim laughs. 'Too many good piss-ups!'

Boarding school punctuated family life: weekends brought their three children Jen, Sandy, and Bruce, back to the farm, brimming with cattle and crops.

But punctuation of a different nature was affecting their lives. Since UDI and the first shots of the 'Bush War' at Sinoia — where seven Zimbabwe People's Revolutionary Army fighters infiltrated from

Zambia — Territorial Army call-ups were a routine fact of life. Captain (Acting Major) Tim Henwood was now getting regular call-ups for six-week stints away on operations … six weeks on, then back home for two months. This pattern applied to most in their twenties and thirties, although farmers were often accorded lenient treatment if it was a busy time of year for them. 'Obviously it disrupted our family, but we just learned to live with it,' says Wendy. 'I would never stay on the farm; I would go with the kids and stay with family in Salisbury. So it wasn't unpleasant.' Partly this was for security, partly for companionship.

Wendy took to walking around home and farm with an Uzi-like machine gun slung across her shoulder, looking menacing, and taking no chances, even when Tim was home. It was not uncommon to see housewives doing the shopping in Salisbury with an Uzi nonchalantly hanging off them.

One day the gardener came to Wendy and said, 'Madam, there's a snake in the chicken house.' She rushed there with her automatic weapon. Tim can't resist jumping in and finishing off a story he's probably told 1000 times: 'She's emptied a few rounds into the snake, and the snake didn't move. After a few shots, the gardener said, "Madam, stand aside, let me kill it." So he proceeded to hit it with a stick and kill the snake! The enemy forces that we were being protected from by Wendy were feeling a lot braver after that day!'

Security was constant: diamond-mesh fences around the farm, alarms, a pistol at the hip for Tim, and even a rack for rifles at the country club door. Yet it felt strangely normal. 'It creeps up gradually,' Tim said. 'You never believe you've lost until you've lost.'

He was all the while active within the Commercial Farmers Union, which was now having to become more of an activist and advocacy organisation as attacks on farms and farmers increased.

Patrol Officer Ian Daniel was by now posted to Nuanetsi, about 100km north of the Beit Bridge border post with South Africa. It was full of childhood memories for him: 'We used to go shooting there to get meat.' His bush district policing duties had morphed from standard duties ('handling murders and stabbings and basic crime') into 'just different, it grew with you'. But as much as he didn't think about it, the reality was they were now in a war.

'I was given the job of visiting farms and finding what we called "Green Routes". In the event of an attack, you don't want to use the main road going in, you want to use the green routes, back roads — the quickest and safest road in.' So his job was to collate this info into a big file in preparation.

He was sent on one TEAMS deployment (Tribal Trust Land Emergency Action Manpower) in north-eastern Mtoko. While the fire forces were dispatched frequently from here, life for the police team seemed 'cruisey'. Ian received an invitation to a party in the house of the local magistrate, a former BSAP member. Enjoying the beers, Ian was somewhat surprised to see a bunch of strippers come in, flown in on the private plane of the magistrate. 'From the strippers' point of view the night was a failure, because the guys were more interested in chatting to each other and getting drunk on all the free beer and wine,' he laughs. 'Such is life on the front.'

Nearby the local government doctor at Mrewa was found to be siding with the terrorists, and 'came around' after interrogation by Ian, and told his job tenure might now be in jeopardy. Thereafter, he was supplied with adulterated medications, which were presumably administered to terrorists. (Post-liberation that doctor allegedly became the Health Minister.)

There were also cases of local shopkeepers supplying clothing laced with anthrax to terrorists, causing mysterious deaths.

Back in Nuanetsi, New Year's Eve came around, being celebrated at the local hotel. Ian wasn't in a party mood, with his head full of the green routes stuff. 'And this woman — a huge jolly lady who I knew from my childhood as Aunt Audrey — grabbed me and said, "C'mon, dance, dance!" But I just couldn't get into it — I was preparing for a terrorist attack, but they weren't aware. They were still living life, but I couldn't tell them, and I left the party early. That really disturbed me, things that were going on that we couldn't reveal.'

His job entailed a lot of advice for farmers on preparing for attacks, such as sandbagging, screens on windows ('not that they'd stop a rocket'), predetermined firing points around the place ('whether they were gonna shoot out of a window or go outside into the sandbags or retreat to the middle of the house'). A lot of them had big security fences erected, typically six-foot high chain-mesh fences and a gate.

A system called Agri Alert was also introduced. It was a rural early-warning system and communication network linking farmers to police and military units. VHF/FM radios, often Barrett or Pye, were set up in homes, farm offices, even in vehicles, with each farm assigned a call sign.

A call of 'Contact! Contact!' or 'Code Red!' or 'Condition Charlie !' meant it was game on. Forces were mobilised, and neighbouring farmers would arm themselves in readiness. Distress calls were relayed further as required to the Police Reserve Air Wing, or the Joint Operation Commands which could mobilise Police Anti-Terrorist Units (PATU), fire force units, Grey's Scouts, etc.

'It gave them immediate contact to outside help if it was possible, 'says Ian, 'but by the time outside help got organised and got to the farm the attack's over, they're gone.'

The white population of Rhodesia peaked at this point, with somewhere between 280-300,000 whites, but still less than five per cent of the population.

After Portugal's pulling out of East Africa, that left an exposed flank with Mozambique and Angola ... now two fronts had to be monitored and manned by the relatively small Rhodesian army. Adding to the degree of difficulty, guerrilla camps were embedded deeply in the Rhodesian countryside, from where training and operations took place. The danger was now within.

General unrest and sabotage activities widened to take in the south and south-west, and in Easter 1976 the shocking news came that a young American couple, Peter and Barbara Fletcher (newlyweds from California), were killed when guerrillas ambushed their vehicle near the Victoria Falls resort area.

Soon, armed convoys were put in place to protect civilians just going about their business or pleasure, from one part of Rhodesia to another.

23

GONE WITH THE WIND

SOUTH AFRICA, 1974. I followed Glendon to boarding school at Cordwalles. I was so excited to go to this school — the open days were always brilliant fun, seeing boys doing mechanics club (building and fixing go-karts), butterfly club (catching butterflies and pinning them to boards), chess club, theatre productions, plus a smorgasbord of sports.

Cordies sits on beautiful grounds, around 20 football fields large, with jacaranda and oak trees aplenty, just outside the historic city of Pietermaritzburg. It looked far more historic than it was (established 1912) thanks to the British colonial style red-brick buildings and arches which dominated it.

Kids came from all points of Africa to be here, especially neighbouring countries. We had a few interesting classmates, such as Van Deventer, who used to arrive at school in his father's 6.3 litre Mercedes 600 with self-levelling air suspension. Clearly a bit of dosh in the family. And there was a rather gangly guy with big ears called Timothy. His father was the infamous Col 'Mad Mike' Hoare, mercenary of note, who was active in the Congo, and depicted in *The Wild Geese* movie by Richard Burton. (A few years later his father led a botched coup attempt in the Seychelles, resulting in a shoot-out at the airport, where he hijacked an Air India plane back to South Africa, where he was arrested and jailed, and it became a big diplomatic incident.)

But no sooner had I been dropped off than the homesickness set in, even though I had my brother there, and a couple of familiar faces. The rule was parents were not allowed to visit new boys within six weeks of them starting. Around two or three weeks after Glen had started, Dad had a conference in Maritzburg, and decided to drop in and enquire how he was getting on. Ronald C Brookes, the headmaster, said: 'Oh, we can call him and ask him yourself.'

'Like a duck to water, apparently,' is how Mum remembers his adjustment. Me, not so much.

On the first eligible Sunday, I saw Mum and Dad arrive in their Mercedes, and park under the trees. I ran to the car, crying, dragging my tartan-checked blue bag of marbles behind me. I collapsed in tears in their car (I guess I always was a sensitive soul).

Brooksey, a pukka Englishman with a master's degree from Cambridge, was a wonderful educator determined to turn us all into fine Englishmen in the colonies. He loved picking up kids on sloppy pronunciation.

'Sir, do we have to take our books with us?' some poor sap would ask. At which Brooksey would pull an exaggeratedly painful expression on his face, and put his cupped hand to his ear, as though struggling to hear or understand.

'D wee avta? D wee avta?' he'd ask.

Then the kid would have to repeat what he'd said, slowly and clearly.

Each week we had a time in which we had to write a letter home, which would be checked for length by the master on duty (often 'Monk' Steer). I loved the feel of writing with a fountain pen on onion skin paper. We had those desks with the ink well in the corner, and as much Quink found its way onto the floor and over the desk, as it did on the page. Being left-handed, I was given exemption to use a Bic biro or Parker ballpoint to avoid smudging as my hand crabbed across the page.

Dormitories (which ran on two levels) were named after inspirational characters like Shakespeare, Pasteur, Columbus, Drake, da Gama. Each night, 'Brooksey' or the duty master, would come patrolling through, checking that we were all reading something — you always had to have a book on the go.

After lights out, Brookesy made sure everyone was still in their beds, not talking, etc. I don't know whether it was the homesickness, but I took to sleep-talking and even pee'd my bed a few times, a great way to get bagged by your new dorm mates. Everyday tricks played on others included 'apple-pie'ing the sheets, meaning you remade somebody's bed, but folded the sheets in half so they couldn't get their body all the way in, and couldn't work out why not. The other cruel one was getting two mugs, one filled with water. Then you'd gather round some poor sleeping sod, and transfer the water from one mug to the other, with resulting sloshing and splashing sounds. This resulted in many a poor bugger reflexively pissing in their sleep.

One time the housekeepers did a raid in the daytime, and I got hauled into Brooksey's study.

'Lloyd, explain these items we found in your dressing gown please.'

He held up Exhibit A, a torch. And Exhibit B, chewing gum. Serious contraband.

'Um, er, ah,' I stammered, tap-dancing my way towards an ingenious lie. 'I used my dressing gown at home during the holidays, and I use the torch to go to the workshop outside, so I guess I just forgot it there, sir.' I offered no defence for the chewing gum. He lifted his chin and looked down at me over his half-frame glasses. He wasn't buying this. The torch was confiscated and I could pick it up at the end of term and take it home.

Wilbur Smith had attended this school, and hated nearly every minute of it because he was not a sports jock nor a fan of religion and hated the food and the cold and... But, as he wrote in his autobiography: 'Fifty years later, I can look back on my career as a best-selling author, and it all started under the blankets in a dorm at Cordwalles.' He praised his English master for inculcating the love of literature and writing in him.

The library was a source of great wonder with its dark hardwood shelves, musty smells, and a great big book which listed in beautiful calligraphed penmanship all the winners of various scholarships over the years. How I wanted to be in that book for all time.

Like Wilbur Smith, I took to reading voraciously. I never seemed to get past the Second World War section. Paul Brickhill's *The Colditz Story* lit the fuse on my imagination. I also picked up *Reach for the Sky* by Douglas Bader, the legless Spitfire ace fighter pilot. As Mum would often remind me, I must have read that book non-stop for the next three years.

The food was boarding school food. Big tubs of generally edible stuff, wheeled out on great big metal trolleys by the kitchen staff, in their not-always spotless whites. Grace would be said by one of the prefects, then there was five minutes' silence enforced, as music was played — often classical if Brooksey was officiating, or maybe something poppish like Simon and Garfunkel — and the slop was served. Scrambled eggs were some kind of reconstituted watery powder.

The best meal was on the occasional Sunday when trifle was served, and none was ever spared. Except for one Sunday (in shades of the Sani Pass Incident) when we were dismissed from the dining hall, but dessert was running behind. As everyone was filing out, I noticed activity in the kitchen — they were about to wheel out the trifle. Some fellows and I sat resolutely at our table, the only table left. Big plastic buckets of trifle were delivered to us, and we tucked in, eating for the rest of Africa. Geez, we felt sick afterwards, but I would do it all again tomorrow.

Marbles was the big thing at school during any break time or free time. Any available flat surface, such as a cricket pitch, was ideal to set up your stall with whatever your special was: 'Six piley!' Six piley!' You'd spend time with forensic actuarial detail working out the odds of somebody hitting your special smoky glass marble stack from five metres away, discreetly placing a little blade of grass or something in the path to load the odds in your favour.

Around this time, I wrote a letter home, boasting of how I'd made my fortune in marbles, bags and bags of them bursting at the seams. But the little PS at the bottom probably betrays the real story of my skill: 'Please send me some more marbles.'

This school was brilliant, there was always so much going on, and everyone could find their 'thing' be it academic, sporting, or a hobby. There was little I didn't participate in.

Highlights were being a tuck shop assistant. You got to serve your mates and slip them an extra bit of this and that to their eternal gratitude. The smash hit of the day were Fizz Pops, a raspberry lollipop with a sherbet centre, a dentist's dream and a 20-cent ticket to heaven. In huge demand, we'd always make sure to put a few aside for ourselves and our buddies.

Academically, I took to Latin with relish. From the first *'amo, amas, amat'* I always aced it. Actually, all subjects, including Afrikaans with Mejuffrou Stein. 'Yiffie' as we called her, was a spinster, and a great human being who lived not too far from the school. On Sundays (when we were allowed out) we'd often pile round to her place for lunch and just hang out for the day.

Mr Edwards and Mr Judd were other really engaging teachers who made maths and science vaguely interesting. They were also both very active in sports coaching. I played rugby, cricket, tennis, hockey, and athletics competitively. I was never a swimmer, which my two brothers were.

Summer terms always started with the ritual of 'knocking in' your bat. All the cool kids used Grey Nichols, now with fluorescent orange stickers. And the secret to Graeme Pollock-like performances (he averaged 74 in tests!) was oiling your bat with linseed oil and pounding it with a rubber mallet so its sweet spot was, well, sweet.

My letters home described fantastic bowling figures which I'm now sure were hugely spin-doctored. Another letter described how I had a sore ankle but played anyway, and was on my way to a sure-fire triple century when this guy bowled and, just as I went to hit the ball, the ankle pain returned, and I dollied it to mid-on for a catch, thus ending my brilliant innings of 12 runs. Brookesy would always be sitting on the sideline on his 'shooting stick 'seat, with Banquo the beagle with his broken tail (allegedly at the hands of my friend AB Taylor's brother, JB) at his side, and always had a 'Well batted, Lloyd 'or 'Well bowled, Lloyd 'to say.

In the first XI cricket we'd have an annual fathers vs sons cricket match. Dad couldn't play because of his wonky knee. But Mum and Dad drove up to watch. Andrew Lund's dad, a Howick farmer, came into to bowl to me. First ball, he bowled this slow looping ball which landed way outside my off stump. I did the sensible thing and lifted my bat, watching it drift safely by … right into my middle stump! Never mind Shane Warne, Mr Lund had delivered the true 'ball of the century'! I looked at my rattled furniture, back at the umpire, and almost said, 'That's not fair, my folks have driven all the way from Tongaat to see me,' before making the long and slow walk of shame back to the changing shed.

On the upside, that gave me more time on the sideline to appreciate Andrew's blonde younger sister Penny, with whom I was truly madly in love, despite never even having said 'hello' to her. I was also truly madly deeply in love with Andrew Rattray's sister Belinda (or was it Melinda?) on the basis of one 'hello'.

Still, I did have shining moments in the baggy brown-and-white cap. Like the time against Highbury where I smashed several sixes into the trees (and for some of those shots I even had my eyes open) to win the game.

We had an athletics event which was the cricket ball throw. Glendon had an amazing arm on him and broke the school record of 62m. That's a long throw for a 13- or 14-year-old!

Cross-country running was also something I loved, as did my father. The school had a great circuit which ran for a couple of kilometres down through the bush to the lower oval, then back up to the school with a couple of cheeky uphill sections. I'd invariably end up in a photo-finish with good friend Mark Tully.

I threw myself into rugby, having a bit of speed and size out on the wing, fly-half, or fullback. Except for one match where we were pitted against Highbury who had a man-mountain in the form of Duncan Willis. He played centre, and I was told that I was to be centre that day, and mark Willis. My testosterone levels kicked up a notch: 'I'll show him who's boss! 'First play of the day they won the ball, it got passed out to Willis, and he was heading straight for me. *Right, bring it on*! I was thinking to myself. I ran towards him, lowered my shoulder to go into the tackle, and the only thing I remember was next thing he was under the goalposts celebrating a try, and I was lying back on halfway listening to sparrows chirping in my head, and watching blue-and-gold stars circling. There may even have been a unicorn in there, too.

For the rest of the match, every time he got the ball, I laid out the red carpet for him: 'Mr Willis, after you, sir.'

I was clearly not living the school's motto of 'Courage Builds Character'. But I do remember one slogan permanently on one of the classroom blackboards chalked in a beautiful gothic typeface: 'Manners Maketh the Man.' I thought I showed exemplary manners to Mr Willis that afternoon.

I was peeved that I got overlooked for rugby 'colours' — apparently for not putting my head deep enough into the rucks one game against Highbury — while Andrew Lund, Charlie Kessler, AB Taylor, and Douglas Tatham were awarded theirs. Still, I got to hold the ball in the team photo.

We travelled over large parts of Natal playing sport. But my favourite was often matches against Clifton Nottingham Road. Because after playing them, often with snow piled up on the side of the field, you'd always be treated to great big steel mugs of boiling hot tea, the most delicious tea I've ever drunk in my life.

We'd be transported to these games in an old Ford Transit, with two rows of bench seats along the back. Hi-jinx would usually ensue after a rugby game with some poor sod often held down and Deep Heat applied to his undercarriage with hilarious laughter from all (except the victim).

On Sundays, us few Catholics at the school would be taken in that same van — still reeking of Deep Heat — to the St Mary's Catholic Church where we'd repent our sins or, if we had been the victim the previous day, to pray that the perpetrators be damned in hell.

But that didn't exonerate us from attending chapel on Sunday evenings back at school. I went one step further and signed on to be an altar boy. I know. The perk of this was we got to set up the chapel in the mornings, and Charlie Kessler and I would often do quality control on the 'blood of Christ' which was stored with the holy water in a little hatch in the sacristy to the side.

Glendon and I were in the choir and loved all the singing and music that entailed, along with elaborate cassocks in black, with a white-over-tunic, frilly collar, and a blue lanyard. It helped that my good mates Mark Tully, Charlie Kessler, and Craig Lardner were also in the choir, with lots of laughs had (especially when our voices started breaking). Charlie went on to become choir captain.

Prof Raven was the choir master. He was a real enthusiast, and had us singing in wonderful multi-part harmonies and counter-melodies. He was also a terrific organist and used to play amazingly strident entry and exit tunes, with his fingers flying, tweaking the stops on the organ for different sounds, his legs pumping away on the pedals to produce the bass notes.

The big event each year was when Cordies took over the cathedral downtown for our annual carol service. Competition for solo spots was fierce. Glendon was a soloist. I got my audition, but the musty air of the cathedral triggered my hay-fever, so *Once In Royal David's City* sounded more like 'Once in royal nasal sniffy ...' Next! I was relegated to the main choir and had to content myself with lyric improvisations such as *'While shepherds washed their socks at night ...'*

I was still learning the piano, although struggling to be enthusiastic under the rather crotchety (pardon the pun) Mrs De Villiers. She was insisting I learn some really boring old stuff, whereas I was now into pop stuff, and wanted to play *Raindrops Keep Falling On My Head.* One day there was a rugby match on at the same time as my piano lesson. Of course I went to watch the rugby game. I made the excuse that I'd given up piano lessons, which everyone found incredulous because I was the golden-haired wunderkind in the music rooms.

Then months later my parents wondered why they hadn't been invoiced for piano lessons.

'Er, I gave up the piano … piano is for sissies,' I said, channeling my inner-Digby Stanley.

'You'll regret it later,' Mum said, 'it's such a wonderful instrument.'

'No I won't,' I said. Yes, I do.

Instead, I took up two things. The organ and the guitar. Mary Turnbull was a music teacher at school and taught me how to play the chapel organ. And, before I knew it, I was added to the player roster for the nightly chapel services.

Sweating profusely with nerves, I played something meandering for the entry song. People filed in, and Brookesy strode up the aisle, and took his seat opposite me to run the service.

'Now we'll have the first hymn, Hymn 304, *There Is a Green Hill Far Away.*' Everyone stood, opened their hymn books, I broke into the chords, and got through the song with no hiccups. So far so good. A few more readings.

'Now we'll have the second hymn, Hymn 304, *There is a Green Hill Far Away* …?' Brookesy looked across at me for confirmation. I nodded, and broke into the song, sang with a little less gusto than the first version. More prayers etc.

'Now we'll have the third hymn … um …' Brooksey's looking at me quizzically, looking around at the hymn board, which shows Hymn 304. I nodded. He frowned. 'The third hymn is Hymn 304, *There is a Green*

Hill Far Away.' And we limped though that, everybody thinking the same thing: Didn't we already sing this before? Twice before even? Then I played the recessional and people filed out laughing and sneaking glances at me. But I was too buried in my sheet music to notice or care.

I quickly added a couple more tunes to my repertoire, but safe to say organist Prof Raven's job was never really threatened.

In the music rooms was an acoustic guitar for sale. Someone had dropped a snare drum on it, cracking the soundboard. It was for sale for $10. I tested it out and *Smoke on the Water* sounded fine, so I talked Dad into buying it for me.

I started guitar lessons with Bruce Gadd at school. He wore his hair in the longer style with some serious platform soles, so he must be good. We started off with D, G and A chords, with little coloured stickers stuck on the fretboard so we knew where to place our fingers. Within weeks I had *Tom Dooley* nailed (well, there was a little pause between the 'Tom' and the 'Dooley' and the 'hang down your head and …' and 'cry' where I had to find and finger a different chord).

Easy, this guitar thing — nothing to it! Until Mr Gadd introduced me to the F chord. Try as I might, I couldn't get my fingers into that shape, and if and when I did, I'd get all this fret buzz. That was the end of my guitar career, for now.

Thankfully extra-curricular options were endless. I joined the chess club, of which Glendon was a keen and competitive member. Dad had returned from some trip with a beautiful wooden chess board and a book which detailed every match and move of the Fischer vs Spassky 1972 showdown, which was the Cold War boiled down to a board game. We devoured that, marvelling at the moves.

I improved and became captain of the Cordwalles Chess B team. One afternoon, we had a match against St Charles, in the back of the old auditorium. I gave my team a rousing pep-talk, and — within about two minutes of the matches commencing — I was sheepishly standing in the corner stuffing my face with sandwiches and orange juice. I had been fools-mated!

Fortunately, soon after, the old auditorium was demolished and a flash new purpose-built theatre constructed in its place, with wings, balconies, lighting rigs, trapdoors, and everything a theatre could possibly want. Glendon starred in many productions, notably as a Russian Cossack in *The Nosebag*. He was a natural thespian.

I made it into the crowd ensemble of *Julius Caesar*, enjoying the toga party atmosphere of the production. One night there were a few girls' schools bussed in to watch. Of course, I'm there — supposedly in the forum as the famous 'We came here to bury Caesar not to praise him' thing is going on — and I'm ad-libbing chants, trying to impress the girls. Afterwards, our English teacher Mr Crookes pulled me aside. 'Er, Lloyd, I don't think words like "cool" and "groovy" were part of the Roman vocabulary back then.'

Then came my star turn in *Olaf and Ogre*. I was Olaf, wearing these great big wellies, playing opposite Andrew Everett, a chunky classmate from Maseru, Lesotho. We ran a few nights, and everything went perfectly. Then one night the play was over and the curtain came down. Hmm, that was rather quick, I was thinking to myself. Indeed, it was. Our teacher came across, flustered, and explained where it all went wrong — I'd picked up on the wrong cue, Andrew had responded to that line, I followed on, and we'd managed to skip entire scenes and background changes, bringing us to the end of the show about half an hour early, the audience clapping yet scratching their heads simultaneously.

The theatre was also used for debating, speeches, and music performances. Debating was a ton of fun, and what a brilliant way to learn to formulate and articulate arguments, whether you agreed with what you were saying or not (this prepared me well for a life of bullshitting my way to the top of the advertising industry).

Even at that age I was formulating ideas for product ads. One I remember concocting was for Brut men's fragrances, with these tough, dirty, smelly rugby players, and the headline: 'These guys need Brut strength.'

We used to do inter-school debating too, with teams visiting us or vice-versa, and had a healthy debating culture within the school, too. One clanger I made: Mum had given me a great quote from Kenneth Clarke, a real mic-dropping knockout punch for my side of the motion. I went to the library and looked him up because I had no idea who he was. She was horrified to hear me attributing that quote to Ken Clarke, a one-term mayor of Durban, instead of the Kenneth Clarke, presenter of the blockbuster BBC series *Civilisation.*

Next, I put up my hand to be the projectionist for the school's Saturday movie nights. It was fun learning to thread spools of 16mm film into the machine, loop it over this thing, lift up that thingy, run it under the thingymajig, then loop it round this whatchumacallit, then back onto the other reel. Press play, and *PRESTO*! A movie!

We showed movies like *The 39 Steps*, *The Plank*, and — happy days! — *Reach for the Sky*. All I wanted to be was Douglas Bader, but I'd prefer to have my own legs if possible.

The art of the good projectionist was to minimise the reload time for a multi-reel movie. You'd have the next one lined up, watching the current reel getting smaller and smaller until, with a clack and a whirr, the loose end would come spitting out. Then you'd whip off the first reel, click on the second reel, and off you'd go again. You'd time your own performance in doing this like an F1 pitstop.

There's nothing like getting the reels out of order (not unheard of) to sow mass confusion! Sometimes there'd be calls of 'Focus!' And you'd look to see this blurred image on the screen.

One time, the camera zoomed into this cat sitting on a bed. The cat's face got bigger and bigger, them seemed to blister and disintegrate. In the days before computer graphics, this was quite amazing. Wait, hold on, what's that burning smell? I turned to the projector to see the film had jammed, and the projector bulb had melted the film. *Shit*! Boos and jeers from the understanding audience! Open the projector, pull out the offending roll, cut it, rethread it, press play. Lights out. Ironic cheers. And we're off to the movies again.

Around this time, Dad noted my interest in photography and gave me his Voigtlander camera. It was an impressive and expensive bit of gear, so the gesture was not lost on me. He taught me all about f-stops and depth of field. I started photographing whatever I found interesting: rugby matches, and the view from the school up to World's View at sunset, which was always stunning, and featured in at least 3,000,000 student drawings and paintings. Then I'd go to the school's dark room and process the film and develop the images. It was a buzz to bring your image into focus on the paper, expose it for just the right amount of seconds, then dip them in various chemical trays to set and fix them for the right amount of time again, then hang them to dry, hoping you'd nailed all the variables and came up with a killer shot.

World's View was part of the old road known as Boesmansrand, which the Voortrekkers had used to reach Pietermaritzburg. It was a thickly forested hilltop with a radio mast atop it, and a popular lover's lane. One of our teen thrills on Sundays out there, was to come across used rubbers — or *frikkies* as we called them — which had been hastily discarded out of car windows.

On Sundays, if you were in Standard 6, you were allowed out into the city. We headed to the city. Our mission this day was to drop in on Penny Lund. Turned up at Wykeham School, announced myself to whoever was running intercept, and was told, 'No, sorry, Penny is a weekly boarder, she goes home at weekends.'

So I transferred my allegiance, mentally at least, to my tennis coach Ruth Stevens' daughter. Every Tuesday morning Ruth would come out and give us tennis lessons. I loved tennis, probably more than any other sport. Mum was a feisty competitor, and I loved the strategy and skill set required. Being a left-hander I was developing this really swervy serve with a massive sidespin that was proving devastating ... if I could only get the bloody ball into the proper box on the court. Enter Ruth's daughter Greer. Blonde hair in ponytails. Tanned. Muscular. Short tennis skirt. Make that a *very* short tennis skirt. She was only 18 at this time but had turned professional in 1974 and was rising up the ranks.

My energy levels shot up whenever she was around. I was serving and volleying and smashing and running like I'd never done in my life before!

Shortly after this, at the Maidstone Open, Mum made it to the final and came up against Greer. It was the moment I was perhaps most proud of my mother. She traded shot-for-shot in long rallies with Greer, creating massive conflicting emotions in me. You've gotta cheer for your Mum, right? Yes, but — *but*! — she's playing against Greer Stevens. *My Greer*! Haha! The match went the full distance, with Mum running down impossible balls, blowing hard in the Natal heat, red in the face, but sticking at it. Finally, Greer Stevens pipped her and won the trophy.

Within a couple of years, Greer Stevens had won the Wimbledon mixed doubles with Bob Hewitt (Australian-born but later took on South African citizenship after marrying a local lass). Within a few more years, she'd added several more titles, and peaked as the #7 ladies singles player in the world. I like to think it was those Tuesdays at Cordwalles that shaped her into the champion she became.

Because she was so busy, I transferred my allegiances once again. To another tennis player. In summer, we used to play every town's tennis tournaments: Umhlali, Maidstone, Empangeni, and so on.

My tennis playing was actually like my chess game. You didn't know you could be fools-mated on a tennis court, but I proved it. I was always the easy-beat of the tournament, knocked out in round one. Every. Single. Time. As a result, I'd pick up umpiring gigs and umpire everyone else's matches, usually competing at Umhlali with Gary Hulett for the umpiring award each year (based on how many games you'd umped, irrespective of how many contentious line-calls you'd made).

Empangeni was always super-fun because we'd go and stay with Dave and Jill, whose house was just over the road from the sports club, and it was wonderful summer fun with cousins Leigh, Joanne, and Michael.

A few matches of note. One year they played a round-robin format, so I was in the tournament for much longer than usual. I'd raced to a 5-2 lead (first to 6 games wins). And I lost 5-6. To this day I'm still traumatised by the result.

Another year, I came up against Glendon in round one (normally he was in a higher age group than me) and he was a good and super-competitive player. You could always tell when he was playing because of the anguished language at high decibels that came from his court. But this day he absolutely wiped me off the court. I got so frustrated at myself, especially when he lobbed one ball back, which looped into the stratosphere, and just made it onto my side of the net. I set myself up for a super-smash to blast this ball back at him emphatically. All I managed in my red-mist fury was to get a top edge and my return ballooned over the fence into the trees beyond. That summed up my day, my week, my summer.

However, it did give me time to fall quietly in love with Mary Deavin. Not that she knew I was in love with her. More, a case of she hardly knew me at all! I fastidiously followed all her matches, gawking from the sidelines. It should've been obvious to me that Eban Taylor, a swarthy good-looking guy, a few years ahead at Hilton, and gun tennis player, was nearby and similarly besotted.

When school term resumed, I wrote her a letter care of her boarding school. A few days later, I received a yellow envelope, with cursive female writing. My heart skipped and pounded wildly. As soon as we were dismissed, I ripped the envelope open. It was from Mary. She wrote: 'Your letter had the stamp on upside down, do you know what that means?' No, absolutely no bloody idea, Mary. Not then, not now. I'd probably not even stuck the stamp on myself because of the way the school postal system worked — you addressed the envelope and they did the stamps for you and charged postage to your parents. That was the end of that non-romance! I was clearly out of my league anyway.

The school offered lots of diversions and distractions. Often there'd be excursions to things like the Maritzburg Agricultural Show, or the local botanical gardens, where we'd be set tasks of finding certain flora, perhaps sketching it, etc.

On a bigger scale we'd go on wildlife camps, where Mr De Berg-White — a Baden-Powell lookalike who worked for the Natal Parks Board — would supervise multi-day campouts in the bush. This was cub scouts on steroids, with all the skills brought into play. We'd leave the campfire burning at night to ward away whatever wild animals may be lingering with bad intent. One night I awoke to a rustling sound. Close. My survival instincts (read: overactive imagination) immediately kicked in. Lion. *Huge* lion. *Pride* of huge lions. *Pride of huge, angry, hungry lions.* I sat bolt upright, heart thrashing, and peered out the zipper of the tent, only to see a single curious kudu bull with impressive corkscrewing horns.

Often Mr De Berg-White would come to the school before or after these events and give us talks on conservation, which he always made engaging and funny, like the guys who'd packed for a camping/fishing trip. Their *bakkie* was loaded to the gills with thousands of cans of beer, plus a single loaf of bread. 'Gee, what are we going to do with all that bread?' one of them asked.

Sometimes there might be a charity visit to a school for blind black kids in the area, or a high-octane visit to the Roy Hesketh race circuit, where

Basil van Rooyen was a local hero. (South Africa hosted F1 races in those days, Jody Schekter winning at Kyalami in 1975.)

On weekends, I would occasionally go and stay with friends, such as AB Taylor and his family, who were on a farm nearby.

This might have been when we started sneaking smokes for the first time. Menthol was all the rage then; the peppermint meant learner smokers could inhale with less coughing and spluttering than with normal tobacco flavours. Consulate was the go-to brand.

Other weekends, Mum and Dad would pick us up and we'd go sailing at Midmar Dam. This dam had been constructed in the mid-60s to be the water supply for Maritzburg and the growing industrial belt towards Pinetown-Durban. We'd stay in caravans, and often freeze our bits off at night, as the wind chill in winter could send the mercury into below-zero territory.

Talking of bits, I'd gone for a sneaky pee behind a tree before getting in the car to return to school. On completion, I'd caught myself in the zipper. In that agonising moment you realise the only way out is to go through the whole process in reverse. I screamed out. Dad came running, expecting I'd been bitten by a mamba or something. What he saw was far less impressive than a mamba! He grabbed the zipper and — with trademark subtlety — reversed the zipper over the offending member to screams of agony and very unmanly tears.

Charlie Kessler and I became really good buddies. He was from Joburg, and we were in cricket, rugby, choir, and everything else together. He came to stay with us on at least one weekend. In return, he and Craig Lardner invited me up to their Joburg homes for the holidays. We caught the bus up with all the other Transvaal boarders. En route the bus took a stone in the windscreen. *CRASH*! The whole thing suddenly shattered. The driver pulled over. Nobody was hurt and we limped on, now with added air-conditioning in the coach.

Craig's folks had a nice place near Sandton City, which was an ahead-of-its-time retail development, and Sandton became the happening commercial centre of Joburg around it.

One afternoon we went to the cinema to watch a film. *Shampoo*, a pretty racy film with Goldie Hawn and Warren Beatty. It was restricted to 18-year-olds and above. So we bought tickets to see something lame then dashed into *Shampoo* just as the movie was starting, hearts pounding at the prospects of being busted.

We were young boys trying to be men. We had Queen's *A Night at the Opera* and ABBA's *Arrival* on high rotation. We got lost in the grooves of those all day. We had a party in the calendar, at Angus Simpson's place, coming up. Every day we'd siphon a little bit of alcohol from Craig's parents' well-stocked bar counter. A nip of gin, a nip of vodka, a nip of rum, a nip of whiskey, a nip of brandy, and so on. It all went into this empty bottle, which we were going to take to the party. Bit by bit the bottle was filled with this lethal cocktail. Unwittingly we had concocted a potent Long Island Iced Tea.

Meantime, we were on the Kool menthol cigarettes, disguising the giveaway smell with Ego deodorant (the Lynx of the day).

After a week, I shifted across to Charlie's place. We were sitting on the roof in the sun one day, enjoying a smoke. Suddenly his mum appeared, and we hid the ciggies behind our backs. But the tell-tale wisps of smoke snaked their way up above us, and she asked what was going on. But she was quite liberal. Charlie's sister Lynette enjoyed starting the day with a little choof of weed, so it proved to be quite an educational break.

Come the night of Angus' party, we turned up with our bottle of magical mystery elixir. It was a really straight affair. More like a movie night at home, with full parental supervision. Which made our mission to get completely pissed for the first time all the more appealing.

But the real fun started when we got home. All three of us were sharing Charlie's bedroom. Of course, the room was spinning violently. I think a big storm had come in, so there was lightning and crashes of thunder. At some point I needed a pee, so tried opening the window, which set off the burglar alarm. Craig was throwing up in the cupboard. Or maybe it was me throwing up in the cupboard and Craig peeing out the window. Or me peeing on Craig. I've got no idea. And into this chaotic scene walks Mrs Kessler. We'd come a long way from sampling the 'body of Christ' at Cordwalles chapel!

To this day I cannot get within five metres of gin (the over-riding flavour of the mix) without a reflex gag.

By the time we got back to school after that holiday we felt we'd passed through the threshold to true manhood.

One of our dorm mates, Michael Brooks, was being driven in a van from his home back to school. His driver had decided to save petrol, so switched off the engine to coast down the valley. Net result: loss of power steering — the van plunged off the road. I believe he lost his spleen in that accident, and it was a while before he was back to school.

The roads of Natal were a crazy place to be at that time (perhaps still are). One afternoon we were all in the family car heading down to Tongaat Beach when this truck turned across us. Dad swerved and we clipped the underside of its tray section. Dad confronted the driver, who was cross-eyed and clearly drunk.

Another time on the main road near Umdloti, which has high embankments on either side, this *bakkie* loaded with passengers on its open back, was weaving along the road. 'I think he's drunk.' said Dad, backing off. The weaving became more and more pronounced as this *bakkie* started going up one side of the embankment, then up the other, almost comically, before he went right up the side and — as we passed it — saw it roll down the embankment.

Ever since the oil crisis of 1973-4, punishments for speeding were being increased to deter offenders, to the point that Dad reckoned if a copper with a new-fangled radar pulled you over for speeding, you would be better off running him over than copping the speeding fine. You got less for murder, apparently!

South Africans often joked that some roads were badly potholed, and you'd have to weave around the potholes. It was easy to tell who was drunk — the guy who just drove straight, without dodging the potholes!

Mum once had to get a lift to Durban with this guy who worked for Tongaat. He drove a mustard-coloured Alfa. He was tearing along the road. Mum gripped the dashboard in white-knuckled terror. Eventually she blurted out that he should be driving a bit slower, a bit more carefully: 'Hell no,' he replied with a certain logic: 'If we have a crash I don't want to be left maimed.' Mum tightened her grip, and I imagine might've invoked a quiet prayer to the Lord.

We mostly caught a chartered bus from Musgrave Centre in Durban to school after the holidays, but usually one or both our parents would pick us up at the end of term.

Mum turned up one day. She'd already collected Glendon from Hilton College (further beyond Maritzburg), and then collected me. It was the end of the school year, summer holidays ahead, good vibes running high. We had the windows wound down, sun shining, Mum had the radio up loud, and she was flying down the highway towards Durban. *Tie a Yellow Ribbon Round the Old Oak Tree* came on the radio, and Mum turned it up even louder. She was sending it! And we were all in full voice on the chorus. We'd never seen Mum so joyously expressive before. Suddenly a policeman pulled us over for speeding. Talk about sucking the oxygen out of the room.

Big news. We were moving houses, to Braeside at Compensation, just minutes inland from Umhlali and Ballito. Compensation was the site of Morewood's first 40-acre farm managed by Ephraim Rathbone that got the whole sugar industry moving. Not that we knew that at the time. (Today a memorial park stands on Morewood's site).

The farm was one of the early sugar farms carved out of the larger Compensation Estate in the late 19th century.

By the mid-1970s, Tongaat-Hulett was one of South Africa's great private empires — it felt more like a world or an eco-system you lived in, rather than a company one worked for.

The stately Braeside homestead was originally built by Ray Hulett but was now owned by Tongaat. 'It was wonderful,' said Jen, 'because of Dad's position we were able to get it.' There were some dark mutterings from the wives of other executives (hello to Mrs Hankinson if you're reading this) as to why we got this grand house.

And may well they have green eyes, for this home was once marketed as a 13-bedroom house and now forms the core of the new Manor Estates development. It was then very *Gone With The Wind.* Double-story, with open balustraded verandahs on every side, reached by a circular driveway ringed by palm trees. The landscaped garden was several acres, with lychee trees. It had a pool. A tennis court. We put in a sauna. Out the back, a big garage and workshop. Our new phone number was Umhlali 123.

Our bedroom — all three of us boys shared one room on the top floor — was as large as a dormitory and had a big balcony. We'd often just sleep on the balcony on sleeping bags on hot summer nights to get the breeze.

Washington, a short moustachioed gardener with yellowed blood-shot eyes from way too much pot came over with his family from Klipfontein to here, and we added a couple of new faces ... John, a tall and pleasant fellow, and Petros, a gentle soul who was in charge of the kitchen and other stuff inside the home.

Washington's wife was pregnant. And one night she went into labour. Dad woke up to drive her to the clinic, but she delivered the baby in the car halfway there. The baby was naturally called Mercedes.

John had a full-time job just mowing the lawns, because by the time he'd finished at one end, he'd have to start at the other. We begged him for a chance to operate the mower, which of course he was only too happy for us to take over. It was a novelty for us.

Umhlali Country Club was minutes up the road, a new social epicentre. The prosperity of the cane industry at that point was staggering. Everyone was suddenly driving Mercedes Benzes. Two local farmers rolled out of the club one night, bid each other farewell, hopped into their brand-new Benzes, reversed out and found themselves facing each other from opposite ends of the car park. They did the thing that seemed to make sense at that moment: have a game of chicken. They achieved full ramming speed, leaving two crumpled heaps in the car park, laughing as they left the scene arms over each other's shoulders. The next day they were back at the dealership again for new models.

The license plate system was such that the prefix indicated where you lived, ie, ND was Durban, NJ was Tongaat, NT was Stanger. One day a guy from Tongaat was heading down the south coast, and pulled into a roadside bar for a swiftie, noticing an NJ plate in the carpark. 'Who's the arsehole from Tongaat?' he said as he entered the bar. And in this way friendships were formed.

Dad drove us to Shaka's Rock one day, a rugged piece of basalt coastline near Ballito Bay and Salt Rock. We peered over the edge to the waves smashing into the tidal pools below. He shared with us that Shaka used this rock as the place to dispose of enemies and prisoners and dissenters, such was his fierce rule and reputation as a Zulu chief. Top-down command and control was their general modus operandi. We believed Dad's version, but it's folkloric.

Stanger was now where Mum went supermarket shopping, the highlight of our trips being this intellectually handicapped black guy we called Foofie Nunu. He had a big round moon-face sporting a perpetual big grin, which exposed three or four bright yellow teeth. His specialty was opening the car door for you — excellent service — then slamming your leg in it before you'd fully got into the car. All the while grinning wildly.

Another great benefit was being closer to the Shuker family who lived in a very stately historic home at Kearsney. Mum's childhood friend Paddy Saunders had married Dr Graeme Shuker, executive director of agriculture for Tongaat Hulett's. Their three kids Iain, Bruce, and Jane were almost identical ages to us so there were many family lunches and outings. And they had the best go-kart ever, a high-octane mean-machine which we'd blast around their circular drive way.

And church became more interesting in Stanger. Sitting in the pew I couldn't help noticing the wonderful shoulders on the lady in front of me. Such perfect posture and poise, and the rest of the figure did not disappoint. 'That's Penny Coelen.' Mum later explained. The former 1958 Miss World, Uncle David's friend (who still lives in the Ballito area). Anneline Kriel won the title in 1974, Roelene Strauss in 2014, and South Africa has always put up a strong showing in Miss Universe, with Margaret Gardiner (1978), Demi-Leigh Nel-Peters (2017), and Zozibini Tunzi (2019), winning the crown.

Then came 1976. South Africa was one of the last countries in the Western world to introduce television, due to resistance under the National Party and their closely aligned Dutch churches who viewed TV as a potential moral and political threat to their puritanical agenda.

South African Television (SATV, later SABC TV) started by dipping its toe in the pool, and broadcasts were limited to the evenings, and featured mostly news, imported shows, and split local Afrikaans/English programming (two hours of each, alternating each evening as to which went first).

Then we got one — *one*! — set at Cordwalles, and suddenly the sanctity of that reading time in dorm was violated by us seniors being allowed to watch *The Bob Newhart Show* and *The Carol Burnett Show* for an hour.

Wholesomeness was clearly the order of the day. *The Waltons, Hawaii Five-O, Mission: Impossible, The Six Million Dollar Man, Kojak, Love Thy Neighbour*, and *The Donny & Marie Show* were all foisted on us.

Braeside gave rise to any number of teenage adventures. Down the bottom of the highly landscaped area of gardens was a path leading down to a small pond. The dogs Peter and Eliza loved to swim there. We took our rods down and I was excited when, within three nanoseconds of my first cast, I had a bite. A solid bite, with a strong fight. I reeled this thing in, and it was an eel. An angry eel, which proceeded to wriggle up my line on to my rod, which I dropped and ran. We finished it off with a stick lying nearby.

There was also an early adventure involving pellet guns (air rifle), which Glendon and I had got for Christmas. We were soon taking pot shots at everything, from cans on a fence to birds in the garden. Indian Mynahs were dispatched by the millions. One afternoon there was a large crow in the tree by the tennis court. I lined him up and winged him. He plummeted to the ground, flapping and squawking madly. I pumped another shot into him, but that only made him flap more furiously. I moved and stood right over him. Poor thing was looking pleadingly up and me, as I set up for the point-blank coup de grace. *BANG*! I put several shots into his head, but he kept looking at me with his tongue out, and pleading eyes. Nothing for it, I eventually picked him up and carried it home, where he became a pet. He joined a talking crested barbet in a large cage in the courtyard outside the kitchen.

The 65 palm trees that lined our driveway were home to a fine colony of fruit bats. By day they roosted in the leaves, hanging upside down. Irresistible targets. The first time we shot at them, this thing plummeted out of the tree, and just as it was about to hit the ground, spread its swings, swooped up, and fell at my feet. I couldn't believe it's little foxlike face. We were transfixed by these things, especially the wingspan, which was easily 80cm across. Each tree had about 30 of these specimens in them. Do the maths — that's a lot of target practice!

One more memorable felling was one that swooped at very low level, and there was a hen that used to cluck around with its chicks in the garden near the worker's compound area. As this thing swooped, the hen reared up, talons extended — like Bruce Lee in *Enter the Dragon* — and brought this bat down, with a messy tussle ensuing on the ground. The chicken left it for dead.

One day, wandering around the estate we came across a large dump truck, parked on the side of this dirt road. No one around. Its big rear tyres presented an irresistible target. I lined up the shot with my pellet gun. *BANG! PhhhwwwiiiiiIIIIRRRRR*!!! The ricocheting slug came whizzing through the air in a swerving arc and Glendon and I watched open-mouthed in slow motion as it buzzed just past my right ear. A lucky near miss.

Another day, there was a mynah on the top of the corner post of the tennis court. I lined it up, fired, the bird flew away, but out of the corner of my eye I noticed Washington — always in bright orange overalls — hopping and skipping and clutching his foot. Time to disappear, I thought … I never owned up to that ricochet.

Which was similar to David Seymour's fishing story, where he was down at the beach, with the fish running a fair way out. There was only one other fisherman, a white guy, about 100 metres down the beach. He loaded up his line with several heavy pyramid-shaped lead sinkers. He swung the rod back for the biggest cast of his life but — as he cast — the line snapped. Out of the corner of his eye, he suddenly saw the other fisherman drop as though shot by a sniper. As you would if hit in the back of the head with a barrage of lead weights. 'I thought I'd killed the poor bugger!' David made a rather hasty exit back to his car.

Those palm trees featured in a couple of other stories. One day I was driving Dad's Mercedes round the drive, a nice circuit, because you could go straight up into the workshop/garage area, or you could turn right and go to the turning circle near the pool in front of the house. I was having a gentle cruise around one day, when Glendon jumped out of a bush in front of me. I slammed it into reverse, and backed down the drive, inexpertly reversing, and went off the track, jamming on the brakes just in time to stop me slamming boot-first into a palm tree. My heart was pounding out of my chest, especially at the thought of explaining that one to Dad.

Near the garage was a palm tree with a hole in its base, which a colony of bees called home. 'Let's smoke them out.' Glendon and I got some paper and matches, and the bellows from the fireplace. What could possibly go wrong? As we pumped the smoke in, the whole fleet made an orderly exit. *Triumph*! But, a little later, as I was walking down the driveway, I heard this growing buzz and a swarm of bees zeroed in on me. *ZAP*! Shrieks of pain! I ran into the house and, in trying to get the stingers out, probably squeezed all the poison in. My left ear swelled to about four times its normal size, turning me into this grossly asymmetrical Mr Potato Head figure. It remained like that for a few days.

We also had some rabbits in a cage under one of the large lychee trees. They lasted about a week until one morning we noticed the cage empty. They'd no doubt ended up in someone's cooking pot. The camphor trees down the bottom of the driveway were shaved each night, making up a part of some witch-doctor's magic potion.

It would be a brave person who decided to take on our dogs Peter and Eliza in the garden. Friendly as they were to us, any stranger that crossed the line of plants near the road onto our property was asking for it. We came home from the drive-in one night to see a motorbike parked near our garage, its rider standing up on the seat trembling, surrounded by two snarling dogs. He gave some fudged excuse about being lost, Dad called off the dogs, and sent the guy packing.

We always understood the standing instructions if there were an intruder: we were to shoot them first, and then fire a warning shot into the ceiling.

There were many other distractions, such as sabotaging our youngest brother. With the veggie patch full of all known things, the chilli bushes presented an obvious opportunity to Glendon and I.

'Hey Rog, try this carrot,' we'd say, holding out an orange chilli.

'Why's it so small?'

'It's a baby carrot, very sweet, try it, you'll like it.' Followed by wails of anguish, and much running to Mum, and much scolding of older siblings.

This was adapted in many guises, such as the old sugar/salt switcheroo. And custard/mustard. We also built a ramp next to the pond and sent him hurtling down it on his bike once, straight into the drink. 'I remember it more as a dam than a pond,' he says of his dunking.

'I seem to remember feeling like you should have "flown" further,' said Glendon.

Taking it out on your baby brother never got old (until he became 6'4" and, well, we're a bit more reverent with him now).

Dad built a 'foofie slide' too, a flying fox which went from one huge sprawling tree down into a lychee tree. This thing would transfer you at rapid pace, hanging on for dear life, many metres above the ground. Mum would be nowhere to be seen, probably on the far side of the house pretending none of this was happening.

Board games were huge distractions too: Mastermind. Battleships. Risk. The latter introduced me to foreign and exotic names such as Madagascar and Kamchatka. We'd added a Subbuteo cricket game to our collection. This was a felt playing field, with tiny plastic action figures of bowlers, fielders, and batsmen. Two teams: one in green caps, the other in blue. You bowled by rolling a ball down a little chute and batted by flicking a plastic bat attached to a small handle. Glendon had bought home a Wisden *Cricketers' Almanack* and this became our bible. All the teams and all the scores from the years' county and test matches. So many stats, so much data. Who was better — Allan Knott or Rod Marsh?

Our tests were always South Africa vs England vs Australia. We all wanted to be South Africa, of course. And never mind five-day tests … these series could go an entire Christmas holiday season. Boycott would be facing Lillee and Thompson. Or Underwood would be bowling to one of the Chappell brothers.

Another favourite game was matchbox rugby. This was played on our Persian rug, with a matchbox, bound in electrical tape for durability. You flicked it with your fingers, and if it rolled over, you got to flick it towards the try line or else got to place-kick for goal. This involved the defender forming goalposts with his fingers and thumbs forming the crossbar, and the arms forming the goalposts.

Action Man was also fun. One Christmas I got an Australian Jungle Fighter figure. He was cool in his flipped-up slouch hat. I remember being vaguely aware of this placed called 'Vietnam' because I remember looking at a map on the wall of our classroom. As memory serves, that Action Man, along with any other number of action figures and toy soldiers were immolated, an often sad yet supremely satisfying spectacle.

Dad had designed a kite called the AeroBat, a dual-stringed aluminium-framed kite which could do amazing stunts because they were infinitely controllable. Dad manufactured these with a small team who worked out of our workshop, where all the jigs were set up. His big marketing breakthrough came when a crew from SATV came to interview him one day and film the kites in action. He made a T-shirt which had 'AeroBat' in simple red felt lettering across his chest. He was totally dismayed when told the segment couldn't be aired because of the blatant commercial 'advertising' on his shirt.

Music always loomed large. Mum could break out a blistering version of Mozart's *Rondo alla Turca* and any number of Strauss pieces such as *The Blue Danube* and *Tales from the Vienna Woods*. I was still regretting giving up playing, but was composing pieces which I transcribed into a music book, including one which was a march to be played at my funeral (inspired by some famous composer who'd done this. Sadly, I've lost that book.) Dad and I were still hammering out *Tom Dooley*, and many fun musical nights were enjoyed, as he'd done with his father before.

We now had a separate turntable set up in the rumpus room. And we were getting some Aussie tunes such as John Paul Young's *Yesterday's Hero* and Sherbet's *Howzat* on our local airwaves.

I bought my first-ever album, *Springbok Hit Parade Vol 7*, which I bought at Game for 99 cents. Track 1: *SOS* by Abba with its wonky piano intro. But the big sensation sweeping the country was Rabbitt, a home-grown glam-rock sensation. They were a true teen-idol phenomenon, causing Beatlemania-like scenes wherever they appeared, singing hits such as *Charlie*. Trevor Rabin and bandmates caused a sensation when they posed nude — backsides only visible — on the album cover of *Boys Will Be Boys*.

All of this sent the Calvinistic government into paroxysms of shock and horror, especially as Rabbitt appealed to all races and all language groups, across all barriers. That year I gave Mum some underwear for Christmas, with the card reading, 'Don't throw these at Rabbitt.'

The moralistic government was losing the battle for hearts and minds as the 70s loosened people up. Rabbit's follow-up was *A Croak and a Grunt in the Night*. Then at the height of their fame, Rabbitt split, with Rabin joining Yes (smashing it with *Owner of a Lonely Heart*). Vocalist Duncan Faure joined the Bay City Rollers.

If there was a single watershed moment in South Africa's history, it was 16 June 1976. On that morning, thousands of black schoolchildren in Soweto began a largely peaceful march to protest the apartheid government's decision to enforce Afrikaans as a medium of instruction. To many, Afrikaans was the language of oppression, and the policy symbolised the wider inequalities of the education system and the authoritarian nature of the state.

As the march progressed, tensions escalated when police confronted the students. Attempts to disperse the crowd led to clashes, with some protesters throwing stones and other objects. Police responded with tear gas and, shortly thereafter, live ammunition. They opened fire on the unarmed crowd, killing and injuring children. The image of the dying schoolboy Hector Pieterson, just 12, carried through the streets, became an enduring symbol of resistance. In the days and weeks that followed, protests spread rapidly across South Africa and were met with sustained and often brutal state force.

That uprising was not orchestrated by the ANC, but Mandela recognised its inevitability. For years, he had argued that 'the armed struggle was a means to force the government to the negotiating table,' yet Soweto showed that a generation of children had seized the moral high-ground first. Their defiance announced what the state refused to hear: that a nation built on fear had finally lost control of its future. Enough was enough.

After Soweto, Mandela came out and proclaimed: 'Those who live by the gun shall perish by the gun. Unite! Mobilise! Fight on!' There was no turning back. In the next four years, there'd be 112 violent attacks — such as bombings — in South Africa.

Probably due to censorship, I was unaware of any of this. And I don't think I'd ever heard of Mandela until several years later. Such was the tight control over the media.

The Soweto uprising galvanised both internal resistance and international condemnation of apartheid.

After seeing these scenes of young ones rioting, Mum realised South Africa was not the future for her young family: 'We must go,' she told Dad bluntly.

'Good god, what do you want to leave for?'

'The boys, there's no future here.'

'No, I cannot leave and start again … I'm at the height of my career,' Dad, then 47, said.

We had seen a letter in the bureau in the study from Dr Geoff Cleasby, chairman of the Tongaat Poultry Division, notifying Dad of a pay rise and bonus entitlements, which took his monthly emoluments to ZAR 1925 (USD $2650 in the day). Glendon, Rog, and I looked at each other, and gave a low whistle: 'Whew … we are rich!'

Mum's argument was that we must all go now as a family, otherwise she and Dad would be left alone as we would eventually leave for overseas after study, or marriage, etc. 'At least we'll all be together.'

Dad came home from work the next day and said to Mum: 'You are right.'

Around this time, there was a lot of emigration. Many we knew had headed off to Vancouver in particular, because Canada was actively soliciting educated professionals with transferable skills. Many in the sugar industry had also chosen Argentina, which was booming at that time.

Which gave rise to a couple of chancers who thought they would go to Argentina and marry into wealthy Argentinian families. The best way? Target the daughters of polo players. But slight problem: they'd never actually played polo before. They moved to Argentina, set up the ironing board in the small flat they shared, and sat astride that as they practiced their polo shots. Last heard of, their plan was successful and they both rode off happily into the Argentinian sunset.

The rumour mill was alive and well at this time. 'The so-and-so family are moving to Canada.' All these conversations were held between parents only, the kids in those days only on a need-to-know basis.

And so we were shuffled off back to boarding school and life carried on.

Life at Cordwalles was getting interesting. In my final year, I was a prefect, vested with the power to send people back to the top of the corridor if they were seen running. 'Back and walk!' As a prefect, you got a wide tie, with broad diagonal brown-and-white stripes. We also got to spend evenings in Mr Brookes' study, shooting the breeze and listening to his massive wooden radio set. I remember the Bee Gees' *Jive Talking* rumbling out of his radio.

The township jive of Soul Brothers was doing a lot of talking too. But the real soundtrack to the revolution was soul: Black artists like Percy Sledge, Booker T (whose organ-based tracks I love), and Wilson Pickett. Because the references were non-political and oblique, the government didn't pick up black joy as resistance, and groove as solidarity. No slogans, just songs of dignity and hope under pressure, dressing smartly, and sending the subtle yet stoic message that this is what black success looks like.

With the intention of sending me to Hilton College, I was invited to sit scholarship exams in order to qualify for a bursary. We became Brookesy's pet 'scholly wallahs'. For the exams, Mark Tully, Martin Davidson, and myself piled into the Ford Transit van one Sunday afternoon, and headed to Hilton where we'd stay for a few days to sit exams in various subjects. Luckily our academic arch-rival Doug Tatham was going to Michaelhouse.

As we drove in through the main gates of the school, I looked across to where Ellis House boarding block was. There, standing stock-still in the sun, was a figure I recognised immediately. My brother Glendon! It turned out that his house master Mr Mackenzie had found him and a friend hiding out on the estate with a rifle. Japanese POW-style, he was forced to stand in the sun as punishment. Glendon was a frequent flyer on Mr Mackenzie's shit list. There was talk of possible expulsion.

Apparently the exams went well because I was awarded two scholarships: the Nicholas Arthur Prize, and the Cordwalles scholarship. I had finally made it into that great big ledger in the library!

Christmas got bigger each year, as more cousins were born, and others — like Uncle Mick and Aunt Paddy and sons — moved down from Rhodesia. Huge family affairs, big tables laid out on the verandah, lunch eventually becoming a lazy afternoon in and around the pool.

Being back home for Christmas holidays was always great. Down to Sheffield Beach, probably only a 10-minute drive from home, where we'd rent a beach cottage each year. Mornings at low tide were spent scouring the rocks for oysters and mussels, lobsters, and the occasional octopus. We'd fill bags and bags, daring to take on the incoming tide as long as we could until common sense prevailed. Usually.

'We were catching mussels once and got smashed by the Indian Ocean on the rocks,' said Rog, becoming better known as The Accident Waiting to Happen. 'They slashed my leg open.'

Then we'd head back up to the cottage and spend the morning shucking the shells and boiling everything up. An absolute feast, fresh from the ocean, and free.

Then we'd go out for some body surfing. The waves came in pretty roughly here, and the big game was to see who got 'modified' most — meaning, intentionally catch a dumper, which would smash you into the sand, churn you around, suck the last bit of oxygen from your lungs, and give you a saltwater enema of the sinuses. The worse, the better. Then you'd stand up triumphantly, and your brothers would rate your efforts through volumes of laughter.

Dad enjoyed fishing from the rocky outcrops at Sheffield, landing some decent rock cod.

It was very social, and the chance to catch Cindy Barry in her neon pink bikini was always a bonus. The Short family was often around too, with their daughters Caroline and Joan, and son Ian. And often at night there was a *jol* (party) somewhere in the area. DJ set-ups were the order of the day, with great big speakers and minimalist light shows. *The Rocky Horror Show* movie was banned in South Africa because of its gender-bending themes, but its soundtrack song The *Time Warp* was a popular hit. JJ Cale's *Cocaine* and Golden Earring's *Radar Love* were songs I'd always hit the dance floor to. The nights would usually end with Frankie Valli's *Can't Take My Eyes Off You*, and you'd dive in for a slow dance if you could.

Tookie Johnson seemed to be at every party, and was always the star attraction, even though he was only about 3'6" (OK, maybe a fraction more than that). He was a great sportsman, a good bloke, and we came up against him on the sports field often. He'd be up on the table or the bar counter, beer in one hand, ciggie in the other. Shirt off. Dancing and singing. Pretty cool for a 13-year-old!

More and more, people would mention, 'Oh, I hear you guys are immigrating?' The volume of the rumour mill grew and grew, until we brought it up at dinner one night. 'Are we leaving?'

Mum and Dad exchanged awkward glances, and Dad then explained that yes, he was looking at opportunities in America, Canada, Australia, and New Zealand. Mum had shot down America before it even got off the launch pad.

'New Zealand!' Glendon and I chorused. We knew the All Blacks, so that's where we should go. Dad had plans to visit all three and decide. Rog was deemed a bit young for such serious discussions and kept out of the loop for now.

Mum meantime had a health issue and had to go for a hysterectomy in Entabeni Hospital, Berea Road, Durban. It turned out to be a cancer. Gran Alys Seymour had moved into an apartment on the Berea, after the passing of her husband George and mum Rosie, and we used to drop in there whenever we were in the area. All the old touchstones were there: the music box, the bottles of Cinzano, the Black and White whiskey. I'm sure she felt a little cooped up there after the spacious homes she'd lived in. But she was now very close to King's Park and the Durban Country Club. She also had a skin cancer cut from her nose.

Hilton College sits on 4350 acres of lush Midlands countryside, near Howick, the site where Nelson Mandela was captured in 1962. Hilton is one of the largest school estates in the world, encompassing rolling pasture, indigenous forest, rivers, dams, farmland, and extensive sports facilities. The Cape Dutch architecture of most of its buildings lends it a timeless charm, and, like Maidstone Primary, it had a slave bell, facing the main admin building. It is an achingly beautiful school.

It had been going for over a century by the time I came along, and this formed a big part of our initiation. All new boys lived in Falcon House for the first year, then got assigned to other senior houses. Across the hall, the dorm prefect was Eban Taylor (of Mary Deavin fame). *Uh oh*! I decided to keep my head down.

Among the new boys were familiar faces, like Tookie Johnson, Duncan Willis, and Paul Rayner (who went on to play cricket for Natal and Western Province). All new boys were regularly quizzed on school history and current affairs. On cue, you had to rattle off all the school's Oxford Scholars, for example. I'll always remember 'B St Clair Moor', because that was Bruce, executive director of the Maidstone mill, a family friend, and father of my friend and new classmate Steven. Or you'd have to rattle off the name of the entire 1st XI or XV before you were allowed to go watch the movie screening on Saturday.

Bed-making took on epic proportions. The corners had to be tight and razor sharp. Or else. Everything came with an 'or else' here.

Prefects were allowed to walk on the grass, other mere mortals only on footpaths. Or else. Matric students could have one hand in their pocket. Others - no hands in no pockets at no time. Or else. Your hair had to be an inch above your ears. Or else. In that case they gave you another haircut on top of the haircut you just had a couple of days before.

The school day started with one class before breakfast. Tuesdays was biology, and one time we were dissecting sheep's eyeballs before breakfast!

Our housemaster was Robert Hofmeyer, who also taught Latin, which remained my strongest subject, so I was on the right side of him. Usually. Except for one end-of-term assembly. He was making the usual housekeeping announcements and mentioned that Tookie Johnson had a cricket bat for sale, if anyone was interested, see Tookie. He then dismissed the assembly: 'OK everyone, enjoy your holiday, and go quietly.'

Just then I spied Tookie. 'Hey, Tookie!' I called out to him.

'*LLOYD*!' yelled Hofmeyer. 'I said go quietly. My office, now!'

I slunk to his office knowing there was only one outcome possible. He motioned me inside towards a comfy chair, asked me to bend over, while he selected a suitable cane from his rack. *WHACK*! *WHACK*! *WHACK*! *WHACK*! Four of the very best. *Holy Jesus*! 'Thank you, sir,' I said and sprinted upstairs to the toilets to bathe my burning bum in the icy cold water of the hand-basins.

To me, Hofmeyer echoed the broader South African government's situation at that point. In 1977 it was at a moment of grim clarity: the apartheid system was no longer stable or reformable, only enforceable — and at mounting human, political, and psychological cost. It was using increasingly bigger sticks.

The border wars with South West Africa and Angola were increasingly serious. National service was increased to 24 months of continuous service, followed by annual call-ups (typically 30–90 days) in the Citizen Force until around age 55. Dad's friends and colleagues at Tongaat, like Mike Heenan and Rodney Cheeseman, would disappear for weeks and months at a time. Disruptive to work and family life. I remember AB Taylor's father coming home one Sunday afternoon from a reservist camp, and laying his FN rifle (a Belgian-made standard-issue warhorse) casually on the chair, with the rest of his army gear. As normal as that seemed, it did give me an inkling that not all was right with this world.

Words like 'Caprivi Strip' and 'SWAPO' became everyday terms. The South West Africa People's Organization was the liberation movement fighting to end South African rule in what would become Namibia.

Dad was just back from his fact-finding mission and picked us up from school. We were eager to hear our future plans.

'New Zealand is a retirement village,' he said.

'I often think of that movie *Sliding Doors*,' Glendon recollects. 'If they'd chosen to go to Canada, they don't play the same sports as us. I'm a shit skater, it would've been horrific.'

Which left Australia. 'I saw Sydney Harbour and that was it,' said Dad, who always loved swimming, sailing, and sunshine.

'Sydney?' I'd never really heard of the place, and it felt anti-climactic. The Australian rugby team was not much good either.

Mum seemed disappointed because in her experience she preferred New Zealanders as they were generally better spoken (really Mum?), whereas Aussies came across as a bit tough. Anyway, she was a bit under the weather from her operation to be phased one way or the other.

Dad had had a grand old time, watching the Centenary Ashes test between Australia and England, in which debutant David Hookes smashed five fours in an over off England captain (South African-born) Tony Greig, and Rick McCosker had his jaw broken but batted on anyway. Amazingly, like the first match 100 years earlier, Australia won by the exact same margin of 45 runs.

Dad brought home some Australian publications. One was a book about 'aboriginals and kangaroos' Glendon remembers, and a newspaper — on the front page was a headline about a murder. Gee, what are we getting ourselves in for? I thought. Then I picked up another one, a travel brochure about Sydney which, apart from photos of the Opera House and some beaches, had a scantily clad showgirl hiding behind a velvet curtain. 'Sydney looks good, Dad!'

Rog was scratching his head: 'Why have we got this big book about Australia?'

We joked about who was going to do the washing up. We joked that we'd just be having BBQs every night, using paper plates. We joked about the accents we might acquire and did our best nasal impersonations of the Aussie twang.

Dad had scored a job as general manager of Ingham's, a chicken business owned by the colourful brothers, Bob and Jack, who were equally famous in the horse-racing world. The stage was set.

We all travelled to Cape Town to apply for the requisite documents, which were British passports which we qualified for by being born in Rhodesia (with the exception of Mum, a South African citizen again).

After returning from that three-week break, my bruises from Hofmeyer's flogging were still purple and easily visible.

Glendon was on his own dubious record-breaking quest — to get the most 'cuts' in Ellis House. Smoking got you six but could also get you expelled. One of his bolder pranks was to black-out the school lights during prep one night. His co-conspirator was an electrician who thought this a wonderfully evil plan so taught him how to access and flick the various master switches. Glendon headed out to the mains board, flicked the switch, plunging the school into a sudden darkness, then bolted back to Ellis House. The next day at assembly he owned up to it, but there was sadly and inexplicably no punishment that would add towards his record-breaking tally of 70 cuts for the half-year.

Ironically one of his most memorable 'cuts' was by the head of Falcon House who was so worked up, that Glendon heard the cane whistling through the air, only to have the master miss his backside with an erratic air swing and smack him clean on the back of the head!

On another night, he set off on a midnight ramble to St Anne's school, a good 9km away. He'd played a mixed doubles tournament recently and met some girl there. 'My heart was actually with some girl in Collegiate,' he says, 'but Maritzburg was too far for a walk.' He set off with a buddy. The walk would take them nearly 1 hour 45 minutes. Reaching the school, he identified the first dorm building as their target. 'It was all ivy-covered. I had sussed out you could definitely climb this thing. We didn't even get as far as halfway up the wall to the second story, and suddenly there was this commotion.'

Sprung mid-action, they had to clamber down and face the music. 'She wasn't the head mistress but gave us this dressing down. Then they just made us walk back, and never told Hilton, never.'

PE at Hilton was run by Andy van der Watt, a Springbok legend, known as 'the fastest wing to play for the Springboks' because he could blitz the 100m in 10.4 seconds. He'd just retired from rugby and would teach at Hilton for the next 37 years.

My first encounter with him was in the gym where he got us all to climb up this big knotted rope to the ceiling. I didn't get very far, and then came the chin-ups. I didn't manage very many. He scribbled furiously on his clipboard, probably a big 'X' next to my name. But as a rugby coach he was brilliant because he pushed us beyond our limits, and you were fit to tackle anything, literally. He put me in the loose forwards for my size and speed. I became captain of the mighty under 14B team, and was proud to wear the black-and-white stripes of Hilton.

What I coveted most was the all-white 1st XV jersey, with the fleur de lys logo on the left chest. I would earn it one day, I was sure.

The big annual match was against our arch-rivals Michaelhouse, where — quelle horreur! — our cousins Bruce and Hal now went to school. And all teams — seemingly hundreds of teams in all ages and grades — would play against them. Parents and old boys would turn out in their thousands, and it was the big event on the school calendar.

I remember some sniggers reading the match program because Michaelhouse had a stocky Chinese scrum half, Michael Ng. Hilton didn't allow Chinese back then: 'second-class citizens' apparently. We joked at how to pronounce this guy's surname. 'Ning? Nug? Naga?' (How ironic I'd end up living happily in Asia for 25 years of my life, very comfortable amongst its local citizenry, many called Ng!)

Glendon used to wear the longest, biggest, widest shorts ever seen on a rugby field. I was super-proud watching him play because he was a fierce-competitor, and that day he ran in a try (as a prop) from about 50m out in front of the massive cheering crowd.

I signed on to be the sand boy for the 1st XV game. Simple, just run on with a tin of sand when the referee signalled a shot at goal or there was a conversion, and bathe in the glory.

I played my match earlier in the early afternoon. I took a big knock, saw some serious stars, and the ref asked me what the score was: 'No idea, sir, but I do know that we're beating those buggers!' was my proud reply.

So I was on duty and the 1st team ran on, Hilton led by captain Carey Millerd. Soon came the first penalty of the day.

I was standing on this side of the field with my tin. But the bucket of sand was on the other side of the field! And people were looking at me, and I was pointing over there, and people were running around headless, and the ref was looking at his watch. The players, including several of my house prefects like Louis Schmidt and Dave Hyslop were glaring at me. And eventually I got some sand to the kicker. An absolute stuff up, to be filed under 'One lousy job, Lloyd!'

If memory serves, my mighty 14Bs were the only team to beat our rivals that day, so the day wasn't a complete loss.

Sundays out on the estate at Hilton were a real pleasure. We'd be free to roam as far as we could, picking up packed sandwiches on the way out. Often, you'd have a tin of condensed milk to feed your acne, just in case it wasn't flaring up enough. Sometimes you'd go splash in a river, risking the rapids in tubes if the water was up. Other times just a walk. Many times, find some hay bales in a shed. And JB Taylor would then bring out his secret stash of *Playboy* or *Penthouse* magazines, because they'd just come back from a holiday in Mauritius.

During school days, some extracurricular activities involved de-sexing the farm animals, and we'd get a crash course docking lambs' tails, or applying a topical anaesthetic/disinfectant, slicing open a pig, popping its balls out, and *voila*!

Much fun could be had stroking pigs behind the ear with a stick. They loved it. So much so that they literally passed out from the pleasure. And sometimes you could end up with a pile of inanimate pigs piled on top of each other in one corner.

To the west, we could see the Drakensberg ranges. A stunning sight to be sure. The bad news was the cold winds that would blast down, and the winters could get decidedly icy. As a result, we all had long thick trench coats — *dlaminis* — hanging in the locker room.

One Saturday night, having satisfactorily answered the questions put to us by dorm captain Mark Welch, we went off the watch the movie. Afterwards, the prefects got us newbies to clean up any mess, straighten the chairs, etc. To this day, I don't know what my infraction was … but Dave Hyslop (first team prop and generally a good guy) singled me out for not doing something right with the chairs, probably in retribution for being a shit sand boy.

And so, on my very last morning at Hilton College, my very last day of school in South Africa, I was awoken at 4am with all the other miscreants, we donned our *dlaminis*, and were marched out and down to the college cemetery. There we were issued a fork and had to spend an hour weeding the cemetery in the pitch darkness of a freezing winter's pre-dawn.

Later that day, as I packed my trunk for the final time, I spotted Dave Hyslop's 1st XV rugby jersey in a pile of ironed laundry. I could snaffle that; it'd make a fine souvenir. I thought about it and decided it might lead to the next level of punishment, which was not just weeding the cemetery, but ending up in the cemetery myself.

I can't remember saying a proper farewell to Steven Moor, Charlie Kessler, or Martin Davidson, nor taking down addresses for future contact. More focused on the forthcoming excitement, I simply left. Gone with the wind.

◘ ◘ ◘

And with the long mid-year break upon us, we prepared to pack and move. We vacated Braeside and headed down to the cottage at Sheffield. We had the Umhlali tennis tournament to play. As usual I was bundled out of the singles in the first round by Guy Mungle and his unplayable serve. So I was in line for the umpire's award again. But wait — I'm also entered in the under-15s boys' doubles draw, partnered by Gary Hulett. We played the first round, made it through. Miracle … I'm in the second round at a tennis tournament. Then we played the second round and won. Amazing. Third round. Semi-final. We won. We're into the final!

The final was an absolute nail-biter. In the last set, we edged ahead, and in the last game, after a long rally I smashed the winning shot down the tram lines. I threw up my hands and let out a huge, 'Yahoo!' We'd won. I got presented a tiny silver trophy, all of three inches high, but to me, that's my World Cup because of what it represents — years and years of being the easy beat. On my last full day in South Africa, I'd won a tennis trophy: Umhlali under-15 boys doubles champions, 1977. No one can ever take that away from me.

In the lead-up to the move, Glendon and I were eager: Bring it on! 'Excited? Hell yeah,' says Glendon. 'Something new, just adventure.' But he was a bit disappointed that he couldn't see out his remaining 15 months till matriculation at Hilton. 'I had the scholarship, and they had to leave money behind, so why didn't they just let me board and then fly to Australia every holiday or second holiday, right?' Mum felt him not being with the family would be detrimental.

But Mum felt Roger, who'd just turned 11, was very stressed and unsettled in this period.

'I wasn't told until we were at Sheffield Beach, a week before we left, ' he fumes. 'Because they were worried I was going to blabber … the whole rats and sinking ships thing, right?' *Loose lips sink ships.*

So Mum and Dad were reluctant to tell Roger about our imminent departure before he left Cordwalles. 'I'd only been there six months, so leaving wasn't a big issue. But because they were scared to tell me, I just left school, and never said goodbye to anybody. It was fucking weird.'

On the way back from Sheffield, Mum was driving through the canc fields of Tongaat and Umdloti, the same area her family had converted to this green gold. As she motored through there for the last time, she took in the beauty of the rolling green fields, knowing that this is what'd she'd miss most about South Africa.

That final night we were staying at Mick and Paddy's at Westville — Mick was then a professor of microbiology at the Westville campus of the University of Natal. I remember Mum coming through to say goodnight, and I burst into tears. All the excitement, anticipation and bravado about moving welled up. 'I'll have no friends,' I wailed.

'I miss Peter and Eliza and Simon Armstrong,' wailed Roger in unison. We'd left the dogs at Braeside with the new tenants, Ted Garner and family, who we knew very well.

'Well, we can get a new Peter and Eliza,' Mum soothed him. 'But you'll have to find new friends.'

24

THE CROSSHAIRS OF CONSCRIPTION

RHODESIA, 1977. Conscription had long been in place, which started as one year's service, then increased to 18 months and would peak briefly at two years' service in the later 1970s. Essentially every 16-year-old male in the country signed a piece of paper saying they were the property of the Rhodesian government.

Cousin Geoff Flint was right in the crosshairs of conscription when he finished school in 1977. 'Everyone went to the army; it had been socialised into you that this is what you do — if you wanted to be part of the in-crowd you've gotta have done your national service.'

'I hated it, but what could I do,' says his mother Kay of conscription. 'All the young men went, do you think I could've stopped them going? The worst part was hearing about boys being hurt or killed.'

Geoff was hoping to do the Officers' course when he fronted up to Llewellin Barracks in Salisbury, named after Sir John Albert Llewellin, the first Governor of Southern Rhodesia after WWII. It was the heavily fortified HQ depot for basic training for the regular infantry. Usually, conscripts were told to head to the unit they wanted to join, where they'd be screened and vetted for suitability.

But on arrival, Geoff got pulled aside. 'Right, Flint, you go and join those guys over there.' About 30 or 40 had been pulled to one side. 'We were identified before we even got there,' says Geoff, who'd played rugby for the Mashonaland Schools team. 'Our Commanding Officer was a rugby fanatic, and his job was to win whatever rugby competitions were going on throughout Rhodesia. He said: "You are going to play rugby." And I had to stay there and become an instructor and play rugby. I played rugby for 18 months, that's all I did!"

Sounds kind of idyllic. 'No.' Geoff corrects me. 'Llewellin Barracks was the worst place in the world, because the dregs of the society were put into Llewellin Barracks — all the guys they didn't want in the Rhodesian

Light Infantry or the Rhodesian African Rifles. These guys were bitter, vindictive, and had a chip on their shoulders. They probably had not had a great education, probably had difficult home lives, but the army was their home. I had to live with and work with these guys.'

First came six weeks of Basics training. 'We all had an FN rifles, nicknamed "the right arm of the free world" because they were so widely used in the Cold War era, then it was all about the grenades, flares, and so on. If you called your rifle a gun you had to recite a verse: "*This my rifle* (point at your rifle) *this is my gun* (point at your dick), *this is for killing* (point at your rifle) *and this is for fun* (point at your dick)".

'Towards the end you'd learn about some of the weapons the so-called terrorists were using, like AK47s. Basically your whole life is spent cleaning, cleaning, cleaning, and practicing your drills for the next day. We were on the parade ground from seven in the morning till about two o'clock, just square bashing, then you'd have to clean up for the next day, make sure you were in pristine condition, and your bedroom was in pristine condition. It was mind-bending.'

But Geoff concedes that the army had a couple of good things going for it. 'It's a great place to learn how to socialise with people from different backgrounds. And you have to work as a team otherwise you're dead. You've got to make it work.'

In modern business terms he sees it as 'forming, storming and norming': 'I still haven't found anything in the world that's as competent at that: the Army gets a group all working together because of process, process, process.'

As a Lance Corporal, he then transitioned to being a Drill and Weapons Instructor, which he also found monotonous and boring because it was mainly teaching people how to look after weapons and keep them clean. 'It was amazing how many people have never used a rifle.' he says. 'A lot of the farmers were very competent, but the city-slickers …'

Then it was rugby o'clock at 5pm each day: 'We'd get on a bus, go and play rugby, get home around 8 or 9pm, then carry on cleaning the barracks. We had a great group of guys playing rugby, absolutely fantastic — but we were told under no circumstances were we to leave

Llewellin: "You're playing rugby". I guess I was lucky, but I hated the barracks.'

The competition — be it club rugby in league or knock-out comps, or against provincial teams — was always very competitive, often with Rhodesia national team players lining up against them in opposition teams.

So the obvious question is, 'Did they win the competitions? '

'We always lost to Police,' he laments.

Speaking of Police, Detective Section Officer 8868 Ian Daniel's ever-morphing role had now become Ground Coverage within the Special Branch (SB).

He was posted to the Matibi No. 2 Protected Village camp, in the Matibi Tribal Trust Lands not far from Nuanetsi. These 'keeps' were internment or resettlement camps built to separate the rural African population from guerrillas (ZANLA and ZIPRA). But the curfews and confinement were understandably not always popular with the citizens they were designed to 'protect'.

The job was working with a section ('stick') of five 'natives', collecting intelligence on enemy movement and support, and classifying the information, on a scale from D1-D5, and submitting it to the local SB offices to see how it tied in with their bigger picture.

The camp was attacked so frequently that two major attacks came in one night. 'The first attack, I called it in and said, "Hey, we are under attack — we're pretty heavily outnumbered here!" And they said, "OK what do you want us to do?" I said, "Well, there's nothing you can do now, I'm just letting you know".' Then the attackers broke off.

But 30 minutes later they were back for another go. 'So I called back again. "Hey' we're under attack!" And he said, "OK we can send an aircraft up with flares so you can see". I said, "Piss off — I don't want them to see me any better than they can!"'

On leave, Ian went to stay with Mick and Kay Flint at Mandara. 'I sat there and stared out the big glass windows at the avocado trees for three days, only going for food and drink when called. After three days I got in my car and returned to the operational area. These days you have terms like PTSD, but in those days, there was no such term ... you were maybe just a touch "bush happy".'

Another time on R&R he suffered from something akin tick bite fever, now known as Lyme's Disease.

Ian and his colleagues understood that if they were doing a good job, the bad guys would be hell intent on trying to target them. 'But if you're doing a bad job, they're just gonna leave you running around.'

There was one Patrol Officer in the north who was obviously doing a good job because a bounty had been put on his head. 'So he came down to relieve me, 'remembers Ian. 'One day we went out together in the Land Rover, I was showing him the roads, where people were, and what have you.'

Ian was dressed typically in shorts (khaki, green, or black) and a T-shirt — throwing in his 'grab jacket', which was a webbing-style jacket which fitted two water bottles, food, and six extra ammo magazines.

On a track used by no one except probably Ian, he was sitting in the passenger side with his NATO FN 762 rifle on his lap, pointing out the door. His guest from the north was driving, and they came down into a small dry riverbed.

'I remember just a bang and a flash. It was fast. The Land Rover got picked up and dumped 13 metres away.' A landmine placed there specifically for his benefit. 'My first concern was, Where's my rifle?' He feared a follow-up attack, which fortunately never came.

He found his rifle barrel-down in the engine compartment, the bonnet having been blown somewhere else completely. They surveyed the scene with ringing ears. They called in a chopper. Ian meanwhile picked up some mementos of a big day out: the wing mirror protection plates and a metal tag off the engine's alternator which he'd seen glinting in the grass.

They were airlifted to the hospital at Triangle where both were diagnosed with perforated ear drums from the blast. 'And Triangle Estate used to give free beer to any servicemen in the hospital. So we were lying in beds next to each other and got rotten drunk!'

The nursing sister was doing her rounds and was supposed to dish out medicines to help relax their muscles and ease the ear pain. 'She looked at us and said, "I don't think you're going to need them, I think you're both relaxed enough!" So we went to sleep.

'Bush happy? Yeah, I guess we were.'

25

THE LAND OF OZ

SOUTH AFRICA, 1977. The SAA flight took us from Durban to Johannesburg, then on to Mauritius. I loved the tropical vibe of the island, with its rich volcanic soil, evidenced by piles of brown rocks repacked as fences on farms and properties everywhere. The minivan took us through cane fields towards Port Louis, then we turned off to the west coast.

What a pity we knew nothing then of the great pioneering adventures of Mum's Rathbone clan there, and their eminent role in the sugar industry.

We stayed at La Pirogue, a dramatically designed resort — like a single sail of the Sydney Opera House — right on a stunning beach, and it was a fabulous week swimming in the shallow turquoise waters and watching water skiers wipeout. When Mum and Dad went for an afternoon nap, the first thing I did was dart off to the resort's shop, where *Playboy* magazines were for sale. The shop assistant must've wondered about this kid who came to the shop everyday but never bought anything.

The seafood dinners were absolute feasts, but no doubt cost a lot more than the feasts we used to cook up at Sheffield Beach. Coming out of dinner one night I looked up and felt that the sky was like a false ceiling because the stars were so plentiful and bright it looked like they were hanging just above us.

A week was nowhere near enough, but we caught the SAA 747 on to Perth, arriving in Australia on 11 July 1977. By the time we arrived in our hotel in the King's Park area, we collapsed in a collective jet-lagged heap. Later that afternoon, we went for a walk around the picturesque city. We crossed the Swan River and went to the Perth Zoo. 'And here were the fucking kangaroos,' marvelled Roger, probably still wondering how he suddenly came to be in Australia.

We also saw a rugby game in progress. We stopped to watch, and immediately our worst fears were confirmed: Australians can't play rugby. Why does the game stop when they're tackled? Why don't they pass the ball? It turned out we were watching our first game of Rugby League.

Later in the hotel, unable to sleep, we were delighted to see the in-house movie was *The Rocky Horror Picture Show.* And we watched that about a dozen times. All the strictures of South African censorship were behind us.

A couple of days later we flew … and flew … and flew … on to Sydney. We were transfixed by the orange barrenness of the Outback — which could do with some Karoo apricot trees! — and landed in Sydney at night. Peter Finlayson — presumably connected to Ingham's — picked us up in his stately Ford LTD, and dropped us at the Camperdown Travelodge, gawking at the bright lights and billboards of Kings Cross en route, and laughing at signposts to places like Woolloomooloo. This was a long way from Arbor Acres and Maidstone.

We assumed we were the first of our family to set foot in Australia, not knowing anything of the brave adventures of 23-year-old seaman Vincent William Seymour — brother of gardener George who had sailed to Durban — who beat us to it, 130 years earlier almost to the day.

Vincent was in the Royal Navy and served with Captain Owen Stanley on the HMS *Rattlesnake*, seeing action in the first Opium War off China, followed by an important scientific expedition charting the Torres Strait, New Guinea coast, and northeast Australia. When they stopped in Sydney in 1847, he chose to settle around Brooklyn, ultimately getting a 40-acre land grant on the Hawkesbury River, where he married Sarah Hibbs, grand-daughter of Peter Hibbs, crewman on the HMS *Sirius* 'First Fleet' vessel in 1788. Vincent spent the rest of his life there and was buried in the pioneers 'cemetery on tiny Bar Island in 1899. The area, although redeveloped, remains named Seymour's Gully to this day. And directly adjacent is Lloyd's Gully (although I can ascertain no direct relationship with our family).

It was mid-winter in Sydney; grey and cold. The Opera House wowed us … it had leapt from the pages of *Beano* to being right in front of me. The tour guide told us that Australians love to bet and will bet on two flies walking up a wall. (Gambling became a big business, losing Australians over A$30 billion annually as of 2026.)

We moved out to the Coachman Inn at Campbelltown, nearer Casula where the Ingham's poultry farm was. Then, this was right on the southern edge of metropolitan Sydney, and pretty dreary. The only highlight was that we had to eat our evening meals in the adjacent restaurant, so it was fillet mignon nearly every night (I believe the company picked up those tabs!).

Dad started work immediately and ran into problems with his two bosses. They'd call for him to come through and discuss something. 'OK, I'll be there just now,' he'd say and get on with finishing the task at hand.

'George!' They'd call impatiently (Dad had reverted from Buster to George).

'Yes, I said "just now".'

'So come on then, where are you?'

It was one of those common inter-cultural misunderstandings — other countries don't have a 'just now' as South Africa does. That, to them means right now. Like 'now-now'.

Soon we were bored out of our brains. Not at school. Not in the house. No playmates. We bought a Mohamed Ali action toy, but our real-life fights were epics. They might start as a playful brotherly pillow fight, but always escalated into something far more brutal as we took our frustrations out on each other. TV at least was 24-hours around the clock.

The Ashes series was on, from England, so we'd stay up all night glued to that, except when Boring Boycott was batting, and cheering on our new home team — although Australia got smashed 3-0, because their biggest names, including the Chappells, Lillee and Thommo, had defected to World Series Cricket.

The Goodies were a bit of fun. *Young Talent Time* was on, and I fell in love with Tina Arena. And rock shows: Ray Burgess hosted *Flashez*, Donnie

Sutherland hosted *Sounds*, Molly Meldrum hosted *Countdown*. There was big hair and high heels everywhere. Yes, I boasted a pair of chunky high heels, and flared jeans that could house a family of five. But the new wave and punk bands were trying to put a stop to all of that.

We soon moved to the Beecroft West Motel at Carlingford. A better area. We now had a plastic soccer ball which we could go and kick around the adjacent Carlingford High School playing field, not having to look over our shoulders in fear of Digby Stanley. One day, we found a 20-cent coin lying on the ground. We were so excited — money!

The exchange rate at the time between the Rand and the Oz Dollar was roughly 1:1. And the USD and the AUD were roughly parity, the Aussie dollar being slightly stronger generally.

We walked nearly 30 minutes to use the coin at the Carlingford Court shopping centre! It was a little excitement to have these sorts of facilities on our doorstep. We played a new-fangled video game.

Mum asked us to go down to the local shops one day to get some veggies for a dinner she was cooking. We got everything on her list, but I couldn't find any potatoes. Conscious of my accent, and trying my best to sound Australian, I asked the assistant: 'Do you have any poraroes?'

Glendon looked at me, Roger looked at me, the shopkeeper looked at me, quizzically.

'Poraroes,' I repeated.

'Aah … potatoes, over there,' the Italian shopkeeper pointed.

Our stuff had now arrived from South Africa, and our Mercedes duly arrived, and looked rather out of place transplanted from Tongaat to the carpark at Beecroft West. But it was a thing of value, to be sold at the soonest opportunity to raise much-needed cash.

Because by 1977, leaving South Africa meant more than packing bags and buying tickets. The state kept a firm hand on departing money because of tightened sanctions and financial flight. Emigrants were allowed to take only a modest allowance with us — somewhere around R2000-5000 per person. Enough, perhaps, to get started. The rest was frozen behind the bureaucratic language of 'blocked rand' accounts, which could only be released in dribs and drabs over time.

As a result, people did literally have diamonds in the soles of their shoes, as Paul Simon sang. Kruger rand coins (being a troy ounce of gold) fetched $150, so were a popular item to stash away in luggage and shipments, er, allegedly.

There were always stories. No one could ever quite say who, or when, or where. Only that it had happened. In the case of being busted with excess and non-declared money and valuables, all were immediately confiscated.

'Dad was so bloody straight,' says Glendon, who believes a sum of R7500 and a couple of Kruger rands was all Dad had brought out.

With Dad at work, Mum was busy house-hunting in the area. She loved Sydney's drivers: 'They were polite, let you in, forgave you when you were lost and made wrong turns, and they stuck to their lanes,' she said. She probably also enjoyed petrol costing only 20 cents a litre at that time.

She'd been out one day and found a place she liked, in 'a treeded area' according to the real estate agent's placard. 60 New Farm Road was a rather modest weatherboard house in West Pennant Hills, the last line of the outer north-western boundary of metropolitan Sydney. Beyond that was bushland and five-acre lots.

Mum was so excited to show this to Dad and, bubbling with excitement, they drove out to look at it. She deliberately made sure they took the approach from Cherrybrook Rd, which featured fancier homes and bigger blocks, for a better first impression.

As they neared the corner of New Farm Rd, she said, 'There!'

'Where?' said Dad.

'*There*!'

Dad shook his head at this very small, plain white wooden cottage. But it was all we could afford and had been marked down to $55,250. Dad bought it, the first property they ever owned. (Current estimates put it at around $2.5 million.)

The small house actually had a lawn tennis court, which formed most of its back yard, and sat on a nice sunny corner. The sweet smell of privet bush dominated, and cockatoos screeched from the tops of nearby gum trees. It was our new home in our new country. And our new lives could now commence in earnest.

Just up the road was a Koala Park, and here we delighted in up-close brushes with kangaroos, koalas, emus, and the weirdly unique Australia fauna such as the duck-billed platypus and numbats. Much safer than the predators we were used to.

We started at school. Glendon had a false start at James Ruse Agricultural College near Parramatta (yes, we laughed at that name, too). We'd gone on a recce tour, and our jaws dropped at the sight of a student with a lush beard. Glendon was accepted but I would have to repeat Year 10. He found his classmates nice and were happy to take him under their wing.

'I think not having Latin was the biggest adjustment.' he says of school. He loved and excelled at Latin. Agriculture was a compulsory topic at James Ruse, and he had to make up his HSC units with 3 Unit (advanced) maths. 'It was like applied maths in South Africa, and I'd never got anywhere near that. And agriculture's not what I thought it was — I thought it'd be farming stuff that I could grasp readily, but it was quite detailed. So I was absolutely swamped. '

Even the start of rugby season didn't improve things for Glendon. 'And I'm sitting there thinking, Jesus Christ my future is going to hell in a hand basket here.' Mum twigged to this. 'I think us moving here was really bad for you,' she said, sympathetically. Glendon repeated that he thought he should've stayed on at Hilton.

He would soon join me at Pennant Hills High School. The school was only about a kilometre walk up Boundary Rd, a cluster of spartan Brutalist grey buildings. It was certainly no Hilton! And it was probably the biggest culture shock of my life.

I was dressed in my uniform of long grey trousers, white shirt, red/blue/white striped tie, polished black shoes. Watching other students pile into the school, there were kids in blue shorts, desert boots or scuffed black shoes, open neck shirts, hair that could easily nest a whole family of pigeons. Hands in pockets! There were prefects but nobody sending anyone back to the top of the corridor for running. Corporal punishment did not extend as far as the cane it seemed, and would be banned altogether within 10 years. (It would take South Africa until 1997 to ban it.)

My first class was mathematics, with Mr Ford. 'Oh, we've got a new face,' he said.

I stood up to speak to him. My new classmates roared with laughter — who the hell stands up to speak to a teacher? It was something I'd had to do all my schooling life.

'Lloyd, sir.'

'Where did you come from?'

'South Africa, sir.' More guffaws, gorilla-noise gibes, and jungle drums.

I sat down, my face bright red.

But I was thankfully and immediately welcomed into a group with Marcus Kuzsmierski, David Furze, Stephen Snitch, and Lance McCabe.

'What kind of music do you have in South Africa?' they wanted to know.

'Oh, the same as you … ABBA and John Paul Young,' I said trying to find some firm common ground. Did I just imagine their eyes rolling? We soon formed a band together, belting out tunes by Elton John, Fleetwood Mac, and Led Zeppelin among other bands. We called ourselves Dire Straits, then soon heard there was another mob by that name in the UK, so changed it to Cobalt Blue. Still, it doesn't stop me claiming I was a founding member of Dire Straits!

We had girls in our school group. *Girls*! Julie, Jenny, Robyn, Margaret. I was going to like this place. Especially Verity with her GG bust (reduced a couple of years later to a more manageable DD). And there were Chinese at this school! The lovely Ho Sisters, Lisa and Sandy. Lisa went on to be one of Australia's foremost celebrity fashion designers.

At morning recess, I queued up at the canteen. A guy came up to me, thrust some coins into my hand, and said: 'Buttafingabunennacannaloim.'

'Pardon?' I said, trying to flatten and broaden my 'a' sound, and having zero clue what he'd said.

'Buttafingabunennacannaloim.'

A can of Lion? They sell beer here? Beer *and* girls, I was going to love this school. Then I ordered. The parent behind the counter furrowed her brow. 'Sorry, what are you after?'

I repeated it as I'd heard it. 'Buttafingabun and a can of Lion, please.' (A buttered finger bun is basically a hot dog but with pink icing instead of a sausage. A diabetes bomb.)

'Lion?' the server asked. 'You mean lime?' I had no idea.

The guy who gave me coins stepped forward. 'Yeah, *loim*.'

Australia then was at the start of an exciting period of identity building, shedding the culture cringe, and ultra-local characters such as Paul Hogan (later star of *Crocodile Dundee*), Norman Gunston, and Dame Edna Everage/Barry McKenzie (both played by Barry Humphries) set Australianism on a strong new course. Local bands were also being championed on radio, fuelling the Oz Rock boom, and mirroring Australian instead of American and UK cultures in songs.

Most of the questions I got about South Africa were about wild animals in the streets, and the death penalty. 'How can you justify killing somebody for killing somebody? 'they'd ask. To me it was a no brainer that didn't need to be justified.

At West Pennant Hills Primary, Roger was having a rather rough initiation. 'I walked into this class and they go, "There's a chair, everybody welcome Roger." And there's a black chair set aside for me, everybody else's was blue. 'They figured I was coming from Africa; I was gonna be a black guy.'

Then a fight was set up between him and a big red-headed guy called Matthew. 'Just because I had a weird accent. A fight to the death — and I've never fought anything in my life before,' laughs Roger. 'Why did I get caught in this shit?' The venue was set near the cricket net, and the whole school turned out. 'On the way down, I'm saying, "Can we just pretend or something?"' But the bigger bloke was having none of that. As the kids started chanting for blood, Matthew moved in to start the rumble. 'Then before you knew it, the teachers were there: "Everybody go away!" It's all over.' Not a punch thrown.

Roger sat in class watching gob-smacked as kids in class around him made primitive tattoos by digging the point of a compass into their skin, filling it with fountain pen ink. But he was more transfixed by a girl called Mandy and another called Toni. 'These days they'd call it stalking,' he laughs.

At the end of that final primary school year, everyone was asked to stand up and give a little chat reflecting on their time at the school. 'I got up and made a speech on racism,' he says. 'We came out of South Africa, we left because of apartheid, but I've never seen anything as racist as what I've seen in this country.' That black chair had clearly triggered the 11-year-old!

Interestingly, Australia had only fully disbanded and walked away from its infamous 'White Australia Policy' in 1973. From the grandstands Australia booed apartheid as if it were a foreign sport, conveniently forgetting it was a land acquired with muskets, missions, and a talent for not asking who used to live there. Aboriginal populations were decimated in near-genocidal levels.

On the first Sunday, we all headed to the top of Boundary Road where St Agatha's Church stood. They announced a family BBQ for the next week. We turned up with our meat and bread rolls and paper plates. And everyone turned in dismay at these uncivilised cannibals from Africa who attacked their food using their bare hands — and thus we learned the hard way that Ozzies use a knife and fork even for a BBQ.

We did a lot of BBQs at New Farm Road, figuring that meat was cheap and healthy, with some lettuce and salad, and the washing up was minimal. Sunday evenings was KFC, because we were supporting Dad's work — Ingham's being a supplier to KFC — and it gave Mum a night off. (Dad would soon quit from there, and buy a plastic injection moulding business, showing the entrepreneurial chutzpah of his forebears. Over ten years he built it up from a single factory running eight hours a day to two factories running around the clock.)

We spent all our spare time on the tennis court playing cricket and tennis. One end of the court was an embankment, which was home to a very fine nest of funnel web spiders, nasty big black critters. The anti-venom was not yet invented so if you got bitten, in a couple of hours you might have developed life-threatening cardiac and respiratory effects. (Since the introduction of the anti-venom in 1981 there have been no reported deaths.)

Even though reptiles and marine predators capture public imagination, animal-related fatalities in Australia are extremely low compared with other everyday risks. Only three or four people per year will die from the Big 5 of snakes, spiders, sharks, jellyfish, and crocodiles here. Australia's legendary 'everything can kill you' environment is far more benign than Africa's.

One day a ball had gone out onto the road. A schoolmate of Glendon's happened to be passing by. 'G'day Julian, 'he called out. 'Could you pass the ball please, mate? Thanks, mate. 'We were trying very hard to integrate. I soon dreamed of playing cricket for Australia.

We'd moved from one revolution to another. Thankfully this was only a sporting one — World Series Cricket changed cricket into a colourful circus, but South African players like Barry Richards got to play against the world's best in this forum after years in the wilderness. We went to watch a few games and collect some autographs from the global who's who of players, few greater than the big cat Clive Lloyd (no relation). We also watched proper test cricket at the Sydney Cricket Ground (SCG), thrilled to be in the background on TV with my home-painted sign: 'Bewdy Thommo!'

And of course, our pellet guns (and Dad's shotgun and pistol) had made the journey too and there was no shortage of shrikes who found the choko vine on our court fence a good place to rest and snack. We knocked them off in their hundreds. And I'm ashamed to say I couldn't resist taking a long-distance crack at a cockatoo, and was really saddened when I actually hit it, and it toppled off its branch. One day I was doing some homework in my room, and I spied a lizard on the concrete verge which ran around the house. I picked up my pellet gun, loaded it, and blew its head clean off. (Many years later I would surrender all our guns during a government amnesty).

Poor Dad was working his arse off trying to keep a roof over our heads and asked for help with lawn mowing and other chores around the house. Even Dad's offer of paying us a few bucks to mow the lawns didn't incentivise me, to the point of frequent friction. Gee, where were Washington and John when we needed them?

Mum had to start working too, doing the books for a Greek mechanic in Parramatta. That would've been a shock to her system, but she knuckled down uncomplainingly, all the while doing the housework — another shock! — and all the cooking (apart from the BBQs).

We were getting some work done around the house, and the tradesman detected Mum's South African accent.

'On the chicken run, are yers?' he said.

Mum was deeply offended. In her mind the reasons for the move were for positive reasons. Moving to greener pastures in search of better future opportunities, as our families had done for the past 200 or more years. She certainly did not see the move as a cowardly act.

Moving countries is always a wonderful chance to clean the slate and reinvent yourself into your new desired image. As a teenager you are trying your darndest to forget where you came from and embrace the new. I hated the South African accent. I hated what South Africa represented, for no other reason than I was a teenager who didn't want whatever my parents were or stood for. A full-blown identity crisis. I went all-in on Australia.

To my regret, I turned my back on my family and my African roots for the next forty or so years.

26

PULLING THE PIN

RHODESIA, 1979. Things changed with the first general intake into the army of black Zimbabweans in 1979; a big change.

Geoff Flint has an over-riding memory of teaching the native recruits how to shoot. 'The concept of aiming was foreign, so we had to start them off with pellet guns.' To make matters worse, many of the conscripts had never left their own Tribal Trust Land area. 'They had no clue how things worked in the army.' reckons Geoff. 'It's a bit like understanding cricket, or a five-day test — unless you've grown up with it, you don't get it.'

The rank and file of the Rhodesian African Rifles (RAR) was African, its Non-Commissioned Officers (NCOs) and Officers were typically whites; an *askari*-style regiment, like the Gurkhas or the Malay Regiment. 'The RAR was absolutely outstanding,' says Geoff. 'They trained the guys hard, and we had to pick up a few training tips from them because we were struggling with these guys who were all aligned with Muzarewa.' Bishop Abel Muzarewa was the black nationalist leader of the United African National Council (UANC).

And into this mess stepped younger brother Lloyd Flint, also now conscripted.

Mick and Kay dropped him at the RLI HQ. 'And you couldn't kiss your mom and dad goodbye because all your mates were watching. So, you just shook Dad's hand and said "Cheers" and Mom was obviously crying, there was terror in her face.'

Lloyd recalls the mixed feelings of excitement and trepidation at the adventure ahead. 'They bused us into the barracks, probably about 600 of us, all shaven, all confused, all entirely discombobulated. There was not one emotion in entirety. We knew what we were going into, we knew there would be some losses.'

The TV news each night would lead off with the news from the battlefronts: 'We regret to announce the death of …'

'It was like a 9 o'clock flush — we had a litany of losses,' says Lloyd. 'Everyone knew someone who'd lost a boy in the war.'

'A good day was when no one was killed,' says Geoff.

Although highly outnumbered, Rhodesian forces achieved striking tactical kill ratios, with elite units at times claiming figures of 30 or even 50 to one, though the overall war ratio was much lower, closer to 10 to one. But it was not your typical military war fought on a single front. An equally important and vicious front was the propaganda war being fought in and around Rhodesia, but also in the international press. The single-minded simplistic story line of 'whites stole this land and must give it back 'was gaining traction in the global media.

But Lloyd was buoyed by the initial feeling of camaraderie and adventure: 'We'll be back in six months after giving them some biff. ' But the biff came from an unexpected quarter: 'Within 30 minutes, you were smashed by your Directing Staff, who told you that you were worthless; you were shat on by these staff who had an IQ no larger than a shoelace. The biggest bollocking you ever got was when you did something and the guy says, "Why did you do that?" And you turn to your Directing Staff and say, "Well I was thinking that …" And the immediate rhetoric reply was, "You do not think in this fucking army. You do as you are told!" The university students really, really struggled with that. That's your first six weeks, you get smashed down. The sense of adventure gets taken out of you.'

The most typical punishment was being sent for a run up the *kopje.*

'The Sergeants and Directing Staff sat in the sergeant's mess with binoculars, and we had to run from the ablutions block, out the gates, up the *kopje* — about a hundred metres high.'

At the top would be an empty 44-gallon drum, which had to be filled with tin mugs of water carried from the bottom. 'And the Sergeants were just getting pissed in the mess and watching us pour these cups of water into the drum, and we were supposed to fill that while they were having Saturday afternoon drinks. We obviously didn't fill it, so guess what? We got our logs [a long, shoulder-borne log used for endurance drills] and we went running. That was the weekend!'

But his lowest moment came when he received a phone call from mum, Kay: 'Gordy's been killed.' Gordy McMillan was a great buddy he played polo with, who'd joined the SAS. 'He didn't get *klapped*, he lost his life laying mines. During training you are very vulnerable, you are fucked anyway. At that point in time you reckon, *Jesus, really, what is this all about?*' The emotion is still palpable over 40 years later when he relates this story.

As an instructor, Geoff had a hand in helping some guys get into the units they wanted. 'I could swing it for them, to places where they wanted to be or with a group of people they wanted to be with. I sent a whole lot of Lloyd's friends to Artillery.'

Lloyd had expressed interest in the Officers' course and was luckily accepted. They were to go to Gwelo (Gweru these days) and were to catch the regular night train down there. Geoff and a few others were assigned to oversee the wannabe-officers on that trip.

'And I said "Look, guys, just take it easy".' says Geoff. 'Have a good doss, take your boots off, just cruise. Your officer is nice. They'll only come and wake you up at nine o'clock, you'll go off for a leisurely breakfast and just start getting used to being an officer.'

But the train stopped at 2 o'clock in the morning. 'And the officers were onto them.' laughs Geoff. 'They were screaming and shouting, and these guys had taken their boots and their caps off. And there was absolute chaos. Lloyd had to run to the barracks with someone else's boots on!'

Here Lloyd met a real character, one of the Regimental Sergeant Majors (RSM), 'a toothless East Ender from way back, hard as rocks', who'd served in the Malayan Emergency. 'He was the hardest bastard that you could think of for the guys in detention barracks — you really felt sorry for them when you sent guys there. 'But it was this unlikely gentlemen who shared a pearl of wisdom with Lloyd: 'The only thing we learned from history is that we don't learn from history.'

Several episodes involved 'The Brothers Grim' — as the Flint duo became known — because they really knew how to tear it up and would take any opportunity to do so. 'We had a lot of fun when we were together,' laughs Geoff.

One time there was a provincial rugby competition in Redcliffe (near KweKwe), trials for Rhodesia under-19s, and Geoff was playing for Matabeleland. 'Midlands put in a side, and mainly it was guys from the School of Infantry barracks, where Lloyd was.' So Lloyd was watching as well.

Matches were played each day, followed by rigorous rehydration, repeated as required each night. Geoff and crew were settling in for a large innings on the last night, the Sunday, planning to return on the Monday. But the Gwelo crowd — including Lloyd — were due back in barracks that night because they were still training.

'We were having a bender of note, 'recalls Geoff. 'There was a guy there called Benkenstein, about to finish his officer training, and he knew Lloyd was my brother. 'Someone gave permission for Lloyd and Benkenstein to stay, pointing out a Land Rover they could use to get back to barracks once the bender was completed. Around midnight, said bender was over.'

Lloyd — who could hold his drink admirably well — said to Benkenstein, 'Sir, do you need me to drive?' But he was waved away. 'No, I'm fine, I can drive.' So off they drove back to Gwelo.

The next day, Geoff and team were on their bus back to Llewellin Barracks. 'We saw this Land Rover that had rolled off the road and it was in the bush, and everyone joked, "Haha, that's probably Benkenstein and Flint!" I said, no, can't be, because I haven't had any news.'

A day later, back at barracks, the news came through: it *was* Benkenstein and Flint, the former with perhaps a broken collarbone, Lloyd unscathed! 'They both escaped absolutely fine because they were so pissed,' laughs Geoff.

From this point, Geoff and Lloyd's Bush War experiences diverged wildly.

'Towards the end, I don't think anyone's heart was in it, 'says the older brother. The white Zimbabweans or Rhodesians wanted to be there. Otherwise, the option was to leave the country. Because it was that fractious.'

The blacks he saw as not wanting to be there. 'I don't think they were on the same team — they really had no interest in fighting our war, they saw it as a white man's war.'

Lloyd was spending a lot of time in lecture rooms, including doing a Shona course, although all commands and instructions in the army were in English. They also spent a lot of time dressing up, and dining, getting 'shiny'. Kay, Mick, and Geoff came down for his passing out parade. 'You then go to the real world.'

2nd Lieutenant Lloyd Flint had been assigned to an independent infantry company, 'predominantly black troops with those national service whites that had been through Llewellin.' His company comprised 90 black soldiers, but his Non-Commissioned Officers and Corporals posed a bigger problem: 'They were all at school with me, but a year ahead, so they'd been kicking my arse at school. And I'd come into this company and I was giving them orders, and they were saying, "Fuck you, sir! I remember you as a gobshite at school." Difficult and awkward. And the black soldiers would look at this and say, "What the hell, how can you tell sir to fuck off?" It made it harder by virtue of the fact that you then had to prove yourself. Eventually they end up calling you "sir" which was glorious!'

Equally glorious was his salary of $45 a week 'and beer in the mess was only 18 cents or something.'

Did Lloyd, as an 18-year-old have a clear understanding of the politics of the war and what they were fighting for? 'No one had a clear understanding of what the politics were,' he says honestly. 'It's only when you start thinking about history, this is pretty much following the same route as the rest of modern Africa … from Zaire, Congo, and all of those places. But at the end of the day there was very much a mentality of 'we are doing the right thing'. We would've followed Ian Smith to wherever, but there was no real understanding of the political situation. The propaganda was immense in terms of what we were fighting for, why we were fighting. But at the end of the day, it was getting harder.'

Assigned to the Eastern Highlands, around Mtare and Nyanga, he was in the hot spot where the guerrillas were pouring over the border from Mozambique into Zimbabwe. They were finding the enemy getting stronger and smarter, thanks to Russian and Chinese backing and training. Also, the 'terrorist' bases were pulling further back, deeper into Mozambique and to places like Tanzania, beyond the reach of easy intelligence. 'Zambia got a pretty good *klapping* — in Lusaka, a lot of their camps got smashed. But they were getting better and better ... the more you attack someone, the better they are gonna get at defending. So it was becoming harder, man.'

Lloyd was thankful for the Shona course. 'Most of the time if you were getting shot at, the guys would be talking Shona to each other anyway, so you could understand what they were saying. But you could also say to them "forward", "go back", "drop". If you talked to them in English, generally they would think "well, this is to be ignored" but if you really wanted to stress a point, you talk in your crappy Shona and they looked at you with a mixture of laughter or "far out, this guy's actually wanting to say something to me".'

■ □ ■

Ian Daniel was asked by his senior officer to go back to ground coverage in Matibi 2 — exactly what he was doing when the landmine blew him up. He gave them a firm 'No'. So his next posting was as a Section Officer in Fort Victoria (now Masvingo), close to the Great Ruins of Zimbabwe in south-central Rhodesia.

Several weeks later an army unit in Matibi 2 got attacked and three Rhodesians died. 'I was sitting in the local urban police station and my boss comes through and says. "There's some bodies being flown into the airport, I need you to collect them and take them to the mortuary".'

Standard procedure in the mortuary was to check the pockets of casualties. 'Always look for letters because you don't want a girlfriend's letter going back to his wife. I found a letter in one of the guy's pockets, from his wife, and it had actually been written the day before — so the mail service to the army was bloody brilliant. And that just hit me ...

his wife had written to him, he had the letter in his pocket, he'd read it, and now he's dead.'

He still gets maudlin over this, reflecting, sighs. 'You lived with it; you basically accepted it because there was no other option; it developed around you.'

But there was something else developing too: an interest in a lady who drove daily to work past the single quarters where Ian was living at Fort Victoria. 'I thought, She looks alright. One day I wandered over to the hospital to where she was working as a radiographer and asked her out.'

Christine Roberts came from an interesting family, with her English father having been born in India, and later flying Lancasters in the RAF. Her mum was Welsh. Post-war they migrated to Kenya where her father joined the police. They then moved back to the UK before emigrating to Rhodesia. And here she was.

So that gave him something positive to be excited about, while he had another change of focus, looking after camps, hospitals, and armoury. The role involved checking that the facilities like tennis courts were all in good order, and stocks (especially the bar of the singles quarters) were well replenished — heaven forbid they should run out of Lion or Castle Pilsener beer!

He volunteered for the Police Anti-Terrorist Unit (PATU). 'I guess I missed the adrenaline!' The role with PATU involved patrols anywhere in the south-east every couple of weeks. Sometimes they'd be alerted to gatherings of terrorists and local farm workers, and go to stake it out, or call in air support (if they could get the radios to speak to each other). Sometimes they'd uncover terrorist camps, or find ambush sites, bodies with lips cut off by terrorists.

'Occasionally you'd get a "Go Now!" That's where my grab jacket became very useful,' says Ian.

As a Stick Leader he could be thrown together with a random squad, whoever was available. One time they'd been sent to find the murderers of a local headman who'd been killed. Ian was leading, following the track. 'I got to this river, which was fairly overgrown. You expect your support to stay right behind you, and I paused and looked back, and these guys were about 80 metres behind me. And I thought, *no, this is not a good feeling.*'

It turns out three of the squad were in their last two days of this assignment, which Ian didn't know. 'They just wanted to go home. It was the last thing they wanted, to get involved in some sort of contact and get shot at.' Fortunately, there was no contact that day.

CID (Criminal Investigation Department) Salisbury was his next stop, which suited him fine, given that Christine was also in Salisbury by now. 'I requested permission to marry Christine and, after background checks came back clear, I was granted permission to marry this delightful lady.'

The Monomatapa Hotel was the CID's local watering hole. Fridays usually involved a damn good lunch, at the end of which the men would return to the station to sign off for the day, and return immediately back to pick up where they left off.

■ □ ■

Sanctions were biting hard, limiting weapons and capabilities of the Rhodesian forces. And guerrillas were now widely embedded within civilian populations in the countryside.

Lloyd Flint: 'The guerrillas would walk into a village and say, "Feed us" and the locals would say, "No, because the army is just down the road." And then they'd say, "Feed us or we're gonna kill you" and then they'd kill them or cut their lips off or cut their ears off. We'd go into the village and say, "Where are they now?" "Ah, we don't know, they've gone." These black soldiers had no mercy for the black civilians — it's always the civilians that get smashed up by both sides.'

Twenty thousand Zimbabweans, mostly black civilians in rural areas, had already died in the previous 15 years of the war.

At this point the Rhodesian army had grown to around 10,000 regulars, plus 30,000 reservists. By 1979 the total security apparatus (including air force, police, guard force, auxiliaries, etc) numbered 150,000. It was all hands on deck. Every male was doing a minimum of six weeks a year in reservists. There was even a third force, made up of those who'd surrendered and converted from the communist forces, and were turned into Rhodesian soldiers. 'Everybody who had anything to do with the army was doing call-up.' explains Lloyd. 'Or was knitting gloves for the army or cooking cakes and teas for the boys. It was a military-run country and there was nothing else.'

His father Mick was a Sergeant Major in the artillery by now 'so they even had frail men like him doing the army … he couldn't even climb into the back of the truck. They called him "the old man" but he was quite good at his job — kicking people's arses and make sure they did things right.'

Geoff meanwhile was noticing that by the middle of 1979 none of the blacks wanted to be in the army. 'No interest, it was very hard, 'he says of trying to keep the momentum going, getting 800 guys moving in the right direction, noticing there was 'always a little bit of conflict 'between the blacks and whites.

He completed his conscription in August but had a six-week call-up in December. He had been keeping up his water polo and was selected for Rhodesia and due to play in December. Luckily one of his teammates was George Walls, whose father was General Peter Walls. 'He said, "Don't worry, I'll get you out of your call-up and you can play polo". Which he did, so I was very lucky,' says Geoff gratefully.

Ironically as the war was nearing an end — with a brokered deal between the two sides on the table — Lloyd was having an increasingly terrible time. His men started asking him, 'What happens when you go?' referring to Ian Smith's army getting moved on. 'Who's gonna look after me?'

'And you'd say, "No, don't worry about it, I'm gonna sign up for the war," because there were all these plans that Mugabe was not going to win the election, we were going to go back to war, and there would never be any peace.'

Meantime, Lloyd headed home on R&R leave and celebrated his 19th birthday. Shares in Castle Lager rose again on the back of that. Unbeknown to him, Kay and Mick had been hustling behind the scenes to get him a place at university in South Africa. 'There was an interview for a scholarship, so I came home for that, too.'

For four decades Southern Rhodesia flew the Union Jack, with only a colonial Blue Ensign to mark its separate identity. Then in 1964, as Northern Rhodesia became Zambia, the settlers unfurled a plain green flag with the Rhodesian coat of arms — their own banner at last. Four years later, after Ian Smith's Unilateral Declaration of Independence, came a starker symbol: a green-white-green triband, the coat of arms defiant in the centre, flying stubbornly over a state no one else in the world recognised.

The breakneck changes that followed were dizzying.

In 1979, Bishop Muzorewa's short-lived government raised the flag of Zimbabwe-Rhodesia: green-white-green vertical bars with the ancient soapstone bird perched on a red star.

Ian Daniel was selected as a Close-protection Officer for the Prime Minister. 'It was not my idea of fun,' he says. Things were very edgy. A second Air Rhodesia civilian airliner had been downed in as many years by Zimbabwe People's Revolutionary Army (ZIPRA) guerrilla forces, killing all passengers and crew. A stunningly demoralising episode and a huge propaganda win for the rebels. Ian was standing outside the church on guard while Muzorewa attended the memorial service inside. 'The CID was idle, I couldn't take it. And they obviously knew because they just removed me.'

Ian noticed, with wry amusement, their house servant Alois would go off on a Saturday and Sunday 'and he had better clothes on than I owned.' But he had a rather disconcerting chat with him one day talking about the elections. The servant had voted for Muzorewa last time, who was not standing in the upcoming elections. Who was he going to vote for? 'ZANU PF,' came the reply: Mugabe's party.

'What if you're going to have to come out and kill people,' Ian said. 'Are you gonna kill me?'

'No, replied Alois matter of factly.' I've got the guy down the road who I have to kill, and one of the other people's gonna come here to kill you.' Ian laughs nervously at the retelling of this, as he thought to himself, OK, well I'm glad we've got our papers in to leave the country.

They were ready to go but the UK government stepped in: If you stay on over the Independence period, we will guarantee your pension. 'So I said, "Well it's only another two months..."'

The Zimbabwe-Rhodesia flag flew for scarcely six months before the Union Jack was hoisted again in Salisbury, as Britain briefly resumed authority under the Lancaster House Agreement.

■ □ ■

On 21 December 1979 the Lancaster House Agreement was concluded in London, signed by the Rhodesian Government, the Patriotic Front (ZANU/ZAPU), and the British government. Under this arrangement Southern Rhodesia — as it was now called — would be under British administration until elections were held. The ceasefire took hold three days after Christmas.

'We were lucky to watch history,' says Lloyd, rotating through Umtali (now Mutare), but at Inyanga at the time observing Echo camp in Zimbiti TTL on the Mozambique border.

'We were monitoring these camps, where all the terrorists were supposed to surrender and go into six or seven camps. But none of the real terrorists surrendered — all we got were women, children, adolescents, and SKs (WW2-era carbines). My troops all knew Mugabe was going to win or could win, and the war was going to end.'

Meanwhile Lloyd had put his name down for the Zimbabwean Army, with a huge pay jump to $120 a week as an Officer there. 'Obviously it was a lure to get people into an interim period in the army to keep some sort of stability.'

He took himself up a hill to watch the seething humanity below and do some soul-searching. 'Where am I going? What's gonna happen now? Have I done the right thing?'

He was flicking through a copy of the University of Cape Town Freshies Week program: 'A barbecue on the beach on the Monday, then Tuesday go to the pub with the ladies of Baxter House ... this place has got sun, booze, ladies, and I'm thinking, *where does this world exist?*' he laughs.

His parents had said his place at Cape Town University was now confirmed and he must take advantage of that opportunity. Versus that was walking away from a $120 pay check. 'Christ, what was I going to do at university? I think it's called Business Studies — I have no idea what the fuck that is.'

More thinking required now that peace has come. 'Collectively relief, we may now have our sons and daughters back. But then the question was raised, "Well, peace means that we've come second. What happens when you come second in war?" So there were a lot of demoralised people.'

A lot of his troops felt the same, fearing retribution for ending up on the wrong side of history if/when the Mugabe government came in.

But the army's propaganda unit was working overtime: there was not going to be a black nationalist victory, things will just go back to the way they worked before. Head-in-the-sand stuff. His commanding officer repeated the same party line, telling them that's what they'd need to tell their troops. 'As a 19-year-old full of worldly wisdom, you think, How the fuck are we gonna keep on going forward?'

Lloyd glanced at the Freshies week program again, and his decision was made. 'Right, I'm going to university. And so there was this elevation from the lowest point in my life to the highest point. It was like being on red drink, but I hadn't even had any sugar!'

He radioed in his decision: 'I'm gone.' He made his way to the airstrip waiting for the next Dakota resupply plane to come in. 'I said nothing to my troops except that we were going back to Inyanga for redeployment. And I got off the plane, went back to barracks, showered, got the cammo cream off, packed my bag, which had absolutely sweet fuck-all in it — I gave everything else to the cooks.'

He then got on a truck. 'I don't even remember looking out the back of the truck to see my troops, as I disappeared off to university and the life that they would never know anything about.'

He confesses to this being a low moment, knowing they were thinking, 'Well he's alright, he's sorted himself out — how do we look after ourselves now? That was probably the last thought I had about it. Poor buggers.' He's never dared to look up the fate of his unit, fearing they all got '*klapped'* later in Mozambique.

Within three days of reading that Freshies Week program, he was in Cape Town. 'It worked out exceedingly well with the girls and the beer,' Lloyd says. 'But do not ask me about how the academic side of it worked out.'

So I asked his brother instead. 'A scholar of note,' Geoff laughs. 'If they had a roll of honour for who achieved the most in terms of socialising, he would be in the Top 10 … of all time!'

Lloyd got involved in the Rhodesian Society at UCT, meeting on a weekly basis. That was the best way to keep in touch in those days of pay-phone callboxes and second-hand news. 'And we'd be hearing about how farmers were getting hit, and wondering do we have to go back, and is there gonna be a call-up? Then we'd go to the pub. And then you forget about it till the next meeting.'

■ □ ■

'They sort of got a hold of your mind and twisted it around a few times, and then you ended up living in Zimbabwe,' says Tim Henwood. 'Mugabe was very clever and we were all very nervous. Wendy and I left the country for the actual independence date.'

At midnight of 17-18 April 1980, the Union Jack was lowered at the Rufaro Stadium and the new Zimbabwean flag was raised for the first time.

Its seven horizontal stripes move from green (the land and agriculture) through yellow (mineral wealth), red (the bloodshed in the liberation struggle), and black (the people themselves), repeating in reverse order — a reminder that struggle, wealth, and land are cyclical, not resolved. At the hoist sits a white triangle, signalling peace, within which stands the Zimbabwe Bird, lifted from the ancient stone ruins of Great Zimbabwe — a claim to a civilisation that predated colonisation by centuries. Behind it lies a red star, pointing to revolutionary ideals and international solidarity.

Later that day, Bob Marley headlined the independence celebrations, performing a powerful emotionally-charged set that mixed liberation anthems like *Zimbabwe* (popular with guerrillas during *Chimurenga*) with beloved reggae classics such as *Positive Vibration* and *Get Up, Stand Up* — a moment that linked his music forever with African freedom.

'Mugabe stood up and made what was supposed to be a statesman's speech and told us we were all safe and he wanted us all to stay and how we could all be happy together,' says Tim. 'And in fact, he honoured that for 20 years.'

There had been a general exodus of white Rhodesians since 1975, when the white population had peaked at around 270,000, representing around 3-4 per cent of Rhodesia's total population.

"But those of us that decided to stay became Zimbabwean almost overnight,' says Tim. 'We adopted the attitude of, "this is our country and we're gonna make a go of it".'

Stevie Wonder trumpeted that peace had come to Zimbabwe in his hit song *Master Blaster (Jammin')*. But it wasn't that simple to achieve Marley's *One Love* overnight. Or ever.

'There was a lot of biff amongst themselves.' says Lloyd of tribe-on-tribe retribution. 'There were a few car crashes for people of notoriety. The traffic became terrible for them at that point.' he jokes of the increasingly popular method of targeting enemies. Foreshadowing genocidal-level horrors down the road.

He and Geoff burned everything pertaining to the war and their memorabilia of it. Only one photo of them in uniform remains.

Ian and Christine Daniel were very unsure about the future of this new country, having witnessed the intimidation happening in the tribal areas. Ian was getting very disillusioned with the collapse of standards in a once-proud BSA Police force. 'I had zero confidence in the future there with Mugabe,' Ian tells me. With Christine being English she could go back anytime, and Ian could be her trailing spouse.

In 1980 they pulled the pin, sold their house, and shipped their furniture and belongings to the UK. But with strict foreign currency controls in place, only a very low amount of Rhodesian dollars could be taken out of the country. 'So we lived the high life,' laughs Ian. 'We went dining and wining and dancing and did everything we possibly could to spend as much as we could before we left. We didn't want to leave anything behind.'

Shares in the Monomatapa Hotel would have risen sharply, as they threw cash over the counter at its many bars and dining areas: Prospectors; Bali Hai; 12,000 Horsemen; and The Homestead.

It's amazing to think that, after all his experiences, Ian was only 23 or 24 when they flew to the UK. He boarded the plane with no particular emotions either way: 'OK, find a future, get on with it. 'He was not daunted by the unknown that lay ahead. 'To be honest, the experience I'd had gave me the feeling of ... invincibility. I can do anything. Nothing phased me.'

But it was to be a hard landing because the UK was in the middle of a deep recession. Nothing was doing in Wales, so they moved further east, but accommodation was hard to find because landlords were scared they were just going to squat and not pay their rent.

As summer approached, they bought a tent. 'We camped out, we toured the UK. We saw Lakeside, we saw North Wales, Blackpool. We had a great time.'

Eventually as winter was coming, they found accommodation down in Southampton. A one-room apartment in a big house where they paid minimal rent and got fed breakfast because Christine was doing cleaning work there.

They bought a big pink blanket to keep themselves warm. 'And it shed pink fluff on anything that came near it,' remembers Ian. 'I was trying to get a job and going for interviews in my suit, and it had all this pink fluff that you couldn't remove completely.'

They met an Australian couple who encouraged them to give Australia a go: 'We've got a contact in the Australian High Commission. We'll introduce you to her and she'll see you're a good bloke.'

'We went up there and this woman refused to see us,' laughs Ian, who says the very thought of going to the big smoke like London (aka 'Harare North' by this stage) induced headaches in him. 'So we put in our application.' A few weeks later they were contacted to attend an interview. 'We walked in the door, this young guy looks at us and said, "That's great. I just wanted to check that you were white." You're in.'

It was then discovered that Ian had overstayed his six-month visa in the UK and his Rhodesian passport was about to expire. Off to the Zimbabwe passport office in London they went, which shared a small section — behind a little prefab partition — in the British passport office.

The Zimbabwean officer asked for his photos. Ian handed them over.

'They haven't been signed,' he said.

'Well, on the form it says whoever signs it must have known me for six years,' explained Ian.

'Aah, just go wait outside.'

Ian went and sat on a chair for half an hour or so until he heard, 'Charles! Charles!' Then shouting: '*CHARLES*!' A head appeared over the top of the partition. 'Charles, I'm calling you.'

'Sorry, people normally call me Ian,' said, er, Ian. He was called inside the office where another man sat.

'Now you go with this young man, he knows what to do right now.'

Outside they went.

'What's the deal here?' asked Ian of the stranger, who'd been taken from Rhodesia as a 3-year-old.

'You've gotta sign my photos and I've gotta sign yours.'

Ian laughs. 'And I thought, this is Zimbabwe … only a few months after Independence and already, we've got the corruption running at a very fine level.'

And so they made it to Australia, and — after processing at the Noalimba Migrant Hostel for two to three weeks — settled in Perth for over 12 years. Ian opened a printing business, 'which set us on firm financial footing in Australia.'

George Lloyd gave him some advice: 'He told me go out, buy a house, and hock yourself to the hilt, you won't go wrong. The best advice I ever got in Australia!' They later settled in Brisbane, Queensland, where median house prices have grown 300-400% (after stripping inflation) since then.

As for his police pension? 'After four or five years, the pensions just stopped coming. Zimbabwe fell into disarray, but the British Government was meant to guarantee it. The guarantee wasn't worth the paper it was written on.'

■ □ ■

Our move to Australia was a catalyst for others. Getting to Australia was quite a relief for David and Jill Seymour in 1985. 'I was 54 when I migrated and it was thanks to Jennifer, because through her local member of parliament, she did a lot of work to get us in — they don't want you when you're 50-something,' says David from his home in the quiet suburb of Pymble, Sydney, adjacent the Saffa stronghold of St Ives. 'It took a while to get everything going with Pretoria, and you wondered whether you were ever going to really get there. But once we were here it was easy, it wasn't too much of a sacrifice.'

He acknowledges it was a big move, especially with three children in the mix. 'But I quite enjoyed my move, because I didn't have a job, so I'd go off and watch the Test matches, and I had quite a few friends here, ex-South Africans like Hamish Drummond. And they'd give me first-class members tickets to go to the Sydney Cricket Ground and watch rugby and cricket. It was a good time, not even really thinking too much about work.' He'd eventually establish his own home-based accounting practice.

It was a big challenge for Jill, with all the domestic duties now falling on her. 'I could not have survived without Jen,' Jill says of her sister-in-law. 'I'd never boiled an egg nor used a vacuum cleaner before. She showed me how, all with a good chuckle.'

'Jill had never cooked a dinner before, and it tasted like it,' laughs David.

What did he miss most about the Empangeni life? 'Having to do everything yourself, no servants. You're doing things that tied you up quite a lot instead of having free time. I really enjoyed my period in Africa.'

Son Michael had just turned 18 in January 1985. He was at school at Hilton when he got the news of the move: 'Mum and Dad told us late in 1984 that we were moving to Australia. I recall probably feeling more excited than apprehensive about moving.'

Despite his good matric result, they were late in making applications to universities. 'Hence I ended up in Armidale, University of New England, a few weeks after we arrived.'

Armidale was initially a bit of a shock: 'No one understood what I was saying and I struggled with an initial nickname of Kaffir, later changed to Boer, then Bush. But the hardest part was losing all my history and not having any connection to Australia, Wallabies, NSW Blues, rugby league, etc.' He also faced some 'strange questions' given apartheid was very much in the Australian news with daily footage of blacks being attacked.

'I soon settled in … rugby was very big in Armidale and luckily I played.' At close to two metres tall he was a useful addition to the second row in Armidale, and later at the Gordon club in Sydney. He went on to reach a CFO position within telco Optus, with expat postings in Singapore and Bangladesh. Sister Josie followed in her mum's footsteps becoming a teacher, and Leigh got into music publishing.

■ ■ ■

In 1988 Dad's brother Dr Mick Lloyd, BSc, MSc, Phd, DIC (Imperial College) was invited to work at the Commonwealth Scientific and Industrial Research Organisation (CSIRO) in Canberra as a visiting scientist. As a professor of microbiology, he had some in-demand skills, so he used that three-month stint to look around. The University of Melbourne was in the process of turning its agriculture college at Dookie, regional Victoria, into a fully-fledged degree program. Mick was offered the job.

'Mainly the move to Australia was for the boys' sake,' Paddy says of sons Bruce and Hal. Bruce had already started studying law at Rhodes, but Hal had to finish matric at Michaelhouse (where he was opening batsman for the 1st X1). 'We saw no future for them in South Africa. We didn't want them to go into the army and didn't agree with what they were fighting for in the army.' This last point is an important distinction — not all whites were on the side of the Nationalist government nor apartheid.

And so they made the move to Dookie, population less than 300. Paddy was partly excited, partly trepidatious. 'Sad to leave Mum who I knew wasn't going to last long. Thrilled and excited to be here. The Dookie people were very friendly and warm.'

But then came the reality. 'The biggest adjustment was not having servants,' laughs Paddy from Sydney where she now lives near her sons. 'I had to learn how to iron and do the housework … a steep learning curve.'

She soon picked up work in the canteen of the college, as a kitchen hand. 'I mopped floors and scrubbed huge pots and saucepans in the Dookie college kitchen. God if Gladys could see me now!' she laughs, referring to their maid in Westville.

But then she soon found work in her real vocation of teaching, at a school in nearby Shepparton.

After successfully getting the degree program up and running, Mick went on to pick up a posting running the sustainable agriculture programs under the auspices of the South Pacific Organisation (SPO) in Fiji, to where he retired. Bruce and Hal went on to partner positions in some of Sydney's most eminent law firms.

'Life is good,' reflects Paddy. 'If you are happy and people around you are happy, that's all that matters. I miss the wildlife of Africa, but I don't miss the political upheaval and soul-searching of African politics.'

Part 3

MAKING RAINBOWS

27

GIVING IT ONE LAST SHOT

ZIMBABWE, MID-1980s. After graduation from the University of Zimbabwe (UZ) with an honours degree in pharmacy, Geoff Flint had been working at a retail pharmacy in Harare, and was back into playing rugby again, more seriously than ever. There was talk that the nuggety hooker might make the Zimbabwe team, which was to compete in the first World Cup, in Australia 1987.

Then one day his phone rang; it was a former lecturer of his from UZ, who was now working for Bayer in Johannesburg. He offered Geoff a position in the medical department, doing clinical research. There were push and pull factors: 'I hated retail pharmacy,' said Geoff, and I thought, I can't miss this opportunity. Zim was pretty dead work-wise, and this was a nice role where I got to travel the world and do clinical trials.'

Rugby World Cup or career breakthrough? 'It was a difficult decision,' he admits, before opting for the career choice. (As it turned out, Zimbabwe's World Cup campaign didn't fare that well, being bested by France 70-12, Scotland 60-21, and Romania 21-20.) Geoff would probably tell you they might've hoisted the trophy had he played!

He already knew Johannesburg well because he had a lot of friends living there, who he visited frequently, so there was a sense that he should be there anyway. He ended up living there for eight years, during which time he met Bridgette, and got his MBA at Witwatersrand University. Her father was Ian Morrison, a patent attorney and — as deputy mayor of Durban — was instrumental in saving old buildings such as the Durban Station and Children's Hospital at Addington from the wrecking ball. He'd worked with the Tongaat Hulett Group on patents for some of their sugar processing machinery.

Geoff and Bridgette married in 1991 and had a son, Justin, a year later. After her three months' maternity leave, Bridgette went back to her job as training manager for Bristol Myers Squibb. 'She broke down in tears, 'said Geoff. 'I can't go back to work and leave Justin behind, I just can't do it.'

Hmm. They mulled over the options. 'I can probably get a job back in Zim,' offered Geoff, 'where you don't have to work.' The thought terrified her: 'She had met some of my friends, and it wasn't a good initiation,' he laughs. And Lloyd didn't help, when, at his first meeting with her, he would only speak Afrikaans to her! 'This didn't go down well with the lady 'who only spoke the Queen's English,' laughs Geoff. Bridgette made it very clear that she was not happy about a move back to Zimbabwe.

■ □ ■

Meanwhile, in 1982 brother Lloyd was back in Zim, studying at the UZ, and had met Carol Little at a party in Harare. 'Lloyd knew my sister, Kim, from the University of Cape Town,' explains Carol, who was working as a secretary at Colcom (a major meat processor) at the time. Kim would marry Steven Saunders, son of Chris, and he'd go on to be chairman of the Tongaat Huletts group. An interesting family backstory emerges of her London-born father and German-born mother: 'Mum went to London to learn English and worked for my father and his first wife as an au pair!' The 'new' Littles then moved out to Northern Rhodesia, Malawi, and then Southern Rhodesia.

In 1988 Lloyd reckoned the furthest he'd ever been away from home was Trennerys (a resort on the Wild Coast of Transkei) where they used to go on family holidays, 'because that's where our father could afford a holiday.' Sanctions meant limitations on travel, except to places like Greece.

Then Carol said she would submit application papers for Australia. 'And I thought, Are you kidding me ... I have to leave the country?'

But it did have some appeal. The Zim dollar was weakening, there was in-fighting in the government factions, and disturbances happening around the country.

They technically qualified for immigration to Australia (especially with points from family in the country already) but were not given the nod because of Lloyd being an accountant; Australia did not feel the need for more accountants. *Don't call us, we'll call you.* They put in papers for England.

'When we landed in the UK — in my shorts and slops — it was surreal for me, mind boggling. In the first instance there were not many black people around. Secondly, how am I gonna navigate through this world I know nothing about? All these things were completely foreign to us.' Underground trains were a whole new thing for him, they ran every few minutes, and you didn't actually have to run and barge onto it for fear of missing it.

'A lot of the guys in the army who were of my ilk were going over for the first time. And they lasted about four weeks over there … they had no warm clothing, they'd had three fights and they'd be booted out of the country.'

He got reassurance from Carol who'd been travelling for some time previously: 'Life does continue outside Zimbabwe, outside Mandara. ' But he found London huge: 'Gobsmacking, and there was no savanna grass and there were no msasa trees.' He found things alienating: 'If you spoke to people about the war, you were somewhat of a pariah.' Gradually he felt a sense of bitterness creeping in, realising the brain drain from Zimbabwe was not going to help the situation. He knuckled down to living in England, realising 'you go on with it, or you've lost it. '

I am reluctant to broach the subject of PTSD. 'I think there was a significant amount of PTSD,' he says, feelings not far from the surface. 'We've lost a lot of guys to suicide, who at the time in the army you would think, Gosh this guy is a pillar of strength. But PTSD for the nation as a whole too, primarily because we were singularly focused on the war as Rhodesians. Suddenly someone says, "Things are going to be OK, there's no adversity going forward". Does life continue as per normal? No it doesn't … there was this progression from a well-oiled machine that facilitated a war with minimal inputs, into a country where you didn't have to worry about a conflagration, but at the same time was crumbling because administratively it was going to be poorly run and no one had any idea what the outcome would be. The evidence of its poor maintenance was very apparent right at the very beginning.'

Australia soon had a change of hearts on accountants, and Lloyd and Carol were accepted in.

Carol arrived six months pregnant with Cameron and stayed with Jen and Buster George for a short time, while they found themselves accommodation. Three years later Kirsten was born, also in Sydney. However, they found the Sydney housing market very expensive, so went back to Zimbabwe in 1995. And then in 2000, a few months before the first farm invasions, they returned to Australia, this time to Perth.

Currently, Lloyd is CFO for three ASX-listed explorer companies looking for minerals 'anywhere other than Africa'.

■ ■ ■

Meanwhile, in 1993, back in Johannesburg, after Bridgette had returned to work after maternity leave, Geoff contacted a good friend of father Mick's, John Swan, in Zimbabwe. 'I had a job the next day. I said to Bridgette, you won't have to work.' So they headed back to Zimbabwe.

Geoff took up his position as General Manager with Lobel's Bread. Lobel's was a popular local brand, whose production capacity peaked at 300,000 loaves per day, a big market share.

They added a daughter Steph and stayed in Zimbabwe for eight years. 'We had the most awesome time ever,' says Geoff. 'Zim was starting to open up again to the rest of the world. Foreign currency restrictions dropped, you could get stuff, things started to work. Zim always had a good black middle class and there was always a reasonable level of education. The government was not ideal, but reasonably competent. And everyone wanted to make a go of it.'

Life was much easier: a wonderful house. A maid. 'Absolutely brilliant, it was really a lot of fun. But the most important thing was you could go to so many wonderful places in the bush. And it was relatively safe.'

Geoff and Bridgette also established a business, an agency for Roche Vitamins and Fine Chemicals. 'It was a lovely import-export business,' says Geoff, 'importing Roche chemicals under the direction of Roche in South Africa, but also working with Switzerland.'

But then as the economy began to slide, and inflation kicked in, the wellbeing of the business turned a bit pale. 'Currency became an issue,' explains Geoff. 'It was difficult to run a business where we had to pay our supplier in US dollars, but the exchange rate was changing once or twice daily — so customers were quoted one price and ended up having to pay a much higher price once their products arrived, which affected their businesses as well as ours — this became untenable.'

It was not uncommon for businesses to explore opportunities with a complex system of banking by mailing travellers' checks overseas for deposit into their offshore accounts. Not that that was foolproof: In one instance, Interpol in the UK called a Zimbabwean business owner to say fraudulent travellers' checks had been banked … and those checks had been purchased directly from a major international bank in Harare! Trust and confidence were at a new low.

It was Bridgette who said, 'Hey there's a problem, we need to go.'

She had been working for the past three years to get the papers together for immigration to Australia, and they'd been approved.

'We are going,' said Bridgette. Geoff wasn't that keen but was happy to do the "look-see-decide" so they went over to Australia for two weeks.

Although he loved Zimbabwe, Geoff could see the writing on the wall, and by March 2001 they had moved to Brisbane.

Why Australia? 'It's the only southern hemisphere country that works,' says Geoff, 'and is one of the sunniest continents on earth, where they play rugby and cricket and have BBQs!

'Leaving the folks was difficult,' he says of leaving Mick and Kay. 'It was sad because I knew we were probably only going to see them infrequently, and because we were starting all over again, leaving everything we had built in Zimbabwe. It broke my heart when I left.'

He takes a minute to compose himself. 'I broke down at the airport — I had all the guys from Lobel's coming to say goodbye … geez, they packed out the airport, all my former employees, black Zimbabweans as well as white. They were all there.'

28

UNFINISHED BUSINESS

ZIMBABWE, 2000. Twenty years after the flags of independence rose over Harare, Zimbabwe stood at a crossroads. What had begun with the Lancaster House Agreement in 1979 — a carefully-brokered ceasefire and a promise of reconciliation — had descended into violence and lawlessness.

The murder of David Stevens in April 2000 shocked the nation. He was the first white farmer killed since the invasions began two months earlier, dragged from his property and shot. Tim Henwood, then president of the CFU, was the man who announced it to the world: 'David Stevens was abducted from his farm in the Virginia farming area and shot to death,' he told reporters. His words echoed across international airwaves; the voice of a farmer-leader suddenly thrust into the role more akin to a reluctant war correspondent.

Tim would be quoted in newspapers such as *The Guardian, The New York Times, The Washington Post*, and several others over the next couple of years.

Just a couple of days later, Tim had the first of several face-to-face meetings with Mugabe. Nervous? 'Aren't you naturally nervous when you meet a president?'

Several things struck Tim. First was the ostentation in Mugabe's office: 'All the pomp and ceremony was there. So flash. All the old colonial stuff was there, including the tea 'boy', and white China cups and silver teapot and the whole bit. And little sandwiches — everybody got given a little sandwich. You could have been in Westminster.'

The second was how astute Mugabe was. 'He was an amazing man. He'd sit through a three-hour meeting with 15 people present and, at the end of it, without lifting a pen, he'd summarise the whole thing and say, "When you said this why didn't you say that?" And he knew exactly what had happened. '

And so they got down to the hard business of that day. 'Mugabe — having organised Stevens' murder — was so apologetic and said, no, he would definitely be protecting us and blah, blah, blah, which was absolute lying.'

Was he openly hostile at all? 'No,' says Tim. 'He was an absolutely smiling crocodile, as I would like to call him. I never knew him when he wanted to be nice to us. I only knew him when he was trying to be pretty nasty to us.'

Mugabe assured the Commercial Farmers Union that the violence would subside.

The very next day — just three days after Stevens' murder, on Zimbabwe's Independence Day, April 18, with nationalistic feelings running high — cattle rancher Martin Olds was gunned down. A farmer from Matabeleland, Olds had sent his wife and teenage children into Bulawayo after repeated threats. In the half-light, busloads of men — perhaps 100 or more, described as war veterans but armed like soldiers with AK-47s — descended on his homestead. Automatic gunfire rattled against the walls, petrol bombs shattered the windows, and the telephone and radio lines fell silent. Olds fought back with a hunting rifle and a shotgun, wounding several assailants. Shot in the leg, he splinted it himself and carried on, turning his home into a bunker against overwhelming numbers.

The siege lasted nearly two hours, a grim theatre of defiance. Smoke poured from the farmhouse as Olds continued firing from room to room. Neighbours tried to raise the alarm, but roadblocks stopped ambulances, and the police made no move to intervene. When the attackers finally broke through, they dragged him from the house, beat him savagely, and finished him off with a bullet to the head. His body was left as both a warning and a message.

The death of Martin Olds underscored the grim reality: the state was no longer simply tolerating lawlessness; it was orchestrating it. The optimism of 1980 was buried.

The former British diplomat Robin Renwick remembered Mugabe's darker instincts. 'During the liberation struggle, Mr Mugabe depended critically on terror as a political weapon,' he wrote. Village headmen who resisted ZANU were executed in front of their people, and in government Mugabe unleashed the same terror on Joshua Nkomo's supporters in Matabeleland. Two decades on, the same tactic was being wielded against white farmers. Renwick was blunt: 'The rule of law has been destroyed in Zimbabwe by the president himself. He is as much responsible for the death of David Stevens as the thugs he incited to abduct him from his farm.'

Violence spiralled. Movement for Democratic Change (MDC) activists Tichaona Chiminya and Talent Mabika (supporters of Morgan Tsvangirai's opposition party) were burned alive in Buhera when a petrol bomb was hurled into their car. Union spokesman Nomore Sibanda lamented, 'The president is encouraging all this anarchy. He seems to be condoning violence.'

The Chipesa farm attack on Iain Kay — who vocally supported the opposition —was typical. Around 60 ZANU-PF-aligned war veterans descended on his farm, near Marondera, about 100km east of Harare. His father had originally bought the land in 1948 as virgin bush, developed over time to grow tobacco, maize, and supporting livestock. He was born and had got married on that farm. Kay's hands were bound with barbed wire, he was beaten and whipped with belts and axe handles, but managed to scarper into a reservoir, where he hid. But the invaders hurled rocks at him in the water. Constable Finashe Chikwenaya, who attempted to arrest one of the occupiers, was shot dead.

Yet still the government doubled down. Information Minister Chim Utengwende told the BBC: 'What is going on in the country is a result of hundreds of years of racist oppression by the British settlers. What is happening now is the unfinished business of the liberation struggle.' When pressed, he back-pedalled slightly: 'We don't support the attacks but we support the acquisition of land for redistribution and we support the peaceful demonstrations by the war veterans, not the attacks.' But the signal was unmistakable — violence was permissible so long as it was cloaked in the rhetoric of history.

On returning from a summit in Havana, Mugabe himself drove the point home. The High Court had just ruled the invasions illegal and Vice President Msika had asked squatters to leave. Mugabe brushed them aside, overruling both. 'This is not a problem that can be corrected by the courts. It is a problem that must be corrected by the government and the people of Zimbabwe,' he told a cheering Harare crowd.

In November 2000 the confrontation reached a new pitch. The Supreme Court declared the occupations unconstitutional and ordered police to remove the invaders. Mugabe's response was contemptuous: 'Whatever the courts might say, the land is ours and we will take it.' That weekend, government supporters seized fifty more farms.

The Guardian erroneously reported that one of the farms taken was the Banket property of Tim and Wendy. Hooligans and would-be invaders had turned up to their farm. 'But never like that, 'says Tim. 'We were actually never evicted. And that was another one of Mugabe's very, very clever tactics, which is that he left all the leadership of the farming organisations more or less alone, so that he could make us look as if we were working on his side. It's a very old communist tactic of divide and rule. And so we personally were pretty much left alone.'

For Tim, it was a bitter vindication. He had long argued that Zimbabwe needed land reform, but through an orderly and lawful process, not through chaos. Now Mugabe set out to silence opposition and cripple institutions. Black farmers aligned with the opposition had their farms targeted too.

Some misconceptions need to be addressed: *In The Last Resort*, New York-based Zimbabwean journalist Douglas Rogers — who writes for *The New York Times, Washington Post*, etc — accepts a calculation that white farmers only accounted for 14 per cent of all farm land ownership and produced around 65 of all agricultural produce. Yet Mugabe's state line was that 'greedy white farmers' owned 70 per cent of all farmland. The latter was a factoid reiterated in the world's media. In reality it was a statistic only applicable to the Mashonaland tobacco-belt around Harare.

Come the revolution, Tim was either going to be first against the wall or spared. 'Yes, there was a deliberate attempt by Mugabe to isolate the farming leadership by appearing to leave us alone. The ultimate result was no different, however.'

Tim circles back to Mugabe's astuteness. 'If you could meet him, and not know what he was, he was an absolute gentleman. I mean, that's where he was so clever. By then he was beginning to lose it, and from there on he definitely became a problem.' Bit of an understatement, perhaps.

The 'Fast Track Land Reforms' program was bought in, creating a feeding frenzy. Drunken mobs turned up in trucks with machetes and guns, chanting at farm gates, throwing furniture out of houses, and threatening certain death to white occupants. The smart ones got the hell out, quick-smart. The police, if they ever responded, just shrugged: 'It's a political matter, out of our hands.'

Each Friday farmers would read *The Herald* to see if their farm was listed as being earmarked for take-over. You can imagine hearts in mouths.

One of the farms taken over in Matabeleland was that of farmer Jim Pocock. He and his family emigrated to Australia, where his son David flourished, becoming vice-captain (and occasionally captain) of the Wallabies, and an independent senator for the Australian Capital Territory.

By year's end, more than 1600 farms had been overrun. International condemnation was muted; Britain and the Commonwealth spoke of ethical foreign policy but delivered little beyond rhetoric. As Renwick warned, 'Mr Mugabe has calculated that no external power, and no one inside the country, is going to be able to prevent him clinging to power by the most brutal means.'

No one, including Tim, would imagine that the now-despotic Mugabe would be ruling for another 17 years. And from there, things in Zimbabwe went into a death spiral, literally.

'After Rhodesia became Zimbabwe, we had 20 very good years there, ' says Tim. 'We can never deny that. We brought up our family there, and we could never have done it any better anywhere else in the world.'

Tim moved on from the presidency of the CFU, which would cite 29 white farmers killed between 2000 and 2016 (although some of those were not directly linked to land occupations or invasions).

‘I think for 20 years, Mugabe could see the benefit of having us there. When he became politically threatened, then he used us as bait. He got to the stage where he had nothing else to offer the people except our land. So he took it away from us and gave it to them.’

He sees the whole thing as being politically motivated. ‘There was an artificially created demand for land by the people that had fought in the war. But, in reality, the demand for the land wasn't nearly what it was made out to be. They were stirred up politically to cause trouble, with the reward being the supposed land that they were meant to want, which they didn't really want at all.'

Push came to shove. ‘The continued chaos and crisis soon made it obvious that we would never want to return. That was a very trying time.’

Initially the Zim dollar was relatively stable, reflecting the country’s strong ‘breadbasket of Africa’ agricultural-based economy. But with the confiscation of farms, agricultural output soon collapsed, crippling export earnings. Without foreign currency inflows, the government turned to simply printing more money.

Inflation started to rocket, from around 50 per cent in 2000 to around 600 per cent in 2004.

Allegations of election rigging in 2002 and the land seizures caused the EU to impose travel bans, asset freezes, and arms embargoes on Zimbabwe. America also stepped in and restricted its access to the IMF, World Bank, and African Development Bank. This in turn triggered capital flight and generated a feeling of lost confidence in the country’s economy.

Tim and Wendy emigrated with their three kids to Western Australia in 2005. With typical positivity and humour Tim saw it as paradise when they first arrived: ‘We’ve got McDonald’s on one corner, and Burger King on the other!’ They live on sixty acres outside Donnybrook, a couple hours south of Perth. It features rolling orchard hills, vineyards, jarrah forests, and winding rivers. They run a few Angus cattle. ‘I know them all by name,’ laughs Tim of his small herd. ‘The rule is simple: if you have a name, you’re safe; if not, you might end up as hamburger.’ And with typical Zimbabwean humour he said: ‘Come for a *braai* — my *braais* make McDonald’s look like a health farm!’

He considers himself lucky that they got out while the getting out was good and has not once regretted their decision: 'Things weren't so bad then, you only needed a wheelbarrow to carry your money. Later, you needed a two-ton *bakkie.*'

He's not joking ... there were two boom industries in Zim at that time. One was wheelbarrows and suitcases to carry the 'bricks' of money required to go shopping. The other was coffins for AIDS victims.

At its peak around 2000, Zimbabwe had one of the highest HIV rates in the world at around 29 per cent of the population. The epidemic slashed life expectancy for black Zimbabweans to the mid-30s (from 61 in the late-80s).

The breadbasket had become a basket case.

In 2006, the currency re-denominated, slashing three zeroes off the old money. In 2007-8 inflation zoomed into the thousands of per cent per year. Mick Flint was having lunch one day with Tim, who'd returned on holidays. At the start of the lunch, the beers cost whatever. The second round cost twice whatever. Shops changed price tags several times daily.

Golfers in Harare took to pre-paying for their half-way-round refreshments, to lock in the price because clubs had to adjust for inflation every few hours.

Bartering became popular. Salaries became worthless within days. A loaf of bread might cost billions of Zim dollars this week, but next week, it could cost trillions. If you were lucky enough to find bread.

'You can't imagine this, if you didn't see it for yourself,' Mick Flint told me. 'You go to the supermarket, this huge store. And there's nothing on the shelves, apart from maybe a loaf of bread here, and maybe a bag of carrots there, that's all.'

Mick loved to tell the story — and you want it to be true! — of a guy who'd taken his wheelbarrow stacked with bricks of cash to do some shopping at the supermarket. 'Parked his wheelbarrow outside, gone inside to shop, came outside to get his money to pay, and some bastard had tipped the money out, and stolen his wheelbarrow!' he laughs.

But reality was biting hard. Mick was largely blind by then, earning a British pension from the Crown Civil Service, because he'd worked for the Minister of Agriculture from 1958 to 1965. This amounted to £52 a quarter, never indexed to inflation because he was living outside of the UK. And he had to front up to the embassy each quarter just to prove his existence. He was fetching at this stage around Z$20 million for a Pound, enough for a loaf of bread. Kay was doing part-time caring work for families who were prepared to pay US dollars. 'Lloyd and I were supporting them, 'says Geoff. 'And as a pharmacist I was able to get all their medications.'

But to keep up with the soaring cost of living was proving impossible. Mick and Kay sold their 'lovely cottage' up at Kariba Dam and then made the painful but necessary decision to sell their marital home, which he paid $26,000 for and they'd lived in since they were married. The idea was the cash it realised would tide them over for the rest of their lives. 'I'm a multi-millionaire,' he'd joke with anyone within earshot. But …

'The money I got for our house was just enough to buy a bowl of apples,' lamented Mick.

By November 2008, Professor Steve Hanke at the IMF calculated inflation at around 79.6 billion per cent. *Monthly*! (Spare a thought for those in Hungary in 1946, the only other nation whose inflation rate has ever been higher.)

More zeroes got slashed off the money. But still banknotes had to include a 100 Trillion Dollar denomination — count the zeroes: $100,000,000,000,000 — the largest-ever banknote amount printed in global history.

Giesecke & Devrient (G&D) was a private German security printing company supplying the Reserve Bank of Zimbabwe. Through the 2000s, G&D supplied the special paper and the presses needed to keep up with Zimbabwe's ever-rising note denominations. Meanwhile the German government came under strong pressure from the EU and human rights groups to stop enabling Mugabe's regime, to the point that Berlin formally asked G&D to cease deliveries of banknote paper, inks, and technology to the Reserve Bank of Zimbabwe. Which they were only too happy to do, because Zimbabwe couldn't pay the bills to print its own money anymore!

By early 2009, the arse fell out of the Zimbabwe dollar entirely, and the government abandoned it in favour of foreign currencies (USD, Rand, Botswana Pula) which became legal tender.

Around this time the British Government tabled legislation which covered repatriation of civil servants who'd been sent out on service, and hadn't had their pensions indexed, and were now living in poverty in various parts of the world.

On Mick's next visit to the embassy he was told he was eligible for a British passport. 'No, I don't think so; Robert Mugabe has said I'm not allowed a British passport.' The British official said to him: 'He has no control over a British passport. You're allowed one, would you like one?' He also outlined the new repatriation legislation.

'Don't worry about that but, OK, I'll just take the passport for now,' said Mick.

With that, Kay was also eligible for a passport.

But they were adamant they'd stay put. 'All my friends are here,' Mick told me.

'Kay didn't want to leave because she was absolutely shit scared,' says son Geoff. 'She had no idea what was going to happen. In Zim she knew how the system worked and she could make it work for her, so that was it.'

Mick for years had been cussing the queen for isolating Rhodesia and Zimbabwe, saying, 'These bloody Poms they've forgotten us and isolated us, we were supposed to be their servant, we've contributed so much …' But now they were being remembered, they were hesitant, reluctant.

Their sons felt they should take the olive branch, but Mick and Kay pushed back. On the ground Tim Henwood and his brother Doug ganged up on them to persuade them to take this opportunity to leave for the UK. 'But if I'm blind, who's going to look after Kay? 'was Mick's final concern. But they eventually agreed to go, having been offered an apartment by the government in Colden Common, Hampshire, free health care, a computer, and a pension.

As the last of the direct lineage of pioneer Henry Llewellyn Lloyd to leave the country, one wonders if they felt any sense of history in their moment of departure? 'I think economic considerations were ahead of historical and lineage considerations for Mom and Dad,' says Lloyd. 'He had US$147 left in his trust account at the time of departure.' So they packed all their belongings into two suitcases. Kay packed a plastic bag containing Rhodesian and Zimbabwean coins and notes, worth trillions in face value, but worthless souvenirs in reality.

And even their departure had a dramatic twist: a Zimbabwean emerged from the shadows of the airport and approached their British government escort. 'These people are not leaving,' the mystery man said, possibly looking to save face for Zimbabwe as they had to leave as essentially economic refugees, or probably to thwart the British outlet for people to leave the country.

'Dear sir, these guys are on British passports, they are refugees back to their country of origin,' replied the British official, forging onwards. (The fact that Mick and Kay had only ever visited the UK once before to visit Lloyd and family on holiday was beside the point.)

When they landed in London, it was 20 degrees colder than Harare. The winter of 2009 in England was 1.5 degrees colder than the 30-year average, so it was more a baptism of ice than a baptism of fire; and neither had ever seen snow before. There was no more violent sunshine, but still they were so full of gratitude for the opportunity.

'Once he arrived over there and Queenie started filling his coffers, he was quite happy with Queenie, mate,' laughs Lloyd from his home in Perth. To Kay, England was 'not like a foreign country, but not like a coming home either.'

They settled in well. And on one visit to the UK a few years later, I caught up with Kay, Mick, and Glendon for a memorably hearty and humorous lunch at their local pub. Afterwards, sitting in their flat talking about Zim, Kay went to her room and re-emerged with a bag of money. She casually pulled one note out of the bag: 'Would you like a souvenir of Zimbabwe? she asked. She placed a 50 trillion ($50 000 000 000 000) dollar note in my hand. 'There you go ... totally worthless,' she said wistfully.

In 2015 the Zimbabwe government officially demonetised the Zimbabwe dollar, and anyone with a local bank account holding up to Z$175 quadrillion — that's 175,000,000,000,000,000!!! — could exchange it for just USD$5.

A cup of Tanganda tea anyone?

29

THE STAY BEHIND PARTY

SOUTH AFRICA, 1994. There was a time in the late 1980s when Roger and Renee Seymour stood at the crossroads of a new life, with maps open on the kitchen table, and the thought of a new life in Australia seemed a sensible option. After all, Roger's sister and brother were already established there, and South Africa was teetering on the brink of the unknown. Roger recalls it simply: 'The family was cleared to emigrate to Aus in 1989. We went on a LSD trip (Look-See-Decide, not the other kind of trip!) to see the country and evaluate work opportunities.'

They admired the sun-washed suburbs and ordered streets, the familiarity of a place that looked a little like South Africa, but without the worry. 'We liked the country and the lifestyle – which seemed similar to South Africa in many respects.' It could have worked. But something didn't spark there.

The numbers made it harder for the chartered accountant — the then-exchange rate of ZAR6:AUD1 biting at every property viewing — and Roger could see a future that felt perhaps more dutiful and thinner on opportunity. 'Buying a half-decent house appeared beyond possibility. Renee and I could see us both working until we were 65+.' (That exchange rate has since blown-out to 11:1)

And so they decided against the move. 'Given all of that we don't have any regrets of not going,' he tells me from Cape Town.

South Africa's moment of independence came not with fireworks or rupture, but with a long, deliberate exhale. In April 1994, after decades of apartheid and years of negotiation, the country held its first democratic, non-racial election, with millions of South Africans voting freely for the first time. Common sense had prevailed. Nelson Mandela and the African National Congress won decisively, and Mandela was inaugurated as president in May. What followed was government of national unity, with an emphasis on reconciliation over retribution.

The new hybrid South African anthem said it all: two songs (the formerly banned *Nkosi Sikelel' iAfrika* and *Die Stem*) sung in five languages (in order: Xhosa, Zulu, Sesotho, Afrikaans, English), with a single plea for harmony despite history, and unity through humility.

The new South African flag was raised for the first time on 27 April 1994, the morning of the country's first democratic election, over the Union Buildings, Pretoria. It didn't matter who won, the country had a new flag. The black, green, and yellow are associated with the liberation struggle and African identity, while the red, white, and blue tie in with earlier flags and European heritage. The central green Y-shape symbolises different paths coming together and, importantly, moving forward together with dignity.

George Lloyd retired aged 60 and took avidly to golf and travelling, including a cruise with Jen on the *QE2*, in which they struck a vicious cyclone between Tahiti and New Zealand. With all Wedgwood crockery smashed, passengers were reduced to using paper plates and cups aboard the luxury liner. In an echo of our Beira voyage, it was only Mum, the captain, and a few stragglers, that managed to make it to dinner one night.

George been back to South Africa and Zimbabwe a couple of times in the mid-80s and early 90s, enjoying seeing that his friends still sat in the carpark at King's Park drinking cold Castles after the game, as they always did. He especially enjoyed the serenity of fishing on Kariba. He was diagnosed with lung cancer on his 66th birthday birthday in 1995, and passed away within months. When I went to collect his ashes from the crematorium, the attendant handed over the package: 'Oh, he must've been quite a large man,' she said, feeling its heft. Well, putting cow shit in your shoes obviously works then! (His brother Mick — following a senior appointment to the South Pacific Commission in Fiji, looking after agro-biosecurity — would retire there, then die of a heart attack aged just 63.) Longevity doesn't seem to favour the Lloyd males.

In his eighties now, Roger Seymour has witnessed history sweep away walls that had stood for centuries. 'South Africa has changed for the better with the abolition of apartheid. We have a wonderful constitution where all citizens now have equal opportunity to flourish and do well.'

As a sportsman he especially remembers isolation, a nation siloed off from the world. Now, South Africa stands on global stages again: 'We are now part of the greater world — whereas we were very much isolated in the 1970s and 1980s.'

On rugby fields, transformation sings: Sia Kolisi lifting the Webb Ellis trophy for the Rugby World Cup high, the whole country roaring through him. Ironic given that years ago the Springboks were one of the most visible manifestations of apartheid. 'Sport has brought most sectors of society together — unifying us as one,' says Roger.

But rainbows never promise that more storms are not on the way. He is blunt.

'Fraud and corruption became the norm; unemployment sits north of 35 per cent.'

And yet Roger refuses to let the negative define the nation. 'South Africa still remains a country of opportunity. People of all races are basically very friendly folk.'

Hope here is stubborn, like *fynbos* pushing through fire-blackened earth.

His son, John, carries that same inheritance — restless feet, bright eyes, a heart anchored in nature and landscape. He tells me his family have been in the Cape nearly a decade now having moved down from Johannesburg, where he was thick in the cut-and-thrust of business in the mining city that is still characterised by grit: 'Cape Town's a much more gentle city, more cosmopolitan, more tourists… it's been good.'

He says that Johannesburg is still the place you go to roll up your sleeves and make things happen, but the Cape gives you lifestyle, mountains on the skyline, weekends in the southern suburbs that smell of sea salt and *braai* smoke. 'I think the Cape is a little bit more balanced,' reckons John. 'There's quite a bit to do outdoors.'

His brother Andrew and family live just a few kilometres away. A keen surfer, Andrew became a renowned physiotherapist for elite athletes.

Yes, John says, the country has changed. Yes, frustration can spill over. 'There's been a big deterioration in service delivery, especially outside of the Cape, and massive corruption.'

But he shrugs it off because none of it is enough to loosen their grip on the life that stirs their blood.

His mum Renee has a very adventurous soul, who in the 70s motorbiked through Portugal on the back of a Harley, slept under the stars on the beach of the Red Sea, and lived in a kibbutz in Israel. John imagines this is where his intrepid nature came from. From his youngest days, his family did trips through Africa. 'And I guess Africa is a bit of a frontier.'

After he finished school at Pretoria Boys High School (Elon Musk's alma mater) he hitchhiked to Victoria Falls, then at university he drove and took planes to spend two weeks on Zanzibar, in the good old days before Instagram and mobile phones. 'I kind of miss that.'

He and wife Nicci have a compass that has always pointed toward adventure. After all she was a chef in many safari camps, with her own book in progress. The title *There's a Hyena in my Kitchen*, based on one actual episode in the bush, says it all. Shortly after they got married, they made a pact: 'We would choose experiences over things.' John goes as far as saying he would spend his last dollar (or Rand) on travel.

Their youngest child is named George Frederick, after that intrepid great-grandfather. They've done a lot of adventurous travel as a family, especially in far-flung parts of Asia, where John says he feels 'free and comfortable'.

Closer to home, he loves Crook's Corner, the outpost that through history has been a hideout for smugglers, poachers, and fugitives. The same outpost where BSA Police Section Officer 8868 Ian Daniel went searching for bad guys. Aside from his main focus on 'alternative equities', John is chairman of a business that owns eco-training camps, skilling up conservation and field guides. One of their camps is at Pafuri, near the border point in the far north of the world-famous Kruger National Park. 'There're no gold tiles and watercolours in the room,' he laughs. 'But that's a place that's quite close to my heart.'

Then there's Zimbabwe which they've visited four times in the past year alone. 'I actually love Zimbabwe, eh,' he says. 'You can still drop off the grid, and it's very remote.' He nominates Hwange National Park as his favourite experience there.

'The lower Zambezi, that's food for the soul,' he says, picking that as his top African destination choice.

Adventure is oxygen here, inhaled daily.

He'd also recently attended a friend's 50th party on a boathouse on Kariba. 'Three decks, 60 people — enough booze for 200 — what could possibly go wrong?' The party went for three days. 'Generally, Zim friends get the social rev counter into the red pretty quickly,' he laughs.

■ ■ ■

Sandy Harley, daughter of Tim and Wendy Henwood, always carried Zimbabwe in her bloodstream. She grew up with the kind of country childhood in Banket that formed her inner operating system: 'Family and friends and community and *braais* and dams ... just big community ... it was a lot of fun,' she tells me from Harare. Like so many of her generation, she left during the turbulent years, but she never quite left emotionally. 'For some reason I just couldn't move on ... there was always a pull back.'

After an underwhelming year in London, she returned to Harare, and met and married Arthur 'Arch' Harley — whose whole immediate family remains in Zimbabwe — and in 2010 they followed the main current of the era outward, relocating to Australia. They lived first in Perth, then Sydney, where both their children were born. To the outside world it looked like a typical new chapter: stable, safe, prosperous. But for Sandy and Arch, Australia was never intended as the final destination.

Their return to Zim wasn't impulsive or romantic. It was deliberate and values-driven, anchored in what they wanted their children to absorb while they were still young enough to be shaped by it. School teacher Sandy puts it simply: 'We always wanted our kids to come back ... we always expected our kids to do schooling here.' Arch expands: 'The schooling system here instills the discipline and the characteristics that I think we wanted in our kids that we saw growing up.' For them, Zimbabwe represented a culture of clearer expectations.

They moved back in 2018, with their son Arthur four and their daughter Ella turning two.

Sandy found herself with something modern life rarely permits: time. 'We have a full-time maid and gardener, which really does make a difference to us. We have more time … I have more time. I'm at home a lot more … when the kids are home, I have more quality time with them. The kids still have to help out around the house, of course, and do their part.'

The maid and gardener live on the property, and receive free food, water, and electricity as part of their deal. (An experienced 'house manager'-level trustworthy long-term maid generally earns up to USD$300-350 monthly based on recent job ads.)

Even now, with Arthur and Ella as weekly boarders, Sandy's rhythm revolves around them. 'Most of my life right now is the kids.' There is sport, travel, and the movement of family life lived at a human pace rather than a treadmill pace. Residents extol the chilled pace of Zimbabwean life.

Arch also has more time for his most loved sport: cricket. He plays for Zimbabwe in the over-40s Masters team, having just returned from a World Cup competition in Pakistan, and is looking forward to the next one in Guyana, West Indies, at the time of writing.

Business-wise Arch returned with a plan: to build something for himself. He started Kalekt Analytics, analysing the basket-level behaviour of shoppers and translating it into decision-making for businesses. It was a field he'd worked in Australia, and he saw 'white space' back home. In Zimbabwe, he explains, they are 'really the only ones doing it here' in that FMCG category-management niche. The opportunity is real, but so are the constraints: the market is developing, but he sees 'a big shortage of skilled people across every sector,' which slows progress and makes growth more difficult than it would be elsewhere.

Zimbabwe, like many emerging markets, demands a strong stomach for friction.

Zimbabwe, rather than Australia, is their comfort zone, yet the couple don't view themselves as adventurous. When people ask why they would reverse the usual migration flow, Arch's answer is blunt, and quietly philosophical. 'There're pros and cons to every place. You gotta weigh up what cons you want to deal with.' Sandy agrees, even if some days it still stirs doubt. 'Some days I think, Why, what am I doing?' But in Zimbabwe the dual citizens recognise themselves again, a familiar place with familiar instincts. Arch's family is still all there, for starters. And they live in a house owned by Sandy's father, Tim.

Sandy confirms what Tim told me: many of their young white friends are farmers and moving back onto the land to work it again.

Harare, they say, is full of contradictions; hardship and momentum braided together. It's very 'poverty' on one side, but also 'development, with shopping centres going up all the time and big property estates being built.' Much of that growth comes with a defensive architecture: gated communities, alarms, burglar bars. Safety is managed, not assumed. 'You don't just leave your door open like Australia … you're constantly locking up gates, doors locked … it's just a part of your life.' They don't live in fear, but they're not complacent either.

And then there are the everyday realities that make Zimbabwe feel uniquely Zimbabwe: not just potholes and rough roads, but the whole obstacle course of unpredictability. 'The roads are terrible. And the drivers. And the dogs, and the donkeys,' they laugh.

Still, they are clear-eyed about time and seasons. When the children are older and move on — probably back to Australia — the equation may change again, especially as medical care and ageing become more important. But for now, this is their window: a chapter lived back where their story began, happily schooling their children not only with lessons, but with the values and texture of the world that shaped them.

When I chatted with John Seymour for this book, he'd just returned from a weekend of fishing at Cahora Bassa Dam in Mozambique, where he and son Max bagged a few 17-pound Tiger fish, which put up a damn good fight, including lively aerial displays.

Though he realises as a white tourist he sticks out and attracts a bit of attention in remote north-western Mozambique, 'physically I've never felt unsafe' he says of being in the very area which, just two or three decades ago, was the heartland of the communist terrorist insurgents.

Business-wise, he visits London for a week each month, but finds it sterile and, having been based in Zurich before, half-jokes that Switzerland would send him quietly mad: 'If you put Nicci and I in Switzerland, I think we'd go out of our minds.'

This strand of the Seymours don't stay because they are stuck. They stay because the place makes sense in their bones. Because they love the edge of life — the way joy must be seized, not assumed. The small things become appreciated, like availability of ice cubes in a remote setting to go in John's whisky. The way community matters. The way the land still shapes people more than people shape the land.

Roger sums up current South Africa in his no-nonsense way: 'More frustrations than negatives for us. We do sometimes wonder about the future of our grandkids …'

Mind you, grand-daughter Jemma has fallen on her feet, working on the private yacht of a global multi-billionaire. He's a keen explorer, so she's been part of his advance party in places such as Galapagos (where she snorkelled on Seymour Island!), Costa Rica, and Alaska. 'The places she has been and seen,' says Nicci proudly. 'Her grit, bravery, and determination is hugely admirable.' As for son George, she recently posted for his 16th birthday: 'Never lose your sense of adventure, your curiosity to travel, your deep sense of compassion towards others, your ability to talk to old, young, strangers or friends!'

Roger and Renee could have left. But they planted themselves deeper. They watched the country stumble and rise and stumble again, and they stayed upright with it.

Because the story isn't finished of this family who dared — and still dares — to build their lives on moving frontiers. And because the perfect country is a myth. 'There is no utopia anywhere in the world!' concludes Roger.

John weighs in: 'When you live somewhere you only notice all the bad things. And when you've left there, you remember all the good. You can still have a fantastic life here,' he says, as is evidenced by their Facebook pages leaping out of the screen with photos of fishing, cycling, whale-watching, game-viewing, weekends away with family and friends. All bursting with love and life and laughter.

'Someone said living here is like it's schizophrenic — when things are going well, it's amazing. And when things are going badly, the world's gonna end.'

And sometimes it can be all that on the same day. Or even at the same time. Sunshine and rain together.

In other words, a monkey's wedding.

EPILOGUE

In 2003, I opened my mailbox in Sydney one day to find a *par avion* envelope, with beautiful cursive fountain pen handwriting, addressed to 'Stuart Lloyd, esq.' It took me a few seconds to recognise the writing and, when I did, a lifetime of memories washed over me. It was from Ronald C Brookes, the former headmaster of Cordwalles.

'I have often wondered what happened to the Lloyd family after you left Natal,' he started, explaining that he was now retired in Cape Town. He'd read a *Weekly Telegraph* article about me and my writing career and was congratulating me on such. 'I was horrified, however, to see a former scholarship student of mine beginning a sentence with a preposition. Unless, of course, you were misquoted.'

Just beautiful! That the man would take the effort of reconnecting after 25 years, by writing to the editor of that newspaper in London, who then forwarded it to me in Australia, summed up his dedication. Mainly to correct my grammar, I suspect.

Remember those imaginary Brut ads I used to concoct at boarding school? I actually parlayed that daydreaming into a wildly successful international career as an advertising copywriter and creative director. For many years South African Airways and South African Tourism were my clients. Then I took Wilbur Smith's lead and started writing books. I still read his books avariciously but can only dream of his sales figures.

I am totally thrilled to be on the judging panel for the Wilbur and Niso Smith Foundation's 'Author of Tomorrow' prize for 2026.

It has taken the writing of this book to bring me full circle to an understanding of who I am — a Saffa! — and where I come from and consolidate those notions within me. That understanding is neither comfortable nor conflicted. It simply is. I look back now with utmost admiration for the resilience, the endurance, the ingenuity, and for the complicated humanity of the cast of characters who made lives in countries that were never simple and never innocent.

History almost always carries unfinished business. People rarely understand the full meaning of their lives while they are living them. Clarity often arrives late, if at all.

Indeed, one of the things that makes me happiest is watching rugby. I support the Springboks wholeheartedly again (after years of being a Wallabies supporter) now that I know my heritage is really South African. When Sia Kolisi sings the national anthem, I feel that the world is in good hands — he strikes me as an incredibly good and humble human being. But the most satisfying thing is to see the stadiums of South Africa full of people of all colours and creeds cheek-by-cheek, celebrating the team and uniform that was once a symbol of apartheid but is now one of the most cohesive elements in the Rainbow Nation. SA rugby crowds go off like no other! It's a full-on life-affirming party.

Having said that, though, with the Zimbabwe Sables qualifying for the 2027 Rugby World Cup, I will have two horses in the race. How brilliant if the final were to be South Africa vs Zimbabwe!

I am close friends again with Charlie Kessler, who I knew from Cordwalles then Hilton, and who now hobby farms in Wollombi, just north of Sydney. Our lives diverged in 1977 when we emigrated. He sought me out on the internet and when he finally found me after 30-odd years, said, 'I'm now living in Sydney'. I'd just moved from Sydney to Thailand a couple of months earlier! But we managed to reconnect.

Apart from cousins, the only other person from South Africa days I'm connected to is Steve Moor, family friend from Tongaat and classmate at Hilton, who went to the UK 'for nine months ... 33 years ago!' He made a career in automative finance in the UK and is a passionate golfer.

My children grew up in worlds that would have been unimaginable to me. My son Justin was born in Singapore — a childhood far removed from mine, yet still full of adventure: turtles and frogs, sailing boats, exotic travel, and the everyday experience of difference. He is Eurasian, raised in a city-state where multi-cultural plurality is not aspirational but ordinary. My daughter Jasmine was born in Australia and then lived and was schooled for years in Koh Samui, Thailand, absorbing languages, rhythms, and perspectives through an eclectic group of international friends. She went on to study food science and sustainable agriculture.

I like to think their childhoods were rich in experience, curiosity, and movement.

When we travelled as a family through Southern Africa — as touched on in the foreword — I found myself seeing the landscape through my camera's viewfinder, and through them. Worlds colliding. It was disorienting. These were worlds I had always held apart — sealed off as memory, as my past, as something I once belonged to but had left behind. Even turned my back on. And suddenly there they were: my children standing at the Maidstone Club. Looking at that smoked beehive in the tree at Braeside. On rickshaws in Durban. On the beach at Sheffield. I remember thinking, with genuine astonishment: What are they doing in that world? Yet I wanted them to know my world, too.

On that trip I took them to Maidstone school, and the headmaster Mike Whitehead told me that the black students (now by far the majority in the school) were way better than white students because they were hungrier for what education could bring to their lives. Roger's abiding memory of returning to Maidstone some years earlier was 'being underwhelmed by the size of the school.'

At Cordwalles, I was due to meet the headmaster, my former choir mate and fellow 1st team cricket player, Simon 'SJ' Weaver. Sadly, he had to rush off to a funeral of someone killed in a home invasion earlier that week. At Hilton College I was gob-smacked by the sheer beauty of the school, and the manners of the boys I encountered. They allowed me to sit on my old bed in Falcon House, with the flood of memories nearly crashing my brain's hard drive. And yes, floggings from Mr Hofmeyer might've dominated those thoughts.

I've returned to Zimbabwe only that once, but to South Africa more frequently. Once in 1980 after finishing school, and my main memory is a number of good parties, and seeing family friends who were in the throes of national service. Many (like Gavin Glover) super-fit because he became a PE instructor in the Army) while others (like Bruce Shuker) definitely heavier on the back of much beer drinking amid the 'hurry up and wait' life of the Army.

In the mid-90s I travelled to South Africa often, mainly to Braamfontein, Joburg, because that's where SAA's marketing department was based. One morning we'd flown in at some ungodly early hour, and — with the jet-lag — had decided to go for a stroll around the block. 'Are you crazy?' Our local clients couldn't believe we'd done that because Joburg at that point was rated the fifth most violent city in the world (the four above it being Latin American cities driven by cartels and drug-war insurgencies).

I was saddened to learn that the Tongaat-Hulett group entered 'voluntary business rescue' (under administration, essentially) in 2022 after its board concluded the company was in 'financial distress' due to huge debts and a severe working capital shortfall (and not insubstantial financial irregularities). Trading in its shares on the JSE was halted after 70 years. Inconceivable back in the day.

As of 2025, nearly 224,000 South Africans call Australia home, and 39,000 Zimbabweans.

Our mother once imagined that when we moved to Australia, we would all be together, geographically.

My brothers and I have each found our spiritual centres far from where we began. Having married an English lass Catherine, Glendon and three kids settled in a small, two-pub town in Gloucestershire (where Pioneer Henry Lloyd's grandfather clock still marks time on the mantelpiece). As a serial entrepreneur, his current pet project is Bonza dog food, a 100% plant-based vegan-friendly dry dog food which he formulated. He's never returned to Africa since we left. Roger has returned only twice, the latest time with his wife Angela before they had children, covering both South Africa and Zimbabwe, and coming away staggering, literally, with the propensity of his Zimbabwean cousins' propensity to party (he being no slouch himself).

He found his groove in Sydney, as CEO of Palisade Investment Partners, which he grew into a multi-billion dollar firm, and with his beloved Crooked River Winery on the south coast of New South Wales, where they run music festivals, wedding functions, and villas.

I spent 25 years in South-east Asia, epicentred firstly on Hong Kong then Singapore, then Chiang Mai in northern Thailand, where coincidentally around 200 Rhodesian families were involved in the tobacco industry at its peak in the early Noughties.

Thailand is where I've lived the longest continuously in my life: 11 years. Is it just a coincidence that its national symbol is the elephant? Since Covid I've lived back in Australia where — due to the brilliant execution of my life's financial strategy — I find myself driving shuttle buses to and from one of the largest gold and copper mines in the world. It's a daily reminder of the pioneering activities my forebears were involved in, and I delight sharing a '*masikati shamwari*' (good afternoon, friend) with Zimbabwean miners Mishek, Charles, Pride, Felix, and Samuel, or a '*hoe gaan jy*?' (how are you?) for South Africans including Lizette, Willem, Clarice, Randolph, and Johan. How Pioneer Henry Lloyd would've loved an air-conditioned luxury coach with reclining seats to get to work at the mine!

When Mum passed away in 2024, we tied yellow ribbons on her coffin in honour of that memorable sing-along speeding fine moment 50 years ago. Sadly, her engagement and wedding rings with their direct line to Dad's family farm in Gwelo and the very soil in Rhodesia, went missing months before she died. An unsolved mystery.

In my living room, I have those Spanish paintings Mum and Dad bought on their overseas trip, plus the Japanese tiles and the Geisha portrait on silk, and still have the Persian rugs that Dad bought at Henri Lidchi's in Salisbury that we used to play matchbox rugby on. I also have one of grandfather George Seymour's paintings of a Cape Dutch house on my office wall. Dad's old Voigtlander sits on a bookshelf, as does the brass bell from the dining room. I ring it from time to time, but nobody comes running!

Having travelled to 75 countries and lived in nine, I generally find First World 'developed' countries anodyne, and Western people often smug, entitled, and generally far less content with life.

Perhaps that is where the old bloodlines show themselves. There may be a trace of Settlers Henry and Alicia Lloyd, and George and Mary Ann Seymour, in all of us — shaped by movement, risk, curiosity, and the belief that life is not meant to be lived from a single vantage point. Perhaps their real legacy is not territory, but appetite for life: adventure and adaptation.

I feel a certain sense of melancholy at the thought that the graves of many of my ancestors lay abandoned and unattended and in unknown condition, strewn across South Africa and Zimbabwe. Have they survived the upheaval over the years? It's a little odd because I didn't even know that some of these people ever existed until a few months ago, but now I care about them deeply, with respect and admiration. Because, without them, there would be no me.

As I write this, Johnny Clegg's *Scatterlings of Africa* is playing. It is a song about displacement, exile, and longing — but also about survival and continuity. Scatterlings are not lost. They move. They adapt. They remember. Perhaps that is the truest inheritance of all: an origin story that travels with you, quietly informing how you see the world.

In Southern Africa there is an idiomatic understanding that one walks forward best when one knows who walked there before … not to follow them, but to know where the path began. So this book is not a map or a manual. It is simply one chapter; observed, remembered, and set down — best as I could — without verdict.

History moves. Jen always used to say that her Granny Rosie Tate lived in the most amazing period: she started in the late 1800s in a world of horse-drawn carts and oil lamps … and lived to see humans walk on the moon.

Even in my lifetime I've gone from having a phone number that was 'long-short-long' on a party line, to an app-loaded iPhone, not to mention the seismic geo-political changes I've witnessed in Southern Africa during that period.

And like all scatterlings, we carry what came before us. Not to repeat it, not to erase it, but to walk forward knowing exactly where our Lloyd and Seymour footsteps began.

The next generations of our family in South Africa and Zimbabwe will write their own histories, shaped by forces I don't understand and cannot predict. I wish I could be around to read their books of their own continuing adventures in Southern Africa.

Because adventure, it seems, is clearly in our blood.

If you've enjoyed *A Monkey's Wedding*, please consider leaving a rating or review on Amazon, Kobo, B&N, Goodreads, Spotify, and Audible to help other people discover this story. Thanks so much!

ACKNOWLEDGEMENTS

Heartfelt thanks to the following who know what they generously did to help bring this story to life:

Rick Antonson
Malcolm Brown (Kwazulu-Natal Family History Society)
Lindy Collins
Ian Daniel
Dawn Eyre
Cameron Flint
Geoff and Bridgette Flint
Lloyd and Carol Flint
Arch and Sandy Harley
Tim and Wendy Henwood
Bridget Hunter (Ancestry.com)
Bruce Lloyd
Glendon Lloyd
Kathleen 'Kay' Lloyd
Paddy Lloyd
Roger Lloyd
Steven Moor
Tony Park
Douglas Rogers
David and Jill Seymour
John and Nicci Seymour
Michael and Sally Seymour
Roger and Renee Seymour

A special shout-out to Bridgette Flint who did the heavy-lifting editing work, challenging my often clumsy sentence structures, picking up time-line inconsistencies with a beady eye, and generally keeping me in line. Thank you for your masochistic generosity!

Also, a special note of thanks to David Seymour, who had laboured on researching the Seymour family history for years. Thankfully I was able to collaborate with him, enjoy many high-spirited conversations and reminiscences, and access all of his collated materials which formed the basis of the Seymour family history. It is with regret that I was unable to present him with a final copy this book before he sadly passed away as we went to print in March 2026. RIP, Uncle Dave.

Also members of Maidstone Primary School Pupils (South Africa) and Frank Johnson Junior School (Pre 1980) Facebook groups for helping me patch together some memories.

Ngiyabonga kakhulu!

BIBLIOGRAPHY AND SOURCES

Foreword:
Have You Ever Seen the Rain? Written by John C. Fogerty. © 1970 Jondora Music, administered by Concord Music Group (all rights reserved).

Chap 1: Sold Down the River
1820settlers.com
Port Elizabeth of Yore: Thomas Pringle's Sojourn at Algoa Bay, Dean McCleland, thecasualobserver.co.za
Rev William Boardman 1768-1825 And His Family, Harold B Lee Library.
The Man Who Would Be Cheops, Thomas Willson and Port Elizabeth, thelondondead.blogspot.com/2018/02
The Reminiscences of an Albany Settler, Henry Dugmore, 1870.

Chap 2: Welcome to Africa
angloboerwar.com
A Social and Cultural History of Grahamstown, 1812-c1845, Richard Marshall, 2008.
The Albany Levy of 1822-1825, Neville Gomm, *Military History Journal*, June 1970.

Chap 3: Green Gold
Natal Witness 1865-1869, bmds
Sugar and Natal Pioneers - Morewood, molegenealogy.blogpsot.com
Sugar and Natal Pioneers - Rathbone, molegenealogy.blogpsot.com

Chap 4: The Desert Dunes of Durban
ancestry.com
digital.nmla.metoffice.gov.uk
George Seymour Obituary, *Natal Mercury*, 2 February 1900.
Passengers to Natal, Catherine, 1862.

Chap 5: Eureka!
anchorenvironmental.co.za
Caractacus Reliance Rathbone, 1879zuluwar.com

Consolidated Gold Fields in Australia: The Rise and Decline of a British Mining House, 1926-1998, Robert Porter, 2020.
History of Medicine: On the Diamond Fields Around Kimberley, N Kretzmar. SA Mediese Tydskrif, 1972.
List of Shipwrecks in August 1842, Wikipedia.
Shipwreck Gold Coins from South Africa, Theheritageportal.co.za.

Chap 6: Turning Emeralds into Gold
When Family Lore Meets Facts, Michael McGee, irishfamilyhistorycentre.com

Chap 7: Circle the Wagons
Founding of a Nation: Rhodesia 1889-1922, A.S. Hickman, 1960.
Rhodesian Genesis, The Story of the Early Days of Southern Rhodesia, Neville Jones, 1953.
Rhodesian Jewry and its Story, Part 1, Eric Rosenthal.
The Pioneer Column's march detailed on maps, zimfieldguide.com

Chap 8: Bulawayo Boomtown
Around Town, bulawayomemories.com
Early Days, bulawayomemories.com

Chap 9: White Man's War
Agriculture in Lydenburg, 1900-1960, Stefan Schirmer, University of Witwatersrand, 1994.
Australian Boer War Memorial, bwm.org.au
Lydenburg News, September 3, 1948.
The Boer War, Thomas Pakenham, 1993.
The Siege of Mafeking, Reuters.
When Family Lore Meets Facts, Michael McGee, irishfamilyhistorycentre.com

Chap 10: A House of Cards
Major William *James Boggie and Jane 'Jeannie' Boggie*, rhodesianheritage.blogspot.com

Chap 11: A Gentleman Named Buster
Dorothy Daniel recollections recorded by Ian Daniel, 2025.
George Ernest Jansen, wikipedia.
Kathleen Lloyd interview by Glendon Lloyd, September 2024.
Kathleen Lloyd interview by Stuart Lloyd, July 2025.
Kathleen Lloyd interview by Cameron Flint, June 2025.

Major William James Boggie and Jane 'Jeannie' Boggie, rhodesianheritage.blogspot.com
Roger Seymour email with Stuart Lloyd 10/3/25
Stella Aurorae: The History of a South African University, Volume 2, The University of Natal (1949–1976), Bill Guest.
Springbok confesses to kick, New Zealand Herald, 30 June, 2000
Third Test – Lancaster Park, Christchurch, 18 August 1956, rugby-talk.com

Chap 12: A Lady Named Jen
Darnall Sugar Mill Avonside, steam-locomotives-south-africa.blogspot.com
David Seymour interviews by Stuart Lloyd, July 2024.
Faithful in Adversity: The RAMC in the Second World War, John Broom.
Jennifer Lloyd interviews by Stuart Lloyd, 2020.
Mr David Brown, steam-locomotives-south-africa.blogspot.com
Sugar and Natal Pioneers - Morewood, molegeneology.com
The Sugar Coast, compiled by Maria Louise Kruger, Makiti Guides and Tours (Pty) Ltd.
The White Tribe of Africa: South Africa in Perspective, David Harrison.

Chap 13: Those Were the Days
A Nice River, callofthestream.wordpress.com
Ballito's Own Miss World, The North Coast Courier, 19 August 2015.
David Seymour interviews by Stuart Lloyd, July 2024.
drifttwoodestates.co.za
Some Memories of Time Spent at Banghazi, Ossie Tedder, 1986.

Chap 14: All Roads Lead to Rhodesia
And the Roots of Rhythm Remain: A Journey Through Global Music, Joe Boyd.
British South Africa Police, bsap.org
Gwebi College of Agriculture, gwebi.co
History of the BSAP, rhodesianforces.org
Mandela, The Authorised Biography, Anthony Sampson.

Chap 15: California Dreaming
Jennifer Lloyd interviews by Stuart Lloyd, 2020.

Chap 16: Batman vs UDI
Beira and Mashonaland Railway, zimfieldguide.com/manicaland/beira-and-mashonaland-railway-stories

redcombgenetics.co.nz
The Beira Patrol: Britain's Broken Blockade against Rhodesia, Richard Mobley, *NWC Review*.

Chap 17: Small Village Charm
Cape Dutch Tongaat: A Case Study in 'Heritage', Peter Merrington, *Journal of Southern African Studies*, 2006.
Darnall Sugar Mill Avonside, steam-locomotives-south-africa.blogspot.com/2009/12
Lindy Collins email to Stuart Lloyd 29/4/26.
Tongaat Brown Eggs, Dr TG Cleasby, *South African Journal of Animal Science*, 1977.

Chap 18: The Chimney in the Canefields
Ian Daniel interview by Stuart Lloyd, 1/10/2025.
Ian Daniel voice memos 3/1/26.
Political Detainees and Nationalist Activities, NAZ: S2929/5/1 – Special Branch Reports, 1960–1964, David Smith & Colin Simpson, 1981.
Roger Seymour email to Stuart Lloyd 4/4/2026.
The Past is Another Country: Rhodesia 1890–1979, Martin Meredith.
Vila Salazar Last Months and Closure 1974, BSA Police Support Unit Association, 2019.

Chap 19: Rucks, Mauls and Religion
A Long Shadow: The 1981 Springbok Tour of New Zealand, Sebastian Potgieter, 2019.
John Seymour email to Stuart Lloyd, 02/01/2026.
Roger Seymour email to Stuart Lloyd, 12/03/2025.
The Residency, eshowe.com

Chap 20: Meanwhile Back in Zululand
David Seymour interviews by Stuart Lloyd, July 2024.
Roger Seymour email to Stuart Lloyd, 12/03/2025.

Chap 21: In Deep (Chicken) Shit
All I Want for Christmas Is My Two Front Teeth, words and music by Donald Yetter Gardner, © 1944 (renewed) EMI Mills Music, Inc. All rights reserved.
Jennifer Lloyd interview by Stuart Lloyd, April 2016.
KZN10.com
Mandela: The Authorised Biography, Anthony Sampson.

Chap 22: The Bush War
Geoff Flint interview by Stuart Lloyd, 16/8/2025.
Ian Daniel interview by Stuart Lloyd, 1/10/2025.
Lloyd Flint interview by Stuart Lloyd, 8/8/2025.
Tim and Wendy Henwood interview by Stuart Lloyd, 31/08/2025.
White Population in Rhodesia/Zimbabwe 1901-2020, White Rhodesian Society, Kenrick.
Why Rhodesia lost its war, despite winning every battle, Willem Petzer, YouTube.
Zimbabwe census summaries 2012-2020.

Chap 23: Gone with the Wind
Glendon and Roger Lloyd interview by Stuart Lloyd, 21/12/25.
Mandela: The Authorised Biography, Anthony Sampson.
On Leopard Rock, A life of Adventure, Wilbur Smith.
RIP Andy van der Watt (1946 to 2025) www.springbooks.rugby 20/1/25.

Chap 24: The Crosshairs of Conscription
Geoff Flint interview by Stuart Lloyd, 16/8/25.
Ian Daniel interview by Stuart Lloyd, 1/10/25.

Chap 25: The Land of Oz
Gambling in Australia, Wikipedia.
Glendon and Roger Lloyd interview by Stuart Lloyd, 21/12/25.
HMS Rattlesnake (1822), Wikipedia.
Michael Seymour email to Stuart Lloyd 1/12/25.
Visiting Bar Island, historyservicesnswblog.blogspot.com

Chap 26: Pulling the Pin
Lloyd Flint email to Stuart Lloyd, 2/2/26.
Master Blaster (Jammin') written and performed by Stevie Wonder. © 1980 Jobete Music Co., Inc.
Michael Seymour email to Stuart Lloyd, 1/12/25.
Paddy Lloyd interview by Stuart Lloyd, 30/12/25.
setlist.fm

Chap 27: Giving it One Last Shot
Geoff Flint interview by Stuart Lloyd, 16/8/25.
Lloyd Flint interview by Stuart Lloyd, 8/8/25.

Chap 28: Unfinished Business
Losing the Plot: The Strategic Dismantling of White Farming in Zimbabwe 2000-2005, Angus Selby, Oxford University.
Mugabe Urged to Intervene, The New Humanitarian, 26 July 2000.
Mugabe Vilifies White Farmers, Washington Post, 19 April, 2000.
Press Statement: Demonetisation of the Zimbabwe Dollar, issued by the Reserve Bank of Zimbabwe, 9 June 2015.
The Last Resort: A Memoir of Mischief and Mayhem on a Family Farm in Africa, Douglas Rogers.
Third Chimurenga and its Implications on the Commercial Farmers Union in Zimbabwe, TW Chibanda and T Mashingaidze, Midlands State University, Zimbabwe.
Tim and Wendy Henwood interview by Stuart Lloyd, 31/08/2025.

Chap 29: The Stay Behind Party
Arch and Sandy Harley interview by Stuart Lloyd, 19/1/26.
John Seymour interview by Stuart Lloyd, 8/12/25.
Roger Seymour email to Stuart Lloyd, 9/12/25.

Epilogue:
Australian Bureau of Statistics (ABS) 2021 Census.
Tongaat Hulett clings to life as rescue drags into third year, The Star, 7 November 2025.

General reference books and recommended reading:

And The Roots of Rhythm Remain: A Journey Through Global Music, Joe Boyd
Born a Crime, Trevor Noah
Don't Let's Go to the Dogs Tonight: An African Childhood, Alexandra Fuller.
Exit Rhodesia: From UDI to Marxism, Pat Scully.
Mandela: The Authorised Biography, Anthony Sampson.
Mukiwa: A White Boy in Africa, Peter Godwin.
The Last Resort: A Memoir of Mischief and Mayhem on a Family Farm in Africa, Douglas Rogers.
The White Tribe of Africa: South Africa in Perspective, David Harrison.
When a Crocodile Eats the Sun, Peter Godwin.

PHOTOGRAPHY CREDITS

Photo page 1:
1820 Settlers landing in Algoa Bay by Thomas Baines.
The 'Catherine' in an unidentified harbour [PRG 1373/28/38] State Library South Australia)
2.
Wagons of the Pioneer Column crossing the Nuanetsi river in 1890, Central African Archives.
Cecil Square, Salisbury, in 1890, Central African Archives.
3.
Ephraim Rathbone, D Kisch, Durban, Natal.
4.
George F Seymour photo courtesy David Seymour.
Silver salver courtesy David Seymour.
Medals John Burridge Military Antiques.
5.
Henry Lloyd photo courtesy Wendy Henwood.
Central Hotel photo copyright BulawayoMemories.com
6.
Henry Lloyd certificate courtesy of Ian Daniel
Henry Lloyd gravesite, Lloyd family collection.
7.
Five-stamp mill courtesy of Kay Lloyd.
Gwelo farm house courtesy of Ian Daniel.
8.
Dick Lloyd and Eileen driving, familysearch.org
Buster and Paddy, Lloyd family collection.
9.
Buster Lloyd portrait, Lloyd family collection.
10.
Dick and Eileen Lloyd and children, courtesy Ian Daniel.
11.
Mick and Kay Flint, courtesy of Flint family.
Dot and Dick Lloyd inspecting gemstones, courtesy Ian Daniel.
12.

George Seymour and friends, Jen Lloyd collection.
Alys Seymour portrait, Jen Lloyd collection.
13.
George Seymour and David, Jen Lloyd collection.
14.
David and Samuel with Bibi, courtesy David Seymour.
15.
Paddy Shuker and Jen, Jen Lloyd collection.
16.
Buster and Jen Lloyd wedding, Jen Lloyd collection.
17.
David and Jill Seymour wedding, courtesy David Seymour.
18.
Glendon and Stuart at Umhlanga Rocks, Jen Lloyd collection.
19.
Stuart in Frank Johnstone uniform, author's collection.
20.
Lloyd family in Beira, George Lloyd collection.
21.
WeWe (Dudley Pringle) Dam, George Lloyd collection.
Roger with balloon, George Lloyd collection.
22.
Roger Seymour rugby, Natal Mercury, Jen Lloyd collection.
23.
McGee family, photo Michael McGee, IrishFamilyHistoryCentre.
Seymour family, George Lloyd collection.
24.
London and Goliat, George Lloyd collection.
Beatrice and Mabel, George Lloyd collection.
25.
Ian Daniel, courtesy Ian Daniel.
26.
2nd Lt Lloyd Flint, courtesy Carol Flint.
27.
Lloyds at Klipfontein, George Lloyd collection.
28.
Tongaat original 1972, George Lloyd.
Re-enactment 2002, Catherine Lloyd.

ABOUT THE AUTHOR

Stuart Lloyd is a sixth-generation Southern African, a global citizen who has lived in nine countries and travelled to 75. He is a self-made multi-trillionaire (in Zimbabwe dollars) who is now an Australian citizen (where he is not). He is married to a Thai, has two Eurasian children and two grandchildren. Passionate about rugby, motorcycle touring, Latin and African music, especially South African *maskandi* and *mbaqanga* styles.

Stuart has published 20 non-fiction books, and hundreds of articles in the *Sydney Morning Herald, The Australian, South China Morning Post, National Geographic Traveler*, etc.

He is a regular reviewer for the *Asian Review of Books* and a reviewer for the Wilbur and Niso Smith Foundation's 'Authors of Tomorrow' prize, 2026.

Connect with Stuart:

Instagram: @RealStuLloyd

stuartlloyd.net

Enjoy a Curated Playlist of all the Songs Mentioned in This Book:

Spotify playlist: search *'A Monkey's Wedding — A Southern African Saga'* http://bit.ly/4rCN9Ew

BOOK CLUB DISCUSSION GUIDE

A Monkey's Wedding: A Pioneering Family's Seven-Generation Saga in Southern Africa — Stuart Lloyd

This guide is designed to encourage open conversation rather than 'right answers'. Some questions may resonate more than others depending on the group — feel free to skip around.

First Impressions & Emotional Response

1. How did this book make you feel overall?
(For example: nostalgic, unsettled, reflective, conflicted, amused, saddened, hopeful.)
2. Was there a moment when you felt particularly close to the author?
What created that sense of intimacy — a memory, a confession, a sensory detail?
3. Which moment surprised you the most, and why?
Did it challenge an assumption you brought into the book?
4. Were there moments that made you uncomfortable?
How did you respond to that discomfort — did it push you away, or draw you in?
5. In what way is this story also part of your story?
This might relate to family, migration, identity, loss, privilege, or belonging.

Story, Voice, & Style

6. *A Monkey's Wedding* blends grief, history, and adventure.
How did the use of humour affect your reading experience?
Did it soften difficult moments, sharpen them, or both?
7. How would you describe the author's narrative voice?
(Observational, self-questioning, affectionate, ironic, restrained, playful, etc?)
8. The book often moves between personal memory and broader history. Did that shifting scale work for you? Why or why not?
9. What felt deliberately left unsaid in the book?

Why do you think the author chose silence or restraint in those moments?

Place, Memory, & Belonging

10. Which setting felt most alive to you, and why?
Was it a place of childhood, travel, conflict, or return?

11. How does the idea of "home" evolve throughout the book?
Is home portrayed as a place, a time, a feeling — or something more unstable?

12. The title "a monkey's wedding" refers to sunshine and rain at once. Where did you see this metaphor playing out in the story?

History, Legacy, & Moral Complexity

13. The book engages with colonial history without offering easy judgments. How did you respond to this approach?
Did it feel honest, evasive, balanced, or challenging?

14. In what ways does colonial legacy shape identity, belonging, and inheritance in the narrative — both materially and emotionally?

15. How does the book handle responsibility across generations?
What is inherited, what is chosen, and what is questioned?

Thought Experiments

16. Would this story be different if it took place today?
If so, how — socially, politically, emotionally?

17. Imagine the book written from another perspective (a sibling, a parent, a local observer, or a later generation).
What might change? What might stay the same?

18. If the author had written this book earlier in life, what do you think would have been lost — or gained?

Ask the Author:

If Stuart Lloyd were in the room, what would you ask him — and why?

(Stuart is available selectively to field questions from Book Clubs like yours, either live online, or via email. See contact details in front matters section.)

AUTHOR Q&A

What inspired you to write this memoir?

SL: This book began as a way to make sense of the stories I'd inherited … and the ones I've lived. I'd had a dump file sitting in my computer for years, but the trigger was the passing of my mum in 2024. I acutely felt the loss of connection to Africa and family stories, and regretted the conversations we never had. Most family histories are a mix of myth, memory, and half-truth. I wanted to explore the truth, and was blown away by what I discovered.

The title *A Monkey's Wedding* is intriguing — what does it mean to you?

SL: It reflects contradiction. Beauty and brutality. Dark humour under a blazing sky. Where I came from, the weather and the people both have a fierce intensity — sunshine can heal … or scorch. My cousin John talks about the 'schizophrenic' nature of life in South Africa. That's a great way of putting it.

You write with humour about some painful experiences. Why?

SL: Humour is a survival instinct and defence mechanism. In Southern Africa, when the world gets absurd — and it often does — wit becomes a shield and a lens. Laughing doesn't mean something isn't serious; it means you refuse to let it defeat you. Another example would be my upcoming travelogue/memoir Motorcycling Cures Cancer*. That's deadly serious life or death stuff, but you need humour to navigate through that mental minefield.

What was the hardest part of writing this book?

SL: Deciding what *not* to say. A memoir isn't a data dump — it's a truth that's shaped. There's tons of childhood memories that I have that didn't advance the story; they're simply a memory. It also opened up some wounds for me — I made myself cry on occasion as I remembered some of our best family times ever, and how our family was never really the same tight unit after we emigrated. Is that as much to do with teenagerdom with dislocation and identity shift? Not sure.

Your book deals with belonging and identity. Do you feel you've found home?

SL: Home, for me, is a mosaic: people, moments, smells, danger, hope. It's less a physical place and more a vibe. Some days I feel I have many homes; other days none at all. The longest I've lived continuously in one country is Thailand, where I'll always be a foreigner. But I'm just as much an outsider in Australia, where I currently live. I've lived in nine different countries, none of them 'the perfect place' although Singapore came closest for me. But these days as long as I've got my wife Mam by my side, that's home. Our retirement plan is in Thailand.

How did the colonial history of Southern Africa influence your storytelling?

SL: It's unavoidable. The past isn't past — it carries forward as a lens. I didn't want a narrative of guilt or denial, but one that acknowledges complexity: privilege and peril, love and loss, the beauty that can exist alongside injustice. That shit happened. It's a colourful and chequered past that contributes to an equally colourful and chequered present and future. I have to own it, but don't need to apologise for it.

What do you hope readers take away from this memoir?

SL: This is my family's story. It's intensely personal in some places, but I hope it's universal to others, too. To those whose families perhaps lived through similar times and in similar places but never wrote their story, hopefully it's wonderfully nostalgic. But also to those who have no connection to Africa and pioneering behaviour, I hope they marvel as I do at the fortitude of my forebears ... their appetite for adventure, and ability to adapt.

Were there stories you were surprised to uncover during your research?

SL: Constantly. It's an amazing cast of characters of whom I knew next to nothing when I set out to write this — I especially felt a kinship with Pioneer Henry and Ephraim Rathbone. Wow, just wow, at the lives they led. Those discoveries changed how I see myself. We are all descendants of the remarkable and the ridiculous. Probably more the former in my case, and the latter in the case of my children!

Music features throughout your writing. Why is that?

SL: Music is memory's first language. A song can transport you faster than a plane ticket — to a dusty road, a first kiss, a battlefield, a beach. It anchors the emotional geography of the book. And African music especially is so primal it affects us on a deep cellular level I'm sure. Hope you enjoy the Spotify playlist!

What advice would you give someone wanting to write their own story?

SL: Have those conversations *now*. Record them on a voice memo, transcribe them. Collate the photos and share them in a dropbox folder. Don't take ancestry.com and MyHeritage as gospel ... there are so many well-intentioned amateurs but few real genealogists supervising their rigour. Question everything and rely on actual documents. Then write. Just write. *Please* write. So down the track everyone knows better who they are and where they came from before it's lost. Surely that shapes 'family'?

OTHER BOOKS BY STUART LLOYD

A Bleeding Slaughterhouse: The Outrageous True Story of the Alexandra Hospital Massacres, Singapore, February 1942.

Bamboozled: The Lighter Side of Expat Life in Asia.

Gone Troppo! My search for Tropical Paradise.

Hare of the Dog: History, Humour, and Hell-raising from the Hash House Harriers.

Honeymoon for One: Collected travel writings from Australia to Zimbabwe (and everywhere in between).

Tales from the Tiger's Den: An Oral History of Foreigners in the Far East 1920-2020.

The Depths of December: The Sinking of HMS Repulse, Prince of Wales ... and the British Empire. (Also in audiobook.)

The Grubby Little Men Who Raped Hong Kong: The True Story of the St Stephen's College Massacre, December 1941. (Also in audiobook.)

The Malay Experiment: The Colonial Origins and Homegrown Heroism of the Malay Regiment. (Also in audiobook.)

The Missing Years: A POW's Memoir from Changi to Hellfire Pass. (Also in audiobook.)

See more at StuartLloyd.net

www.ingramcontent.com/pod-product-compliance
Lightning Source LLC
LaVergne TN
LVHW041101080826
845145LV00007B/1642